ational Library of Sociology

ded by Karl Mannheim

r: John Rex, University of Warwick

iae

e of the books available in the **International Library of Sociology** series of Social Science books published by Routledge and Kegan e found at the end of this volume.

Phenomenology,
the s

Inter

Four

Edit

Arbor Scie
Arbor Vita

A catalo
and other
Paul will

Phenomenology, language and the social sciences

Maurice Roche
Department of Sociology,
London School of Economics and Political Science

Routledge & Kegan Paul
London and Boston

First published in 1973
by Routledge & Kegan Paul Ltd
Broadway House, 68-74 Carter Lane,
London EC4V 5EL and
9 Park Street,
Boston, Mass. 02108, U.S.A.
Printed in Great Britain by
The Lavenham Press Ltd.
Lavenham, Suffolk.

ISBN 0 7100 7546 4

Library of Congress Catalog Card Number: 73-79112

Contents

Introduction

In modern philosophy there have been a number of self-styled 'revolutions' and 'movements'. This book is an examination of two of them, phenomenology and conceptual analysis (or ordinary language philosophy). The main questions it tries to answer are these. What are the views of the two schools on the explanation and understanding of thought and action? Are they similar to each other in any important respects? And how do such views relate to psychological and sociological analyses of thought and action?

Answering the first question has called for a fairly detailed description and analysis of the main texts and arguments of the two schools. This provides for the answer to the second question above, viz. that the two schools *are* similar in important respects, to be proposed. The overall argument here is that phenomenology and conceptual analysis have what may be called 'humanistic' features in common. Both are opposed to the application of natural scientific procedures, theories, analogies and aspirations in the human and social sciences. They are particularly opposed to the mechanism and reductionism of philosophical standpoints like logical positivism or empiricism. Both advocate a descriptive approach to human experience as an important method for philosophy and the social sciences. And finally both can be seen to rely on virtually the same theory of man.

Their common 'humanism', like that of the young Marx, thus appears in their theories of knowledge and of being. Other more loose and less analysable usages of 'humanism', in anti-theological moralising for instance, are not relevant to our use of the term here.

The third question mentioned above concerns the relation of this humanistic philosophy to the social sciences, here understood to include psychology as well as sociology. The overall argument advanced is that psychological theories tend to be mechanistic and reductionist whereas sociological theories tend to be anti-psychologistic and humanistic. The dichotomy in philosophy between humanism and positivism is played out in the social sciences in the dichotomy between psychological and sociological explanations of human action. Mental illness, for instance, can be understood psychologically in terms of genetic abnormality, or inborn personality traits, or environmental conditioning, or fixation of the personality at a certain stage of its sexual and super-ego development in infancy, or a mixture of these factors. For such explanations and the forms of therapy based on them, the actor's, or patient's, experience and accounts of his own actions, are symptoms of processes not experienced by him. Thus only the scientific psychological observer and not the actor can give some account of them. Sociological explanations on the other hand accord the actor's accounts some value as explanatory in themselves, and not as symptomatic of unseen explanatory processes. To take an extreme case, when the 'paranoic' claims that his mother/his father/his job/his love-life/his psychiatrist/his country, or whatever, 'is driving me mad', the sociologist takes this seriously. It offers him an insight into the actor's experience of the world, how the actor conceives and perceives meanings in his social situation. The sociologist attempts to reconstruct the main features of the actor's developing situation, the successive interactions between him, members of his family, his friends, police, doctors, judges, and ultimately asylum staff and inmates who are involved in the labelling and defining of the actor in his career of madness. How the sociological humanistic approach to mental illness emerged in part as a reaction against the reductionist implications of Freud's psycho-analytic approach, will be discussed in some detail in chapters 6 and 7.

Even conventional and classical sociology has significant humanistic elements, in spite of its too common positivistic and scientistic veneer. This veneer, generated in particular by the institutionalisation of sociology as a 'profession' in the United States, has been cracking up and falling away in recent years. Minus the veneer, sociology reveals itself as singularly lacking in solid achievements, and as naively unaware of the implications of its entanglements with the buyers of information and the manipulators of men, and as profoundly and inextricably enmeshed in everyday common-sense reasoning.

By making clear the nature of the humanistic philosophical critiques of psychology and sociology, I hope to add a few more voices to the rising tide of criticism of the blinkered pretensions of conventional sociology which reflect, where they do not serve, the dehumanising features of mature capitalist society. This is not at all to recruit Wittgenstein, Husserl and the others with whom I am concerned in the book, to the role of social criticism and radicalism. The imaginative re-writing of philosophical history which that would require is beyond me. But it is to indicate the complex problem of mutual relations of philosophy, sociological 'knowledge' and social reality. At the very least, philosophy always has some degree of autonomy *vis à vis* social reality, some degree, however minimal, of transcendence. Humanistic philosophy may well be analysed by sociology as being a parasite on the scientific culture of a secular, rational, technological society, or further as 'bourgeois ideology'. But then sociology itself is subject to the same sociological analysis. And like sociology, philosophy is never *merely* parasitic and *only* ideology. The philosophy of a society like the religion of a society and like the 'madness' of an individual is never merely a symptom, a reflex response. It is, like religion and madness, a form of consciousness. And forms of consciousness, given that they are intrinsically social, as we will observe in the course of our argument, have a degree of autonomy and integrity in their internal structures of meaning. A humanistic sociology lives with the complexity that this imposes on its so-called 'sociology of knowledge', without dissipating or reducing that complexity. And part of this complexity is the fact that the philosopher's argument besides being sociologically explained can be listened to as having implications for sociology's self-consciousness, if not for its practice. Periods of re-evaluation of belief systems and their methods necessarily involve an inherently philosophical maneouvre of 'going back to basics'. The present is such a period of re-evaluation for the belief systems and practices comprising sociology. And as such it requires, besides political critiques of sociology as a practice, philosophical critiques of sociology as a belief system. Its beliefs concern social action and social structures, their relations and the methods most appropriate for their study. The humanistic philosophies of phenomenology and conceptual analysis have important arguments concerning these topics which thus deserve the sociologist's attention. The emergence within sociology of a movement like ethnomethodology, whose various proponents explicitly invoke the terms and concepts of both schools, adds to the necessity for the sociologist to do more than merely 'explain away' phenomenology and conceptual analysis. He must, besides, try to understand them. The clarification and criticism of the two schools that is attempted in this book is addressed to this need for sociology to understand and to come to terms with humanistic philosophy.

A word about organisation. The book is divided into two main parts, the first giving an account of phenomenology, conceptual analysis and logical empiricism (chapters 1, 2 and 3 respectively) as schools of philosophy. Chapter 3, in particular, attempts to define the reductionist idea of psychological and sociological science against which humanistic philosophy has developed.

Part two is mainly devoted to tracing out the reductionist idea in psychological theories, and the two versions of the humanistic critique of this idea as it appeared in the different theories. Behaviourist psychology, Gestalt psychology and Freudian psychology (chapters 4, 5 and 6 respectively) are progressively more ambiguous formulations of reductionism. Phenomenology and conceptual analysis have both produced important critiques of reductionism in these three areas. Similarly, Weber's sociology, committed as it was to a humanistic method, has nevertheless generated critiques, albeit fraternal ones, by both schools. These are examined in chapter 8. Chapter 7 discusses humanistic psychiatric and sociological approaches to the specific area of mental illness which counter the ultimately reductionist implications of Freudian psycho-analytic theory. And chapter 9 concludes by stating the broad underlying themes of the two forms of humanistic philosophy, and indicating how they relate to problems of theory and method in sociology.

part I

The philosophical schools

1 Phenomenology

There is some truth in the argument that each successive phenomenologist produces a different meaning for the term 'phenomenology'. If this were completely true then the notion of a phenomenological 'school', or of a phenomenological 'movement' (Spiegelberg, 1969, vols 1 and 2)[1] would be hard to justify. However, the argument is not completely true, and there do exist common denominators which will be outlined here.

One such common denominator is the injunction, accepted in theory and practice by all phenomenologists, to 'be true to the phenomenon'. That is, to describe that which is given in experience, that which you and others experience, that which appears to be the case, etc. This would seem to be no more than the traditional empiricists maxim: 'know the facts'. But phenomenologists interpret the injunction more readily in terms of the Socratic maxim: 'know yourself'. This is because they hold that description of experience reveals facts about consciousness, about the *ways* man experiences the world, as well as directly revealing facts about the world.

It is useful to keep a simple theme like this in mind when analysing the ostensibly disorderly developments of phenomenological ideas by successive philosophers. We deal, in the main, with the contrast between Husserl's pure phenomenology on the one hand, and existential and ontological phenomenology, epitomised by Sartre, Merleau-Ponty, Schutz and Heidegger, on the other. This contrast is introduced by a discussion of the contribution of Brentano to the ideas of the phenomenological school.

Brentano

Brentano was the first major figure of the phenomenological school. Much of what he wrote was later rejected by his pupil, Husserl, but, with the later re-assessment in his turn of Husserl's work by existentialist phenomenologists, we can now see more clearly Brentano's importance.[2]

Brentano founded the idea of a phenomenological psychology in his *Psychology from an Empirical Standpoint*, first published in 1874. He supported the idea that philosophy had to base itself on the investigations and discoveries of such an empirical enterprise, rather than be a self-justifying activity of reason.

Brentano also founded one of the main epistemological ideas in phenomenology, that of the intentionality or 'aboutness' of conscious activity. And since an epistemology always implies an ontology (in that a theory of knowledge implies a theory of being, concerning a knower and something known, in order to give any sense to the analysis of the knowing-relation between them), Brentano also made ontological claims as to the basic nature of human existence in a way characteristic of later existentialist phenomenology.

Brentano's phenomenological psychology was presented as a purely descriptive study of the mental acts of persons. He was primarily concerned with classifying and categorising modes of experiencing, and types of consciousness. One major source of data would be each individual's description of their private domains of experience. Brentano disliked the term 'introspection' and preferred to use the term 'inner perception' to refer to this source of data and this method of investigation. The difference is quite a fundamental one, and has been missed by critics of phenomenology. They tend to label phenomenology as a form of introspection, and they can build up a sound case to show that the notion of introspection is a confused and inapplicable analogue of ordinary visual concepts and experiences. Brentano himself poked fun at introspective psychologists who had only come up with 'a tumult of confused ideas and numerous headaches', from their observations of inner goings-on (quoted in Rancurello, 1968, p. 31).

Introspectionists basically held to a 'bucket' theory of the mind, in that they were looking for 'contents', sedimented accumulations of sensations, associations and the like. Brentano held that consciousness is an activity, constituted in relations between the active subject and the object he is conscious of. That is, consciousness is always 'consciousness of' something; in the activity of thinking, there is something thought about; in the activity of believing, there is something that is believed; in the activity of loving there is something loved, and so on for all forms of conscious activity. Mind or consciousness exists in these intentional relations, functions and uses; as Sartre was to put it in a somewhat different context years later, consciousness exists 'as a wind blowing towards objects'. And much as one would not feel a wind if one were looking in still air, so introspectionists, looking for mental things 'in' a passive mental receptacle called the mind, would not feel the work of mind in the subject's activity. What could they expect to find in their mind-bucket, a thought perhaps, or maybe a sensation? Assume they are successful and that their mental fishing produced at the end of the line a Thought. How are they to describe this catch? What name are they to give it, what is it called? In the end it will be seen that the only way to describe the catch is to say what the thought was a thought of.

Let us say that the introspectionist has fished up the Thought that 'the Earth moves around the Sun'. What is distinctively mental about that, what does it tell him about the nature of his mind? The oddity of the whole procedure may unsettle our introspectionist, he may even switch to hard-headed no-nonsense behaviourism or even further to neurology, convinced that consciousness is a hoax. He has looked 'inside his mind and has found out something about the solar system outside'. But while introspection has failed to reveal a distinctively mental thing, in its own terms, Brentano would assert that the paramount fact of intentional objective reference by the conscious subject *has* been revealed. What has been seen is that a correct description of consciousness is required from the very beginning, and this is a description of referential activity, not a description of some hypothetical inactive mental receptacle. It is just such self-awareness of one's own mental activity that Brentano is getting at with his term 'inner perception'.

Inner perception is simply knowing what one is now doing, being able to put one's own conscious activity at any particular moment under some description such as, for instance, 'daydreaming', 'calculating', 'lying', 'missing the point', etc. Inner perception is an ordinary comprehensible reflective turn, whereas introspection is an extra-ordinary, incomprehensible mental contortion.

So the main source and the main method of Brentano's phenomenological psychology was to be 'inner perception' of on-going conscious activity. Another source was held to be individuals' memory of past conscious activities. Both of these sources suffered from the main methodological problem accompanying any kind of self-testimony subjectivism, that is the impossibility of inter-subjective checking of the alleged facts, and thus the possibility of dishonest witness. His final source was less suspect from these angles. It was the 'externalisation of the psychic life of other persons' in verbal communication, autobiographical accounts, 'human achievements and voluntary acts' (ibid., p. 32). And he specifically mentioned study of the behaviour of infants, adults in primitive societies, the mentally ill, socio-cultural phenomena and even animal studies.

However Brentano proposed this programmatic descriptive psychology of experience in harness with what he called 'genetic' or 'explanatory' psychology. That is, he took very seriously 'the weakness of all non-physiological psychology' and granted that the foundations of such a psychology 'would always remain insufficient and unreliable' (ibid.). Therefore he proposed that psychology is basically a split-level psycho-physical study, part phenomenological description of experience, and part neurological explanation of the genesis of experience by reference to organic brain-cell processes. Yet these two studies would be as different as chalk and cheese and Brentano fully recognised this. In fact he was a great propagandist *against* what he called 'physiological reductionism' in psychology.

In spite of his conception of the 'bipartite psycho-physical' nature of the psychological enterprise, he was able to write in 1874: 'Not only the surrender of psychological investigation to physiological research, but also the admixture of the latter to the former seems by and large counter-indicated. On the whole, to this day, there are only a few ascertained physiological facts which are suited to shed light on psychic phenomena' (ibid., p. 72). Nearly a century later, it could be argued, this state of affairs still holds true. However, having differentiated two distinct psychologies (phenomenological-descriptive on the one hand, and genetic-explanatory on the other) Brentano provided no justification for keeping them together. He merely papered over the basic differences by referring to them both as equal constituents of the one study—psychology. Having recognised the 'weakness of all non-physiological psychology' he proceeded to outline the programme of just such a psychology. He also devoted considerable effort to criticising the inadequacies of the current English school of physiological psychology (ibid., p. 73). The general impression given by Brentano's tacking to and fro between physiology and phenomenology is that of his respect for the prospective extension of science to the area of Mind, being modified by his desire to make such an extension fully self-aware and adequate to the distinctive nature of Mind.

In this way he was unlike Wilhelm Dilthey, who in the 1880s launched a critique of the new science of psychology, in so far as it had any resemblance to, and inspiration from, the natural sciences (see Hodges, 1969 and Rickman, 1961). Dilthey's distinctions between mental/cultural phenomena and physical phenomena, and between the methods adequate to them, take almost the same form as Brentano's distinctions. And Dilthey's contribution to phenomenological interpretations of sociology and psychiatry, through Max Weber and Karl Jaspers respectively, with the concept of *Verstehen*, is probably just as important as Brentano's various contributions to the phenomenological school. Yet Brentano declared himself as the interpreter and guide of scientific psychology whereas Dilthey repudiated the very idea of it. Brentano is in this respect out of step with a main characteristic of the phenomenological school, which has been to contrast its own methods, theories and findings against natural scientific claims, in the area of human action and experience. Dilthey proposed such a clear contrast, whereas Brentano argued that in the area of psychology, in particular, phenomenology can *complement* natural scientific methods and findings, rather than compete with them.

Brentano's outline of the programme of a phenomenological psychology was, thus, not embedded in a fundamental critique of the claims of natural science to the humanities, (on this point see Husserl, 1970a, pp. 233-5,298 and *passim*). But the elements of such a critique were present in Brentano's psychological and philosophical writings, and when drawn together appear as an anticipation of the existentialist phenomenology of Sartre and Merleau-Ponty.

All philosophers, wittingly or unwittingly, make use of ontological axioms and assertions, concerning what kinds of things, in the final analysis, can and do exist, and in what way they exist. Phenomenology, unlike most other modern philosophic fashions, makes explicit its ontological commitments. Although these do change from one phenomenologist to another, they all tend to hold that mental phenomena have as real and as unavoidable an existence, albeit in a different way, as have physical phenomena. And in some cases an idealist kind of primacy of mental over physical existence emerges. Instead of accepting the materialist thesis that only things that can be touched, smelled, heard, seen or tasted can be said to exist, which would make mental phenomena non-existent in that they cannot be sensed, the idealist argues that judging, naming, discriminating, etc., are primary and that physical things only exist secondarily as the correlates of these mental phenomena, that is as 'the named', 'the discriminated', etc.

Brentano had begun in more or less the idealist manner indicated above, even though he expressed a dislike for the German tradition of idealism. He had differentiated two main classes of existents, mental and physical. But mental phenomena were basic because they contained the class of 'physically active subjects', in terms of which mental states and physical things had their existence (Rancurello, 1968, p. 46). Thus mental phenomena such as knowledge, joy and desire, like physical phenomena such as a fire or a table, all exist as 'immanent objectivities' in (a) consciousness. They exist as the intentional objects of some mental activity and orientation on the part of the individual conscious subject. However, knowledge, joy and desire also exist 'actually' as these subjectively generated objectivities, whereas tables and fires exist 'phenomenally' in subjective consciousness (see Farber, 1943, p. 13). This idealistic type of argument has the effect of making desire, etc., more real to consciousness than tables, etc. Brentano later went back on this ontological analysis when he saw the extremes it was taken to by his students, Husserl and Meinong, and he became unwilling to allow 'irreal' mental objects any status at all, compared to physical realities (Rancurello, 1968, p. 36; Spiegelberg, 1969, vol. 1, p. 48).

But until this change of view, Brentano had, in his philosophical writings, asserted the existence of consciousness and analysed its central operating principle, that of intentionality. While in his psychological writings he had asserted the existence of individual personal consciousnesses, and had analysed the principles of operation of personal consciousness in outlining the programme of phenomenological description.

Apart from Husserl, most of the phenomenological school, particularly Sartre and Merleau-Ponty, have a great desire to relate ontological analyses of consciousness in general, to descriptions of individual consciousness in action. With Brentano they analyse consciousness in general in order to better understand it in particular, in order to understand the world of people, human existence better. Thus it is always an assumption of the phenomenological school that there exists a world of people, whose distinguishing characteristics include the 'possession' of individual consciousness. There exists a world of numerous subjective unities of experience, called Selves or Persons. This is the rock-bottom of assertions about being made by the phenomenological school. From it can be reconstructed their analyses of the being of consciousness, etc. But their most basic ontological assertion about the furniture of the world always involves the assumption that there are at least Persons, and Persons have, besides organic and other defining characteristics, the paramount defining characteristic of being unities of consciousness, interpretative centres of sensory and communicative information, both in terms of acceptance and of generation of such information (see chapter 9 below).

Brentano implies such an ontology of Persons when he discusses the concept of Self in his prospective psychology. He believes that a subject, the self, underlies 'the totality of our psychic life' at any given moment. It is the 'common belongingness (of our psychic acts) to *one* real thing', he asserts, 'which constitutes the unity of which we are speaking'. Conceived in this way, he considers that the unity of consciousness is 'one of the most important tenets of psychology (Rancurello, 1968, p. 42). Because of the interaction in phenomenology between psychology and philosophy it would be fair to say that what is axiomatic to the one is axiomatic to the other, that what is an untestable meta-theory to the psychology is an ontological assertion to the philosophy. We will consider this at greater length when we deal with existentialist phenomenology proper. Suffice it to say that Brentano, almost unwittingly, anticipated this turn in phenomenology because of the close relation he felt ought to exist between philosophical and psychological studies and because of the way he felt free to introduce ontological notions into psychological studies. This has led one of Brentano's biographers to write of his 'existentialist metaphysics' (ibid., p. 67).

Before finishing with Brentano it is worth looking a little closer at his own analysis of consciousness, which he considered as a contribution to the phenomenological description of experience. As has been seen, he considered his main discovery to be the intentionality or 'about-ness' of all mental phenomena. Thus he wrote: 'a common feature of everything psychical consists in what has been called by a very unfortunate and ambiguous term, consciousness, i.e. in a subject-attitude, in what has been termed *intentional* relation to something...' (ibid., p. 45). It follows that the various 'modes of consciousness' or 'fundamental classes of psychic phenomena' are simply particular manifestations of such an 'attitude'. The basic task of descriptive phenomenological psychology consists in revealing and sorting out the various possible 'attitudes of the subject to the object', or 'modes of relation to the object', describing them, and showing their dynamic interrelationships.

Brentano himself identified three major classes of intentionality, or subject attitude to object, and they were—representation, judgement and affectivity. Representational intentionality refers to primitive awareness of something by the subject; for instance, mere awareness of what it is that is imagined, or thought, or sensed by the subject. Concerning this Brentano said: 'We speak of representation whenever something appears to us' (ibid.). Judgemental intentionality is an attitude by the subject to an object whereby the subject accepts the object as true, or rejects it as false. And affective intentionality is an attitude by the subject to the object which expresses love or hate of the object by the subject. It is a class of intentionality defined by what is not included in the previous two classes, and as such it includes what Brentano calls: 'The phenomena of love and hate', 'emotions', 'feeling and will', and 'interest'.

In explicating this analysis further, Brentano feels obliged to extend his conception of that 'unfortunate and ambiguous term', consciousness. The formula: 'All consciousness is consciousness-of', is extended to 'All consciousness is consciousness-of, and is self-conscious' (ibid.). As a statement of some kind of universal fact, this extended formula is as unacceptably as the original formula was acceptable. It is the case, for instance, that when I am immersed in a chess problem that the problem is an intentional objectivity established and sustained as such by my attention and intellectual effort. But it is not necessarily the case at all that I know what I am doing under the description of it just given. Or, to take another example, hating somebody is doing just that, it is *not* being self-consciously aware that hating is 'what I am doing'.

What *is* the case is that every person is *capable* of being self-consciously aware of their mental acts or what they are doing. Thus it would be correct to say: 'All consciousness is consciousness-of, and is necessarily *capable* of being known/reflected upon/being brought under a description by the subject'. But it is simply inadequate phenomenology to say that every consciousness is *ipso facto* a self-consciousness. So it is better to interpret Brentano's statement: 'Every psychic act... implies the consciousness of itself' (ibid., p. 46), in this light of possibility. It is only in this light that a descriptive psychology of consciousness makes sense. Every subject is *not* already completely self-conscious of all that he is and all that he does simply by virtue of being a conscious agent. It requires a reflective turn to know about oneself, and few of us make that turn for few of all the possible occasions that we could. Thus Brentano's notion of 'inner perception' could be simply interpreted as a request to us to be more self-conscious, to put more of our ongoing experiences under descriptions. Of course, the descriptive psychologist would be concerned with other sources and methods than this, as already indicated, but he would also be required to be self-aware in this way.

Brentano's statement, then, that 'Every psychic act... has a double object' (ibid.), its primary intentional object, and itself as a psychic act, is unacceptable as phenomenological description, because possibly the majority of human experiences are lived-through, not reflected upon. But it is acceptable as a statement of what we are capable of, indicating the main area of investigation of a phenomenological psychology. And for prospective investigators it would have been better had Brentano expressed the concept of intentionality more rigorously in the following fashion: 'Every psychic act has an intentional object of *another*, and *later*, psychic act'. Brentano's conception of 'inner perception' as description of 'ongoing psychic processes' indicates his lack of rigour in this respect. He allowed a completely unanalysed notion of the possible co-temporarity of thinking something, and describing *that* one is thinking, to lead him to assert that the psychic act of thinking something necessarily involves its reflective description by the subject. In fact the co-temporality is spurious. When a man is describing that he is thinking of something he cannot be thinking of the something. And when he is thinking of the something, he is not doing something else like describing what he is doing. There is thus an intermixed temporal sequence of two distinct kinds of acts, for the active investigator, not the co-temporal ongoing of two halves of the same act, as Brentano seems to assert.

Generally we might sum up Brentano's position in the phenomenological school as follows. He gave the school some of its basic inspirations, although in a relatively unsystematic way. Both the notion of phenomenological psychology, which he first explicitly used as a term (1888 lectures), and outlined as a programme (1874), and the notion of intentionality as the defining characteristic of consciousness, stem from Brentano. In his work the ontological primacy of some concept of Person first emerges. This anthropomorphic, man-centred ontology, as developed in later writers, is a defining feature of the phenomenological school.

The other main feature of the school, which could be called 'experiential empiricism' also first emerges with Brentano. He was prepared to take issue with the epistemology of traditional sensory empiricism; with its restrictions on the kinds of experience that are there to be studied, and with its restrictions on the kind of evidence we can bring to justify knowledge-claims. He also began the phenomenological school's effort to disassociate itself from naive introspection. Finally, he was an explicit, if sometimes ambiguous, critic of physiological reduction in the study of conscious agency, as were all later phenomenologists. Brentano's psychological programme inspired much of the work of both Carl Stumpf and William James (ibid., ch. 3; see also Spiegelberg, 1969, vol. 1, pp. 55 and 66-9), while his personal sense of mission, as much as his philosophy, inspired Husserl, to whom we now turn.

Husserl and pure phenomenology

Husserl's intellectual development went through several distinct stages, but generally speaking the stage of pure phenomenology is recognised by phenomenologists as being the most important.[3] This recognition is ambiguous because it is fair to say that few of his disciples and pupils actually try to practise the specific reflective techniques of pure phenomenology. In fact most are prepared to criticise Husserl for the Platonic idealism inherent in pure phenomenology. And yet the ideas exert a fascination that makes a comprehensive rejection of them almost impossible within the school. But perhaps the most interesting stage of his writing is the final one, the decade up to his death in 1936. Here, at last, he began to tackle ontological and existential problems concerning man's existence and coexistence among men. Here we find also his growing suspicion that his pure phenomenological concepts did not fit the new problems. The First World War and the rise of Hitler in pre-war Germany could also be said to have had its effects on Husserl, reinforcing his desire to understand history, culture and inter-subjectivity.

Husserl's early philosophical work began with an attempt to apply Brentano's descriptive psychology to his own special area, mathematics.[4] However, he became disillusioned with this project, and instead launched an attack on the 'psychologism' involved in trying to base logic on empirical psychology (1970b, vol. 1, pp. 90-197). He radically reformulated Brentano's conceptions of descriptive psychology and inner perception to mean rather the intuition of essence by the subject (1967, p. 23). He then attempted to found logic on such self-evident insights and essential intuitions (1969). 'Phenomenological description' thus took on a sense different from that given to it by Brentano. Husserl used this new sense to drive home his antipathy to traditional Humean empiricism as a theory of knowledge (1970b, vol. I, pp. 115-29, 402-26).

He liked to portray Hume as the first and greatest, although unwitting, descriptive phenomenologist. And he claimed that Hume deceived himself into thinking that he was some kind of empirical psychologist 'introspecting' particular sense-data, and building up generalisations to account for ordinary mental phenomena like thinking, remembering, calculating, etc. Husserl claims that on the contrary, Hume's object is to exhibit the essential in the particular, and there is no attempt to generalise and compare case-histories of such things as rememberings. His method is direct and intuitive. All of the 'contents of the mind' are divided into 'impressions' and 'ideas' by Hume, and he does not make Locke's mistake of differentiating them in terms of their respective sources, say, without and within. Rather mind is built up of impressions which depend for their recognition on the 'intensity' with which they appear to the subject. Without going further into this, and suspending the question of whether such an interpretation is valid or not, one can see how Husserl was led to call Hume the first phenomenologist, in so far as Hume described what appears in experience (1967, pp. 23 and 183).

Husserl shared Hume's and Brentano's conception of psychology, in one shape or form, as the 'queen' of the sciences. But he argued that, as one natural science among many, psychology could not occupy such a pre-eminent position. The understanding of mind, must therefore take a distinctive form, which would serve equally as a basis for physics as for a natural scientific psychology. Husserl took it upon himself to outline this distinctive understanding of mind which could serve as the basis and the horizon of all natural scientific knowledge. As with all idealism, the Absolute beckoned Husserl on in his grandiose mission. And in his early works on arithmetic and logic he was beginning to evolve the notion of subjectivity, which was to inflate into the Absolute in his philosophy of transcendental idealism.

Husserl wanted to create a philosophic study that would transcend the empiricist account of the nature of knowledge, and that would put into perspective, and give meaning to, the sciences based on objective empirical principles. This would have to be a study of subjectivity, of experience from the 'inside' as it were, but unlike Brentano and the later existentialists, Husserl wanted to study 'pure' subjectivity, uncontaminated by such incidentals as the fact that subjective consciousness has an existential situation 'in' a socially and organically differentiated being, called a Person. It is in this context that Husserl developed the two main concepts of his pure phenomenological period, the 'thesis of the natural attitude or standpoint' and the 'epoche, or phenomenological reduction'.

We will discuss these two concepts in turn and try to highlight what it was about them that led Husserl's followers to largely *ignore* pure phenomenology in their developments of phenomenological description, and which led Husserl himself *away* from his 'pure' researches into an attempt to demonstrate their relevance and application to the lived world, in his later philosophy.

First, then, we turn to the 'natural attitude or standpoint'. The 'natural standpoint' is the point of view that all of us cannot but adopt in the course of our everyday lives. It indicates that we must, and do, accept certain things as 'real' and indubitable in order to live and act in ordinary everyday life, and it describes these 'objectivities' which include values and aesthetic features, as well as facts and states of affairs, social facts as well as physical facts (ibid., pp. 101-7). It refers to the naive everyday realism embodied in our beliefs that in our world there are good paintings and bad ones, useful objects and useless ones, good weather and bad weather, good men and evil men, socially powerful men and socially powerless men. In this attitude these sorts of things are 'out there', their dependence on our judgement is ignored. We live in a world of objectivities which confront us, with which we have to deal and 'push our way through'—so as to speak—in pursuing our aims and acting intentionally. In the natural attitude there is not just this 'my world'. Rather I accept that there are many 'my worlds' besides my own, and each man believes as I do that he is one among many.

The natural attitude knows nothing of solipism. We manipulate and pass between each other the 'same' physical object. We agree and disagree about the 'same' cultural object. Husserl does not develop his argument to the analysis of language and communication in the natural attitude. But even so he establishes a point that such an analysis would make more conclusively, which is that the world of natural attitude is, in a fundamental sense, taken to be an intersubjective or social one.

By a movement in spatial location, each 'I' considers that, and acts on the assumption that, it is capable of having the 'same' environment of perceived physical objects and the 'same' perceived horizon as any other 'I'. Similarly, by empathy and imagination, each 'I' considers itself capable in principle of valuing things, in the 'same' way (whether morally, aesthetically or practically) and of having the 'same' environment of valued objects as any other 'I'. These are the *possibilities* that must be present if the world is to be meaningful for men as an 'intersubjective world'. As regards valued objectivities it is clearly possible for there to be such deep disagreement over their natures, that they may appear in the natural attitude as 'contested objectivities or realities'. A trivial example might be the Mona Lisa's smile, is it a beautiful or an ugly object? A more serious example might be a social object, thing or reality like a parliamentary system of government. In an historical situation where such a thing is both denounced and supported within a national society, as say in Germany during the rise of Hitler, then we have in the everyday attitude of Germans, besides the awareness of the system as a 'good' or 'bad' thing, also the awareness that it is a 'contested' thing, which involves the possibility of it ceasing to exist, and of it being made to cease to exist.

The social 'objects', social 'realities', have an often contested, and always perspectival 'existence', in the eyes and minds of different men in the natural attitude. There is thus an ongoing practical problem of intersubjectivity in the natural attitude. And, as we will see (chapter 9 below), this practical problem, the everyday social construction of social reality through men's thought, action and talk has increasingly become a focus of interest for sociologists, particularly ethnomethodologists. Husserl, however, never really addressed this problem of intersubjectivity. But he did address, without in any way solving, the problem of intersubjectivity that his own epoche method generated at the transcendental or reduced level.[5] We will look at the trap of solipsism, into which the absolute or pure ego falls, a little closer later, and also at Husserl's increasing emphasis on the natural attitude or Lebenswelt in his later philosophy. (Although this change of emphasis always remained within the suspect solipsism of the pure phenomenological point of view.)[6] But in his earlier preoccupation with pure phenomenological, for and in itself, Husserl was only interested in the 'natural attitude' as the quickly disposed of foil of the pure phenomenological 'epoche'; we will now briefly outline what is meant by this concept.

In the epoche the philosopher attempts to suspend his naive belief in the natural attitude (ibid., pp. 107-12). He puts the 'real' world of objects, instruments, values and people 'between brackets'; he puts them 'out of play' and attempts to do without them in his subsequent investigation of consciousness. Schutz expressed the relation between the natural attitude and the epoche well, when he called the former a 'suspension of doubt' and the latter a 'suspension of belief' (1962, pp. 229). In each case it is not so much a question of denying, but of ignoring and doing without, doubt and belief respectively.

As a way of 'getting back to basics' it might be argued that Descartes had forshadowed Husserl with his method of systematic doubt until one reached the indubitable 'I think/doubt, therefore I am, the "cogito".' Husserl recognised a considerable debt to Descartes, more than to Hume and Kant, even calling one of his best known works, *Cartesian Meditations*. But he was clear to distinguish his method from that of Descartes, which he did not think was radical or sustained enough as a philosophical project (1960a, 1969; p. 227). One must go further, suspending the 'fact' that 'I am', and that it is the concrete self 'I' who thinks; one must ground the 'cogito' itself as a pure possibility generated by the meaning-constituting activity of transcendental subjectivity, the realm of 'absolute being' (1967, p. 153), of Truth and the (Platonic) essences.

The epoche is a method of coming to terms with the fact that 'reality in itself', the 'objective world out-there', is without significance, unsignified, meaningless apart from man's conscious attention to it. This holds for social 'reality' just as fundamentally as it does for 'logical objectivities', and more than it does for material reality, although Husserl mainly confined himself to the latter two.

In epoche, the brute existence of a blossoming tree is ignored—its meaningless aspect is ignored—and we only deal with its meaningful aspects, those that are given to it, as it were, by consciousness. In doing this we are trying to grasp the essence of the phenomenon 'this blossoming tree'. A linguistic analogue of this procedure would be if we ignored the occurrence of the phrase, 'this blossoming tree' as part of a speech-act, and instead viewed the phrase from a different standpoint. We would concentrate on its grammatical structure, the references of the words and their function together as a phrase, within the sentence of which they are a part. We could 'think away' the occurrence of speech-acts altogether and still be left with phrases and sentence structures. Similarly, according to Husserl, we could 'think away' the existence of this blossoming tree altogether, destroy, it in our imagination, and still we would be left with a meaningful conception of the tree. This would be its essence or 'eidos', that which is essentially given in the experience of seeing the tree. When we come to Sartre it will be seen that there are other interpretations of the essential nature of perceptions. Sartre's account of being overwhelmed and sickened by the meaningless brute existence of a tree, in his novel *Nausea*, is a good example of the different concerns and interpretations of experience given by existential phenomenology compared with Husserl's pure phenomenology (1965b, p. 182).

Followers of Husserl, like Sartre, agreed with him that philosophical activity must be more and other than simply a parasitic analysis of the achievements, methods and logic of the natural sciences. The logical empiricist and positivist restrictions of philosophy were rejected by both of them, but in the name of different projects. Husserl's involved the quest for a 'higher science' of transcendental subjectivity, which would reveal the ground of logic, mathematics and theoretical science in the meaning-constituting activities of pure consciousness. For Husserl, these forms of knowledge were really only very sophisticated enclaves and dimensions of the natural attitude, which also incorporates, as we have already mentioned, our more naively realistic beliefs about the physical and social world. In his pure phenomenological stage Husserl uses a speculative philosophical method to reveal and analyse essences and 'essencing' activities. He is not interested in proceeding there by way of, or towards, a critique of science, which on the contrary he hopes to 'ground' and justify. His interest in the cruder, more vague and pervasive dimensions and enclaves of the natural attitude is minimal; he seems to think that any thinking man would in any case suspend their relevance, and he is not much interested thereafter in grounding and justifying the superficialities and trivia cluttering up common sense. As compared with this, Husserl's existentialist sociological followers have set themselves precisely the project of studying this 'clutter', and the everyday life which generates it, in close detail, and partly by means of a trenchant critique of natural scientific, empiricist and positivist claims and analogies. That is, they reject Husserl's transcendental project, together with all scientific and scientistic methods drawn from the sophisticated enclaves of the natural attitude, in order to study the natural attitude more or less on its own ground and in its own terms.

My case in this book is that conceptual analysts, following the later Wittgenstein, took a remarkably similiar view to these dissident Husserlians, given all of the differences in style between them; and that furthermore, both schools set themselves tasks that only humanistic sociologies like ethnomethodology can tackle. Both philosophical schools in their different ways, see a project and a method, a topic and a resource, in the lived world of the natural attitude. And both indicate that this project establishes a role, not only for philosophy, but for sociology also, and in particular for types of sociology that are at present regarded as unconventional, unnecessary and uninteresting by conventional sociology.

It is interesting to note, regarding conventional sociology, that the taxonomic 'theorist' Talcott Parsons, has had recourse to Husserl's transcendental essentialism. He made use of Husserl's notion of the phenomenological essence of something being that which 'cannot be thought away' from the experience of the thing. Parsons wrote, in the *Structure of Social Action*, that what he called the 'action frame of reference' was 'the indispensable, logical framework in which we describe and think about the phenomena of action' (1937, p. 733). Thus it had what he called 'phenomenological status', in that it involved 'no concrete data that can be "thought away".' The 'essence' of action was thus alleged to be given in Parsons' analysis of 'the action frame of reference'. On the other hand, space and time cannot be thought away from any conception of the physical world. Thus the 'essence' of physical objects, the area of the natural sciences, was alleged to be given in any analysis of the 'spatio-temporal frame of reference'. The sciences of action are in this way distinguishable from the natural sciences, according to Parsons, and investigation in terms of the one framework necessarily involves the irrelevance of the other (ibid., p. 764).

It was a similar sort of position that the existential followers of Husserl endorsed when they demanded a critique of, and suspension of, natural science in order to see and study man's existential situation better, in a clearer light. With Parsons, they are prepared to make ontological-type assertions as to the basic nature and being of things given in and by consciousness, and are prepared to base their investigations and studies on such assertions. Husserl began from the natural attitude, and using his distinctive philosophical method, reached essentialist assertions. His followers and, perhaps unwittingly many social theorists, begin from essentialist assertions and work towards describing the natural attitude. In the previous section on Brentano it was noted that an important characteristic of the phenomenological school was its assertion that, at the very least, there exist Persons, and its analysis of the essential nature of personal existence, which implies an analysis of consciousness and of what it is to have bodily and social existence.

At the same 'untestable' level, various types of sociology have given us 'man the role-player', 'homo sociologicus' (Dahrendorf, 1968), 'other-directed man' (Riesman, 1950, ch. 1), 'animal symbolicus' (Schutz, 1962, p. 356), etc. Again, at the same level, conceptual analysis, influenced by the later Wittgenstein, has given us 'man the rule-governed actor' (Peters, 1958, p. 5), the language-game player (Wittgenstein, 1956, pp. 31-2 *passim*), the 'free actor' (Melden, 1967, pp. ix, 179, 213, etc.), the 'Person' (Strawson, 1959, ch. 3) and soon. All three forms of study utilise these ontological-level assertions and conceptions of the essential nature of man's existence,—whether in the mode of working hypotheses, ultimate bounds of sense, regulative principles of experience and concept formation or whatever—when they describe and investigate concrete examples of such existence. Later we must discuss the 'idea of a social science' as propounded by logical empiricist philosophers of science (see chapter 3 below). And further we must discuss the relevance of this level of assertion in social science (see chapter 9 below, and chapter 7 and 8 *passim*). But preparatory to such discussions it is useful to know that two major philosophic schools are themselves as deeply involved with such assertions, both implicitly and explicitly, as sociology itself is in practice.

Enough has been said about Husserl's period of pure phenomenology and its main concepts of (a) the natural attitude, (b) the method of suspending this attitude, and (c) the realm of pure subjectivity which one is supposed to reach as a result of the suspension. We can now pass on to the final stage of Husserl's writing, where the difficulty involved in reconciling anti-existential subjectivity with existential personal subjectivity and intersubjectivity, produced further ambiguities and contradictions in his work.

The point of pure phenomenology was to show how all meaning issues from pure transcendental subjectivity, and how all meanings are constituted by consciousness. From this standpoint, having grasped the essence of wordly realities by removing their existence from them, we are in a position to allow existence back in again. The latter was a stage that did not occupy much of Husserl's effort in the period when he was developing the idea of a pure phenomenology, but which came to be very important in his later work (1970a, 1960a; see also Ricoeur, 1967a, chapters 4 and 5). For here he tries to build up and reconstitute the natural world, the world of the natural attitude, having taken it apart to get to its foundations in pure subjectivity. This would be a synthetic movement, as opposed to the original analytic one. To use Sartre's dialectical terms, this would be a 'progressive' as opposed to a 'regressive' movement 1963b, ch. 3), or to use Galileo's scientific terms it would be a 'compositive' as opposed to a 'resolutive' movement (see the discussion of Husserl's and Carnap's methods in chapter 3 below).

But the question arises as to precisely how Husserl can reconstitute anything. All it seems that he can do is to restore existence, where he had previously taken it away—to restore by philosopher's fiat what he had taken away by philosopher's fiat. We can reasonably hypothesise that the answer lies in the influence that Dilthey, Heidegger and Lévy-Bruhl, the French anthropologist, came to have on Husserl, and also in the pre-war environment of German internal and international politics.[7] The former influence was an intellectual one, convincing him that he had ignored the distinctive nature of the 'human sciences' for too long. The latter influence was a practical and moral one, convincing him that he had ignored his own society, culture and history for too long.

Heidegger, his student, and Dilthey, with whom he corresponded, influenced him, if not to accept then at least to discuss man's being-there-in-the-world and man's spirituality, respectively. And the rise of Nazi irrationalism led Husserl to write about the 'crisis of European man', which he saw as the failure of European rationalism, from its Greek philosophic beginning, to provide a scientific account of subjectivity and consciousness equal to its account of the natural world (1965; 1970a). Instead European thought had become lost in 'objectivism' and 'naturalism', and had allowed the success of natural sciences to obscure the possibility that a science of subjectivity and consciousness might take a radically different form from that which the natural sciences had taken. Because there had been no rational/scientific (in this widened sense) account of subjectivity and consciousness, a vacuum had been created which had filled up with irrationalist debris, according to Husserl. The Nazi ideology was such a piece of debris. The crisis of European man, on the intellectual level only, could only be resolved by determined efforts to provide the missing rational/scientific account of subjectivity and consciousness. Needless to say, Husserl was advocating the adoption of his own philosophic programme, an essentialist phenomenology of pure subjectivity.

Thus the critique of the 'natural attitude', which was outlined in the 'pure phenomenological' stage of Husserl's development, is superseded by a specific critique of the claims of natural science to exclusively embody the European tradition of rational thinking. Husserl now differentiates the 'natural attitude' and natural science, whereas before he placed them in the same category. This differentiation, as was mentioned above, was made quite explicit by Husserl's followers, who considered that they could suspend and criticise the natural sciences while still being able to study the world of the natural attitude. That Husserl eventually felt the need to make a similar differentiation, shows how inadequate and ambiguous was his portrayal of the 'natural attitude' in his 'pure phenomenological' stage.

Particularly, there was Husserl's ambiguity over what theory of knowledge he held to be implied by the 'natural attitude'. Was it the version of naive realism epitomised by sensationalistic empiricism Or was it the version of naive realism epitomised in historical and sociological empiricism that views all men as the creators of common practical and cultural objects? The first version must be phrased in the passive, received mode, while the second must be phrased in the active, creative mode. The first version builds up the intersubjective nature of the world from sensory inputs received by the individual sensor. The second version simply asserts, as its basic axiom, that the world is an intersubjective construction. Thus the first version asserts that the common world of everyday objects is a spatio-temporal world of things. Whereas the second version asserts that the common world of everyday objects is a meaningful world of things-as-instruments, other persons, social actions, social communication and social structures. There is a dichotomy between these two versions of naive realism which remained unexpressed in Husserl's earlier writings (see Husserl 1967) but which he began to express in his later writings.

Husserl effected this differentiation of two interpretations of the natural attitude, by introducing the concepts *Umwelt* and *Lebenswelt*—the environing world and the lived-in world—which he used interchangeably, to refer to the socio-cultural version of naive realism present in the natural attitude. The other version, the sensationalistic one, he characterised as the philosophic background to the natural sciences, against which the change from empirical generalisation to theoretical formalism in science must be seen.

Husserl's later work, particularly his thesis of the crisis in European thought (1965, 1970a), was put forward largely in terms of a contrast between the concepts involved in man's 'life-world' as against the concepts involved in the natural sciences. He was particularly keen to make the point that natural science itself is an activity engaged in by a community of men, adhering to certain common standards and norms. Thus that in so far as it fails to understand, in general, such common social activities and common social objects like norms, then it fails to understand its own nature. (That science is an enclave within the social and historical world is well shown by Kuhn (1970a)). To Husserl, natural science is 'lost' in the world of things, lost in its own objectivity and desire to 'be objective'. It can no longer view itself as one more activity-of-many-subjectivities among a world of such activities-in-common. Rather, it attempts to stand outside the 'life-world' and in amongst the material objects it spectates and correlates (1965, pp. 184-7).

But just as suspension of the natural attitude was originally Husserl's method of reaching 'pure subjectivity', so now his method of reaching the same realm of essences lies in suspending natural science while retaining and analysing man's 'life-world'. Husserl's followers saw that this attempt to salvage the original pure phenomenological project in the face of the new phenomenological project (to analyse and describe man's consciousness in-the-world) was ultimately a failure. Either the phenomenologist is oriented towards the essence, or he is oriented towards existence. He cannot be oriented towards both, (although Merleau-Ponty did claim to locate essence *in* existence (1962, p. vii)). Either the phenomenologist is concerned with impersonal transcendental subjectivity, or he is concerned with socially and organically embodied personal subjectivity. He cannot be concerned with both.

The phenomenologists who put this argument most strongly were the French existentialist philosophers, Sartre and Merleau-Ponty, to whom we now turn. In a later section the extent to which Schutz and Heidegger also helped in this weaning-off of the phenomenological school from Husserl's programme will be outlined.

Existential phenomenology

Sartre

So far, it has been seen that Brentano contributed the ideas of 'intentionality' of consciousness, and description of consciousness to the phenomenological school, while Husserl contributed the ideas of 'pure consciousness' (the transcendental realm of essences), the 'epoche' of existence and the 'natural attitude' or the 'lived-world'. Sartre and Merleau-Ponty, like Heidegger and Schutz, contributed different versions of man's existential condition to the phenomenological school in a general reaction against Husserl's emphasis on essence. Consciousness was no more to be thought of as some Godhead, outside the world, painting the things in the world with the meanings of Platonic essences. Now consciousness had an organic embodiment and a social situation relative to other such entities, in the writings of Sartre and the other post-Husserlians. Consciousness *is* personal existence, not impersonal essence, as Husserl asserts.

Two of the main problems that confront a philosopher trying to understand personal existence are the senses in which both the personal Body defines the person, and in which Other Persons define the person. Sartre and Merleau-Ponty devote a lot of their writings to these problems and also to ways in which personal consciousness transcends such definitions in ongoing life, revealing, questioning and testing all limitations not only possibly in thought, but necessarily in action. And this is the problem of Freedom which so clearly characterises existentialist writings.

As regards Sartre, it could well be objected that the 'phenomenological ontology' that he sets out in *Being and Nothingness* (first published 1943) is proposed on a very transcendental level. For instance, Sartre pictures 'Nothingness', or consciousness, as a completely impersonal stream of creativity in which all human beings participate. In an earlier critical analysis of Husserl's concept of transcendental subjectivity (1962c), Sartre set out to show that Husserl's epoche revealed a 'transcendental ego'. It did not reveal an ego-less conception of the being of consciousness, as Sartre thought it should have. In other words there is a case for interpreting

Husserl and Sartre in completely the opposite way from the general way I want to interpret them here. It could be said that far from having an impersonal conception of consciousness at the transcendental level, Husserl has an ego-logical conception. And it could be said that, far from having a personal conception of consciousness at the transcendental level, Sartre has an explicitly impersonal one.

The way of dealing with this objection is simply to point to the philosophic work that each philosopher put his ideas to. Husserl worked at the transcendental level, while Sartre has worked mainly at the existential level. If Husserl talked of a 'transcendental ego' then it explicitly had no bearing whatsoever on the existentially situated entity 'person', 'self', 'me', or 'ordinary ego'. Sartre's work, on the other hand, has a bearing precisely on the existential person (see also his criticisms of Kant's transcendentalism, 1966, p. 276). He puts his conception of Nothingness, of transcendental ego-less consciousness, the impersonal stream of spontaneity manifested in every person, to work in the effort to understand human existence and life. In fact he gives his terms so many applications to concrete examples, particularly by tying the Nothingness to Freedom and responsibility, both moral notions, that the original transcendental interpretation of the terms almost becomes redundant and irrelevant: 'One must be conscious in order to choose, and one must choose in order to be conscious. Choice and consciousness are one and the same thing' (1966, p. 565). In connection with this Spiegelberg writes: 'It is this tacit dropping out of the transcendental dimension and the implied humanisation or "mundanisation" of consciousness which constitutes the most significant change in Sartre's version of Husserlian phenomenology' (1969, p. 481). It is in the light of this development in Sartre's philosophy towards analysis of consciousness in terms of personal existence that we must view his analysis, in *Being and Nothingness*, of consciousness as the abstraction—the 'for-itself'.

The point that needs to be made concerning the style of post-Husserlian phenomenologists like Sartre is that they did not give up the claim to make essentialist metaphysical statements, but unlike Husserl they did not regard this kind of statement as the goal of philosophy which could only be attained by a specific reflective technique. Rather they derived such statements directly from descriptions of their own on-going non-reflective experience and immediately applied them and exemplified them in further descriptions of actual and conceivable real life experience.

Sartre's semi-autobiographical novel *Nausea* (1965b) relates the kinds of experience from which the ontological conceptions in *Being and Nothingness* arose, while the outline of an 'existential psycho-analysis' in the latter work (1966, p. 696) shows the concern Sartre felt to relate these conceptions back to these realms of personal existence and experience from which they came.

The experience from which the ontological conception of Being as 'in-itself' is derived is well represented by the feelings which assail Roquentin, the 'narrator' in *Nausea*, when he sits contemplating a tree. He feels repelled and frightened by the absurd, unjustifiable, unknowing solid existence that the tree has. And then it appears that all of the things that confront him share completely this same form of existence, and thus that their individuality, as 'tree' or 'grass' or 'bench' is a façade which melts away to reveal them as being all the same 'stuff', 'soft, monstrous masses, in disorder' (1965b, p. 183).

Sometimes Sartre refers to the form of being in-itself that this exemplifies in anthropomorphic terms, so that it 'threatens', 'seduces' or 'resists' us. Partly this is merely Sartre's over-emphatic imagination and exuberant style. And partly it is a device allowing us to see the co-existence of consciousness and things. That is, this is more than a mere repetition of Brentano's thesis that 'all consciousness is consciousness *of* something'. It pulls this thesis from the realm of definition into the realm of existence. It means that consciousness exists unfulfilled, and in a radically different way than that which fleetingly fulfills it. Consciousness exists as a lack, a nothing, an emptiness in the face of things which exist solidly and for no reason. It is not a matter of mere definition that you cannot have consciousness without there being an object of consciousness; according to Sartre it is a primary datum of our experience. But that does not mean that it is merely contingent and possible either; rather it is held to be a certain and absolute structure of existence. Sartre can refer to experience and talk of existence, and yet come away with certainties and absolutes in the way that no empiricist would when basing his arguments on experience and existence. This is why one has to be very careful in dealing with Sartre's formulae such as 'existence precedes essence' (1965a, p. 26), and with his rejection of Husserl's essentialism, because Sartre's analysis of existence is shot through with unsupported and unsupportable essentialist intuitions.

It is then something of a 'synthetic *a priori*' proposition for Sartre that consciousness arises in the face of things, and that it exists in a different way than things do. The nature of their co-existence is that of antithesis. Consciousness is precisely what being in-itself is not, and being-in-itself is precisely what consciousness is not. Moreover, consciousness 'wants to become' its opposite and so attain absolute self-sufficiency. Or, in more ethical terminology, Sartre sometimes puts this idea as that consciousness wants to escape from its nature and become thing-like, in bad faith and self-deception. On the other hand, being-in-itself is represented in the anthropomorphic postures of threatening and seducing consciousness, its opposite. But while it is in the nature of at least one of these co-existent modes of being to want to be like the other one, it is also in their essential nature that this is impossible. The result is a picture of the Cartesian Mind-Matter dichotomy cast in the form of an Hegelian dialectic that is eternally fated to have no synthesis.

The revelation of the being of consciousness and the being of matter arose from an experience which, it is reasonable to assume, is not a very common experience among people in general, and not a very regularly recurring experience among those afflicted few, in particular. Sartre does not like to remain at this kind of distance from ordinary life experiences for too long, as can be seen in any of his philosophical writings by the number of concrete examples he illustrates his arguments with (and sometimes loses them in). The third form of being which occupies a considerable amount of space in *Being and Nothingness* is attested to by much more common experiences, and that is what he calls 'being-for-others'.

'Being-for-others' is simply the awareness I have that I am seen as body by other people. It is an awareness and a form of experience common to all men, and is exemplified in awareness of the gaze of others at oneself, leading in some cases to experiences of timidity, shyness and anxiety and in other cases to efforts at conforming to the picture that others hold of oneself. Sartre calls this an 'ontological dimension' on a par with 'being-for-itself and 'being-in-itself'. In a sense it is one of the main areas where the grand ontological struggle between the latter two dimensions is enacted. Whereas Sartre's picture of inanimate being 'threatening' and 'seducing' consciousness was set out in unjustifiably anthropomorphic terms, his later picture of the gaze of others threatening consciousness is a little more justifiable. He speaks of the 'profound truth' that lies in the myth of Medusa's gaze which turned men to stone (1966, p. 525).

While personal existence, or personal consciousness need not become a thing merely by co-existing as a no-thing among things, it is conceivable that it could become a thing by co-existing with the Medusa-like influences of other people. This possibility is more clearly seen if we give personal existence/consciousness the interpretation Sartre preferred to stress as he developed his argument in *Being and Nothingness*, that is as absolute freedom. 'I am free to think any thought I choose'. If we extend this formula from thought to action we get, 'I am free to act in any way that I choose'. And if my actions define the person that I am, then we get, 'I am free to choose myself, the person that I am'. Sartre rounds off this line of interpretation by adding that I am 'condemned' to this absolute freedom, this absolute choosing. Becoming 'thing-like' is something of an abstraction, but losing choice and freedom is an interpretation of that abstraction which we can understand a lot more directly.

On the level of his earlier ontological analysis, being-in-itself by its mere presence threatened to transmute being-for-itself into being-in-itself. But in the light of the introduction of being-for-others and the concept of being-for-itself as personal freedom it now appears that the presence of others is the main threat. Whereas ultimately it is physically impossible to become a thing like a stone, it is quite socially and experientially possible for a person to become the thing that others want him to be. This is a social interpretation of reification which refers to a real process, as opposed to the physical interpretation of reification which could never be more than a metaphor. And it came to be used increasingly by Sartre as the paradigm for the existential threats with which personal consciousness has to contend.

His social philosophy is, if you like, a philosophy of anti-sociality. 'Hell is others' (1947). I have to struggle with the other to keep my own consciousness and freedom which he wants to turn into his objects. Similarly he has to struggle against my invasion of his life and liberty. Sartre's pessimistic dialecticism has taken another turn.

On this point Sartre takes issue with Heidegger, who proposed that Others are revealed to us 'being-with' us, in community with us (*Mitsein*), at the most basic ontological level (1966, p. 522). If this primordial community is given in the term 'Us', then Sartre asserts we are implying the existence of a third entity whose gaze at us constitutes us as the 'us-object'. Two men fighting become 'us' in the presence of a third man. All of humanity becomes 'us' in the presence of God. At best then this is a secondary and not a primordial form of community. On the other hand, if this community is given in the term 'We', or 'we-as-subject', Sartre asserts that this implies an 'undifferentiated transcendence' which could not account for the reality of individual, distinct, personal existences. The only kind of personal reality it could account for would be that of the completely anonymous and interchangeable personalities that, in modern society, are the objects of mass advertising, mass transport and mass government. If the 'we-subject' implies the concrete 'we-who-stand-in-a-bus-queue', or the 'we-who-buy-cigarettes', then Heidegger has succeeded only in defining pseudo-community.

So according to Sartre the experience of being *with* other people 'has no value as a metaphysical revelation' (ibid., p. 523), rather it is the experience of being *against* other people that has metaphysical value, revealing one of the basic ontological dimensions. The essence of the relationship between consciousness is not *Mitsein*; it is conflict (ibid., p. 525). If we were to substitute the notion of necessary personal bodily needs for Sartre's notion of necessary personal freedom of consciousness, then we would get a mirror image, in the area of ontological speculation, of Hobbes' political speculations. But to what a different end. Hobbes wants to demonstrate the need for an authoritarian structuring of civil society, and thereby its rightness. Sartre would seem by his conviction that it is right to be true to one's existential nature as an absolutely free thinker, chooser and doer, to be forced into the position of condemning civil society for its institution of bad faith in its production of some degree of harmony and order between people.

In the most recent stage of Sartre's philosophical progress, which we will not deal with here, that of his fraternal critique of Marxism, he repudiates his doctrine of absolute freedom and absolute choice (see Sartre, 1960; 1963b; Laing and Cooper, 1964, ch. 3; Odajnyk, 1965; Desan, 1966). In relation to this it is interesting to note Sartre's sociological premonitions in *Being and Nothingness*. There his allegedly ontological objection to Heidegger's analysis of *Mitsein* is exemplified mainly in terms of class conflict (1966, p. 524). The kind of 'all against all' that is implied on the ontological level by the co-existence of my freedom and others' freedom receives no illustration in terms of ordinary interpersonal existence from Sartre. Thus it is tempting to say that Sartre merely reproaches Heidegger for not being sociologically perceptive, rather than for being ontologically inaccurate.

For both Heidegger and Sartre there is no sense in solipsism. Myself and others the same as myself are really there, really given. Their only disagreement is over the nature of relations between all the 'myselfs' and all the 'others' of which the human social world is composed. As existential phenomenologists they begin with an ontology of persons derived from the everyday realism of ordinary experience, their disagreements arise after this point.

Sartre's existentialism overcomes his transcendentally proposed ontology. Being-for-itself is in the world, it is embodied in a person who confronts other persons. It is embodied in a unique visual perspective, which has a unique centre and a unique horizon. It is embodied as a unique set of organic instruments and tools and as the directive centre that uses them. It is embodied in such a way that it knows itself first, as unlimited abilities and choices, while others know it first, as a limited set of bodily and personality characteristics. In contrast, Sartre thought that '(in Husserl) we begin with the world of our knowledge, we leave it by the phenomenological epoche, and we never return to the world from the epoche' (Spiegelberg, 1969, vol. 2, p. 478). Sartre's philosophy is continually a return to the world from transcendental metaphysical intuitions and assertions that are alleged to have their root in our experience of the world to begin with.

Sartre's own phenomenology of lived experience has covered descriptions of imagination (1948b; 1962a), of the emotions (1962b), of what it is to be a Jew-hater (1948a), besides social phenomenological accounts of the lives of Baudelaire (1963a), Genet (1964b), Flaubert (1971) and himself (1964a). These exemplify, to some extent, Sartre's own programme of 'existential psycho-analysis' which is to understand men's lives, experiences and products, including their own personalities, as the result of their own free choices in the face of the knowing influence of other people and in the face of the unknowing influence of the material conditions of the world. Except in his critiques of the claim of natural scientific methods in psychology to cover the same area, Sartre is necessarily unsystematic and relatively disorganised in his contributions to existential psycho-analysis, which is evidently a vast undertaking. We will examine this undertaking in more detail in chapter 7. For the moment it is enough to remark that existential psycho-analysis is a phenomenological enterprise based on an ontology of persons. And as such it marks a concern for the 'lived-world' and for the 'natural attitude' that Husserl could not admit without jeopardising his methodological suspension of this realm in the epoche. As such also it implies a proximity to the speculative analyses of man, society and action which lie behind such modern psychology, psychiatry and sociology.

Merleau-Ponty

Existential phenomenology is the exploitation of the emergent contradictions of Husserl's later writings. This assertion has a limited application to Sartre's development. But it has a greater application to Sartre's colleague, Merleau-Ponty, who made a study, apparently brief and unsystematic (see Tilliette, 1970), of Husserl's unpublished manuscripts before writing in 1945 his major work: *The Phenomenology of Perception* (1962).

Where Sartre was not much interested in the nature of phenomenological ideas for their own sake, but rather used them in his philosophy of being and existence, Merleau-Ponty was concerned about the nature of phenomenology. He saw the ontological and existentialist use to which Sartre and Heidegger put phenomenological description and experience, and he saw the intimation of this development in Husserl's later writings. He seemed to see his own task in philosophy as that of re-establishing the evolutionary rather than revolutionary nature of this development. Thus the flight from the world to essence required by the epoche had to be made compatible with the description of consciousness engaged in the world required by existentialism.

Merleau-Ponty attempted to demonstrate that these were compatible in the following way. First, he considered that the epoche required only a flight from natural science's conception of the world, but not, for instance, from the 'pre-scientific' knowledge we have of the world given in perception. And second, theories, deductions and ideal types in psychological and sociological studies were, according to Merleau-Ponty, kinds of essence that Husserl would have accepted as having phenomenological status in the sense that they were 'that which could not be thought away from' phenomena. We have seen that at one stage Parsons offered this interpretation of the nature of his sociological axioms concerning the 'action frame of reference'. We have also seen that, despite his slogan 'existence precedes essence', Sartre's theory of the nature of consciousness and material things in general is nothing other than an assertion concerning the essence of things, which is purely intuitive and incapable of being tested. As another example Merleau-Ponty refers to Durkheim's shift, in his analysis of the nature of Australian aborigines' religion, from this concrete problem to the essentialist, abstract or universal problem of 'what is religion' (1964a, p. 85). Durkheim asserts that the *essential* nature of religion is its sociological aspect of expressing group solidarity. And further, he goes on to state that the essence of society is that it is a moral community which needs to express its togetherness in such ways as religious ritual. Similarly Max Weber's 'ideal type' method would be, for Merleau-Ponty, merely another way of stating the essence of some social reality in order to compare and to correlate divers empirical approximations of such a reality (see chapter 8 below).

With more or less rigour, all these thinkers make essentialist assertions, and Merleau-Ponty sees this as some justification for continuing to take Husserl's attempt to reveal essence seriously. He grants that the epoche, and the meditative effort which Husserl envisaged as constituting the suspension of belief in existence, need not be taken seriously; neither may Husserl's belief that the revelation (or more honestly, the assertion) of essence revealed Absolute Truth, the idealist philosopher's Promised Land. Merleau-Ponty believes that in spite of all this, some sense and usefulness remains in the notion of 'essence', and thus in a conception of phenomenology which aims at the revelation of essence, understood in this qualified sense.

Merleau-Ponty's first point, that the epoche required a flight from natural science's conception of the world, rather than from the 'pre-scientific' realism of the 'natural attitude' or of ordinary perception, exploits the ambiguity which Husserl, as we have seen above, found himself in on this question. Either interpretation could be justified by selecting from Husserl's text. Merleau-Ponty's interpretation is embodied in his major work *Phenomenology of Perception.* Here phenomenology still retains its goal of revealing essences, but has no royal road to a realm of pure essences, a 'complete reduction' is 'impossible' (1962, p. xiv). It must embroil itself in existing personal consciousness and in existing social and material things. Its only epoche must be of the natural scientific version of reality: 'Husserl's first directive to phenomenology, in its early stages, to be a 'descriptive psychology', or to return to the "things in themselves" is from the start a rejection of science' (ibid., p. vii). It must investigate the naive realism in which a world of existents and realities is given to every man; it must investigate 'pre-scientific knowledge'; it must investigate the 'natural attitude' and the *Lebenswelt.* Thus, for Merleau-Ponty, it must investigate perception. And this is understood, by him, less as an investigation of the perceiving act, and more as an investigation of the world as perceived. If the epoche has any function it is that of helping us to make this area an object of study and analysis by revealing our engagement in, and commitment to, our naive realism. The epoche, rather than diverting us to the transcendental realm, as it is supposed to do, helps us to see the ordinary as strange and in need of some explanation.

Merleau-Ponty devotes much of his analysis to what embodiment means. He expands greatly on Sartre's analysis of the Self's Body as being both a socially defined thing-for-others and a directive centre which uses instruments situated in space for intentions directed in time.

While it is not true that Merleau-Ponty is in any sense a copy of Sartre, it is true to say that their personal relationship for a number of years as editors of *Les Temps Modernes*, lent a great deal of similarity to their philosophical work (see Sartre, 1965c, pp. 227-326; Rabil, 1967, pp. 116-42). Typically, Merleau-Ponty increasingly became, both philosophically and politically, a cautious and considered critic of Sartre. Philosophically he does not use the melodramatic examples and the exaggerated metaphysics of Sartre. Freedom for Sartre is absolute and unconditioned, for Merleau-Ponty it is situated, conditioned and possibly 'pre-conscious' (1962, pp. 434-56).

According to Sartre we are 'condemned to freedom', while according to Merleau-Ponty we are 'condemned to meaning' (ibid., p. xix). Merleau-Ponty brings out more clearly the intersubjective nature of existence which, as we have seen, is present in Sartre's ideas but which he wants to paint in the colours of conflict. For Merleau-Ponty, speech and language are at least as basic bridges between Self and Others as are the allegedly Medusa-like gazes by which each Self attempts to reify the Other (see Merleau-Ponty, 1962, pp. 346-68; 1964a, pp. 43-96; 1964b, pp. 84-97). Trained as a child psychologist, he was prepared to back up his belief in the intersubjective and social nature of man's conscious existence by referring to psychological research on child development, particularly Piaget's work on the development of children's concepts of space, time, morality, etc. (see 1964a, pp. 96-158).

Perhaps his greatest divergence from Sartre was over the Cartesian dualism of Mind and Matter that lay behind the cosmic battle between 'being-for-itself' and 'being-in-itself' in Sartre's ontology. Merleau-Ponty rejected this dualism in theory (1962, pp. 369-410) as Sartre was to do more and more in practice. As we saw above, Sartre comes to base the concept of the reification of individual consciousness and freedom more on threats from society and other people and less on threats from the mere presence of things, as he had originally outlined in *Nausea*. Merleau-Ponty realised that a thoroughgoing existentialism which investigated man's existence as engaged with his world could only have one concept of being, and that he called '*être au monde*', or 'being-in-the-midst-of-the-world'. Man's existence was not an essentially divided existence, part angel and part animal as Descartes and Kant would have us believe. Man, as we know him, is the possessor of manual and linguistic skills of which only his embodiment as an organic entity, and only his co-existence with other persons could make any sense. The only way he could be pictured as divided is in abstraction from his natural setting, and this kind of abstraction is the one thing that existentialism most clearly rejects.

Merleau-Ponty's positive contribution to phenomenology is to give his interpretation of the *Lebenswelt* in his analysis of the naive realism embodied in everyman's ordinary perception and in the perceived world that he inhabits. His other, more negative, contribution is his critique of natural scientific aspirations in psychology, outlined in his first book *The Structure of Behaviour*, and in other works, including *Phenomenology of Perception*. We will discuss this side of his work further in chapters 4 and 5, and we will investigate his views on Weber in chapter 8. For the moment, our overview of existential phenomenology must be rounded off with some brief comments on the contributions of Heidegger and Schutz.

Heidegger

Heidegger has not yet written a systematic outline of his philosophy of Being, and it is reasonable now, because of his age, to presume that he never will. His major work, *Being and Time* (1962), first published in 1927, was intended as only an introduction to a study of the concept of Being, which was never published (ibid., p. 64). This introduction concerned itself with human being, and with the temporal and historical nature of human being. It was interpreted at the time, quite rightly, as an anthropological and existentialist treatise. However, to the reby interpret Heidegger's phoisophy as existentialist was quite wrong. His real interests and commitments, intellectual ones that is, excluding his Fascist politics, lay elsewhere, in the study of Being, of which particular human beings and other existents are but manifestations. Unlike Sartre, who put his ontology to work in understanding human existence, Heidegger wanted to put his understanding of human existence to work as an introduction to his ontology. (Only the first part of this programme, and a section on Kant from the second part, has ever seen the light of day. Heidegger has produced a number of works since then, on Hegel (1970) and on poetry (1949) for instance, which have not substantially developed or changed his earlier position.)

Whether as an existentialist work or not, we are more concerned with the effect that *Being and Time* actually did have, rather than with the possibility that this effect was the result of misinterpretation. One of the most obvious effects was that the stylistic effort to 'write profoundly', to coin new terms, and to convolute, became fashionable. Sartre's style of writing in *Being and Nothingness* shows Heidegger's influence. As Ryle pointed out, in a review of *Being and Time* (in *Mind*, 1929), such a style runs the risk of lapsing into 'windy mysticism'. Also the logical positivists of the Vienna Circle in this period were able, so they thought, to present *Being and Time* as a good example of the meaningless use of words that metaphysics requires (see for example, Ayer, 1971, p. 59).

But, questions of style apart, the main effects that the book had were to symbolise the 'dead-end' to which Husserl's pure phenomenology had come, and to contribute to the growth of existentialist philosophy. As to the first, this was something of a personal tragedy for Husserl who had placed great hopes in Heidegger to turn pure phenomenology from a programme into a reality. Husserl enabled Heidegger to succeed him as professor of philosophy at Freiburg on Husserl's retirement in 1928. But his attempt to get Heidegger to collaborate with him over a brief definitive outline of phenomenology for inclusion in the *Encyclopaedia Britannica*, in 1927, had already failed. After a study of *Being and Time*, Husserl became convinced that Heidegger's lack of mention of the phenomenological reduction to transcendental subjectivity meant that he had lapsed into a naive anthropological or psychologistic approach (Spiegelberg, 1969, vol. 1, p. 282). Husserl concluded that Heidegger had not rid himself of the prejudices of the 'natural attitude'.

But we have seen that Husserl's view of the 'natural attitude' was short-sighted. The fact is that one cannot relinquish, or suspend, or reduce, ways of looking at the world which one lives but which one has not investigated for their own sake. Living something is not intellectually knowing about it, and in the epochal reduction only what one knows can be reduced and not what one lives through. Thus, even if the programme of a pure phenomenology was adhered to, it still required a *thoroughgoing* investigation of the 'natural attitude', or the *Lebenswelt*, if only as a means of ensuring a valid epoche. Thus at the very time that Husserl was, indirectly, criticising Heidegger for his anthropological investigations of the *Lebenswelt*, he was himself developing the concept of the *Lebenswelt*, and considering how the intersubjective world could be built up from an investigation of pure transcendental subjectivity. The latter project implied a reversal of the direction of the phenomenological programme, one explicitly taken up by Merleau-Ponty, for instance, as justifying the existentialist interpretation of phenomenology. It would be tempting to say that Heidegger's attempt to be independent of Husserl's philosophic influence had the effect, not only of profoundly disappointing Husserl, but also of pushing him into a degree of 'bad faith' and rigidity in the face of important problems within his conception of phenomenology.

However, it is ironic that, in spite of his own ultimately mystical and transcendental aim in philosophy to understand Being, Heidegger rejected Husserl's phenomenology precisely because of its transcendentalism. According to Heidegger, phenomenology, in its role as a preliminary to ontology, would have to be hermeneutic (1962, pp. 49-63). That is, it would have to understand and interpret human existence, as it is, as '*Dasein*', or being-there, as 'being-in-the-world' and as 'being-with-others'. Heidegger himself interprets human existence as having a temporal structure, as being a constant projection towards the future and a constant reassessment of the past. The knowledge of future personal death, of becoming nothing, of ceasing to be, imposes this temporality on human existence, and also imposes a general anxiety (*Angst*) on the human condition. Fear is specific and functional for survival; general anxiety, on the other hand, according to Heidegger, has a more profound influence on daily existence.

Since it is always possible to die and become nothing, Heidegger is able to anthropomorphise this possibility into the Nothing which threatens beings and Being. The driving force lying beneath our everyday lives, then, is our anxious attempt to escape from becoming nothing, although it is our ultimate fate and destiny to fail because of the necessity of our own death. In the light of this, Heidegger analyses our everyday forms of escape into inauthentic and non-thinking social pursuits, being socially successful, being preoccupied with work or trivial conversation and communication with others, or just trying to be 'like everybody else'. The result is that the everyday life of human beings is marked by a repression and forgetfulness of the fundamental *Angst* of the human condition, and this forgetfulness issues in an inauthentic 'concern' about practical dealings with others and aspirations in terms of others.

Although it is not difficult to see why, on this kind of analysis, theologians have turned to Heidegger for an allegedly non-religious confirmation to theological revelations, psychiatrists also have tried to use Heidegger's hermenuetic phenomenology in the study of mental illness, particularly Binswanger (1963). There is a similarity here to Sartre, in the way that the British psychiatric school of Laing and his associates has attempted to implement Sartre's conception of existential psycho-analysis (see chapter 7 below). For both Binswanger and Laing the psychiatrist must make an effort to understand the internal coherence and meaningfulness of the 'mad' patient's perceived-world. And this effort in itself, by establishing the patient as a worthy and equal contributor to the therapeutic relationship, is held to be the most effective aspect of the therapy.

Heidegger's analysis of everyday life has also stimulated various features of the work of sociologists in and around the area of ethnomethodology (see Zimmerman, Pollner and McHugh in Douglas, 1971, and chapter 9 below). Hermeneutic phenomenology of everyday human existence, that is of the naively perceived and lived world, which inhabits everyman's consciousness, as much as everyman consciously inhabits it, was always, for Heidegger, an introductory and preliminary matter. And this is the case in spite of the fact that his creation of the idea marked a major turning point within the phenomenological school, and that others like Sartre and Merleau-Ponty were quick to follow his lead.

Schutz

For Schutz, on the other hand, phenomenology conceived as the investigation of the natural attitude, the *Lebenswelt*, was never a preliminary, but always a goal to which his sociological studies were oriented. And, like Merleau-Ponty, he drew on Husserl's later work, particularly the attempt to 'constitute' an intersubjective world in the phenomenologically reduced realm of transcendental subjectivity, or the pure ego which Husserl made in the Fifth Cartesian Meditation. Again, like Merleau-Ponty, Schutz held that while there were great difficulties in reconciling study of the intersubjective *Lebenswelt*, or natural attitude, with the programme of a pure phenomenology, still some reconciliation must be attempted. Both of them were interested in the problems of the nature of the human sciences, and they both believed that such problems as 'what is social action?' and 'what is society?' are basic questions, requiring an answer, and that any answer would necessarily be some statement of essence. The phenomenological reduction was a method of comprehending essences, therefore it must continue to have some role to play, even in a phenomenology completely committed to description of man's concrete engagement with his concrete world.

But more generally it would be true to say that what Schutz owed to Husserl was not a method but a problem. The problem was how to reconcile Husserl's insistence on building up the meaning of the world from the reduced sphere of the *single* transcendental ego, with the idea that there must actually be *many* coexisting transcendental subjectivities, as many as there are potential meditators, i.e. every person on earth. So at the transcendental level, there was the problem of solipsism, of how equal other-egos could be known (Schutz, 1962, pp. 165, 167, 195, and 197; 1966, pp. 51-84). Philosophers have been more used to stating the problem of solipsism at the mundane level. Solipsistic philosophers question the possibility of knowledge by an actually existing person or other actually existing persons. They are sceptical of the naive realism of everyday experience which sees no problem in the existence of other people.

It is interesting that Schutz, in effect, abandons the problem on the transcendental level, and he puts forward his concept of intersubjectivity as a fact about ordinary experience, at the mundane level, hopefully countering philosophic scepticism and endorsing naive realism. Schutz's 'general thesis of the alter ego's existence' is a statement about ordinary knowledge, in the natural attitude. It is as such that he puts it forward as a 'sufficient frame of reference for the foundation of empirical psychology and the social sciences' (1962, p. 175). Thus it has the same 'phenomenological status' that Parsons gave to the concept of action. The idea is that our knowledge of others can be more direct than our knowledge of ourselves. We have grown used to thinking that the opposite of this is the case. But Schutz draws attention to the facts of communication. When the Other speaks and I listen, I am absorbed in the 'vivid presence' of the Other's thought. Just as the Other cannot see his own facial expressions, so he cannot catch his own expressed thought as a 'now'-thought. He can only catch his own thought by a reflective turn, that is in the 'just-now' area of time. At the moment he expresses his thought I know the Other in a very different and conceivably more direct way than he knows himself. The opposite holds when I am the speaker, performer or communicator, and the Other is the listening, watchful audience. Then at the moment of performance he knows me in a different way, and conceivably more directly than I know myself, at that moment.

Man is always in state of society and this calls, almost constantly, for performance, expression and communication. So, in everyday life, I have a constant and necessary access to, and knowledge of, others, and they of me. As with other philosophical problems, scepticism as to the existence of others could only arise where the fact of man's social condition had been overlooked. This social condition Schutz (ostensibly following Scheler, but implicitly recognising Heidegger and theological existentialists like Marcel and Buber) calls the 'We'. The pure sphere of the 'We' is the ongoing socio-temporal reality—communication in the present.

If we take the general thesis of the later ego's existence, together with Max Weber's analysis of social action as rational and intentional, and as understandable in those terms, then we have the essence of Schutz's approach to the basic nature of the social sciences. His contributions have tended to be elucidations of Husserl and Weber's concepts, rather than independent analyses. He has elucidated both the concept of action (ibid., pp. 3-47 and 67-96; 1964, pp.3-19), and the concept of the natural attitude, (1962, pp. 207-356; 1964, pp. 20-62, and 226-73) following Weber and Husserl respectively. Perhaps his greatest claim to originality lies in his outline of a sociology of knowledge which would investigate the social structuring and social distribution of everyday, taken-for-granted kinds of knowledge (1962, pp. 149ff; see also Berger and Luckmann, 1967).

Thus, in effect, Schutz moved away from the idea that phenomenological description of the natural attitude must lead us on to show the genesis and constitution of the meaningful world from the realm of the transcendental ego, as Husserl advocated. For Schutz, phenomenological description did not imply pure transcendental phenomenology, rather it implied sociology. The given, meaningful world of naive realism or the natural attitude, is best seen as generated by the interaction and co-existence of men in society, rather than by a non-existent egoistically conceived subjectivity, that stands outside of all culture and history.

In the final analysis the sociologist and the descriptive phenomenologist in Schutz overcame the transcendental phenomenologist in him. It is for this reason that we tentatively classify Schutz as part of the existentialist turn in phenomenology. Indeed the existentialist motif of *Angst*, or fundamental anxiety, *is* present in Schutz's analysis of the natural attitude (1962, p. 228). As with Heidegger it is the knowledge of one's own impending death that underlies everyday activity. But unlike Heidegger, Schutz does not suggest that social activities and communications are thereby inauthentic escapes from confronting this problem, Rather, the thought of death is presented as one form of 'shock' that occasionally intrudes into everyday life and that jogs the individual out of the natural attitude and into religious or philosophical meditations, or into immersion in some other sphere of activity. Schutz presents the thought of death as factual shock to naive realism, not as an allegedly more authentic and valuable project than social life, as Heidegger presents it.

Enough has now been said to enable us to sum up the main ideas and developments of the phenomenological school.

Conclusion

The main ideas of the phenomenological school have been as follows:

(*a*) *Man's basic distinguishing feature is his ability to know that he is aware of things.* That is, he can be conscious of being conscious-of. Every man can prove to his own satisfaction that he 'possesses' consciousness. Phenomenologists rarely state this belief in the reality of the conscious individual, because it seems to them so self-evident. It does, however, need to be stated as it is not self-evident and non-controversial in the view of, for instance, the philosophy behind behaviouristic psychology.

(*b*) *Consciousness is intentional.* Every conscious act refers to an object of some kind, be it tangible of imaginary. The only 'contents' that consciousness 'has' are these objective correlates, these referred-to objects. When we describe the contents of a consciousness therefore, we have no 'inner' receptacle into which we look, or introspect. We can only describe that which is believed, imagined, desired, calculated, etc. And, when linguistically expressed, such descriptions are phenomena of the 'outer' world-in-common, as much as they are expressions of an 'inner' private life. The term 'consciousness' covers the ongoing stream of referential acts that any individual lives when he is not asleep or anaesthetised. Having spoken of the objective correlates of consciousness, we can now turn to the subjective correlates. These are mental activities manifested in and resulting in the form that the reference to objective content takes. The subjective correlate of consciousness is activity that creates a specific way of relating to an object. Imagining, believing and desiring, are the kinds of terms that describe this activity of form-giving, or modifying, which the conscious individual is destined to undertake. Phenomenology wants to understand this form-giving activity, but recognises that there is no way of approaching this subjective correlate of consciousness apart from through a study of the objective references of consciousness.

(*c*) *Phenomenological description: phenomenological psychology:* There is no way of studying the conscious activity of the experiencer apart from a study of that which he experiences. This is the sense behind the notion, introduced by Brentano and taken up by Husserl, of phenomenological description and of descriptive or phenomenological psychology. We cannot settle any epistemological or psychological questions until we accurately describe the phenomenon, that which is given, that which is the objective reference of our awareness. In the light of the maxim 'back to the phenomenon', both traditional sensationalistic accounts of knowledge and reductivist neurological accounts of knowledge are premature. For phenomenology, it is never correct to foreclose on the possible information that description of consciousness could produce. It may well be extremely difficult to repress one's inevitable prejudices and habits of thought, which have the effect of foreclosing on the phenomenon and of obstructing the view of it. Nevertheless, it is always philosophically more authentic to try to understand the phenomenon than to prematurely 'explain it away' as for instance, sensationalism and neurology do in different ways (see chapter 3 below).

(*d*) *The transcendental reduction.* This was Husserl's radical way of confronting the phenomenon in as presuppositionless a manner as he could. The main presupposition, or prejudice of thinking, for Husserl, was that of naive realism, which ascribes real existence at one level or another, to all the objective correlates of consciousness. Even imagined objects, like centaurs and dragons, have a mythical world where we accept them in some sense as existent. They can exert a real influence on a man's way of life, if for instance a man devoted himself to the creation and communication of myths and imaginary worlds in the way that novelists, artists or poets might do. If imagining has existential or realistic implications, albeit subtle, with regard to the imagined object, then believing and knowing have all the more so with regard to believed and known objects. Husserl wanted to suspend, or put out of play, these senses of realism and existence with which we concretise our experience in the natural attitude. He wanted to study the objective correlates of subjective activities purely as unities of meaning that have no further existential import. He wanted to see subjective activity as the genesis of meaning. Thus he removed the problem to the transcendental realm by ignoring the concrete existence of the subjective consciousness, and the concrete existence of the objects of consciousness.

Against this the existential phenomenologists have asserted that essence and meaning are inextricably associated with existence. Further, they assert that by ignoring existence the phenomenologist cannot possibly come to an adequate grasp of essence, meaning and subjectivity. If any suspension of thought-prejudices has to be undergone, then it must be limited to the suspension of the natural scientific picture of the world and of the associated positivist and reified features of everyday common sense which treat the world as pre-given.

According to existential phenomenologists, and, indeed, to the later Husserl, the natural scientific picture of the natural world is a secondary interpretation grounded upon our lived perceptions of the world, and as such must be approached secondarily and not primarily. The positivist natural scientific picture of psychological, social, historical and cultural reality, on the other hand, cannot be inferred from any actual achievements in these fields as a picture of physical reality could be (no doubt unjustifiably) inferred from actual achievements in physics. So in these fields, where phenomenology is most involved, the positivist natural scientific prejudice in thinking is essentially ideological and programmatic. For existential phenomenology, reduction is never to the transcendental level, but rather is a specific effort to rebut positivism and the natural scientific programme, particularly in the humanities. One of my main aims in this book is to document this effort.

(*e*) *Natural attitude: Lebenswelt.* We can render these two Husserlian ideas, which became central for existential phenomenology where they had been peripheral for pure phenomenology, in terms of 'naive realism' and 'the perceived and lived-in world', respectively. The latter is a cultural and historical version of the former. They both imply that man in a state of society takes all measure of things for granted as real and concrete. Values, purposes, rules, social organisations, instruments, other people as the same kind of entity to myself, other people as players of social roles very different from my own, all of these kinds of thing are given as real to us in our everyday lives. We could not go about living if we refused our complicity to all of these kinds of reality all at once. It is this existential situation of man in a state of society that existentialist phenomenologists are most concerned to describe and understand.

(*f*) *The trajectory of the phenomenological school, up into the clouds of the pure ego, and back to earth with existent man, represents one reaction of philosophy to the growth in explanatory power and social importance of the natural sciences.* Phenomenology presupposes that there is useful work for philosophers to do outside of elucidation of the nature of natural science. It presupposes that philosophy can still be the primary activity that it had traditionally been until science grew away from it. It need not now be parasitic upon science. Nor need it argue that science is false.

Husserl had hoped that philosophy could be saved by a transcendental project aimed at constituting, as a sphere of philosophical work, a transcendental sphere to which only those who had performed a uniquely philosophical reflective technique would have access. The existential phenomenologists realised that this flight from the world was no way to save philosophy. According to them there is a positive need for philosophic clarification and analysis in the spheres allegedly covered by the aspirant sciences of psychology and sociology. There is a need to re-establish first, ontological questions concerning the nature of the being of personal and social reality, and second, epistemological questions concerning the knowledge of these realities.

Husserl offered a transcendental idealist approach to these problems, and Heidegger offered a difficult and deep form of questioning and seeing. Existential phenomenology (excluding Heidegger for the moment) tended to be pragmatic rather than consistently principled about such transcendental and metaphysical perspectives and devoted just as much of its energies to descriptive, illustrative and exemplary accounts and encounters with the problems of personal and social being and knowledge.

In this book I will argue that very similar problems and a similar ambivalent concern for both a descriptive and a constitutive approach to them characterises the philosophical school founded on Wittgenstein's later writings. And I will argue that the school arose in response to, and in clear recognition of, positivism and the need to find a vocation for philosophy outside of positivism's parasitism on natural science. This has had the result, as we will see, that the philosophy of historical, psychological and social studies is of a markedly different nature than the philosophy of natural science. There is far more in the nature of almost ideological conflict between pro- and anti-scientific philosophies in the humanities.

For all practical purposes this conflict can be resolved into a disagreement over what is admissable on the level of theory in the humanities, and what is admissable on the level of empirical description. Phenomenology typically takes a far less rigorous view of this than pro-scientific viewpoints. Phenomenology proposes that ontological axioms concerning the nature of persons and of social coexistences are admissable on the level of theory. In fact it is possible to argue that sociological theories already imply such axioms or explicitly use them, in the mistaken belief that they are scientifically respectable (see chapter 9 below). Phenomenological sociology thus is in part reflection upon the ontological presuppositions and grounds, the very possibility of sociology. Indeed as models for such reflexive analysis, Heidegger's questioning of Being, and Husserl's search for and investigation of transcendental subjective grounds, are in the final analysis possibly more important and interesting than existential phenomenology, particularly in its more concrete and empirical aspects which I will be emphasising throughout my account. However, in other respects the existential phenomenology of Sartre and Merleau-Ponty is just as instructive for, and resonant with, sociology's humanistic features. Generally, for instance, it proposes that any and all forms of experience are possible candidates for analysis and formulation, that is that any and all forms of experience are evidence of a human world. No prejudgement of experience as corresponding or not to an external physical world is indulged, for instance, That is, there is no specific form of experience such as sensory perception (or rather sensory *re*ception) which confers any privileged kind of validity. In relation to this, it is possible to argue that sociology could have operated if it had not, for instance, made use of experiences of social action, of goals, of means, of others, and of social structures that are not primarily sensory receptions.

The anti-scientific philosophies of the humanities involve at least these elements of a personalistic ontology, and an experiential empiricism distinct from sensationalistic empiricism. Phenomenology has been shown to involve these elements. We may now pass on to a consideration of conceptual analysis, which will show that this school shares these broad features with the school of phenomenology.

2 Conceptual Analysis

The main tenet of the school of conceptual analysis is that the analysis of the ordinary concepts of everyday language and of mundane communicative experience is the 'royal road' in philosophy. This is held to be the only valid direction of philosophical interest, the only way to tackle, and hopefully to 'dissolve' the problems that historically have troubled philosophers, and which still 'bewitch' the modern mind.

As a cultural phenomen the school has received a number of names, none of which is any better than the names given here it. It has been called 'Oxford philosophy', due to the activities of such as Ryle, Austin and Waissman there, although much of the stimulus came from Wittgenstein, and to some extent J. Wisdom, who both taught at Cambridge. It has been called 'ordinary language analysis', and while this is a more informative name than the previous one, it does not get across the sense in which the school is as much a philosophy of mind as it is a philosophy of language; this name applies best to Austin's distinctive influence.

It has also been called simply 'linguistic philosophy', which again is informative, but not very discriminating, since the philosophies that the school arose in reaction against, logical atomism and logical empiricism, were also linguistic philosophies of a kind. Neither is the name given it here any more discriminating, since there are all manner of concepts which we could conceive of as being fruitfully analysed by philosophers, including the concepts of the natural sciences, for instance. Perhaps a better name would include the information that the analysed concepts are those of everyday living and experience, particularly those we ordinarily use to talk about our thought, our action, our status as agents, and the kind of physical and social world we confront. Conceptual analysis is, to a large extent, a form of investigation of what was described in the last chapter as the naively realistic 'natural attitude' in terms of which people typically live their everyday social existence.

Although, on his return to Cambridge in 1929, Wittgenstein was formulating a philosophical position very different from the logical atomism of his earlier work, the *Tractatus*, his influence only really began to be widely felt in the early post-war years. G. E. Moore in the inter-war years had made reference to 'common sense', philosophically respectable. And he had helped to create the atmosphere, in post-war British philosophy, where every philosophic mountain was suspected to be a linguistic molehill, or to put it another way, where linguistic molehills brought forth mountainous 'philosophic' effort.

Since Wittgenstein's *Philosophical Investigations* (1963) were not published until 1953, and had until then enlightened only a relatively small band of Oxford academics, the first widely known example of the new philosophical approach was probably Ryle's *Concept of Mind*, (1963) which appeared in 1949. In the 1950s, when the approach became the orthodoxy in Britain, and widely influential in the USA Austin's concern for linguistic minutiae became a common motif of the school (see Austin, 1970a; 1970b; 1971).

The end of the decade, 1959, brought signs of new developments from within the school (P. F. Strawson's *Individuals*, and S. Hampshire's *Thought and Action*) and brought more than signs of total disenchantment from without, in E. Gellner's *Words and Things*.[1]

In dealing with the phenomenological school, we were able to trace the course of a major change in direction within the school which provided an historical pattern, and point to the ideas which could be reflected to some extent in our account of them. By contrast the conceptual analytic school boasts no fratricidal feature on a par with the existentialists critique of the pure phenomenological programme of Husserl. Family squabbles there are in abundance, but no drama. The themes are, then, concerned with the way in which conceptual analysis is a humanistic philosophy, like phenomenology.

One major theme common to both schools is the ontological one of trying to understand what kind of being a human being, or person, is. Typically, both try to describe and analyse the nature of man as it is, *in situ* that is, for phenomenology, as it is in social coexistence, and for conceptual analysis, as it is in a state of language. The latter position is necessarily symbiotically related to the former in that language is necessarily social, and social coexistence is necessarily communicative and hence linguistic. The other major common theme is the critique of positivism and sensationalistic empiricism as sufficient to understand the subjective or objective poles of experience of social beings. Phenomenological description of experience has its echo in the Conceptual Analytic description of the uses of language and their contexts of communication. There is, however, a difference here, in that what can be called 'experiential empiricism' is for phenomenology something of an end-in-itself, dialectically woven in, as it is, with ontological and constitutive analyses, whereas for conceptual analysis its linguistic variant of experiential empiricism is more of a means to the end of therapy for philosophical puzzlement. Austin's approach may be an exception to this.

With these themes in mind, of personalistic ontology and experiential empiricism, we deal, in this chapter with (a) Wittgenstein's general position, his neo-behaviourism and his conception of persons; (b) Ryle's confused attempt to 'dissolve' the Cartesian conception of Mind; (c) various accounts of the ordinary explanations we give of action; (d) Austin's alleged 'linguistic phenomenology'; and (e) Strawson's and Hampshire's explicit accounts of the nature of persons and of the nature of the non-solipsistic reality that man in a state of language confronts.

Wittgenstein

The *Philosophical Investigations*[2] contains among other things: an attack on the logical atomist theory of language and meaning as put forward in the *Tractatus* (1961), a new theory of language and meaning; a theory of the nature of rules, and of the relation of rules and behaviour; a theory of the nature of philosophical activity; and numerous examinations of the uses and concepts relating to mind and to action. The book is unsystematic and the style is aphoristic, and in this sense it expresses its author's personality more clearly than it expresses his ideas. From the beginning it had the requisite ambiguity and intimations of profundity that any 'text' needs in relation to any prospective band of disciples. It could be mined and worked over, interpreted and reinterpreted, providing a vocabulary, a reference point and purpose for the school which followed. Exactly the same had happenedin respect of Wittgenstein's *Tractatus*, which became something of a basic text for the logical positivist and logical empiricist movement of the Vienna Circle (see chapter 3 below).

Wittgenstein had hoped to present his later views in a volume, together with his earlier ones, in order to show the dialectical form of development of the ideas, from thesis to antithesis (1963, p. viii). However, in some senses the later ideas are not antithetical. For instance, in both the *Tractatus* and the *Philosophical Investigations*, it is assumed that language, the linguistic structure of meanings, is the primary reality. There is no way of getting outside of language and of confronting the external reality that is supposed to be mirrored by language. Thus philosophical activity can never aspire to being more than clarification of meaning, and hence language. Any movement beyond language is a movement into the realms of the necessarily meaningless and inexpressible. The limits of language, the form of language, and the concern to distinguish and stigmatise as meaningless, particularly philosophical thinking that ignores linguistic forms and limits, are features common to both stages of Wittgenstein's philosophy.

The *Tractatus* ideas have had two kinds of influence. First, they appeal to no-nonsense, hardheaded, commonsensical empiricism by claiming that the propositions of aesthetics, religion and ethics are beyond the pale of meaning. This was alleged to be so because such propositions are not capable of analysis down to elementary propositions which assert the atomic facts of which the world is held to be made up (e.g. 1961, sections 4.1 and 4.11). This appeal is all the stronger in that elementary propositions can be interpreted as sense-datum propositions, which endorse a sensationalistic theory of knowledge, mind, meaning and language (see Pears, 1969). Some of the Vienna Circle writers have interpreted elementary propositions in this way. Second, they appeal to the metaphysician because, although there are great areas of meaninglessness in the realms of ethics and religion, about which nothing can be said, yet Wittgenstein held these areas to be important. Not least because they include most of the *Tractatus*, according to the author himself. The logical form that 'expresses itself in language, *we* cannot express by means of language' (1961, section 4.121). So the *Tractatus*, as precisely a theory of the logical form of language, cannot be meaningful as it is an attempt to express the inexpressible.

Another area of the inexpressible is that of subjectivity, which has some relation to the use of the expression 'I'. The subject, or subjectivity, is the limit of the world, never an object in the world which can be known, according to Wittgenstein. It is like the eye in relation to its own visual field. 'Nothing in the visual field allows you to infer that it is seen by an eye' (ibid., section 5.633). The eye cannot see itself or its own workings, and so cannot attest to its own existence in the way that we can attest to the existence of the objects in the visual field. If the visual field is all that is the case, then the seeing eye cannot be said to exist. Similarly, if, as Wittgenstein asserts,' 'the world is all that is the case', then 'there is no such thing as the subject that thinks or entertains ideas' (ibid., sections 1 and 5.631). The 'I' is like the eye.

This treatment of subjectivity as the metaphysical boundary or horizon of the meaningful world is continued in the *Philosophical*

Investigations, within the otherwise different philosophy, when, for instance, Wittgenstein writes that: '"I" is not the name of a person, nor "here" of a place, and "this" is not a name' (1963, p. 123). 'I' becomes a way of distinguishing between my person and other persons. But more than that, Wittgenstein implies that its use differentiates the using person, *as* a world-giving subject, from other persons, as a variety of objects in the subject's world. 'I' does not name any person, but alludes to a boundary of meaning, that of subjectivity, which transcends all determinations and definitions which would make it only some variety of objectivity.

His position is similar to that of the social philosopher, G. H. Mead. Mead distinguished between two features of any human self, the socially and objectively defined and determined 'me', and the undetermined, active, transcendent 'I' (1967, sections 22, 25, 27 and 35). It is tempting to say that Wittgenstein's distinction between 'I' and 'person' echoes Mead's idea. However, we will go into Wittgenstein's notion of human subjectivity further when outlining his ideas on mental and action concepts.

So far the continuity between his early and later philosophy has been mentioned in respect of both the concern for language and meaning, and the notion of subjectivity as some kind of meaningless horizon for meaning. The discontinuity between the early and later philosophy is most marked over what the actual nature of language and the linguistic structuring of meaning is like. The early view held that this structuring of meaning in language took one form only, that of naming or reference to atomic facts, embodied in elementary propositions. The later view held that there is no one form, or one structure of meaning in a natural language. Meaning in a natural language cannot be legislated and prescribed from our understanding of logical relations and truth-functions, as the *Tractatus* had implied. Rather meaning had to be described and discovered in the uses to which words and concepts are put in ordinary communication.

In the *Tractatus* the prevailing metaphor had been that of a picture; language pictured reality; meaning was constituted in the truth of picture as a representation of the world. In the *Philosophical Investigations* the prevailing metaphor came to be that of a tool-box; language has sets of concepts and words like a tool-box has sets of instruments; concepts, like tools, have numerous uses, they can be used for numerous purposes (1963, p. 6). But purposes and uses are specific, and tools that are used for the wrong job, in the wrong context, are like concepts used in the wrong way—useless, meaningless and irritating. Meaning is concrete, socially situated in the communicative games that people play (ibid., pp. 11-12). Taking concepts out of their concrete situation, unhitching them from their ordinary uses, considering them in the abstract where they have no work to do, is an attitude of mind that philosophers are prone to, and is how most philosophical problems arise, according to Wittgenstein. Philosophy must be a therapeutic activity aimed at avoiding this 'bewitchment' of our minds by abstract misuses of ordinary language (ibid., p. 47).

Gellner has pointed out that this approach tends to sanctify ordinary usage. It argues that what uses there are, are what there ought to be. It militates against linguistic reform and the choosing of new ways of putting things, and against the emergence of new forms of life.[3] It involves 'paradigm case' argument from what is actual usage in ordinary language to what is correct usage in philosophical discussion (1959, pp. 30-7). For instance, we ordinarily can claim that we can understand what somebody else thinks, or sympathise with what they feel. We can quote paradigm cases of correct uses of the notion of understanding another's thoughts. According to the philosophical thesis of solipsism, we cannot know another's experience, and so cannot establish his objective existence as a subject like oneself. This would imply that there can be no correct uses of the notion of understanding another's thoughts. Since there are correct uses, then the philosophical thesis is, *ipso facto*, wrong. If it is stated, then it is as a typical philosopher's pseudo-problem. If a concept exists in ordinary language, there must be at least one paradigm case of its correct application. Similarly there must be areas where it could not be used, things to which it does not apply, and jobs which it was not built to do. This, according to Gellner, is the 'contrast theory' of meaning (ibid., pp. 40-3). Together with the argument from the paradigm case, the argument from the actual to valid usage, and the metaphor of language as an agglomerate of a great variety of uses of words and concepts, this constitutes his rendering of Wittgenstein's revised theory of language, and the main features of linguistic philosophy in general.

The main line of Gellner's critique is directed against the presumption that philosophical problems have the linguistic nature that Wittgenstein said they had. And it is directed against the associated presumption that language has the form of numerous, more or less distinct, games, the correct description of which is the main or even the only antidote to philosophical puzzlement. Since the second point also involves the position that nothing general, or overall, can be said about language games, the critique is well justified. If a general solution cannot be offered to a general philosophical problem, then what exactly is philosophic about Wittgenstein's approach? Gellner holds not only this but also that accurate analysis of particular usages and specific language-games is impossible, let alone philosophically insufficient. This is because in a natural language, if the language-game scheme applies at all, it applies realistically, that is messily.

Language-games overlap, contradict one another, involve more or less people, have more or less significance in social structures, and they are historical, they grow and die, they change and adapt. An accurate analysis of any one is impossible apart from a wider sociological historical and cultural analysis, which Wittgenstein hardly envisages.

Language consists of usage games, and meaning is in use; the notion of a rule is introduced by Wittgenstein as the sense behind the notion of use of concepts (1963, pp. 80-8; for sociological relevance see Garfinkel, 1967; Winch, 1958, ch. 1). The use of concepts in actual discourse consists in the application of a rule embodied in the concept. We do not decide beforehand to make a particular application of the rule; rather, the rule is *exhibited* in the concrete use, much as logical form was held to be exhibited in particular elementary propositions in the *Tractatus*. And, like inexpressibility of logical form, rules in general are difficult to talk about. '"Obeying a rule" is a practice' (ibid., p. 81), says Wittgenstein it is an exhibition, its general nature is almost inexpressible. I say 'almost' because, as with inexpressible logical form in the *Tractatus*, Wittgenstein makes an effort to express it. What the general notion of rule establishes is the social and conventional nature of meaning in language. It is inconceivable that there be a social convention that applies to only one man; similarly it is inconceivable that there be a language that only one man uses, a private language. Rules, criteria and concepts are public, social conventions which arise primarily from practical and not intellectual agreement between people. Language is social, not in the sense that it is decided upon by co-existing people, but in the sense that it is the practical form of their communicative coexistence (ibid., p. 88).

Society exists where there are right and wrong ways of doing things according to everybody, that is when mere coexistence has become normative and conventional coexistence, and when individual behaviour has become normatively bound and guided. This has been part of sociology's conventional wisdom since Durkheim and before. Wittgenstein appears to have given sociology's conventional wisdom an unwitting and important semantic and linguistic twist. Language and meaning exist where there are right and wrong ways of communicating things, according to everybody; that is when individual communicative effort is governed by rules and criteria of sense and nonsense. For Wittgenstein and the conventional sociologist, that which is individual and idiosyncratic about behaviour is ignored; while that which exhibits 'normative orientation' or concept/rule guidedness is all important. However, Wittgenstein attempts to describe how actors view and conceptualise this, while conventional sociology tends to 'theorise' by presumptively categorising social action and ignoring the actor's-eye-view, (but for recent, more descriptive, developments see chapter 9).

A theory of language and meaning like that of the sense-data school of philosophy, which held that the meaning of an uttered proposition lay in the reference the proposition made to the speaker's private and idiosyncratic sensations, must necessarily be false, according to Wittgenstein. This dispensed with, for instance, Bertrand Russell's interpretation of logical atomism (see Russell, 1956), while the further observation that natural languages have many sorts of rules and criteria of use of terms, rather than having the one logical form of proposing, dispensed with Wittgenstein's own *Tractatus* version of logical atomism. It is behaviour in the light of public criteria and rules that determines meaning, not mental goings-on behind the scene, in private. As regards meaning, subjectivity is irrelevant and inexpressible. This includes the empiricist's subjective feelings of sensation, and the idealist's subjective intuitions of thoughts. Meaning is the government of *behaviour* in linguistic expressions and usages, by socially recognised rules and criteria. Claims by the subject as to 'understanding', to 'belief', to 'knowledge' and so on, must all be interpreted in terms of the concrete behavioural situations in which they are uttered, and in terms of the behavioural rules which they exhibit.

For instance, Wittgenstein writes: 'When someone says "I hope he'll come"—is this a *report* about his state of mind, or a *manifestation* of his hope? An "inner process" stands in need of outward criteria' (1963, p. 153). This interpretation of mentalistic terms stays within the province of meaning, according to Wittgenstein. To retreat into hypotheses about mental states, private and inaccessible to others, is to go outside of the province of meaning, and to try and say something that cannot be sensibly said. This is where Wittgenstein's notion of meaning as rules, and meaningful behaviour as rule-governed behaviour connects with his numerous analyses of mental and action concepts.

In learning a language we are acquiring skills, which we exhibit in correctly putting terms to use in communication with others. We can say that we 'possess' a skill, but the reality of a skill is in exhibition and in applications in particular situations. My testimony does not guarantee that I am a chess player; my performance does. Similarly, my testimony that 'I understand' a mathematical series does not guarantee that I do, and hence does not mean much. But my practical 'knowing how to go on' when asked to continue the series does guarantee my claim, and indeed is what my claim means, if it means anything at all (ibid., pp. 59-60, 72-73 and 82-3; Winch, 1958, pp. 24-39). This method of argument is both like and unlike traditional behaviourism. It is like behaviourism in that it dissolves the meaning of mental-state assertions into the meaning of assertions about behaviour. It is unlike behaviourism in that it conceives of behaviour not as reactive, reflexive, conditioned and epiphenomenal, but rather as skilful, reasoned, governed by rules and not an epiphenomen of neurological and nervous systems. We must elaborate this equivocal behaviourism of Wittgenstein's a bit further.

Thoughts, understandings and so on could be thought of as the meanings going through one's mind as one made a statement. Wittgenstein therefore asks that we identify them. For instance, we could first make a particular statement while we are thinking it; then we could try and say it without thought; and finally we could try to think the thought without the words (1963, pp. 59 and 107). The peculiarity of these mental gymnastics shows, he thinks, that the idea of mental states, as distinct from linguistic activity, perhaps accompanying it silently and conferring meaning upon it, is basically wrong. But then he goes on to point out that it is only this picture that is wrong, and that in denying the picture he is not denying any reality (ibid., pp. 102-3). It is a point of grammar, or of the logic of mental concepts that they are meaningful in that they are used in practical communication, and that they are not meaningful in that they refer to any (inner) reality.

He asks himself the question whether this is not merely disguised behaviourism, and whether, at bottom, he is really saying that everything except human behaviour is a fiction. And he replies: 'If I do speak of a fiction, then it is of a *grammatical* fiction.'[4] The consciousness of thinking, of understanding, of intending, of believing and so on, given in the expression 'I think', 'I understand', etc., is a grammatical fiction, completely unrelated to the meaning of my expressed thought, my expressed understanding, my expressed intention, etc. This is so much the case that Wittgenstein is prepared to hold that the only correct application of the present tense of some mental verbs is in the third person, while application of them in the first person is meaningless. So, 'It is correct to say "I know what you are thinking", and wrong to say "I know what I am thinking"' (ibid., p. 222).

This looks weird, but what lies behind Wittgenstein's thinking here is what Gellner was getting at with the notion of the 'contrast theory of meaning' mentioned earlier. It is possible that I could be wrong about what it is that you are thinking, that is that I could have misused the concept 'know' or used it incorrectly. Correct and incorrect uses imply the application of a rule, and the possibility of contrast. However, it is not conceivable that I could be wrong about what it is that I think. Since there can be no incorrect application of the term 'I know what I am thinking', then there can be no correct application either; there is no contrast, and no rule being applied. Gellner reports that Austin used the same forms of argument to refute the idea of 'sense-data', which is a contrast-less idea and hence meaningless (1959, p. 41) and Wittgenstein commented on the contrast-less nature of subjective perceptions (1967, p. 77).

Wittgenstein elaborated his distinction between first person and third person uses of mental or psychological verbs in *Zettel* (1967, p. 84) where he wrote that the former are in the present tense not verified by observation, and are akin to expression, whereas the latter can be verified by observation, and are informative. Strawson's thesis in *Individuals*, discussed below, is that this undoubted distinction in the way we verify knowledge claims about ourselves and others, should not lead us in the direction of solipsistic scepticism, on the one hand, or subject-less behaviourism, on the other. In learning the use of a mental verb, we learn both first and third person uses; we do not learn, as Wittgenstein seems to imply, that most first person uses are to be suspected.

Wittgenstein's suspicion of first person present uses of mental verbs, as in 'I believe', and 'I know' (1963, pp. 190-2 and p. 222), appears as an undervaluation of the importance of subjectivity in relation to meaning. In both the *Tractatus* and the *Philosophical Investigations* the notion of a thinking subject denoted by the term 'I think' seems to be some kind of a superstition, some kind of a fallacy. But in the earlier work the impression is also conveyed that we must avoid the superstition of the subject because it is too important, too metaphysical, to get lost in. Whereas in the later work the impression is conveyed that we must avoid the superstition of the subject because it is too unimportant and too mundane to get side-tracked on to if we want to understand language and meaning. But this is to overstate the contrast, because there is continuity, if not in relation to the notion of the thinking subject, then at least in relation to the notion of the willing subject.

In the *Tractatus* and *Notebooks* the notion of a thinking subject is set out, not as a part of the world, but as 'a presupposition of its existence' (1969, p. 80). On the analogy of the relation between the eye and its visual field, which we referred to earlier, the world is my world, but 'I' cannot be inferred from my world. This demarcation of the area and importance of subjectivity corresponds quite well with Husserl's ideas in his pure phenomenological phase. The great difference between the two philosophies is, however, that Husserl attempted to investigate that which to Wittgenstein was inexpressible, i.e. the realm of the metaphysical subject in whose gaze the world has its being. For Wittgenstein meaning lay hidden in language, whereas for Husserl meaning lay hidden in the meaning-conferring activities of the transcendental subject. The techniques of displaying meaning were therefore correspondingly different for both; on the one hand linguistic analysis down to elementary propositions, and on the other hand suspension of belief in naive realism. In lieu of a more adequate comparison between these two philosophies the point might be made that the similarity in their conception of the metaphysical subject led them both to a similar solipsistic position. In both cases also the subsequent development of their philosophy was an attempt to get away from solipsism. Wittgenstein did this by simply overturning his earlier theory of language. Less radically, and less successfully, in his own eyes, Husserl developed the notion of the intersubjective *Lebenswelt*, as we saw in chapter 1.

In the later philosophy the metaphysical subject no longer beckoned Wittgenstein from the realms of the inexpressible. Solipsism and communication are conceived as mutually contradictory ideas. Thus one cannot describe our ordinary communication without dissolving solipsism as a comprehensible problem. As regards the thinking subject, therefore, the early and later viewpoints are radically discontinuous. But there is continuity if we consider the willing subject, rather than the thinking subject.

In the early philosophy Wittgenstein (1969, p. 79) simply asserts, following Schopanhauer, that the willing subject is a reality. In the later philosophy Wittgenstein indicates and insinuates that the willing subject is a reality; the point being that there cannot exist uses of language without there existing willing or will-full users of language. There cannot exist communicative skills without the presupposition that there exist skilled communicators. There cannot exist rules without there existing rule-acknowledgers, rule-followers and rule-breakers. There cannot exist a game without there also existing players. There cannot exist forms of life unless there also exist persons who 'inhabit' them, whose dealings constitute them. All of these presuppositions, I propose, lie beneath Wittgenstein's later philosophic activity. It is part of what we must mean when we say that this philosophical activity was embryonic sociology. Conventional sociology's theory of the normative orientation of action requires a conception of the normatively oriented actor as much as it requires a picture of the structure of norms. Description of social action, for its own sake and in order to help the conventional sociologist understand the nature of historically specific social structures, requires a description of personal experiences which are basically only accessible through actors' linguistic formulations (see chapter 9). Wittgenstein's descriptions are unsystematic, his theory of language is not presented as a theory, and his reliance on some conception of persons as communicators has to be excavated out of his writings. But it is in the light of these elements that the school following him has had such a markedly humanistic and anti-scientific approach to psychology and sociology (see part II of this book). It is also in the light of these elements that a comparison with existential phenomenology can be made. But more of that comparison later. For the moment we can return to the continuity mentioned above between the early and later views on the reality of the willing subject.

In the *Notebooks* Wittgenstein writes: 'The thinking subject is surely mere illusion. But the willing subject exists. If the will did not exist, neither would there be that centre of the world which we call the I, and which is the bearer of ethics' (1969, p. 80). Thus the willing subject is a reality because doing right and wrong, acting for good or evil, are experienced realities. Will is involved in action, but is not a non-caused cause of action. 'The act of will is not the cause of the action but is the action itself' (ibid., p. 87). Thus the fact that I will an action consists in my performing the action, not in my doing something else which causes the action.

The early philosophy therefore already contained the notion of willing as a reality revealed in actions. The willing subject is exhibited, so as to speak, in the acting person. The theme that the later philosophy takes up is, what could be meant by an involuntary action, and what could be meant by trying and failing to will (1963, pp. 159-62). Willing is not any kind of an inner experience that accompanies action, or that causes it. Wittgenstein embarks less on a demolition of the concept of willing, than on a kind of tugging at the sleeve to draw attention to exhibitions of will, that is to all the infinite variety of actions that each of us can and do perform. His advice to philosophers is not to try and pin down a faculty of the will, a backstage location for it, but just to sit and watch communicating performers performing.

There is no more to will than that, but no less either, There is no more, in the sense that it is not the case that every man's every action is produced by him consciously and wilfully. There is no less, in the sense that every man's every action is potentially describable as wilful, intentional and conscious. As general terms 'will' and 'consciousness' and 'intention' are usually ignored in the characterisation of an action because their general implications are accepted in practice. They say too much, they do too much work, more than is needed in ordinary communication. We do not continually need to be reminded that we can think, that we can will things to happen, and that we can intend things to happen.

As such, these kinds of terms are redundant where their implications are exhibited, in ordinary interaction, and are used most where their implications are questioned, in philosophy and psychology. It is the game of philosophy, and not any more normal game, that Wittegenstein criticises when he writes: '"Nothing is so certain as that I possess consciousness". In that case, why shouldn't

I let the matter rest? This certainty is like a mighty force whose point of application does not move, and so no work is accomplished by it' (1967, p. 72). Ordinary life does not need this expressed certainty; but it *is* such that this certainty is exhibited. Wittgenstein makes this point when he considers whether we could imagine that our friends, the people that we deal with, or even those we see crowding the streets, are automata of some kind (1963, pp. 126 and 178). This would be weird because everything we do presumes that they are persons and not automata, and we know what the difference is, even if we are rarely called upon to make general distinctions like this in ordinary life.

It is in the light of this presupposition concerning the wilful, conscious and intentional nature of persons which underlies and fills out Wittgenstein's conception of ordinary language, that we must see his alleged behaviourism (see chapter 4 below; Saunders and Henze, 1967; Hicks, 1961).

We have seen that Wittgenstein's later philosophy contains a theory of the genesis of philosophical problems, and of correct philosophical method, and a theory of language and meaning contradicting his earlier *Tractatus* views. But we are more concerned with his unsystematically presented views on (a) the nature of mind concepts, (b) the nature of action concepts, and (c) the nature of concept-using persons. These views have had their influence on the development of ideas within the school of conceptual analysis.

(a) Wittgenstein's analysis of mental concepts as active performances in communication games, that do not refer to hidden inner accompanying processes, and the suspicion that first person present uses of some mental concepts are expressive and not otherwise informative, gave an aura of behaviourism to the conceptual analytic school. It is tempting to see Ryle's argument in the *Concept of Mind* as an exaggeration of this apparent behaviourism.

(b) Wittgenstein's analysis of action concepts as, on the whole, willed and intentional performances, which heavily qualifies the behaviourist interpretation, was taken up by, among others, Melden, Peters and Winch. Action is intentional and action is conventional. Both of these features of action make it impossible to explain action as a caused phenomenon, according to these writers.

(c) Finally there, is Wittgenstein's conception of the nature of persons which is presupposed in the picture of them as concept-users. This presupposition has been elaborated both in the analysis of action concepts, and in more general terms by Strawson, for instance.

In the ensuing sections we will look more closely at the development of these themes, referring to the authors mentioned. The point is to see in what way the school of conceptual analysis is essentially a humanistic philosophy, and thus essentially comparable to the school of phenomenology. Its weakness as a humanistic philosophy springs from its being tied to a therapeutic conception of philosophy.

In this respect it is unlike phenomenology, for which descriptions of interpersonal experience and conceptions of the essential nature of personal existence and interpersonal co-existence, are a primary matter, and not a secondary means to a therapeutic end.

In this section we have covered Wittgenstein's ambiguously stated position on the nature of mental and action concepts. Our conclusion must be that whether or not his position can be called 'behaviourist' in some new definition of the term, it has no real similarity to the kind of behaviourism traditionally expounded as a psychological programme, (see chapter 3 and 4). In the next section we will see whether the conscious acting person became any more of a myth in the hands of Ryle than it had in the hands of Wittgenstein.

Ryle

Ryle took the behaviourist interpretation of mental concepts further than any other conceptual analyst but, as with Wittgenstein, this was not very far, and appeared more radical than in fact it was. Later writers in the school have tended to retreat from even this weak form of behaviourism. In this section we will discuss Ryle's position and some of the reactions to it within the school.

The precise nature of Wittgenstein's influence on Ryle, or even if there was any influence in the reverse direction, is hard to establish. During the period in which Wittgenstein returned to academic philosophy to face his growing doubts about his *Tractatus* position (from 1929 on, after a break of a number of years), Ryle published a paper stating his own disenchantment with the logical atomist theory of meaning (see Ryle, 1932; 1970). Also Ryle's *Concept of Mind* saw the light of day as a publication in 1949, four years before Wittgenstein's *Philosophical Investigations.* But in spite of this there is little doubt that the decisive innovator was Wittgenstein and not Ryle.

In the *Concept of Mind* Ryle criticises what he calls the 'official theory' of the nature of mind, the Cartesian one. This theory is supposed to hold that every human being is a mixture of two kinds of entity, and of two kinds of process, Mind and Body. Body is a spatio-temporal entity, subject to the physical laws that govern any other physical entity. Mind is an entity outside of space at least, and its workings are not subject to physical laws. Body is public, accessible to other's observations and knowledge. Mind is private, inaccessible to other's observation and knowledge. The Body—

Mind distinction, as a distinction between both types of entity and their mode of behaviour, is summed up in the picture of the 'Ghost in the Machine'.

Ryle criticises this general picture by comparing its implications with the way we normally use mental concepts, in particular concepts relating to knowing, willing, emotion, self-knowledge, sensing, imagining and observing. Ryle does not argue that the concrete things that are explained by the abstraction Mind do not exist. On the contrary, he spends most of his time giving examples and sketching these concrete things, actual learnings and heedings, skilful performances and talk about skilful performances and so on. What Ryle objects to is philosophers' expression of the particular in a universal, or their expression of the concrete in an abstraction.

He also argues that, given that we are wrong to abstract to Reason, the Will, Mind and other ghostly conceptions, we are more wrong if our abstraction bears any resemblance to the abstraction, Body or Mechanism. Hobbes was among the first to conceive of action and thought as epiphenomena of physical processes. His 'illegitimate abstraction' was the notion of man as a machine, albeit an organic machine. Descartes' 'illigitimate abstraction', a reaction to this picture, was to conceive of thought and action as epiphenomena of ethereal ghostly processes called Reason, Mind or Will. What was worse, Descartes' abstraction was couched in mechanical, or para-mechanical terms. Rather than being a really radical departure from the mechanist's way of thinking, it was, on the contrary, a curious reflection of it.

In presenting this critique of Descartes, Ryle would seem to be implying that Mind as an abstraction would have been more acceptable had it been formulated in a radically different form than mechanism; that is, if there were no insinuation that Mind was 'a kind of' thing, 'a kind of' cause a 'spectral machine', or a bit of 'not-clockwork' (Ryle, 1963, p. 21). But this implication cannot be drawn very seriously, it merely indicates that Ryle's sympathies are more with the doctrine of the mind that he criticises, than with any mechanistic view.

Ryle's underlying themes are the need for therapeutic activity in philosophy, and closely associated with this the need to get a clear picture of particulars before one attempts generalities in philosophy. Both of these harmonise very well with Wittgenstein's concerns, as outlined previously. The particulars that Ryle wants to get clear are the ordinary uses and contexts of mental concepts. Descartes and Hobbes, idealist and mechanist, proceeded too quickly to general pictures which were inaccurate and misleading. Ryle sympathises with the idealist that he criticises, because idealism merely mystifies the ordinary uses of mental concepts, whereas mechanism completely subverts them. And yet Ryle's style of argument echoes mechanism in that it can be called behaviourist.

However, there is behaviour and behaviour, and Ryle, along with Wittgenstein as we have seen, considers human behaviour predominantly in the sense that it is communicative. That is, he conceives of it basically in terms of the communication of intentions between people according to conventions. He differentiates between concepts appropriate to this kind of behaviour and concepts appropriate to the behaviour of things that have no language, like animals and machines. This is the whole point behind his argument about 'category mistakes' and the need to 'rectify the logical geography of concepts' (ibid., section 3, chapter 1).

A category mistake is made when thinkers describe the concepts and uses within one category in terms derived from another different category. Or, if we use the idea of logical geography, there is a need to rectify the drawing up of maps of our concepts which blatantly rearrange the concrete distribution and structure of meanings; which pretend to *describe* the uses of concepts but which in fact *prescribe* new and different uses. Such mistakes and rearrangements were made, according to Ryle, by both idealists and mechanists.

Mechanists transgressed the existing category boundaries of ordinary language when they attempted to describe human behaviour in terms that only correctly apply to the behaviour of machines and caused events. Idealists transgressed the category boundaries when they attempted to describe human behaviour in terms that have no direct correct application in any category, but which are most like those that the mechanists use.

This argument of Ryle's implies at the very least that he is willing himself to give a correct overall outline of the logical geography of concepts, or a correct identification of the categories in terms of which mistakes are supposed to have been made. But, as with Wittgenstein, Ryle's philosophical credo is that only the particular can be identified, the generality can only be insinuated. So he is in the position of needing to say something general, but feeling excessively coy about doing so.

With Ryle even more than with Wittgenstein it becomes apparent that at least one of the general things he needs to say is something about the distinctive nature of human persons; not in any abstracted individualistic sense, not as pre-social, but precisely *in situ*, as social, and as users of language. Perhaps not very much can be said; perhaps what can be said is self-evident; but things would have been far clearer in the deceptive profundity of Wittgenstein's remarks and in the deceptive clarity of Ryle's thesis, if something general had been said. Instead, the generalities are allowed to leak out in an embarrassed kind of way.

For instance, talking of the way the general picture of the will as some occult, backstage, machine-like cause is wrong. Ryle says: 'Men are not machines, not even ghost-ridden machines. They are men—a tautology which is sometimes worth remembering' (ibid., p. 179). And once again, talking of the picture of man that the natural sciences provide, and their tentative assertion that man might be 'a higher mammal', Ryle comments: 'There has yet to be ventured the hazardous leap to the hypothesis that perhaps he (i.e. man MR) *is* a man' (ibid., p. 310).

The generality that leaks out is that 'Man is a man'. The embarrassment is that Ryle feels he can leave his position hanging on such an unclarified assertion, insinuating both that it is a tautology and that it is not a tautology. Humanism it undoubtedly is; thoughtful humanism it undoubtedly is not.

Ryle feels he can only exhibit in particulars what being Man is, just as he feels he can only exhibit in particulars how the category of concepts relating to Man's intelligent behaviour is defined, and distinguished from other categories of concepts. These two kinds of exhibitions are associated, in that the concepts relating to Man's intelligent behaviour are the main means of portraying what being Man is.

The concepts relating to Man's intelligent behaviour have meaning, according to Ryle, in that they indicate the possession of behavioural skills, abilities, dispositions and propensities; this is their basic type of use. When we say that a man is vain, we mean that in certain sorts of situation he tends to act in a certain sort of way (ibid., pp. 83 and 87). When we say that a man knows how a tune goes, we mean that he has 'acquired a set of auditory expectation propensities' (ibid., p. 217). In general, when we use mental predicates to characterise people we are not describing occult and private processes, rather we are describing the way people conduct parts of their public behaviour. It is true that we do 'go beyond' what we see them do. But this is not a 'going behind'. 'Going beyond' considers 'powers and propensities of which their actions are exercises' (ibid., p. 50). It does not consider any hidden stage where faculties of Reason, Will, etc., like puppeteers, are working in their mysterious ways making the person dance.

This kind of account is deceptively clear and easy. In fact Ryle's attack on the Cartesian picture he sets up is confused. There is the confusion we have already seen in Ryle's therapeutic conception of philosophy between implying a general position when exhibiting particular uses, and denying that any general position can be taken in philosophy. Also there is the point that 'auditory expectation propensities', and Ryle's other substitutes for mental activities, seem just as weird and mysterious as those mental activities are made out to be (see Chomsky's linguistic criticisms of Ryle (1966, p. 13) and Geach's Wittgensteinian criticisms of Ryle (1957, p. 7). Finally, Ryle tries to moderate his anti-causal behaviourism with the idea that we come to know about one another's behavioural propensities and abilities via inductive law-like hypothetical generalisations (1963, p. 87). This last confusion needs a little more elaboration, as it is the point at which later conceptual analysts depart from Ryle's analysis.

We have already seen how Ryle's intimations of the distinctive nature of Man and of Man's behaviour compared with other kinds of things leak out in statements like 'Man is Man' and so on. We have seen how Ryle is antipathetic to any attempt to account for human behaviour, and the concepts relating to it, in mechanistic and causal terms. So, one might assume, Ryle would endorse Wittgenstein's analysis: that the distinctiveness of human behaviour is revealed in the exhibition of a skill; that the prime examples of skills are linguistic ones; and that the exhibition of linguistic skills takes place in terms of linguistic rules and in contexts of communicative application of rules. Ryle does endorse this picture of skills as moves in a game that are governed but not dictated by the rules (ibid., p. 75). But he also endorses a different picture. Instead of understanding intelligent, skilful behaviour as rule-governed, he also claims that we understand such behaviour as the regular exhibition of acquired propensities, dispositions and habits. In the former case our understanding is of a game which only humans can play; in the latter case it is of a law, which is a form of proposition we can use far more accurately in the realm of non-human behaviour and events. In the latter case human behaviour is being explained by either of two types of disposition; either 'habit', that is, 'in complete absence of mind'; or 'motive', which is some kind of presence of mind (ibid., p. 89). Similarly non-human behaviour, like the shattering of glass, can be explained by referring to the disposition of glass to shatter in certain conditions.

What attracts Ryle to this kind of position is the fact that it makes no mention of the notion of 'cause'. We say that the glass broke when struck because it was brittle. This is a dispositional explanation, and not a causal explanation. A simple causal explanation would be an account of a specific sequence, such as: the glass broke because it was struck. The dispositional explanation, on the other hand, makes no mention of cause; it gives a 'reason for' something rather than a 'cause of' something. When we cite the reason for something happening we usually are citing a law-like hypothetical proposition; e.g. 'if these conditions occur, then the thing in question is disposed to react in this kind of way'.

According to Ryle, we would be making a bad mistake to interpret law-like dispositional explanations as if they were causal explanations. A disposition is not an event and so cannot be a cause.[5] Human behaviour is never susceptible of causal explanation; it is always susceptible of dispositional explanation. We explain human behaviour not by reference to the 'cause of' it, but by reference to the 'reason for' it. And what better reasons for a piece of behaviour than the agent's own reasons? By a somewhat circuitous route we have reached the central distinction with which conceptual analysis has been concerned—that between the causal and the rational explanation of human behaviour.

Ryle dislikes the idea that there could be causal explanation of human behaviour, and wants to endorse a mode of explanation of behaviour which dispenses with cause. Thus he turns to dispositional explanation. What his followers and interpreters have worked their way towards is that there is a distinct species of dispositional explanation that could be called 'rational explanation'. They have gone further than this in their attempt to make rational explanation distinctively human and unlike the kinds of explanation appropriate to non-human things and events. They have claimed that rational explanation utilises the notion of following a rule (see Winch, 1958, pp. 40-65; for his criticisms of Ryle, see pp. 80-3; and for a discussion of Winch, see chapter 8 below). They have also claimed that rational explanation utilises the notion of directedness, the envisioning of some future state of affairs to which the action is orientated, the description of which sufficiently describes, justifies and explains the action (see Peters, 1958, ch. 2; for his criticisms of Ryle, see pp. 32-3;[6] and for a discussion of Peters, see chapters 4 and 6 below).

Ryle recognised these two aspects of rational explanation, rule-following and directedness, but chose to interpret human behaviour and human behaviour concepts in terms of dispositions. This inevitably produced a confused sense of lack of direction in his account. The question he never faced is whether, since all disposition explanations are of the same kind, he would accept an account of a particular, intelligent piece of human behaviour in terms of the disposition or propensity of a certain neurological organ in the actor's brain to behave in a certain way under certain circumstances. From what he implies elsewhere in his thesis about the distinctive 'Man is man' humanism that underlies his conception of human behaviour as intelligent and skilful, one would think that he would distinguish between 'human' and 'non-human' dispositions (including human body organ dispositions in the latter category). In which case the gain in philosophical wisdom of interpreting human behaviour concepts as law-like, hypothetical statements about dispositions seems to be lost.

In the philosophy of history there has been a debate between those who believe that the explanation of a particular historical action lies in understanding the agent's reasons and his perceived situation (e.g. Dray, 1964), and those who believe that the only valid form of explanation is subsumption of an instance under a 'covering-law', (e.g. Hempel, 1959). In this debate Ryle has been cited to support the former position. But such is the ambiguity of his thesis that he could, without too much distortion, have been cited to support the latter position. That is, he insists that human behaviour is explained by the motives, skills and habits of the actors, whether attested to by self or others; as against any type of causal explanation, whether it asserts a specific causal sequence or a lawful very general causal sequence. And this supports the proponents of the 'rational explanation' point of view.

On the other hand, as we have seen, Ryle also holds that the explanation of any piece of human behaviour necessarily involves the subsumption of that piece as an instance of the effectiveness in given circumstances of a certain disposition, which we express in a law-like hypothetical proposition. And this gives some support to the proponents of the 'covering-law' point of view.

Enough has now been said about the nature of Ryle's account to demonstrate that its appearance of clarity and ease of argument conceals a lot of difficulties and contradictions. Conceptual analysis since Ryle, where it has been concerned with the nature of mind and action concepts and explanations, has tended to endorse the rational explanation point of view outlined above, and criticise the covering-law point of view. It has tended to endorse the thesis of the distinctiveness of human behaviour present in Ryle's account, and to criticise those contradictory elements of his account that make no distinction between human and non-human behaviour.

From Ryle and Wittgenstein conceptual analysis has acquired, or rather excavated, a straightforward kind of humanism. Like the existentialists, they take the view that man is what he does. This is not presented in the existentialist light of man defining himself by his acts, but as a clarification of the apparent tautology 'Man is man'. What man does is intentional and conventional; it is reasoned and motivated in some specifiable way. This is so because what man does he does in the presence of other men; therefore what he does is expressive of himself and communicative in terms of other selves.

Intersubjective comprehensibility is what is established by communication conventions. The major form of communication convention is a natural language. 'Man is what he does' becomes, on this line of thinking, man is what he communicates. He is what is comprehensible to others. This is not to mean that he does what others say he does, but that alongside of this, or in the face of this, he can say what he does also. However, it does mean that, in a state of society, man cannot do that which in principle he could not describe (see MacIntyre, 1962, pp. 58-60). Neither can he do nothing at all. Rather he is condemned to his intentions and to his conventions. It is these kinds of ontological intuitions, straightforward enough when expressed, but only coyly alluded to in the texts, that make it possible to compare conceptual analytic humanism with phenomenological humanism.

Hampshire and Strawson make more of an effort to express this kind of position in general terms. But before we come to this, some mention must be made in the next section of the attempts to clarify Wittgenstein's and Ryle's account of mind and action concepts. The views of J. L. Austin on the nature of philosophy as the clarification of language and words, and, more particularly, on the nature of concepts relating to action, are discussed in the section following the next one.

Action theories

Ryle repeatedly criticised the Cartesian 'two-worlds' myth, as was outlined in the previous section, but he implied a new dualism between the world of personal action and world of the behaviour of non-personal things (see Abelson, 1965). With the concept of 'behavioural disposition' he attempted to keep a foot in both worlds, which only led to 'systematic ambiguity' (to steal his phrase) in his thesis. The development of conceptual analysis in the twenty years since the publication of *The Concept of Mind* has mainly been in the direction of making the school more explicitly humanistic. That is, the world of personal action has been readily attested to as distinctive and as incapable of being explained or satisfactorily discussed in terms derived from the world of the behaviour of non-personal things. The dualism and the humanism are as old as the hills, or at least as old as Vico. What is relatively original is the statement of such a position in terms of the facts of ordinary linguistic uses, rules and concepts. It goes without saying that, for my purposes, phenomenology exhibits the same kind of dualism and humanism; a point which is made in greater detail at the end of this chapter.

A species of 'two-worlds' myth, then, underlies a considerable amount of the argumentation of conceptual analysts, particularly over the question of whether or not personal action is causally explicable. In this section we will outline the characteristic arguments used. The point throughout is not to see whether the arguments are true or false, rather to see *that* they are humanistic, and to see in what way they are so.

There are too many papers, articles and books expressing the conceptual analytic position for us to deal adequately with even the major ones. They fall into two groups upholding, at first sight, apparently distinct and contradictory positions. In this section we will discuss and criticise these positions in general, but nobody's position in particular (see discussions in White, 1968b; and Wilson, 1970).

The two positions are: (A) The explanations we ordinarily give of our own and other's actions, as expressed in ordinary language, are of a type that is logically distinct from, and untranslatable into, causal explanation. This is the major position held, in one form or another, by the greatest number of writers including Abelson (1965), Anscombe (1968), Daveney (1967; 1966-7), Hamlyn (1964), Kenny (1963), Melden (1967), Pears (1963; 1968), Peters (1958), Urmson (1968), Waismann (1955), Warnock (1963), White (1958) and Winch (1958), besides Ryle and Wittgenstein. (B) Our ordinary explanations are not logically different from causal explanations but rather are a species of them, or translatable into them. This is a comparatively minor position held in one form or another by Finn (1967), Madell (1964; 1967), MacIntyre (1966; 1967; 1968) and Davidson (1968).[7]

Both positions agree that the explanations we ordinarily give of our own and others' actions in everyday life are, in the main, ascriptions of particular motives, intentions, acts of will, choices and the like, in the light of which the action appears as reasonable and comprehensible. They disagree over what, in terms of this agreement, is almost marginal, that is whether particular motives, intentions, acts of will, choices and the like can be said to have actually caused particular actions; or, to put it in less realistic terms, whether they can be said to exhibit the logical featuers of causal explanations. I say that this disagreement is marginal, because whether ordinary explanations are causal or not, both positions are at pains to endorse the picture of the actor as a voluntary agent. According to both positions, the physical determinism of explanations that refer to brain-cell processes, for instance, cannot provide an adequate account of our experience as actors, or of the language we use to talk about our actions. Neither position A or B would accept a materialistic determinism (see Armstrong, 1967; MacIntyre, 1968).

Position A holds that actions cannot be identified or described except by a description, provided by the agent, of the reason, purpose or intention that justifies the action. There is a logical connection between a prediction and the state of affairs that fulfils it (Daveney, 1966-7), or in the same way as there is a logical connection between a command and the state of affairs which fulfils it (Kenny, 1963, p. 238). The connection is not the contingent one between two distinctly describable events that, for instance, Hume's conception of causality requires. Actions are not discrete physical events, in that there is much more to a description of an action than merely a description of the movements in space and time of an organic body. The 'much more' is the intention or reason for which an action was performed; and this also is not an occurrent event with a discrete description. Therefore actions cannot be called effects of any cause, and intentions cannot be called the cause of any effect.

Position B holds that some sense of cause must be appropriate to the relation between an intention or reason and an action in that there is such a usage in ordinary language, as when we say that a person did something 'because...', and then go on to cite a reason. Intentions, while not some mental analogue of contingent physical events, can be pinned down in space and time by finding out when and where the person was when 'he first thought of doing that'. Similarly the description of the ensuing action can be pinned down in space and time, and by descriptions of movements. To say then, that intentions, choices, reasons or whatever, causally explain actions need not be to wander far from Hume's analysis at all.

Position B is certainly more true to life, in that ordinary explanatory usage is far more messy than position A conceives it to be. Ordinary usage has little respect for the consistency that would rule out the use of the term 'cause' from its accounts of action. But B suffers, as a clear position, from its attempt to reflect this inconsistent usage. The point is that if we can independently identify intentions and reasons as if they were discrete events in an antecedent, and therefore causal, relation to subsequent actions, it must also be possible to give a causal explanation of the intentions which would make them effects of another preceding sequence of events. This is simply the traditional problem of free will versus determinism. As far as conceptual analysis goes, the problem is settled by reference to ordinary language and concepts, and to the communicative life of which this is the dominant expression. Reference is made not to what science has discovered to be the case, but to what we all believe to be the case. That is, in the terminology used in the first chapter in relation to phenomenology, reference is made to the naive realism of the natural attitude, and physical science is 'suspended'.

According to the phenomenological account at least one of the classes of reality that we implicitly accept and act upon is the class of all personal agents, which includes myself. We do not conceive of ourself, or of other selves, as determined robots. It is true a few people do believe something like this, but we call them abnormal, and make therapeutic attempts to recall them to our reality. If we approach the natural attitude linguistically, as conceptual analysis does, the picture is basically no different. Our ordinary conceptual schemes and uses do not carry the implications of a thoroughgoing determinism. As we have seen, Wittgenstein and Ryle explicitly rejected the notion that man could be any kind of mechanical automaton, and that his actions and interactions could be described as resulting from anything other than personal agency.

As regards the traditional problem of the freedom of the will, as against determinism, conceptual analysis has never taken the side of determinism; it has always endorsed some version of the freedom of the will. Position B is no exception in this respect. The sense of causality which it recognises in ordinary explanations of action is the anthropomorphic one of an agent 'causing' something to happen, being the master of his own actions (see the discussion of Austin below). But this is a very different sense of causality than that present in, let us say, explanations of actions in terms of the effect of chromosomal abnormalities, and other such things. This sense of causality is the original 'hidden causes' model in terms of which Ryle presented his critique of the concepts of the mind and the will. The Cartesian version, as we have seen, came in for criticism in so far as it imitated the 'hidden causes' aspect of physical, chemical and biological explanations. The gulf is not nearly so deep between the anti-causal rational picture of action illustrated by Ryle (A) and the rational-cause picture (B), on the one hand, as it is between both of them and the 'hidden causes' picture of action, on the other.

Most interesting in relation to the conflict between a freedom of will attested by ordinary experience and ordinary ways of talking, and a determinism attested to by natural science, is the position of sociological explanation. From Marx to Durkheim sociologists have relied on the experience of coercion and the manipulation of individual action by social wholes and super-personal structures, if not to validate their analyses, then at least to make them intuitively acceptable. Gellner has referred to this as the 'pushing-about' feature of institutions. In ordinary everyday life this is a commonplace. But in ordinary life, as we have just mentioned, it also is a commonplace that men act freely, that is on the basis of their own intentions and reasons.

So it appears that there are at least three types of cause that could be cited for actions; personal, societal and physical. But there are still only two relations in which an actor can stand in relation to these causes, he can be aware of them as a matter of course, or he can be unaware of them as a matter of course. My own intentions and the demands society makes of me, the personal and societal causes, I am aware of as a matter of course. My brain-cell processes, or other physical causes, I am not aware of as a matter of course. What I am aware of I can communicate to others, what I am not aware of, needless to say, I cannot. In both these senses of 'hidden' (what I cannot know, and what cannot, thus, be communicated to others), physical causes are hidden and societal causes, like personal intentions, are not. I have to experience the demand of society for it to be an effective causal agency. A man cannot obey the orders of an organisation if he has not heard and understood them; a consumer cannot buy what advertisers want him to buy if he has not heard and understood, or misunderstood, their message in the direction they want. There are a number of sociological approaches which, however, do make use of a special version of the 'hidden cause' approach, such as Merton's concept of the 'latent functions' of items of a social structure (1936; 1957b) or Marx's concept of the 'false consciousness' of classes, or Popper's concept of the study of the 'unintended consequences' of social action (1961, p. 158). But in general it is still fair to say that if sociology, the archetypal 'soft science', springs from any hard-headed intuition at all, it is the sense that each of us has, that all that he does is not what he would want to do but rather what one or another of the social forces of his experienced environment want him to do. This is not to say that men never do what they want to do, but that, at least part of the time, they do not, and that they know that they do not.

But again the picture is not as clear as it might be, for we also commit ourselves, in social life, to a number of institutions, more or less willingly; institutions whose directives we do not feel as coercive, that we have chosen and want to implement, such as voluntary associations and religions and so on. It is an unsteady line that we draw between externalising the directives of an organisation as 'societal causes' of my action, and internalising them as 'my reason' for acting.

Philosophies like conceptual analysis and phenomenology rely heavily on a sensitivity to our ordinary mundane experience, and particularly to our social and communicative experience. But both make straightforward assertions about the freedom of mind and action that display a lack of sensitivity to those coercive and persuasive features of social existence and social experience from which sociology has derived its inspiration. Phenomenology is perhaps less culpable in this sense than conceptual analysis, for at least it reserves the right to be suspicious of intersubjective reality, and merely sets out to describe it. On the other hand, conceptual analysis relinquishes its right to be suspicious of intersubjective conceptually structured reality, because it derives its standards and criteria from that which it describes. Also its self-ordained mission is the redemption of thought from its fallen state, in philosophy, to the good path, in mundane experience and talk. The good path, by definition, is not suspect.

A serious analysis of reasons for acting typically given in ordinary explanations and justifications would reveal at least this element of societal coercion of which we have been talking. In the light of this, the positions A and B are equally inadequate, and lead to an over-easy endorsement of the freedom of thought and action, whether A, in the sense of reasons as causes of actions, or B, in the sense of reasons as the non-causal explanation of the action (although for some mitigating discussions of coerced and 'unfree' action, see Urmson, 1968, p. 165; Austin, 1968; and White 1968a). This is not to say that we do not experience ourselves as free agents, and talk of ourselves as such. Social existence and social action are lived as an interplay between this experienced freedom and this experienced determination that conceptual analysis seems rarely to have suspected.

Perhaps the implicit contradiction, in some conceptual analytic accounts between talking of action in terms of intention, on the one hand, and in terms of convention, on the other, is some suspicion of this interplay. It could be said that a man is free in that he does what he wants to do, and does not do what he does not want to do. But conventions sometimes get us to do what we do not want to do. That is, it is possible to interpret the stress on the rule-governed nature of action as some kind of a contradiction of the 'free will' stress on the intentional nature of action in their accounts. At a first glance it appears acceptable to say that a man is acting freely if he deliberately breaks specific conventions and acts unconventionally. That is, his behaviour is not predictable from a knowledge of the convention. If Kant's view is taken, a man is free in virtue of moral rules and duties that he imposes upon himself, not in virtue of rules and duties that society imposes upon him. But the conceptual analytic account of rules manages to avoid contradictions by saying all things at once. A man's self-imposed rules and duties are communicable rules just as social conventions are. They constitute a 'way of life', a game for one player (but not a 'private language'), not so different from more communal 'ways and forms of life' and games for many players. And in any case, rules govern, they do not dictate (see Winch, 1958, pp. 52-3). One could not play chess if the rules did not exist which constitute the game; but while the play is 'within' the rules, and hence governed by them, the rules dictate no specific move.

But some social games have infinitely less variety than that allowed by the rules of chess. Winch gives the example of a monk's actions in a monastery. Here there are rules that do indeed dictate moves, and there are rituals and regularities of action. Here is where we would say, with Wittgenstein, that 'Following a rule is analogous to obeying an order' (1963, p. 82). An order does not govern, it dictates. Other social games, such as that of (playing at) being an anarchist, another of Winch's examples, offer far more of a variety of moves. The anarchist's activities are rule-governed in the weak sense of being self-imposed and not very much like dictatorial orders.

The examples of the anarchist and the monk, however, do not quite bring out the sense of contradiction that can be present in the explanation of action, either by reference to the agent's own intention or by reference to socially imposed conventions, rules and regulations. The sociological point that conceptual analysis rarely see is that conventions are sanctioned and enforced to a greater or lesser degree. They do not 'govern' behaviour in some neutral sense, they are *used* to govern behaviour. They do not merely allow the exhibition of purposive action by the rule-follower, as if their *raison d'être* were somehow philosophical. Their *raison d'être* is not nearly so enriching, it derives from social coexistence and the social structuring of power. Rules do not allow the exhibition of purpose as much as they are themselves the manifestations of purpose, the manifestations of power, and power is the ability to get somebody else to do what you want him to do. They do not ensure the freedom of action as much as they display the social determination of it. They are thoroughly equivocal, and the actor's relation to them is equivocal also. Rules may enable him to do what he wants to do: in the subtle conceptual analytic account, they enable him to have a comprehensible intention in the first place. But they may also prohibit him from doing what he wants to do; and they may get him to do what he does not want to do at all, depending on their social power and enforcement.

This means that the 'new' dualism we spoke of at the beginning of this section, between the world of personal action and the world of the behaviour of non-personal, physical things, is misinterpreted if it is thought of as a dualism between human freedom and physical determinism. It may be, as both positions A and B hold, that personal action is incapable of explanation in terms of physical antecedent processes of which the actor can know nothing, in his brain perhaps. But it is not the case that another, sociological, form of casual explanation of action need not apply. It not only can apply, but does in fact apply, because we do ordinarily give explanations of our actions in terms of social influences, coercion, pressure, etc. Knowingly doing what we want and knowingly doing what we do not want are, if you like, phenomenological data, given in any serious description of our mundane experience. The criticism we have made of positions A and B, whose disagreement over what to call personal agency is marginal, is that they have paid little attention to the experience of societal determination, while purporting to derive their account from ordinary explanations of action. The analysis of action in terms of rule-following merely endorses this inadequate account. It assumes that all social rules are like communicative conventions, existing for the purpose of exhibiting intention, rather than that many of them exist for the control and manipulation of intention.

The next section deals with J. L. Austin's version of philosophic method and his views on the nature of action. From a discussion of his method and programme for description of social experience, we return, in the section on Strawson and Hampshire, to the nature of this experience, which we have been discussing in this section.

Austin

J. L. Austin contributed a great deal to the style and practice of conceptual analysis in the decade of its entrenchment as the philosophic orthodoxy in Britain, from the very early 1950s to the very early 1960s. As with Ryle it would be misleading to suggest that Austin was directly and obviously influenced by Wittgenstein. His approach was in many ways quite distinctive, and those who followed him could be said to have formed a school within a school. His philosophy shared, with the wider school, Wittgenstein's picture of philosophy as the activity of analysing the ordinary concepts of everyday language; but it was the way this (rarely articulated) belief was applied that made his approach distinctive. The analysis of ordinary language, for Austin, was its own justification; whereas for Wittgenstein it was justified by the need to understand the nature of philosophical puzzlements, how they establish a grip on the mind, and how such a grip can be shaken off. This is not to say that Austin himself did not share a similar view of the nature of philosophical problems and of the possibility of therapy for them by reference to ordinary language. It is just that the minute analysis of clusters of associated uses of words held a fascination for him almost irrespective of whether or not a philosophical problem lay within the cluster, or nearby, or even anywhere around. A very different personality from Wittgenstein, one gets the impression that he enjoyed analysing language in a way that Wittgenstein could not have enjoyed it. Austin approached ordinary language not as a philosopher, troubled, but as a connoisseur, titillated.

A connoisseur's approach to his subject is necessarily descriptive, and therefore in a sense empirical in the extreme. He wants us to share with him every nuance and nicety, every sophistication and subtlety of the work of art before us. And a natural language is truly a work of art, sustained by the skills of its users, so Austin was to some extent justified in presenting it for the appreciation of his discriminating philosophical colleagues.

The approach which savours the detail for its own sake does not necessarily imply that all there exists to be savoured are details, without general form and structured association. However, Austin appeared to hold that not only would he say nothing general about ordinary language, but also that there was nothing general in the nature of ordinary language about which anything general could be said. There are only the details of particular uses of ordinary language, there are no Wittgensteinian 'forms of life', or 'depth grammars'. And the existent details are all endlessly different, not at all like the earlier Wittgenstein's 'atomic facts', which all at least shared a common logical form of statement.

But the philosopher should not be overawed by the wealth of detail that surrounds him on all sides, like an alcoholic in a brewery, not knowing which vat to jump into first. He should proceed soberly and with system; he should get drunk on his details with dignity, and discrimination, like a connoisseur. So, in his paper *A Plea for Excuses*, Austin outlines three 'systematic aids' and 'source books' to use and to work with (1968, pp. 27-30).

The dictionary should be consulted to discover the extent of the 'family circle' of words one is concerned with; here words related to excuses, accidents, misconceptions, mistakes, etc. Second, common law, particularly the law of tort, should be consulted as this provides a great repository of the use of such words, and of the social contexts in which they arise. And finally, psychology, including anthropology, and animal studies, can be consulted as here also there are stored innumerable accounts and cases of behaviour. Some of these will be relevant to, and descriptive of, excuse-making, responsibility-avoiding, etc. Indeed, some of them would undoubtedly have passed unnoticed and unremarked but for the psychologist's interest. There is another 'systematic aid' to the selection and the savouring of the detail, besides one's own memory and imagination, and that is the seminar. This is its own depth sample of language usages and practices, and Austin thought it should always, in principle, be able to agree on what was correct usage in any area (Urmson, pp. 24-5, in Fann, 1969, part I).

This last 'group-think' procedure was Austin's way of countering the charge that the usages he described and analysed might be loose or eccentric usages, not the kind of thing a normal user of the language would say in the same situation. By reaching agreement in a group of users of the language we are guaranteed avoiding loose or eccentric usages. Given this, and given that the abnormal illuminates the normal, Austin held that 'a genuinely loose or eccentric talker is a rare specimen to be prized' (1968, p. 26).

Another charge that Austin takes into account is the one which later figured in Gellner's attack, that, according to this way of doing philosophy, ordinary language was the 'last word' on what is good or bad thinking. Austin's reply that, while it is not the last word, it *is* the first word, misses the force of this attack. The attack is against the version of the 'naturalistic fallacy' embodied in saying that what is the case ought to be the case; and embodied in the belief that what we ordinarily thoughtfully say ought to be a criterion for judging the worth of what we say in philosophy. Austin believed that ordinary usage ought to be a major criterion for thought in general, because he believed that it held within it the accumulated wisdom and 'inherited experience and acumen of many generations of men' (ibid., p. 29). Thus for all practical purposes he presumed that it was the 'last word'; and even if its status was limited to being, in theory, the 'first word', Austin never got beyond this beginning in practice.

Austin's consideration of another possible objection is also revealing. The objection is the blunt one that linguistic analysis is only about words and not about reality. Given that the objection is extremely imprecise and confusing if left unelaborated, Austin takes it as it stands, almost in the sense of there existing a language, and there existing an extra-linguistic reality which it is the job of language to name, describe and refer to. He then says more or less that in analysing our linguistic references to, and our talk about, reality, the philosopher is coming to know that reality better, and that this is the hard centre that justifies the soft covering of the connoisseur's approach. He says (ibid., p. 25):

> When we examine what we should say when, what words we should use in what situations, we are looking not *merely* at words (or 'meanings', whatever they may be) but also at the realities we use the words to talk about: we are using a sharpened awareness of words to sharpen our perception of, though not as the final arbiter of, the phenomena.

Because of this he states that his way of doing philosophy is best characterised by the term 'linguistic phenomenology' (ibid.).

Austin is using this term presumably in the sense of the description of mundane experience, and not in any pure phenomenological sense. In chapter 1 we saw that mundane experience was characteristically naively realistic, and that all manner of realities are fully used, and partially erected, by the ordinary person in everyday life. We saw also that everyday life is a social, interpersonal life, existentially in the midst of others. Thus the realities in terms of which we live and act, and which are rarely reflectively analysed by the ordinary man, are not idiosyncratic or incommunicable in terms of each individual. Rather, they are similar in structure for everybody; the naive realism of mundane experience presents an intersubjective shared world. A natural language constitutes the possibility of, and the means of, sharing experience. Learning how to see a language at once socialises thought and action; so much so that a whole philosophic school (conceptual analysis) has been able to survive almost solely by criticising philosophies that looked for thinking and acting outside the parameters of thoughtful talking and linguistically describable activity. It is important to study language because it helps us to understand the social genesis, the social form and the social orientation of personal experience. The study of language uses is the study of social situations, social games, social dealings and social interactions. This is the justification behind the turn of phenomenological sociology and ethnomethodology to language study (see chapter 9 below).

Austin is therefore right if he states that the study of words illuminates reality; for it illuminates the social realities confronting and channelling personal experience. And Austin is right if by calling his study 'linguistic phenomenology' he assimilates the study of words to other ways of studying the social situation of personal experience, particularly existential phenomenology. Unfortunately, on both counts, interpretations which lead in a different direction can be put on his few cryptic words on the subject.

It is simply not clear from Austin's remarks what kind of reality he is talking about, whether social reality or physical reality. He talks of 'prising words off the world', of holding them apart from and against the world, so that we can realise 'their inadequacies and arbitrariness', and can 're-look at the world without blinkers' (1968, p. 24). Probably unwittingly, this was a very phenomenological and existentialist way of putting his point. We can almost imagine Austin sitting in a park, perhaps in Le Havre, gazing at a chestnut tree; prising the names of these things off his experience of them; achieving his presuppositionless experience of ... of what? Of 'soft monstrous massed in disorder' such as Sartre described in *Nausea* (Sartre, 1965b, p. 183)? Then a better description of his method might be 'linguistic existentialism'.

Perhaps this is too cynical. The method Austin proposes is certainly one of phenomenological description, as presuppositionless as possible, of the experience we have of physical things. But in chapter 1 it was seen how the most significant development of phenomenological descriptions has occurred in relation to our experience of social things. And the trouble with these relatively intangible realities is that, very often if you prise away their names, and people's behaviour, in the description of which the name figures, you are not left with anything. Take away the linguistically expressed goal and the goal-oriented behaviour of people from the social reality that is an organisation, and the reality seeps away. (In the social world nominalism is not opposed to realism, it is identical with it.) This means that Austin's remarks, if they are meant to apply to social reality as well, as he indicates elsewhere, must be ambiguous. It may be easy to distinguish between language and reality when one is talking of the relationship between words and the *physical* tangible things of everyday experience, but one cannot make the same kind of distinction between words and the *social* realities that populate our everyday experience. One can make even less distinction between speech acts, that exhibit the natural language, and social actions, that sustain and exhibit the conventions of social institutions. Speech acts are necessarily social acts, performed in the context of communication with others: and social acts are necessarily capable of being linguistically described by the actor. Perhaps, exercising our imaginations in a most un-Austinian way, we can understand how words could be 'prised off' the physical world, but how can you prise words off the social world? Austin was ambivalent about this dualism in any case, as elsewhere he states that 'The total speech act in the total speech situation is the *only actual* phenomenon which, in the last report, we are engaged in elucidating' (1971, p. 147). Philosophy becomes sociology via linguistics.

Existential phenomenology studies mundane experience of the social world. Conceptual analysis describes mundane uses of language. Without going into it further at this point, it is conceivable that the two interests and approaches are parallel. Austin appears to state explicitly such a parallelism when he calls his own analysis of language linguistic phenomenology. And yet, because of the uncharacteristic distinction he makes between language and reality, we cannot be sure that the parallel Austin was recognising is the same one that we are trying to propose as holding between existential phenomenology and conceptual analysis. In any case, regardless of his own ambiguities, it is in virtue of his savouring of the communicative morsel, with its specific background story and elucidation of social context, that we could call his approach 'descriptive linguistic phenomenology'.

His paper on excuses is a good example of this concern to describe mundane social experience. In aesthetics philosophers are too concerned with necessarily out-of-the-ordinary experiences of 'beauty' and should, according to Austin (1968, p. 25), concentrate on the quite ordinary experiences, no less aesthetic, which lead us to call things 'dainty', 'dumpy', 'nice', etc. It is in the same spirit that he suggests that philosophers interested in the nature of action, and particularly the common successful act, would do well to look at the equally common experiences of, and speech acts relevant to, actions badly performed, fumbled or botched, for which excuses become appropriate (ibid., p. 23).

But, as with his advocacy of dictionaries, law cases and psychology case histories, as systematic aids to the sampling and savouring of details of social experience, his remarks are largely programmatic. Austin's own papers exhibit a concern for minutiae, for bits and pieces, to which he aspired.

Yet lurking beneath this descriptive particularism, there was the contradictory desire he sometimes expressed to found a new science of language, and a general theory of speech-acts, and even a general theory of all forms of action. Apart from preliminary classifications of a number of different types of speech acts, Austin never converted any of these dreams into reality, and so, never encountered and tackled the problems to be met regarding the idea of a social or psychological science.

It is difficult to see how Austin would have reconciled his practice of observing disparate details with any general or theoretical account. As was previously mentioned, in 'A plea for excuses' (1968) he makes it clear that there is no 'one single', total model or scheme of the doing of actions, for instance (p. 41). And he is more concerned, there, to describe the disparate forms of the language relating to the doing of actions than he is to impose any classification upon them.

He shows that talk of *the* action, and *the* cause for it, or *the* reason for it, in any particular situation, is usually over simple. An intention to do an action can be fulfilled in numerous describable bodily activities. For instance the intentional action, described as 'the posting of the letter', can be enacted by running or walking to the post box, driving to it or catching a bus to it. Or 'the' action could be described by a sequence of such activities, the temporal stages in which we executed the intention. On the other hand, a single activity may be the fulfilment of several different intentions, and we may be able to give a number of distinct reasons and considerations which prompted the activity. So from both directions, the intention to act and the enactment of the intention, the picture of action can be complicated and fragmented (ibid., p. 40).

Broadly speaking, Austin would have endorsed the anti-causal picture of action, position A of the last section, if he could have brought himself to speak of whole pictures rather than of fragments. However, the few words he did spend on the notion of 'cause' were interesting. He pointed out that while 'cause' may well be part of 'the inherited acumen of many generations', a picture resistant to change, *he* was not having any truck with it as regards intentional actions and excuses. At least he was not having any truck with philosophers' interpretations of the notion of cause. He saw these as attempts to reform the ordinary language uses of cause away from their anthropomorphic foundations; to depersonalise and de-purpose cause, in fact. Rather, Austin believed that the ordinary language uses of cause were originally 'taken from man's own experience of doing simple actions' (ibid., p. 41), and 'causing' things to happen. What men could not cause, the weather for instance, they ascribed to man-like, that is purposeful, agencies like the gods. Once again, then, the presumption that man is an intentional actor, a causing agency, and that this is given by his ordinary experience and his ordinary use of language is present in Austin's account, as it was seen to be present in Wittgenstein's, Ryle's and their successors'.

If anything, Austin was more emphatic that first person present uses of verbs indicated personal agency, than Wittgenstein who, as we saw, was very guarded over how to interpret them. Austin fully accepted the point that such uses were not referential or descriptive of any 'back-stage mental goings-on and that they were not truth-claims of any kind (see 'Other minds; in Austin, 1970a). If I say 'I promise to do...X', I am not saying 'A promise-to-do-X is my present mental state, which somehow exists in my mind'. Rather, I am performing the act of promising. To accept that such a usage is meaningful is automatically to reject the view that the only meaningful uses of language are descriptive uses, of which it makes sense to ask whether or not they are true. The rejection of this latter *prescription* of meaningfulness, in favour of *description* of meaningfulness is the hallmark of the conceptual analytic school.

In the case of the first person present uses of verbs, Austin held that they are not descriptive, and hence not capable of being true or false. However, he held that they are meaningful in that they are what he called 'performatives', they perform an action. The speech-act 'I promise to do X' does not describe, or refer to, the mental state of affairs called 'promising X', which 'occurs' 'within' me. Rather, it actually performs the action of promising. Unfortunately this conception of 'performative speech-acts' has turned out to contain some difficult problems. These include, for instance, what to do with the speech act 'I state that X', which looks like a performative, but is in fact making a truth-claim. Also there is the problem that, given the context, speech-acts which look purely descriptive, such as 'Your house is on fire', may 'perform' as warnings, that is, do the same job as 'I warn you that your house is on fire' (see Black, 1969; Chisholm, 1969). Irrespective of the truth or worth of his classification, however, it remains the case that a sense of the 'I'-using person as an intentional actor, a performing agency, is present in Austin's account of language and action, as it is in Wittgenstein's, Ryle's and the others' accounts of language and action.

This point can be summed up by saying that there is an ontology underlying ordinary language philosophical analysis, in the work of Austin, as in the work of the others. And this is the humanistic ontology that there exist persons who have certain characteristics, and that persons exist only in the midst of, and in the terms of, interpersonal coexistence. The understanding of ordinary language, then, is one way of understanding the reality of personal and social life. In chapter 1 it was held that existential phenomenology implied the same kind of humanistic ontology of persons.

It was also held that the main ideas of the latter school implied a radical and descriptive approach to experience, a presuppositionless empiricism, unlike sensationalistic empiricism. On this count also Austin bears comparison with the existentialist phenomenologists. He demolished A. J. Ayer's logical empiricism (see 1970b) precisely by reference to ordinary linguistic and interactive experience. In this humanistic anti-positivism and in its descriptive attention to mundane communicative experience and action, Austin's approach was phenomenological, although not in a very clear and self-aware way. Austin's philosophy, and his methods, pointed to the detailed study of men's practical actions and their situated talk. It pointed to issues that phenomenological and ethnomethodological sociologists are only now turning their attention to.

We now turn to Strawson and Hampshire's work where the descriptive and empirical theme of Austin's work, the connoisseur's savouring of communicative details, is far less in evidence, and where the general ontological implications of conceptual analysis receive more attention.

Strawson and Hampshire

These two writers bear comparison in a number of ways, not least in that, while committed to taking their reference point from the concepts and uses of words present in ordinary language and ordinary experience, both have moved away from the therapeutic and particularistic doctrines of Wittgenstein and Austin respectively. That is, we can call them conceptual analysts, even though they disagree on the one hand with Wittgenstein's doctrine that philosophy ought to be a doctrine-less, substance-less activity of dissolving philosophical puzzles, and on the other hand with Austin's doctrine that philosophy ought to be substantive socio-linguistics and have only a casual relation to philosophical puzzles. They both accept, in contrast, that philosophically interesting general statements can be, and ought to be, made both about, and by means of, concepts embodied in ordinary language. The general statements that Strawson makes in *Individuals: An essay in descriptive metaphysics* (1959), and that Hampshire makes in *Thought and Action* (1959), tend to make explicit the kinds of features of the conceptual analytic school which we have been discussing as implied, or coyly alluded to, by Wittgenstein, Ryle, Austin and others.

As the titles of their respective works indicate, there is a difference of emphasis between Strawson and Hampshire. The former wants to describe the actual structure of our thought about the world. Whereas the latter wants to discuss the nature of thought and action, and in particular the way in which the need to discuss such topics arises from the practical reasoning everyone goes through in the ordinary course of living. Strawson's thesis exhibits the logician's desire to be clear about ordinary thinking; while Hampshire's thesis exhibits the moral philosopher's desire to be clear about ordinary acting, and about the thought that goes into ordinary acting.

But, given differences of emphasis and style, the two theses are otherwise not too dissimilar. For instance, both are completely opposed to any idea that the solipsism is even a comprehensible philosophical position. And this is a natural concomitant of their versions of the standard conceptual analytic position that man exists in a 'state of language'. Men are born into society and language, without choosing it, and they learn to speak and communicate because there is no alternative to co-existence which they *could* choose. Given the ability to communicate, the acquisition of linguistic skills and general competence, it is extremely difficult to seriously doubt the existence of others, like oneself, with whom one communicates. Solipsism is not a going proposition, either on the level of practical life, or on the level of philosophical reflection. Strawson and Hampshire both make out arguments along these lines to refute solipsism, and to demonstrate the necessarily socialised nature of every man's experience of the world. Reality, or the experienced world, is essentially an intersubjective structure of meanings that holds as well, and in the same way, for you as it does for me. We met this theme when we discussed the nature of the 'natural attitude' as the phenomenologist sees it. We can now look at two expositions of the conceptual analytic view on the intersubjective nature of reality.

In the 'natural attitude' Husserl explicitly included, besides material tangible things, such intangibles as values, social groupings and other personal subjects. All of these things we attest to as real in our everyday life; all of these kinds of things we claim to know about and act in terms of. Traditional empiricism would claim, on the other hand, that we can only claim material tangible things to be real, as these are the only things whose existence we can 'directly' attest to by our sense organs. Not only must we be sceptical as to the existence of other personal subjects, since all we can see are behaving organisms, but we must even be sceptical as to our own existence as a personal subject.

There are, then, a number of ways of stating the position that reality is intersubjective, which all amount to the same thing. One way would be to criticise the theory of knowledge of sensationalistic empiricism. Another way would be to criticise any theory which puts all its eggs in one subjective basket, and which leaves room for solipsistic doubt of the existence of other subjects. This includes equally the rationalistic reflection 'I think, therefore I certainly am', as well as the empiricist reflection 'There are sensations spatially focused over time, therefore I possibly am'. Another way would be to criticise the empiricist theory of language. This is a modern variety of empiricism that acknowledges the intersubjectivity of physical reality by accepting the communicability of information about physical things through ordinary language. But this acceptance is tied to a presumption that the only, and most important, function of language is to refer to physical things. Thus, a final way of reiterating the naive realism found in the natural attitude is to argue that language does more and other jobs than reference, and that in any case it refers to other classes of existents than physical things, namely to persons at least.

This last alternative is the one taken up by Strawson. Hampshire's argument attacks sensationalistic empiricism, the first alternative, and both of them take up the second alternative, that of attacking solipsistic theories. We will turn to Strawson first.

Strawson claims that our everyday language embodies a conceptual scheme which refers to certain classes of 'objective particulars' (1959, p. 15). His 'descriptive metaphysics', then, describes our everyday ontology, that which we believe to 'really exist' (ibid., p. 247). His description of this ontology is specific to no particular language, culture or historical period (ibid., p. 10). It covers all human beings who have been, are, or will be, existing in a state of language. In all languages we can indicate, specify and refer to things, and all languages give us stable things, persistent over time, to refer to. Our everyday ontology consists in the specification of 'objective particulars'.

To establish this point Strawson tries to envisage a world in which the only form of sensory experience was auditory experience (ibid., pp. 59-86). This would be as near as we could get to the conditions for a disembodied solipsistic consciousness which could get away with making no distinction between its own states and those of an objective sensed world. But even in this situation Strawson claims that the differentiation of the hearer from that which is heard is conceivable. Sound particulars could be re-identified on the basis of pitch and intensity. Objective particulars, and rules and criteria of reidentification of the 'same' sound, are conceivable even in this almost totally deprived, auditory world. If this is the case in such a world, then how much more so in our everyday world of numerous and alternative sensory means of relating to objective tangible particulars? Strawson holds that material bodies are basic objective particulars in our everyday ontology, because they can be identified and re-identified without reference to particulars of other types or categories than their own.

But he also holds that our everyday ontology peoples the world with another class of basic objective particulars, besides the class of material bodies, and this is the class of Persons. The concept of a Person, like that of a material body, is basic, primitive and unanalysable (ibid., pp. 101-2). The most likely candidates which look at first sight more basic and primitive than this, in relation to human beings, are Body and Mind, the Cartesian duo. But Strawson argues that what lies behind our everyday talk about actions, intentions, thoughts, feelings, perceptions, bodily location, etc., is not, to echo Ryle, a ghost, or a Machine, nor yet a Ghost-in-a-Machine, but rather a Person (ibid., p. 94).

Descartes is wrong when he says that ascriptions of thought, etc., are made to a thing called Mind, on analogy with the ascriptions of spatio-temporal phenomena we make to our bodies. Descartes is wrong if he thinks that the term 'I' can be used interchangeably, now to denote a personal body, now to denote a personal mind. Similarly Strawson holds that Wittgenstein, in so far as he implied a 'no-ownership' view of the self, in his suspicion, mentioned earlier, of first person present uses of some psychological verbs, was also wrong (ibid., p. 95; see also Moore, 1954). Wittgenstein, like Descartes, forces a dualism on our everyday ways of talking. Only *this* dualism is that between a personal body and what Strawson calls a no-subject (1959, p. 98). According to this dualism, 'I' sometimes denotes a personal body and its possessions, like pains, clothes, etc. At other times it is a term which is waved in the direction of the transcendental subject, the boundary of meaning, which cannot be an object to itself, which cannot possess or own its states of mind (because there is no sense in which they are alienable, transferable and hence ownable), and which is thus a confusion best ignored (ibid., p. 95f). Against this Strawson simply objects that states of mind are, as a matter of everyday experience, ascribed to 'possessing' persons, each of which can rightfully use the term 'I' when talking about his state of mind, as in 'I think that. .X'. Wittgenstein, in his 1930s lectures, was tempted to avoid this kind of usage by reinterpreting such statements in the form 'there is a thought X', which is clumsy and unnatural. The use of the term 'I' does not involve the possibility of solipsism as necessarily as Wittgenstein might have thought, so there was no need for him to have gone to a no-subject position in order to be anti-solipsistic.

The use of the term 'I' is one way of referring to a person, it is my way of referring to my person. It applies equally to ascriptions of material things to my body as to ascriptions of thoughts to my state of mind. It is a use that is licensed under the conditions that 'I', 'you', 'he' and 'she' are all of an equivalent status, as ways of referring to persons and their attributes. There may be different ways of coming to know about personal attributes such as feelings, intentions, thoughts, physical abilities, etc., depending upon whether one is the author and 'possessor', or whether one learns about another person by listening to him and watching him. It is true that one knows the person that is oneself necessarily in a different, more direct, manner than one knows about other persons. But the meaning of the expressions 'I know X', and 'He knows X' is not at all dependent on these different methods of verification. Both uses are *equally* ascriptions of a state of mind to a person, and neither use has any grammatical priority. Consciousness-predicates like 'knows X' are learned in terms of both personal pronoun modifications. Strawson states (ibid., p. 108): 'To learn their use is to learn both aspects of their use. In order to *have* this type of concept one must be both a self-ascriber and an other-ascriber of such predicates, and must see every other as a self-ascriber'.

In a state of language it is inconceivable that man could be solipsistic, either doubting the existence of the physical world, or doubting the existence of other persons like himself. The everyday ontology that Strawson claims to be describing, thus comprises of two types of objective particulars, material bodies and persons, that we all utilise as the basic reference points of our conceptual schemes. In this way his account coincides with Husserl's description of the naive realism we ordinarily adopt in everyday life, which also was held to be intersubjective and to give us persons as realities as well as physical tangible things.

Hampshire makes the same kind of general point by a more direct critique of the sensationalistic model of reality and of one's knowledge of reality. Like Strawson he holds that the conception that physical reality is established for a human being by the passive reception of sensory impingements is misguided. Sensation and perception are abilities and skills that are learned as the child is socialised into a state of language and society. They embody the application of criteria to denote what is 'the same', and therefore what is 'different' in the objective world that is sensed and perceived. They are also means, not merely of establishing physical reality, as if the learning human being had only an aesthetic interest in the world, but also of establishing the personal reality of agency, the ability to interfere with things, to cause things to happen, to be obstructed by things, to manipulate things in order to bring intended states of affairs about. The physical world is thus far more than the sensorily registered world, it is the socially classified world and it is the world that both obstructs and allows the implementation of practical purposes (Hampshire, 1959, ch. 1.).

Hume's empiricism would restrict the physical world to that which is sensorily registered by some hypothetical asocial creature who has no practical interests to implement, and who can thus conceive of the world, almost aesthetically, as an infinitely fragmented patchwork of colours, sounds, etc. Hampshire would say that this just does not correspond with our experience of the world, or with the facts of our social condition (ibid., pp. 20-1).

Again, as with Strawson, Hampshire holds that there is, in any case, more to the real world than physical objects. There are other persons, and each one of us develops from childhood as a personal agent in terms of our relationship with the obstructions, intrusions, help and assistance of other persons like ourselves. Men in a state of language and society cannot entertain solipsistic doubts because they cannot live by them; philosophers cannot live by them either, but pretend that they can seriously entertain them.

Thus Hampshire (ibid., p. 89) says:

> No one has ever succeeded in stating a philosophical doctrine that could properly be called solipsism. We can be endlessly doubtful about the criteria of truth and sincerity in the communication of feelings. But I cannot doubt that there are in fact other thinking beings who present me with thoughts that were not originated by me and who refer to me as 'you' exactly as I refer to them, each of us perceiving the other from our own positions in space.

So Hampshire guarantees the existence of other persons, and that their nature is the same at his own, by existentialist reflection on his own situation in the social state of language, whereas Strawson reaches the same conclusion from a consideration of the existential implications of everyday concepts.

Both of them concur that each person's everyday experience is of physical things and persons, and of attributes appropriate to both types of things. That is, everybody experiences the same kind of reality, by virtue of having been socialised and having learnt how to communicate in a natural language. Strawson does not view this general picture as establishing the relativity of 'reality' to specific languages in the way that the anthropologist, B. L. Whorf (1956) did, for instance. Hampshire similarly is not interested in pointing to the differences that can arise between culturally disparate versions of intersubjective reality. For both, it is enough to show the typical intersubjective form that the real world has, and the typical kinds of thing that every man holds to populate the real world, given the existence of language and society. Neither would be interested in the fact that, in historical slave societies, entities that we would call persons were dealt with and experienced as things. It would be enough that, in such societies, there was at least one class of persons, citizens. Neither would either be interested in Whorf's thesis that the language of the Hopi, a North American Indian tribe, gives a different experience of physical reality than a European would have, for instance, because it lacks the subject-predicate form and noun-verb distinctions of European languages. It would be enough that there was at least some differentiation of objective reality in Hopi as in any other language.

The concept of the intersubjective nature of reality and the real existence of such entities as conscious persons was present in Husserl's idea of the natural attitude, and has been present in philosophical sociology from Marx to Mead, to Merleau-Ponty. But in the rarified air of modern philosophy, such an idea is controversial. The sensationalistic empiricist's account of either knowledge or language can imply either a solipsism with regard to the very existence of the objective world, or a solipsism with regard to the existence of other selves respectively. In the former case the objective world is a construct from subjective sense-data, and hence doubtful. In the latter case, only language referring to the physical world is meaningful and language referring to personal states of mind, for instance, is meaningless. Thus in philosophy there are controversial positions, and it is this fact that rescues much of Strawson's and Hampshire's accounts from being mere unwitting reiteration of phenomenological and sociological commonplaces.

The 'man is man' humanism of Ryle has become a little more explicit in Strawson's view that consciousness and action predicates are correctly ascribed to that class of entities called persons. Similarly it has become a little more explicit in Hampshire's conviction that men 'are social animals' (ibid., p. 99), and that they are also 'essentially intentional animals' (ibid., p. 135).

When we were discussing the conceptual analytic position on whether action could be said to be caused by intentions or not, Winch's view that intention is non-causally linked to action through the notion of a rule was mentioned. Actions can be said to be meaningful because they are conventional, that is they exhibit, or apply a rule of some kind. Similarly actions can be said to be meaningful because they are intentional, that is they exhibit a point, or purpose of some kind. Conceptual analysis has typically seen no contrast between intention and convention; the former implies the latter, and vice versa, on their view. Hampshire takes this view also: 'Every convention or rule that I accept is an intention that I declare', 'If there is a use of a language, there must be the intention to follow a convention or rule', he writes (ibid., pp. 99 and 136).

As against this there is the possibility that intentional action is in some sense the opposite of conventional action. This was the possibility we discussed in relation to the idea of 'society' causing action, by the enforcement of conventions. It is the possibility that when we explain our own or others actions in terms of conventions then we often tend to be avoiding responsibility for them, and sometimes condemning them; whereas when we explain our own or others' actions in terms of the intentions they implement we tend to be accepting responsibility, and sometimes praising them. Perhaps it is unwarranted, but usually some relation is assumed to exist between what a person wants to do and what he intends to do. For instance, Hampshire says: 'Some minimal consistency in the relation between statements of wants and ambitions and actual habits of performance is essential to the idea of intentional action' (ibid., p. 147). But very often in our social experience we can say that we do something that we do not want to do; we avoid responsibility for the action which we knowingly did, and say that we were 'obeying orders', or 'doing what everybody else did', and cite a societal and conventional cause to take responsibility for the action.

This means to say, at the very least, that there is a conflict between the notions of intention and convention, in so far as the former relates to what we do want to do, and in so far as the latter relates to what we do not want to do. Given this, conceptual analytic accounts of man as 'essentially conventional or rule-following', and at the same time as 'essentially intentional', misrepresent our ordinary experience of action if they claim that these two ontological descriptions imply one another. It would be more true to our social experience to say that both of these descriptions apply, but as standing contradictions of one another, not as mutual implications. And to say that convention and intention are dialectically related in ordinary social experience is not to overlook the fact that sometimes one wants to do what the convention dictates. It is just to offer the reminder, in relation to this fact, that 'sometimes' is not the same as 'always'.

Conceptual analysts would like to say, not that one always does what the convention dictates but that, when using language at least, one always does what the convention allows, in so far as one communicates successfully. The existence of linguistic conventions is precisely the existence of the means of communicating what one wants to communicate; and no sense could be attached to a coercive interpretation of such conventions whereby they would be seen as somehow getting a person to communicate that which he did not want to communicate.

However, it is ennobling, but a misrepresentation, to think, on this analogy, that most social conventions constitute possibilities of doing what one wants. Rather they very often constitute the reliability that one will do certain things whether or not one wants to. A case could be made out that communicative conventions are a completely distinct species of social convention; that the life of ordinary language, its uses in social situations, can be described independently of social interactions in social situations. But this would be a difficult case to make out, and one that conceptual analysis has no interest in clarifying. Usually it presumes, rightly, that analysis of concepts requires analysis of 'language games' and social 'forms of life' (Wittgenstein), or that analysis of speech-acts requires analysis of social action (Austin). But from this it goes on to presume, wrongly that communication conventions are paradigms of their environmental social conventions, and that a use of language stands in the same kind of relation to a communication convention as a social action stands in relation to a social convention. But even our most naive reflections contradict this. For instance, we say that on the one hand language is a tool of man, and not vice versa, and that on the other hand man can be a tool of society, and society rarely be the tool of man. Language is a means, society sets ends; language provides the means of communication of individual purposes, whereas society can coerce individual purpose into the service of a common purpose.

Hampshire is aware, to some extent, of these very general distinctions between linguistic conventions, which permit the communication of individual purposes, and social conventions, which are more determinative and coercive of individual purposes. It is part of his moral position that we ought to increase our self-consciousness concerning the factors in the physical and social environment that affect, obstruct, or determine us in any way (1965). And that this increase in self-consciousness is a necessary preparatory step to increasing our freedom of thought and action, which is both good and possible. He considers that the philosophical activity of the 'philosophy of mind' is therefore always required to assist this self-consciousness, and in every period in history takes the form of a recognition and critique of the particularly social features of our environment that influence us (1959, p. 272).

To conclude, Strawson and Hampshire both hold that our everyday conception of reality has an intersubjective, because communicable, form, and that the real things it contains are at least material bodies and persons. As to the distinctive nature of persons, both writers accept that it is some kind of embodied agency, to whom it is logically proper to ascribe both body and consciousness predicates (Strawson), and of whom it is existentially proper to say that it arises in the presence of social influences and physical obstructions to become an intentional social actor and an intentional manipulator of its physical world (Hampshire). These extremely general views of the distinctive being that a person is, we can call a 'personalistic ontology' in the same sense in which this term was held to apply to existential phenomenology in chapter 1. And the analysis of the non-solipsistic nature of our everyday realism which we have described, bears comparison to the phenomenological idea of the 'natural attitude', also discussed in chapter 1.

Conclusion

Both existential phenomenology and conceptual analysis represent a return by philosophy to what is concrete. Hampshire says, for instance: 'Whether as linguistic analysis or as phenomenology, contemporary philosophy tends to find the reality of distinctions in mental life in the concrete examples with which the distinctions are illustrated' (1959, p. 235). As humanistic philosophies both aim to understand man, the thinker and actor of everyday experience, and this cannot be done without a return to, and description of, man's existential situation. For phenomenology this means description of man in a state of society, and description of personal experience as it arises in the midst of and in the presence of other persons. For conceptual analysis this means description of man in a state of language, and description of personal experience as it arises in contexts of communication with other persons. It may be that the former school pursues its humanistic course under delusions of profundity, and it may be that the latter school pursues its humanistic course in a conspicuously trivial way, but apart from stylistic differences the courses are essentially similar.

This similarity is not at all jeopardised by the superficial reflection that phenomenology is an inherently metaphysical approach, while conceptual analysis, although born from a reaction against logical positivism, has remained within the anti-metaphysical orientation of that philosophy. One of the main points that I have tried to establish in this chapter is the surprising degree to which conceptual analysis is sunk into ontological axioms and convictions concerning the nature of persons. As Gellner has pointed out (1950-1) analysis in philosophy is usually associated with ontology, in that excavation must reach some form of bedrock.

For conceptual analysis the explicit bedrock is the socialised reality given in everyday experience and communication, and the implicit bedrock is the nature of man as a thinking and acting person. These two ideas are closely related, and the latter assumption is justified by descriptions relating to the former, in conceptual analytic accounts. The socialised reality of everyday experience consists of at least physical objects and persons, two distinct classes of objective existent, in relation to which we, each of us, pursue our intentions and purposes, and which we encounter as obstructions or as means, or as simply present. Description of this 'natural attitude' to the *Lebenswelt* is built up into an argument that we are what we ought to be; that naive realism is not so naive; that we ought to be free actors, and behold, we actually do interact on the belief that we are free agents, so there are, as there ought to be, free actions. The moral ideal that man ought to be, and the ontological suspicion that man is, a free-thinking free-actor is continually bolstered up, in conceptual analytic accounts, by selective descriptions of communication experience.

In discussing ordinary explanations of action the point was made that description of everyday actions and their social context can just as well portray actions as caused by social forces, conventions and the power of others, as it can portray them as caused, willed or intended by the actor. Selective descriptions of communicative experience, as long as they remain over-concerned with the grammar of the utterance and not concerned with the social situation of the utterance and the social conventions and forces that impinge upon the situation, will always tend to endorse the free-thinker free-actor picture.

If one is selective it is not difficult to argue that I can always say what I want, because that is what language is there to allow me to do; saying is a performance, a species of doing; therefore, in some sense I can always do what I want to do, and thus I can freely enact what I freely think. If this line of thinking is applied to any normal range of social experience, however, it becomes apparent that it is a gross misrepresentation of much of that experience. If saying is truly an act which can only be interpreted in terms of its specific context (Austin), and if it is truly a move in a specific language game, a contribution to a form of life (Wittgenstein), then there is no reason why reference to the wider social and political context cannot also be made, to understand its occurrence in these specific contexts. For instance we might interpret the informative speech-act 'My mother is driving me mad' in relation to the language game called 'Let's drive him mad' often played in schizogenic families (see chapter 7). And we might interpret this specific game in terms of wider social conventions, legal structures and labelling processes. But perhaps this would be a little too realistic, for we would be involved in describing the destruction of a personal agent, and this would be in no sense an ennobling bolster to the conceptual analyst's belief in the reality of the personal agent. This is not to say that such a belief is wrong, but simply to say that what truth there is in the belief has to be captured, alive as it were, in the existential situation the social dialectic which confines and defines the person and his actions, and in terms of which he continually defines himself.

To say that man is a personal agent in his state of language and society is only equivalent to saying that a human body is an object that floats when it is in deep water, when what we want really to say is that it swims and makes its own course in the water. We really want to believe that tides and currents would make no difference, and yet we know that they do. We want to believe that swimmers cannot drown; or, to leave the metaphor, that persons cannot drown in society. But people commit suicide, they go 'mad', they live the death of the spirit required by industrial organisations and so on.

Conceptual analysis confines its attention in practice to grammatical features of language uses, and in programme to the local social context of language uses down to the conversational context of the utterance. But it does this in such a way as to miss the sociological and phenomenological implications which are there to be discovered. It treats the ordinary and the mundane as if it were truly ordinary and mundane, and as if it contained none of the dialectic and none of the existential significance which phenomenology and sociology can reveal.

In relating a personalistic ontology to our everyday lived realities, and in holding experiential empiricism, or description of such a natural attitude in our *Lebenswelt*, to be at least a high priority in philosophy, conceptual analysis bears a direct comparison with existential phenomenology, despite differences of style. Its, at times profound, concern with language is very suggestive for both phenomenology and sociology, but as an overall school it tends to have an optimistic and superficial vision of the social world and of the freedom of action available within it. As a school which preaches naivety, it is remarkably successful at times in practising it.

3 Logical empiricism and the reductionist idea of psycho-social science

It is a common presumption that modern philosophy is an analytical activity with no commitments to any position. This would appear, superficially, to be most true of philosophical schools like logical empiricism and conceptual analysis. It would not apply in the same way to either pure or existential phenomenology where commitments are clearly visible, and where they may even outnumber relevant justifications. But analytical activity does not go on in a vacuum, and the kind of commitments that conceptual analysis implies, and that it sometimes explicitly states, have been discussed in the preceding chapter. Logical empiricism too has its commitments, which we will discuss in this chapter.

But why discuss logical empiricism at all? The answer to this is first that we are involved in revealing the similarity between two, broadly speaking, humanistic schools of thought, and logical empiricism is recognised by both schools as an enemy, as a standing contradiction of their approaches. To understand the nature of the common enemy, and why it is *common* to both schools, is to understand the similarity between the schools a little more clearly. And second, the 'idea of a social science', by which we mean here the idea that studies like psychology, sociology and so on can and ought to become natural sciences, has been most categorically asserted by logical empiricism. Conceptual analysis and phenomenology both repudiate this 'physicalist', 'naturalist' or 'reductionist' idea, in general, and also where it appears as the programme of a particular psychological or sociological school.

The first stage of the investigation into the similarity between conceptual analysis and phenomenology, chapters 1 and 2, has been the analysis of their general philosophical positions. The second stage will be the comparison of their critiques of the reductionist idea, in relation to behaviourist, Gestalt and Freudian psychologies and

Weberian sociology, in chapters 4, 5, 6 and 8 respectively. But before this comparison is embarked upon, the reductionist idea itself, and the kind of philosophical thinking upon which it is based, must be made clear.

As a distinct school, logical empiricism crystallised in the inter-war meetings of the Vienna Circle, which was a group of philosophers who came together to discuss, among other things, the implications of Wittgenstein's *Tractatus*. They wanted to unite the empiricist view of the world with twentieth-century advances in logical analysis on the one hand, and with twentieth-century advances in theoretical physics on the other. It is, therefore, necessary to describe the traditional empiricist view of the world first, in order to understand its modifications by logical empiricism. The British empiricist tradition has had a subdued current of materialism running through it from the time of Hobbes. As an ontology, or theory of being, this originally held that everything was a form of matter, and that everything, from human beings to solar systems, was equally subject to mechanical laws of motion. But the dominant feature of the tradition, exemplified in the philosophy of Hume, Locke and others, has always been a theory of knowledge which gives pride of place to sensation, and the sensory relations of the human organism with its environment of stimuli.

Sensationalism

In its traditional form the sensationalistic epistemology holds that 'There is nothing in the Understanding, but what has past through the Sense'. That is, it was a psychological theory of the genesis of men's thoughts and ideas, speculative psychology as much as philosophy. It was a theory of induction which tried to show how generalisations and theories about the world are built up from the accumulation of particular bits of information about the world.

Hume (1735) believed that all complex ideas are built up out of simple ideas. All simple ideas are copies of previously experienced simple impressions. Thus all our ideas are ultimately derived from impressions, and whereas impressions are immediately given and vivid, our ideas are secondary and pale.

But ideas are meaningful, not meaningless second-hand impressions, arbitrarily strung together as they are received. There is logic to them. And Hume tried to account for this as the product of mysterious cerebral mechanics that go on in the faculty of the imagination, whereby one idea is seen as like another, and is thereby linked with it. But this process could not, according to Hume, cover up the arbitrariness and contingency of human ideas and meanings. Basically ideas are associated by regularly and habitually arising together. Thus the idea that something causes something else to happen arises, in Hume's view, from the regular impressions that the one thing always precedes the other. The idea can be analysed down to this; while the 'excess' meaning, produced by the imagination, that something we call a cause actually generates, somehow, its effect, must be discarded on analysis as not empirically demonstrable. The concept of causality, like all other concepts, cannot be attested to by the senses.

Such a theory of knowledge was an important element in liberating thinking from dogma and obscurity in its day. It performed the same kind of critical and sceptical function for thought in general as Hobbes' and Machiavelli's analyses had performed for political thinking. But every revolution becomes established, and what had been a liberating scepticism became refined and reified into a belief and commitment to a narrow class of certainties, the 'certainties' of what a man's senses 'tell' him.

Ernest Mach (1914) applied the sensationalistic model to scientific knowledge, a little more systematically than had previously been done.[1] Mach held that the aim of science was, and should be, the most complete, precise and economical description of facts. Thus scientific laws were concise summations of a great mass of facts, and facts were made up of elements, or sensations, standing in certain relationships with one another. When we describe facts we are, ultimately, describing the resemblances and differences between these elements or sensations. Therefore, physical objects are complex constructs or related sensations. And description of physical objects is more complete the more it breaks the object down into the basic elements or sensations which make it up.

In most versions of sensationalism there is an uneasy alternation between an objective and a subjective frame of reference. What starts out as being a hard-headed materialistic account can often become a suspiciously soft-headed idealistic one. The problem is in what exactly is supposed to be certain, the objective world or the 'raw feel' of the subjective sensation.

The problem occurs in Mach's account. His basic 'elements' into which the objective world can be analysed, like colours, shapes, textures and tastes, are all unanalysable into anything else. And they are all given to us in sense experience. The objective bedrock is subjective sensitisation. What is 'ultimate' and 'unanalysable', what is 'certain' and 'given', are all categories that can migrate from public and objective application to private and subjective application. This is one of the problems that has dogged the subsequent empiricist hunt for certainties in the direction of 'raw feels', 'sense-data', 'sensa', 'qualia' and so on. They are all supposed to attest directly to the objective world, they are the world somehow, they are all there is;

and yet, like your pain, your sense-data, the data of your senses, your raw-feels, are none of them accessible to me.

I can ask you about how you see the physical world in our environment and, given honesty and effort, it would be extremely unusual and weird if we could not come to some agreement about what there is and what there is not in our physical world. That is, you have a knowledge of the world that is perfectly accessible to me. It is commonplace, and commonsensical; we know the same things and know that we know them. And yet if we rely only on raw-feels that are private and inaccessible to any other person but oneself, as the empiricist might bid us, it is hard to see how this provides for our intersubjective knowledge of a public world. It does not seem to be translatable into that knowledge, or even be the building blocks upon which that knowledge is erected. The public world I describe phenomenologically appears to be a different world from that which privately tingles me, or pains me, or impinges upon me in some other sensory way, and which I can hardly describe at all.

The logical empiricist doctrine of physicalism, which we will come to later, was an attempt to take the first-person, subjective perspective, and the indescribable, extra-linguistic, raw-feels out of empiricism. That is, it was an attempt, and not a very successful one, to stamp out the kind of suspicions and problems we have pointed to, and to redirect empiricism back on to its hard-headed course. But what happens if the problems are not so rigorously dealt with? The sensationalist must come to either of two dead ends, a causalist one or an idealist one. The causalist dead end is reached when all conceivable differences and disagreements between subjective raw-feels are eliminated by fiat. That is, it is speculated that human organisms are so constructed that they cannot but all register the same sensations if placed in the same stimulation situation; we all record the world like all cameras record the world; we all are equally passive receptacles which the world causes to be filled in the same way. Of course the physiological speculation is gratuitous and the use of the term 'same' begs every question. The causalist option is a dead end philosophically because, given it, there is no problem of knowledge; the world causes our sensations, therefore there is no question that our sensations could ever give a false picture, or that we could ever be mistaken.

The idealist dead end is at the other extreme from this. It is reached when the empiricist can assert that sensation is all there is, that there is no bifurcation between external reality and internal feeling, or between some Kantian noumena and phenomena. What is internal, phenomenal and known is not caused one-to-one by something that is external, noumenal and unknowable. Rather, my sensations are all there is, the world is all of my sensations and this is very close to the idealist's 'the world is my idea'. Once again the dead end is that the position is over protected, it is so 'right' that it cannot be wrong, and hence there is no such thing as a problem of knowledge, we cannot be mistaken about what we claim to know.

The idealist option, subtle versions of it of course, was popular with philosophers like William James, who influenced Bertrand Russell in this direction (see Russell, 1921, introduction). But the causalist option has also had its influence, not least in behaviourist psychology.

One of the most subtle and systematic versions of the more idealistic type of sensationalism was produced by Carnap in his *The Logical Structure of the World* (1967). Carnap himself, and the rest of the Vienna Circle, soon came to be critical of sensationalism, and therefore of this work, in favour of a modified position which they called 'physicalism'.[2] The physicalist modification was an attempt to take the solipsism, and hence one of the incentives to idealist backsliding, out of sensationalism. It was an attempt to reinstate the publicly attested-to, physical object as the empiricist's bedrock, rather than the private sensation. But it also denied the materialistic ontology which would have to be a consequence of this modification. In the ensuing sections we will deal with Carnap's original thesis and with the later physicalist thesis. For the moment, some closing remarks on the sensitivity of the modern philosophic scene to ontological and other metaphysical, and hence 'meaningless', positions.

With the modern advances in logic and systematic analytical methods philosophers became more interested, so to speak, in cleaning windows rather than looking through them. That is, they became very interested in the linguistic and conceptual schemes in terms of which we know the world, the linguistic window we must look through. They became good at polishing up these schemes and structures of thought, and convinced themselves that the only meaningful philosophical problems were blemishes on the window, accessible to polishing. All more inaccessible problems could be by-passed as 'pseudo-problems', as 'meaningless', 'metaphysical' and so on. If Russell, Frege and others provided the tools to analyse language, Wittgenstein provided a lot of inspiration, in his *Tractatus*. Language can be analysed, metaphysics can only be gestured at. The imperative, to avoid metaphysical positions and to stick to the analysis of, construction of and reconstruction of, language and symbol systems, in philosophy, was taken most seriously by the Vienna Circle. Oddly enough, it was taken least seriously by its propounders Russell and Wittgenstein.

Russell, having helped to provide the technical tools of systematic logical analysis, was, in his own writings on the theory of knowledge and other general topics, quite content to write commonsensically and not technically or very systematically. He did not write loosely, but he allowed himself the luxury of informality, even to the extent of endorsing metaphysical versions of sensationalism. Wittgenstein, too, repudiated the formality and logical strictures of his *Tractatus* position in his later philosophy. And while, unlike Russell, he never allowed himself to state philosophical theses openly in his later philosophy, he did allow himself to insinuate them. Russell, Wittgenstein and the Vienna Circle are related in general as follows. Russell took both systematic logical method (which he had helped to build) and the imperative to 'look to language', less seriously than the Vienna Circle. Wittgenstein also, in his later philosophy at least, took the method less seriously than the Vienna Circle. But he took the imperative far more seriously than they did, as we have seen.

Carnap, Husserl and reductionism

Carnap's thesis, in *The Logical Structure of the World* is a systematically presented sensationalistic one. In some ways it exemplifies the idealist option that was mentioned in the discussion above. But one has to be careful in applying this interpretation. A relevant check can be made with a truly idealistic philosophical thesis, one that makes no pretention at being in any way empiricist or sensationalist, that of Husserl. The comparison upon which we are about to embark is not meant to indicate any deep-seated similarity between logical empiricism and pure phenomenology, which on most issues are at opposite ends of the philosophical spectrum. Least of all is it meant to indicate any, even superficial, similarity between logical empiricism and the existential version of phenomenology, for it is the antipathy between these two schools of thought that we are most interested in. Pure phenomenology, however, has some superficial similarities of organisation to Carnap's logical empiricist thesis which are worth noting.

But first, the general direction of Carnap's argument. He tried to systematically and logically reconstruct the whole apparatus of concepts in all of the fields of knowledge to which we bear witness in ordinary experience and in ordinary language, and the reconstruction was to be erected upon a foundation of concepts that refer to what is immediately given. That is, he wanted to assert that it is in principle possible to 'reduce' all concepts to those referring to basic elements, and to the relation that holds between basic elements. The basic elements are sensations, and the relation that holds between them is taken to be the remembrance or recollection of similarity, by the subject. The procedure is thus characterised as 'methodological solipsism', and is alleged to be neutral with regard to any substantive metaphysical thesis (1967, p. 102).

It uses the data pertaining to one self; this is called the 'auto-psychological basis' of the reconstruction of knowledge concepts. Carnap chooses this not merely because of formal considerations, such as simplicity, but because he believes it to be in any case actually 'genealogically' primary in the process of acquiring knowledge that we all go through (ibid., p. 101). Formally, the plan is to construct a system of concepts whereby all of the concepts we hold pertaining to knowledge about the world can be deduced from, translated into, or reduced to, the set of concepts referring to the auto-psychological domain. Substantively the implication is that the objects of knowledge, physical objects, other minds (called 'hetero-psychological' objects) and cultural and social objects can be shown as successive constructions by the individual sensing subject; that is, that there is a genealogy, a family tree of epistemological levels, that characterises man's experience of the world.

In chapter 1 it was seen that Husserl, in the *Cartesian Meditations*, attempted a very comparable kind of reconstitution of the realities of experience from a solipsistic basis. Only Husserl's solipsistic basis was the transcendental ego, whereas Carnap's was the mundane self's stream of experience. Indeed, Carnap refers to Husserl's notion of bracketing-off, and withholding judgement about, the reality of things experienced when characterising the autopsychological domain, the basic streams of experience, the given (ibid., p. 101).

As with Husserl, the basic stream of experience, although it is interpreted in personal and ego-logical terms, is in fact characterised in an impersonal and ego-less manner by Carnap (ibid., p. 103). For both of them, the notion of 'self' and 'mine' are subsequent constructions, arising together with the notions of 'other selves' and 'not-mine'. This is a subtlety that critiques of Husserl's and Carnap's solipsism are inclined to overlook, but which are not, on that account, wrong. If we can put it in more concrete terms for a moment, the situation might be seen like this. An impersonal stream of experience where there is no differentiation between 'myself' and the world, of objects and other people, where no criteria exist for the differentiation of the real from the unreal, and of the concrete from the illusory, is the kind of magic and mystery that perhaps newly born children experience. It in no sense characterises the experience of any human being who has ever lived, who has been socialised and has developed to live in a society as a social person.

Presumably philosophers investigating 'knowledge' cannot afford, in the interests of relevance, to rely over heavily on models that do not apply to man as he is, and that rather only seem to apply to entities such as babies, that, strictly speaking, cannot be said to 'know' anything at all. All knowledge is some person's knowledge, thus streams of experience are personal streams of personal experience. Existentialist phenomenology reasserted this irreducible level in an attempt to demystify Husserl's assertion that the irreducible nature of man's experience is only to be found at the transcendental level, outside of any realistic context.

Carnap's baby-like notion of a subject-less know-nothing stream of experience was matched by Husserl's god-like notion of an allegedly ego-logical know-all stream of experience. Both are of dubious relevance to the understanding of ordinary human knowing and knowledge, be that mundane or scientific. Husserl got stuck in his irrelevance. But Carnap passed quickly on, prepared to overlook his own strictures and to interpret the stream of experience, the given, as 'mine' and as 'owned' by the socially and physically differentiated personal individual that we all are. 'The self is the class of auto-psychological states' (p. 241), he writes.

From the sphere of the transcendental ego, Husserl tries to show (1960a) how the individual self, or 'monadological sphere of ownness', can be established; then the analogical understanding of the Other self; then the intersubjective sphere of Nature, or public physical objects; and finally the intersubjective sphere of Spirit or Culture, which referred to the specific socio-historical *Lebenswelt* of any individual self.

More systematically and logically Carnap tries to show that, from the sphere of the auto-psychological, concepts referring to physical objects can be constructed; then concepts referring to hetero-psychological objects; and finally concepts referring to cultural objects. The basis of the individual stream of experiences consists of predominantly sensationalistic elements. And it is the relation of similarity-remembrance between these elements which constitutes the basic concept of the construction system. For Husserl the levels of reality we ordinarily take as real, such as the cultural level and the existence of other selves, are all derived from, and hence reducible to, the intentional activity of the transcendental ego. For Carnap the levels are epistemologically secondary and derivable from the primary auto-psychological sphere. And just as Husserl's grandiose scheme of epoche-analysis and 'reconstitution' came in for criticism from existential phenomenologists, so Carnap's grandiose scheme of analysing the logical structure of the world down to autopsychological sensations and reconstructing all knowledge systematically from this basis was criticised by conceptual analysis.[3] For both sets of objectors such attempts at large scale analysis and reconstruction of personal experience misrepresents its nature, and is not based on a sufficiently sensitive description of the variety and heterogeneity of personal experience. And for both sets of objectors, solipsism, methodological or otherwise, is a philosopher's confusion, irrelevant to the understanding of personal experience which has an intersubjective or social nature. Existential phenomenology deals with man in a state of society, and conceptual analysis deals with man in a state of language. The world as a solipsistic construction and the world as an intersubjective construction are, of course, two mutually exclusive ideas.

Husserl's transcendental solipsism embodied the desire to make philosophy into the most basic science. It would be *the* study within which both the natural and the humanistic sciences would find their place. At a pinch one might call this the idealistic version of the unity of all science. The empiricist copyright version, exemplified by Carnap, exalted natural science and not philosophy. On this interpretation philosophy would become a logical and analytical activity, parasitic upon natural science. And there would be no distinctive humanistic sciences and humanistic methods of explanation, such as would find their place in Husserl's master plan. But in spite of this, and in spite of the necessarily fundamental differences between any explicit idealism on the one hand, and any explicit empiricism on the other, there remains the similar reductionist and reconstructionist method with which both Carnap and Husserl organised their ideas. Existential phenomenology, as we have already seen, discarded Husserl's reductionist mode of organisation of ideas, and criticised both the form and the sensationalistic basis of logical empiricism. In this, existential phenomenology was joined by the school of conceptual analysis which also was critical of reductionism and sensationalism. Carnap's logical empiricist colleagues were more fraternally critical of Carnap's methodological solipsism which they considered to be a little too forthright. We may now look at how these fraternal criticisms modified the logical empiricist approach.

Physicalism, reductionism and scientific explanation

The difficulties of accounting for the public concepts of public knowledge by the essentially private means of subjective sensations, as tried by Carnap, soon became clear to the Vienna Circle, and to relevant outsiders like Karl Popper (1959; 1965, ch. 11). But within the Circle, it was Otto Neurath in particular who influenced Carnap in the direction of what came to be known as 'physicalism'. Neurath's argument was basically the point that the logical analysis of any language, be it everyday, technical, theoretical or scientific language, cannot be based elsewhere than in the intersubjective field. That is, while Carnap's constructional system was formally sound, its basic elements should not have been auto-psychological sense-data and their relations. Rather, the basic elements should have been simply physical things and the observable properties and relations of such things (Carnap, 1967, p. vii-viii; see also Reichenbach 1938, p. 129). Things and the behaviour of things are in the public and intersubjective field, sensations are not.

In Carnap and Feigl's later formulations of physicalism a gesture is still made in the direction of subjective sensationalism. According to Carnap, the 'principle of empiricism' (Carnap, 1963, p. 882; see also Feigl, 1963) is that a person regards as meaningful for them whatever they can, in principle, confirm subjectively. But this is only a gesture, for the 'first thesis of physicalism' (1963, p. 883) holds that whatever is subjectively confirmable is also intersubjectively confirmable. The 'second thesis of physicalism' enunciated by Carnap explicitly states the unity of the science ideal; 'All laws of nature, including those which hold for organisms, human being and human societies, are logical consequences of the physical laws, i.e. of those laws which are needed for the explanation of inorganic processes' (ibid.). But Carnap acknowledges that present knowledge hardly approaches this ideal of physical reduction and deductive unification of all scientific knowledge.

According to its proponents physicalism was an attempt to 'liberalise' empiricism by weaning it away from the sensationalist and hence the subjectivist account of knowledge. This shift from a first person to a third person approach needs more clarification, but at least one point can be noted. That is, that whatever is meant by 'liberalisation' it certainly does not imply that logical empiricism had become less rigorously positivist in its attempt to depersonalise its view of the world and its view of knowledge in general. Quite the reverse. Physicalism was a more, and not less, unacceptable interpretation of the nature of knowledge, and of scientific knowledge in particular, as far as humanistic philosophies such as existential phenomenology and conceptual analysis were concerned.

In its first person sensationalist, and in its third person physicalist versions, logical empiricism remained committed to eradicating the notion of persons as distinctive kinds of entities to which both of the humanistic schools we have analysed were so much attached. In the earlier phenomenalism or sensationalism, terms indicating personal 'possession' of sensatory experiences could, allegedly, be dispensed with at the most basic level. So, in the phenomenal or sensationalistic language, 'my' and 'I' would be redundant. There would only be phrases like 'now a red spot in the visual field', 'now toothache', etc. We saw earlier that Wittgenstein advocated a complete avoidance of the metaphysical 'I', which sees the world but which cannot see itself as in the world, in the *Tractatus*. And Carnap's 'methodological solipsism' is a family relative of this idea.

In his physicalist afterthought Carnap accepted that such a language could only be used for soliloquy, and not for communication between people. And solipsistic soliloquy is the philosopher's artifice. He accepted that everyday knowledge, and the concepts and language of everyday knowledge, could not be analysed in solipsistic terms. Rather, some concession has to be made to the fact that we communicate in language which has personal indicators. But the basic job of any language, he believed, is to describe inter-subjectively observable, spatio-temporally localised things, or the events of their behaviour. So the depersonalisation of physicalism was that, while it accepted at a basic level that there are things that we denote 'persons', and that there are valid uses of personal indicators like personal pronouns and so on, on the other hand, it held that such things could only be analysed in terms of observable behaviour. That is, we must take the same perspective with persons that we cannot help but take with physical things. We can only describe their behaviour in the same kind of terms we use to describe the behaviour of things.

Not only was the third person perspective advocated, but it was a very Spartan third person perspective from which most of the normal kinds of things that a person might say in describing the behaviour of another would be eradicated. In particular reference to motives, intentions, purposes, that distinguish human action from mere animal behaviour, would be eradicated, along with all reference to mental qualities and events. All of these 'mentalistic predicates' are always to be interpreted, in the physical thing language, in terms of the behaviour, movement, etc. of physical things like bodies.

But there is more to it than this. Behaviour, particularly of an organic body, can be either macro- or micro-behaviour. That is, it can describe gross movements and dispositions to move of the physical organism as a whole, on view 'outside' as it were; or it can describe micro-structures of the human body, such as brain cell or hormone processes, systems and the like, on view 'inside', to those with the instruments and the interest (see Carnap, 1951; 1967, p. 86). Ordinary third person observations would normally be of macro-behaviour. But scientific and technical third person observations could range from macro- to micro-behaviour, the psychologist or 'behavioural scientist' being more interested in the former and the neurologist, bio-chemist, etc., being more interested in the latter. However, the presumption of physicalism is that the former is always in principle reducible to the latter, both as regards description and, more important, as regards causal and theoretical explanation (for a recent revival of this kind of view see Armstrong, 1967).

The pseudo-behaviourism of dispositional explanation which Ryle offered in *The Concept of Mind*, and which we discussed in chapter 2, is relevant here. Ryle attempted to abolish once and for all the Cartesian Mind-Body dualism, and to analyse mind concepts in terms which referred only to the behaviour of the human body and its dispositions to behave in various ways. This attempt was disingenuous in two ways. First, it both asserted and denied the distinctive nature of human dispositions compared with the dispositions of physical things, and the consequent distinctive nature of explanations of human behaviour compared with that of physical things. And second, it remained purely at a very loosely interpreted macro-behavioural level as regards human action, implying that it might be consistent with micro-behavioural reductionist explanation of action. But elsewhere in the argument it is clear that Ryle is too much of a humanist to seriously accept this implication of his argument.

Carl Hempel, a logical empiricist, has interpreted Ryle as contributing to the physicalist and behaviourist argument (1966, p. 109), but this conversion of a conceptual analyst, albeit an inconsistent one, into a logical empiricist, albeit an embryonic one, cannot be justified. The situation is this. The first step of physicalism in relation to mentalistic predicates was to propose the following analogy (Hempel, 1969; Neurath, 1959). When we talk about a human being in terms like 'intelligence', it is just the same as talking about a clock in terms like 'precision'. Just as we may suspect that intelligence is some kind of thing in a person that makes him do what he does, so we may suspect that precision is some kind of thing in a clock that makes it do what it does. But clearly this is stretching things a bit. So just as we can accept that precision is not some ghostly entity in the clock making it behave the way it does, so we ought, on the physicalist account, to be able to see that intelligence is not some ghostly entity in the human organism making it behave the way it does. All that either of these two terms mean is that clocks or humans have a disposition to do certain things under certain conditions. Ryle's position was something like this first physicalist step.

The second step of physicalism in relation to mentalistic predicates is to accept the principle that the aim of science is, and ought to be, to define behavioural dispositions in terms of the 'actual properties' with which they are associated. For instance, the characterisation of temperature as a disposition to produce certain thermometer readings can be replaced, in kinetic theory, by a micro-structural definition in terms of molecular kinetic energy (Hempel, 1969, p. 178). Or, to use the clock example, the behavioural disposition of the clock, to which the term 'precision' referred, can be further defined in terms of the principles of clockwork mechanical systems, which are exemplified in the actual internal workings of all clocks. And this reduction applies in just the same way to the analysis of mentalistic predicates like 'intelligence' in terms of behavioural dispositions. It would mean that such dispositions would in principle be explicable in terms of the intra-organic and micro-structural processes that underly them, and which cause them. The scientific explanation of human dispositions must, on this account, be micro-structural and theoretical; this is a basic presumption of the reductionist idea of science proposed by logical empiricism.

This second step is certainly not one that Ryle either took, or ever envisaged taking, and yet it is a comprehensible progression given the first step, which he convinced himself, mistakenly in my view, that he had taken. Had Ryle taken the second step, however, it would have made explicit the implicit confusion of his claim that dispositional explanations have got no connection with, and are totally unlike, causal explanations. It could be said that they are themselves summations of causal laws. For while dispositions, arguably, cannot be spoken of as causes, they can be said to be caused by micro-structural processes. And in this sense, and possibly in other senses also, they can be 'unpacked' into causal and theoretical accounts. Then the point of Ryle's claim, which was to give some logical respectability, at the same time, to reason-giving as a form of dispositional explanation, and (off-stage) to human dispositions and behaviour as distinctively rational forms of explanation, would have been lost. The humanistic nature of is general position nevere allowed him to endorse physicalism, reductionism and behaviourism in any thoroughgoing and consistent way.h Hempel did not recognis this ambivalence in Ryle's thesis between humanism and anti-humanistic reductionism. And this means that his assimilation of Ryle to the latter position, Hempel's own, and that of logical empiricism in general, is premature at least.

Physicalism can be interpreted, and is so here, as having realistic, existential and ontological implications, basically those of a monistic materialism. But Carnap, Neurath, Feigl, Hempel and their associates proposed it as a thesis about language, and about the nature of scientific language in particular. It is a kind of democratisation of language and concepts. No matter what a man's qualities, in a democracy he is formally a political unit, a voter, and identical in this respect to every other man. Similarly, in the physicalist unification of all empirical and theoretical science, every concept is formally equal. They all have a complete translation into the terms of the physical-thing language. And this language includes the terms of theoretical physics as well as the terms of everyday things, accessible to casual observation.

Psychology, according to the physicalist account, is therefore one with physics, just as chemistry, bio-chemistry, biology and other natural sciences are supposed to be one with physics. That is, like these other sciences it ought, in principle, to be reducible to and deductively unifiable with physics. In fact, of course, not even bio-chemistry, let alone biology or psychology, is reducible to physics at our present state of knowledge. So it must be borne in mind that reductionism is an *ideal*, a programme behind scientific endeavour and behind some philosophical interpretations of science. For psychology this ideal programme would mean that its special area would be the macro-behaviour of the human organism, closely linked with neurological and other investigations of the intra-organic micro-structures relevant to behaviour. Sociology, then, on this scheme, would be concerned with the group of human organisms, but its explanations would be reducible to, and unifiable with, explanations of behaviour at the psychological level of the individual organism. This would be the most positivistic interpretation of 'psychological reduction' in sociology.

There are some approaches within the study of psychology which proceed with the physicalist picture in mind. The behaviourist tradition in American psychology, from Watson up to Hull and Skinner, fits the requirement of dealing with human action as the behaviour of an organism, environmentally conditiond, but with the conditioning mediated by intra-organic nerve, neural and other processes (see chapter 4 below). Behaviour is accounted for by 'outer' stimulation, or 'inner' stimulation, both of which are mediated through intra-organic processes. An example of the 'outer' stimulation approach might be found in the extensive literature on reward-punishment theories of learning (e.g. Hull, 1943; Skinner, 1957). While an example of the 'inner' stimulation approach might be found in the equally extensive literature on 'drive' theories based on needs of the organism, for food, sex, tension-reduction, aggression or whatever (see Peters, 1958). There are also many attempts to marry inner and outer physicalistic approaches such as Eysenck's accounts of criminal (1970) and political (1954) behaviour based on the connection between environmental conditioning and hereditary physiological determinants of personality.

These are the kinds of psychological theories that have come in for criticism from both existential phenomenology and conceptual analysis. And in part 2 of this book the nature of these criticisms will be investigated further. For the moment it is enough to note the relationship of such psychological theories to their general philosophical background and perspective, that of logical empiricism.

This perspective holds that just as psychology is reducible in principle to physics through various physiological, bio-chemical and other levels, so sociology is reducible to psychology in its turn. Such reduction, as had been seen, is related to the alleged epistemic primacy of the physical-thing level over all other levels.

The logical empiricist reductionist ideal of the unity of all science has found opposition, not only among the humanistic studies like psychology, sociology and history, but also within natural science from biology. Although it is controversial, it is not heretically irrational to hold, in biology, that the organic and animate level of material things, the life-level, cannot be reduced to the inanimate level of matter, or explained in terms of purely physical theories. However, the great advances that are taking place in bio-chemistry, such as the discovery of the molecular structure of D.N.A. and so on, mean that *some* form of deductive unification of natural science, and *some* form of reduction, must be accepted as feasible

The situation with the humanities, however, is much as it always has been. Psychology and sociology continue to be loosely organised federations of varying approaches, varying types of theory and varying types of empiricism. And most of these sub-studies have some commitment, either to the level of the conscious and purposive individual, or to the level of social structure, which they hold as irreducible levels. Humanistic methods of explanation also have tended to be anti-reductionist, in particular they have tended to be one form or another of teleological explanation.

There are two basic forms of teleological explanation used by the humanities. One uses the goals and intentions that a person announces, or that a person can be interpreted as following, to explain why the person does what he does. This can be called the personalist, or individualist form (e.g. Weber, see chapter 8 below). The other form uses a total state of society that all of the various elements of the society can be interpreted as functioning to produce. This can be called the holistic form (e.g. Parsons, 1970). It has a number of variations. The social state that the elements function to produce, according to one theory, is an equilibrium state, an unchanging reference point. The model for this might be any cybernetic or homeostatic system, such as the thermostat, which keeps things like refrigerators, cookers, boilers and air-conditioning systems at a steady temperature. A sophistication of this theory accommodates change by positing the system as an evolving and structurally differentiating one, like an organism (e.g. Parsons, 1966). But this view has no analogy for organic death. A theory which *does*, holds that all of the elements function to produce a constantly changing reference point, where deviance 'amplifies' and the system ultimately ensures its own break-up (see Buckley, 1967, ch. 6). Examples of this line of thought spring readily out of social history and economic theory. One can think of uncontrollable inflation and economic depression, both in theory and in recent history. Or one can think of the international system of interaction we call 'escalation' and 'brinkmanship' which precedes the qualitatively different system of war.

Both types of sociological functionalism have many different dimensions in which they can be interpreted. One of these dimensions has to do with consciousness and with the personalist teleology mentioned previously. The steady/unsteady states that elements of a social system function to produce can be portrayed as goals consciously held by interacting groups, communities and classes of men. On the other hand, such states can be portrayed as things which nobody in the society knows anything about, which nobody works to produce, and which are the result of 'unconscious'/'latent' processes (see Merton, 1957a; Machotka, 1964).

According to Freud, the individual's purposes and intentions can also be unconscious. Similarly, according to psychologists of other schools, the individual's needs and drives, which motivate his behaviour, are not known about by the individual in the same way that the scientific observer knows about them; they are unconscious. So, to sum up, teleological explanation in the humanities can be analysed into personalistic and sociological types. Both types appear in forms which either make use of the notion of consciousness, or conversely, which make use of the notion of unconscious needs and goals. The sociological type, further, appears in forms which either make use of the notion of equilibrium states, or conversely, which make use of the notion of accelerating disequilibrium. Within the humanities, then, there is clearly vast disagreement possible between the different interpretations of teleological explanation. And this is reflected in the long-standing arguments which, in sociology at least, are little closer to solution now than when the founding fathers, Marx, Durkheim, Weber and others, first voiced their opinions and their differences of opinion. But the general point is that without imposing any false unanimity upon the humanities, they all equally stand criticised by logical empiricism, and by its reductionist and physicalist conception of science. Teleological explanation makes the humanities distinctive and cuts the unity of science, as propounded by logical empiricism, into two. But, according to logical empiricism, all science is woven in the same way, and has the same explanatory form. Science explains something by deducing a statement describing it from a law or theory, and by showing what the cause of it was; that is, scientific explanation is logical and empirical, respectively. Teleological explanation, on the other hand, is pseudo-explanation, because logically it does not provide a rigorously deductive account, and empirically it does not show what the cause of any particualr thing is. Of course, the criteria of theoretical deduction and of causal explication are mixed up together in any actual natural scientific explanation. They have to be analysed out, but they are respectively sophisticated and loose presentations of the same line of thinking. That is, the terms 'cause' does not appear in the most rigorous (mathematical) statement of any natural scientific theory. However, we would still say that the theory enables us to understand the causes of things.

But surely much humanistic explanation, which we have discussed as being teleological, could, nevertheless, in a loose sense of the term 'cause', be said to be causal? For instance, it is possible to say that a man's intention to do something caused him to do it (see chapter 2). It is also possible to say that, because the goal or 'preferred state' of a social system is such and such, that this causes a specific social item to behave in the way that it does. We have also remarked on the very interesting connection of the notion of cause with the notion of coercion, both in everyday life and in sociological theory. An institution or group of men can cause men to do things they might otherwise never do, by power, intimidation, the threat of violence and so on. But this coercive type of causation *presumes* that man is a rational actor, and that he is a thinking and willing entity. Unlike other determinisms this does not negate man's rationality and freedom; in order to obey a command man must hear it, understand it, and bring himself to act on it. This coercion-causation, most emphatically proposed in Marxist historical materialism, is a complex area, and has a complex relationship with sociology. For the moment the point is that all of these senses of cause are at least different from, and more loose than, the sense of cause which has traditionally been part of the empiricist approach. The mechanistic materialism of this empiricism is a very different creature from Marxist historical and dialectical materialism, for instance.[5]

The mechanistic empiricist interpretation of 'cause' excludes all of the teleological versions we have mentioned. It holds that a cause is any event that is observed to regularly precede any other. Causal generalisations and causal laws have their foundation on this observable regularity of sequence. Therefore an early casualty of this interpretation is the idea that men act on the basis of reasons, intention, will and so on. None of these subjective 'goings on' can be observed by a third party, and there can be no causal correlation between what is unobservable (mind) and what is observable (behaviour). (For an important sociological rejection of this kind of empiricist positivism and for a formulation of 'motive' as an observer's rule for describing sources of action see Blum and McHugh, 1971).

Another immediate casualty of the interpretation of a cause as an event which temporally precedes its effect, is the possibility that the 'preferred state of a social system' could be a cause, in this sense, of the behaviour of elements of the system. The goal, or preferred state, is an unrealised *future* state of affairs when it realises its effects in the present. It is not the achieved or realised goal or state of affairs which the teleologist points to in his explanation. It is the unrealised future state of affairs which is effective. So the effect would have to be held to *precede* the cause. And in any case, the functionalist analyst in sociology, for instance, does not inquire into the causes of any social element. By definition he looks for its functions, that is for its effects. The functionalist analysis of any particular social element is never an explanation of the element; rather it is always an explanation of things that happen to *other* elements because the element under consideration functions in the way that it does. And, as for our final example of coercion as a form of causation, this suffers in the same way as the first example from the elimination of mind in the logical empiricist account. The subject's understanding of commandments and their sanctions, his decision to obey, or disobey, and the way he subsequently brings himself to do what he does, are all 'unobservable goings on', and as such must be excluded from all causal accounts.

Generally speaking, then, explanation in the humanities is teleological in one form or another. Some of these forms can loosely be called causal, but this does not make them compatible with the traditional empiricist interpretation of causal explanation. Only statistical correlations, in sociology and psychology, could be put forward as tying in with the empiricist vision of what a science should look like. But then, as we have mentioned, this vision is more developed and more subtle than just the notion of causal explanation. Logical empiricism, as the name of the school implies, requires scientific explanation to be logically ordered as well as empirically based. That is, scientific explanation must be lawful and theoretical, and must be able to deduce its empirical instances from a body of systematic laws and theories.

Just as, in some senses, humanistic explanation can be called causal, so some organisations of explanatory ideas in the humanities, such as functionalism in sociology, can be called theoretical and lawful. But equally, just as the logical empiricist version of causality excludes most humanistic versions, so too does its version of theoretical explanation exclude most humanistic versions. Indeed, Hempel (1965), Rudner (1966) and other logical empiricist analysts have put sociological functionalism under close scrutiny, revealing its logical 'inadequacies' compared with physical theories (see also Isajiw, 1968; Gellner, 1970, pp. 21-2). Some of these inadequacies have already been mentioned, particulary the equivocation over causes and effects. In teleological theories, like those of sociological functionalism, this makes the theory difficult to test empirically, and suspiciously circular in its logic. For instance, let us assume that the equilibrium of a social system (A) is produced partly by people's participation in religious rituals (B), i.e. B causes A. So we can say that the rituals function to maintain the social equilibrium. But then the rituals can be said to be produced by the need, goal or preferred state of the system, which is that of equilibrium, i.e. A causes B. The adoption of the functionalist theoretical framework need not always bring circularities as crude as this; but then a subtle or insinuated circularity is, nevertheless, still circular.

Humanistic thinking which becomes pretentiously theoretical and systematised must accept the very likely fate of being deflated by logical analysis, as sociological functionalism has been. It may be unfortunate, but most of the interesting theories in the humanities cannot be stated with crystal clarity, cannot be easily proved or disproved, and they coexist with other theories in disagreement and debate. Logical empiricism imports into the humanities standards of crystal clarity and criteria of empirical proof and disproof which belong elsewhere, and which the humanities in practice ignore, to a large extent. Where sociologists and psychologists take such standards seriously as ideals, they are pushed into a 'waiting for Newton' posture. But, if so long for their Newton, how long for their Einstein?

Conclusion

What we have seen so far then is that, as a general philosophy, logical empiricism is opposed to humanistic philosophies. And also, as a philosophy of science, it is opposed to any special claims for the nature of humanistic studies such as psychology, sociology, history and so on. The general background to this anti-humanism was seen to be its sensationalistic theory of knowledge, its implied materialistic theory of being, and its physicalistic and reductionist thesis of the unity of all science.

In mitigation it might be mentioned that there were less rigid and more sensitive analyses of the problems of humanistic philosophy and humanistic study at large within the Vienna Circle. For instance, there was Schlick's concern to understand ethics and experiences of values, (1962). There was Neurath's loose interpretation of the unity of scientific language as 'universal jargon', his view of science not as a theoretical enterprise but as a predictive and utilitarian service for the good of mankind, and his commitment to Marxism. There was von Misess concern to understand metaphysics, art and poetry (1968, ch. 23-8). And also there was Carnap's own very guarded approach to the realm of cultural realities in his original constructional system (see for example, 1967, p. 230).

However, the main theses of the school are opposed to the kind of theses which phenomenology explicitly, and conceptual analysis more implicitly, are committed to, and which were discussed in the first two chapters. Even if it is a simple generalisation, nevertheless it is useful and informative to portray conceptual analysis and phenomenology as united in a common humanistic opposition to logical empiricism. The later school of thought is the clearest expression of a long tradition, which can usefully be seen as anti-humanistic in the senses discussed in this chapter.

The anti-humanistic reductionist idea of the unity of all science conceives of all sciences, studies and explanations as unifiable in principle with physics. This is an ideal, a vigorous expression of commitment to scientific progress and to the idea that the future lies with physical science. As an ideal, the reductionist idea had its influence on the self-consciousness of humanistic studies. It has captured the imagination of psychologists and, to a lesser extent, sociologists. So in some psycho-social studies reductionism is very explicit and is taken neat. But in others it is disguised and hopefully mixed in cocktail with humanistic commitments and teleological methods. It is into this complex area that we must next pursue the comparison between conceptual analysis and phenomenology.

In the first two chapters some of the theses which these two schools have in common were discovered. These positive similarities will emerge again in the course of our analysis of the discussions by the two schools of behaviourist psychology and of Gestalt psychology, Freudian psychology and Weber's sociology in part II of this book. But, even clearer than this will appear the negative similarities, most particularly the rejection by both schools of the reductionist idea in the humanities. Now that reductionism and its philosophical background has been made clear, this common rejection can be understood in greater depth.

part II

The relationship of the schools to psychology and sociology

4 Behaviourist psychology

As an approach to the study of man, behaviourist psychology is hard-headed and unromantic. Yet to its critics it appears caught in the labours of a lost love, the toils of sterile romance. The object of its dogged attentions is the ideal of a natural science of human behaviour. It is an approach which claims that its feet are planted firm on the ground of evidence. This is indisputable, althought it appears to many that this ground is so narrow and restricted as to be almost invisible. Behaviourism would not accept so readily that its head is lost in the clouds of an aspiration. But it is this aspiration that phenomenology and conceptual analysis are most concerned to identify and to criticise.

Before these criticisms are given an airing it would be useful to point briefly to the main features of the behaviourist position. Historically it developed from two main sources, Watson's (1928) rejection of introspectionist psychology and Pavlov's (1927) animal experiments, both in the early years of the century. In the ensuing decades it grew rapidly in America where it acquired the paraphernalia and respectability of an experimental science. Its major maxims to experimenters might be summed up as follows: pretend to know nothing about human being, forget that yourself and others think and act; now see what you can find out about other people while pretending like this; and now measure and quantify this hard won 'reality'. For an allegedly simple approach these can be rather complex operations. But on the other hand, it had advantages for its supporters, for clearly if the object of the game is to achieve no-knowledge, no-insight, no-imagination and so on, then it is a great help if one does not happen to possess these qualities in the first place. Perhaps this is unfair; behaviourism is also a romance with a great scientific ideal, an ill-fitting vocation for the unimaginative and the dull. But then there are those who would argue to the contrary that the vocation is tailor-made for this cast of mind (see Wahn, 1969; Koestler, 1967).

Ordinary imagination allows us to think and act in terms of other people as if they also thought and acted purposively most of the time. The behaviourist maxims, on the other hand, are incentives to an extraordinary level of dullness about other people. Human behaviour must not be explained in terms of purpose, consciousness or any other such mundane tomfoolery. Rather, men are nothing but organisms, and if we are careful enough we can avoid using any other frame of reference when explaining their behaviour. Rats and pigeons are very instructive organisms, and it is amazing how rat-like and pigeon-like human behaviour can be made to appear if one really works hard at it. It is a fact that behaviourists rarely extend their list of organic analogies of man to include embarrassingly intelligent animals like monkeys, apes or dolphins. They believe that animal behaviour can be explained in terms which make no reference to the animal's purpose, and that in this respect human behaviour is no different from rat or pigeon behaviour. They rarely acknowledge that the exorcising of mental and purposive terms from ordinary or experimental descriptions, and from theory, requires a logical rigour which they have never actually achieved, even with rats, let alone with humans (see C. Taylor, 1967, chs. 7 and 9).

If not purpose, then what? The answer from the behaviourist camp for the last fifty years has been stimulus and response. This has been the main frame of reference of their approach. The behaviour of the organism is presumed to be explicable, in the final analysis, as a response to the stimulation of the organisms sensory receptor organs by the impingements of the physical environment. The basic schema may be exemplified on the human level as follows. Doctor applies mallet (differential impingement of the physical environment) to patient's kneecap (specific area of receptor organs), patient's leg jerks (organism's response evoked—or determined, or caused, or 'controlled'—by the stimulus). So behaviour in stimulus response terms is basically reflexive.

With an attempt at sophistication, behaviourism has posed as a theory of learning, as a theory of how the organism adapts to its impinging environment. But to be more accurate, it is a theory of conditioning. It tries to show how habits, associations, dispositions and other response patterns are conditioned in an organism by the organism's physical environment. Certain responses, evoked by the environment, are reinforced time and time again in the organism by the satisfaction each time of some of the organism's need by the environment. So the theory of conditioning requires a picture of the organism as having certain basic needs and drives. These drives progressively step up the nervous activity and anxiety of the organism until some satisfaction of the drive crops up, and the drive is temporarily 'reduced'. A simple example would be the survival need or drive which produces the drive to get food. Other drives might be associated with sex, territory, aggression, etc. (see Hull, 1943; Nissen, 1964; Lorenz, 1966; McClelland, 1953; Peters, 1958, ch. 4).

Thus, as well as there being 'outer' stimulation of the organism by the environment, the picture is modified by there also being 'inner' stimulations, drives and needs. What determines the habits, dispositions and general patterns of behaviour that the organism demonstrates, is the way that these inner and outer pokings coincide. The thinking behind this approach to conditioning is equally well expressed in the language of reward and punishment (the carrot and stick frame of any donkey's reference). The organism has to do something; it has to behave in some way in order to feed itself, for instance. But the way that it feeds, what it feeds on and so on, is determined by the rewarding and punishment aspects of its physical environment. It is this environment relative to the hunger drive of rats and pigeons that behaviourists have most often attempted to manipulate and control in their experiments. The animals can be conditioned to perform certain operations, such as bar-pressing, by the experimental control of their hunger and the satisfaction of their hunger.

At first (and second?) sight, this kind of approach would not appear to be applicable to very much human behaviour. Some human behaviour is undoubtedly reflexive, some is undoubtedly controlled, in conditions of extreme deprivation, by drives for food, sex, aggression and so on. But most is not, most is thoughtful in some sense or another, and purposive in some sense or another. But, the behaviourist might object, the very production of this written sentence occurs at a speed which rules out thoughtfulness. And it is true, I do not have to interpose some act of will, some distinct thought of each letter, before I actually type it. It is somehow reflexive; the production of the sentence is almost thoughtless. Like most skills, if one had to think slowly over every aspect of their performance, one would be incapable of performing them at all. Here it is almost as if thinking rules out performance rather than generating it.

But to buy this argument the behaviourist has to sell his main thesis. It is quite clear that while the typing of a sentence may be reflexive and thoughtless, the concept of the sentence and the motive to perform the operation were quite the opposite. They were thoughtful and generated by me, not evoked in me as a reflex by some crudely conceived stimulus. It is true that one may say that an idea, sentence, theory or whatever arises somehow as a 'response' to a problem, as a response to the 'need' to solve an intellectual problem. But the use of these words in this context has an entirely different meaning than the behaviourist would like to pin on them; they have an analogical and metaphorical relation to his use. The context of his use is a deterministic explanation of behaviour. The context of my use is the claim that my behaviour is created (determined?) by my intellectual interests, in this case.

In general then, the behaviourist hopes to avoid the 'higher' skills of which human beings are capable. He cannot buy the argument that much skilful behaviour is reflexive without also buying the very unpalatable argument that the most important aspects of skilful behaviour are not at all reflexive. The very reasons (causes?) they are performed at all have nothing to do with reflex, but have everything to do with intellectual judgement and the evaluation of a situation. The behaviourist's main thesis is that human behaviour can be explained deterministically because it is caused by stimuli. But the major distinguishing feature of human skills is that they can be performed in a variety of very dissimilar conditions and situations, which provide a number of very different rationales for the action. That is, no one stimulus controls the skilful 'response', skills are stimulus-free. And if they are stimulus-free, then they cannot be explained deterministically.

The language theorist, Noam Chomsky, has applied this argument most effectively against behaviourism, in his critique of Skinner's work on 'verbal behaviour' (see N. Chomsky, 1964; see also C. Chomsky, 1970; Brown and Fraser, 1963; Asch, 1968; Bever, Fodor and Garrett, 1968). It is quite rare that a behaviourist has ventured into the area of the higher behavioural abilities of humans, and so Skinner must be complimented for his courage, if for nothing else, (Skinner, 1957; Russell and Staats, 1963; Staats, 1968). But Chomsky shows that the linguistic skills of the normal human, like all of the skills that distinguish man from even the highest animal, cannot be explained in the simplistic terms of stimulus and response. For in language, as in these other skills we are dealing with a competence which is to an important extent creative and stimulus-free. The very ordinary and everyday phenomenon of someone producing a sentence is almost impossible to account for in behaviourist terms. Most sentences that we produce contain words that, naturally, we have heard before and come to learn. But the most important point is that their arrangement in a sentence is usually completely novel. We do not produce sentences because we have learned and have been conditioned to produce just those sentences. We produce combinations of words that we have never heard in that specific combination before. The possibilities of grammatically correct combinations are practically infinite, so the scope for our very mundane and ordinary skill of talking is as good as infinite. Behaviourism, which envisages a deterministic process at work, is very hard pressed to produce any account at all of the creativity required by such a skill as talking.

Behaviourism has explicitly allied itself with the logical empiricist physicalist version of the unity of science which was discussed in the last chapter (see Stevens, 1951; Bergmann and Spence, 1951; Hull, 1951; Boring, *et al.*, 1945), and it has propagated this ideal more effectively in the humanities than the Vienna Circle philosophers have been able to, in the sense that it has provided something concrete for potential converts to look at, rather than merely an abstract argument and programme. But this is not to say that its reductionism has been very successful or far reaching.

It has been seen that behaviourism has failed to account for most of the more distinctively human skills. But also it has made little effort to ground its theories on the intra-organic micro-structural nerve and brain processess which Carnap and Feigl, and other proponents of the reductionist programme hold to be essential to the programme. It is all very well just to observe that when a certain stimulus goes 'in' to an organism a certain response comes 'out'. But the reductionist, and the scientific investigator in general, cannot declare the 'inside' of the organism as some kind of black box of intervening and mediating processess that are either irrelevant to behaviour or relevant but unknowable.

It is true that the behaviourist does rely on very simple goings on 'inside' the organism because he relies on the organism's drives and needs, but these are simply hypothesis about the general nature of the organism, and nothing like the kind of complex facts and equally complex theories which are required to provide a more complete picture of the inner workings of the organism. The study of the brain is still in its infancy and imposes an infancy on the putative reductionist account of man's behaviour. Perhaps it is impatience with the slow progress of science in this field that makes behaviourist psychologists suspect that the brain is almost as unimportant to human behaviour as they believe consciousness to be.

What of the relation between behaviourist psychology and sociology? The relation must be, on the reductionist programme, that of reducibility of sociological to psychological explanations. What holds for the single organism holds also in principle for a collection or group of organisms, their individual and collective behaviour is determined according to the same stimulus and response principles (see Argyle, 1957, pp. 81-4; Eysenck, 1954; 1970). But then behaviourist psychology is not really psychological, in the sense that it is not primarily concerned about the individual organism, rather it is concerned with the relation between an individual organism and its environment. So far we have identified this environment as the purely physical environment, the presence or absence of food, the climate and so on. But it is equally the case, even with most animals, that the environment is also social, perhaps predominantly so.

Thus to look at the conditioning of an individual human requires a consideration of the social environment of other humans who reward and punish the behaviour of the individual from infancy and so determine its main dispositions and features. So in a sense, for behaviourism there is no distinctive science of the individual organism that is not also a science of the collectivity of organisms, the society. There is only the one science of human behaviour. And it is this that is reducible in its turn to intra-organic laws and processess. The principles at work in the herd are a simple multiplication of the stimulus-response principles governing the behaviour of the individual animal; there are no 'emergent' phenomena of herd-ness, there are no irreducibly social phenomena. There are only behavioural phenomena, and these are dependent upon organic structure and micro-structures, ultimately.

Skills and abilities are socially learned; they are social in man. A man cannot be a skilful chess-player or talker where there are no social institutions and games known as talking and chess-playing, where there are no social rules and criteria, where there are no other players to teach him the game and so on. And yet behaviourists try to account for these social skills in exactly the same stimulus response terms that they account for purely physiological phenomena like pain reflexes, etc. Not only are there no distinctively conscious and purposive phenomena in the behaviourists' schema, there are no distinctively social facts either.

Conceptual analysis, which we begin with, bases its critique of behaviourism and reductionism on these two aspects of the behaviourist conception of man, the non-sociality of the conception and its non-purposiveness. These two aspects come together in the behaviourist tendency to avoid giving any account of the distinctively human skills like using a language, and, although in most respects conceptual analysts' arguments on linguistic skills are very different from Chomsky's, they share a common consequence, that of attacking behaviourist and reductionist psychology.

Conceptual analysis

Conceptual analysis, particularly some of the writings of Ryle and Wittgenstein, could be, and have been, interpreted as a species of behaviourism (see Holborow, 1967; Mundle, 1966; Hicks, 1961; and chapter 1 above). And further, they have been interpreted as providing a philosophic rationale for behaviourist psychology. The logical empiricist, Hempel, draws this sort of conclusion from Ryle's

Concept of Mind, for instance (1966, p. 109). This argument was examined in chapter 3, and the more general points about conceptual analysts as behaviourists were discussed in chapter 2. The conclusion in both cases was that neither Ryle nor Wittgenstein, and certainly not the majority of their successors, can be said to provide a philosophic rationale for behaviourist psychology. Logical empiricism provides such a rationale, conceptual analysis definitely does not.

This is not to say that some kind of behaviourist analyses are presented by both Wittgenstein and Ryle, although this element of their philosophies can too easily be exaggerated. Nor is it to say that Ryle was not dallying with behaviourist psychology in the *Concept of Mind.* In a sense he was trading on the currency and prestige of a psychological vogue which had appeared so clearly to inherit the future. But he was ambiguous to the point of contradiction in his attitude towards it; if behaviourism by some mischance squandered its inheritance, Ryle's thesis would not sink into bankruptcy with it. He kept his options open. Neither Ryle nor Wittgenstein, to restate the point, ever explicitly endorsed behaviourist psychology. And it would take a virile imagination, and a capacity to ignore many other features of their philosophies, to extract any such endorsement from their writings.

The 'other features' of their positions one would have to ignore in the extortion of this kind of endorsement are their antipathy to scientific explanation of human experience and action, and their commitment to some idea of man as a conscious and purposive actor. Allied with this latter feature is the commitment all conceptual analysts make to a social conception of man. They stress that man is what he is because he exists in a state of language; his possibilities are the possibilities present because he exists in communication with others; without the social fact of language no individual man could be what he is. Behaviourist emphasis on the importance of the environment to the conditioning of the individual organism could at best be only presented as some pale parody of this social perspective. In the main, behaviourism is concerned with the conditionable nature of the individual organism. And to make conceptual analysis consistent with this organic perspective one would have to ignore its own particular type of social perspective.

Man as consciously purposive and man as a social entity are two ideas that, as we have noted on a number of occasions already, come together in any analysis of action and of skill, as far as conceptual analysis is concerned. Suffice it to point out at this stage that behaviourist psychology is not in any way compatible with these sorts of ontological commitments and insinuations on the part of conceptual analysis. Behaviour must be presumed to be an essentially reactive and reflexive phenomenon to the psychologists, but it must be presumed to be active and purposive according to the philosophers.

In this section it will be more useful to pass over these considerations (to return to them later) and to concentrate instead on the other conceptual analytic feature mentioned, its antipathy to scientific explanations of behaviour, and to the reductionist idea in general.

The specific cue from which most ensuing conceptual analytic accounts of psychology begin, and which most of them quote, is the following opinion expressed by Wittgenstein at the very end of the *Philosophical Investigation* (p. 232):

> The confusion and barrenness of psychology is not to be explained by calling it a young science: its state is not comparable with that of physics for instance at its beginnings ... For in psychology there are experimental methods and *conceptual confusions* ... The existence of the experimental method makes us think that we have the means of solving the problems that trouble us; though problems and methods pass one another by.

Whatever other approaches in psychology this statement was aimed at, it is clear that one of the targets was behaviourist psychology with its emphasis on experimental method. In the isolation of individual stimulus-response links it is necessary for the scientific investigator to try and control the influence of all factors apart from the one he is interested in. He can then measure exactly the features of the isolated and uncontrolled factor. Physicists are very good at this kind of thing, therefore it would be wise to imitate them. Experimental isolation and measurement are the high point of the empirical approach according to this view, and if psychologists want to reach this high point, then they too must be prepared to build laboratories and wear white coats.

According to the alchemists, a man in the possession of the right instrument can transmute base metal into gold. It is with something of the same optimism that behaviourism puts so much emphasis on acquiring the instruments and the general appearance of a physical science. Perhaps this, in itself, will transmute psychology from being merely a study of man's actions into being a science of his behaviour. Wittgenstein was not the first, and has by no means been the last, to criticise this belief in the powers of imitation. What was fairly novel in his criticism, however, was the implication that problems in psychology, to which the experimental method was irrelevant, required no kind of empirical or theoretical solution at all. Rather he held that they required therapy, or *dis*solution, by philosophical analysis. Such problems were 'conceptual confusions', and such confusions require conceptual analysis so that they no longer confuse.

But it could be argued that physics and astronomy in late medieval times, when they were embryonic sciences, also had their fair share of conceptual confusions laced with experimental methods irrelevant to them. That is, for instance, theological terms had not been exorcised from theories of matter and of the movement of the planets. God's purpose was present in theoretical accounts together with calculations of physical movement—all very confused by our standards. So perhaps experimental psychology is not at all unlike the very early physical sciences. The problems that trouble us now, for example 'Why do men act in certain ways?', are basically no different from the sort of problems which troubled men then, for example 'Why do planets behave in certain ways?' And what is more, problems about action are due for the same kind of scientific resolution that problems about planetary movements have achieved.

But Wittgenstein would not accept this at all. The two cases remain different and not comparable because, even if it is agreed that early physics was full of conceptual confusions, these sorts of confusions are of a very different nature than those that Wittgenstein believed to be present in psychology. The confusion in physics could be dealt with by the expansion of empirical knowledge allied to precise measurement in the service of precise theories and hypotheses. The confusion in psychology, according to Wittgenstein, cannot be dealt with by any such expansion of knowledge and development of theory. We already know enough about ourselves and others' minds and acts, there is nothing more to find out. All that we can do is be very clear about what we do know, and, more pointedly, about what we can know about minds and acts. The problems and general head-scratching of psychologists epitomise a yearning to go beyond the bounds of sense, to go beyond what we do know and what we can know. The basic problem of psychology, then, in this view, is that there are problems in psychology. The basic conceptual confusion is that there can be conceptual confusions in psychology. There ought to be no problems and no confusions, and the way to this nirvana is to analyse the concepts that psychologists use, to note the way these uses are twisted away from their ordinary everyday uses, and to reassert the importance of these ordinary uses as against artificial distortions.

Then what? Nothing, the inquiring mind rests in peace. Just as the Buddhist ultimately desires to do nothing but contemplate the Void, so the Wittgensteinian ultimately desires as (regards psychology at least) to do nothing but contemplate the harmony of a natural language. This is perhaps the most unsympathetic interpretation that can be put on Wittgenstein. It means that the philosopher gazes complacently and uninterestedly on the progress of knowledge in the physical sciences, and also that he imposes his complacency and lack of interest on attempts to expand knowledge in the psychological and social sciences. The physical sciences are allowed to ignore the complacent gaze, the psycho-social sciences must achieve this very complacency.

This interpretation is very unsympathetic to the need of psychology and sociology to study the world at all and to theorise at all, let alone to do it in a pseudo-scientific way. Elements of this interpretation can be found in Wittgensteinian accounts of psychology, like that of Peters, and of sociology, like that of Winch, both of which we will come to later. Criticisms of this interpretation have also been given a good run for their money, particularly by Gellner. What I am trying to do in this book is to reveal aspects of Wittgenstein's position and of the positions of subsequent conceptual analysts which are more sympathetic to the need for there to be study of the social world, and of acts and of minds. This is not to say that the less sympathetic interpretation is basically wrong, which it is not, but rather that it does not tell the whole story.

Wittgenstein could only warn against all description and confrontation with psychological and sociological facts of the world at the risk of being completely inconsistent, and in fact he advocated a descriptive approach occasionally, 'Don't think, but look' (1963, p. 31). The therapeutic analysis of conceptual confusions, at the very least, implied a description and classification of certain uses of concepts and of the types of context or situation in which they arise. The logic and grammar of any given natural language is a social fact, it is something that exists in the world. Analysis of various structures of meaning in a natural language, similarly, is analysis of the world. If only as a means to a therapeutic end, Wittgenstein described sociological (linguistic) and psychological (actions and experiences) facts of the world, possibilities, and typical features of communication. This was his whole method.

The deflation of puzzling concepts into non-puzzling mundane concepts cannot be understood unless both the former and the latter can be clearly seen and described. The importance of returning to ordinary usage, and of restoring ordinary uses, cannot be registered without a clear knowledge of what ordinary usage in any given situation is. It may not be possible to codify this type of knowledge very much, but it must be possible to state it. And Wittgenstein was emphatic that we must understand the system of thought, the social game we play around and with any concept, the form of life it enters into. All of these are social facts about a given natural language and a given culture. They are subtle of course—cultures within cultures, forms of life within forms of life, games within and overlapping games—but they must be described and stated. The descriptions and statements are the means to the therapeutic end of dissolution of the confusion. But, to dissolve a conceptual confusion in psychology or sociology, Wittgenstein and his followers have had to indulge in amateur forms of psychological and sociological study themselves. To further imply that there is no sense in psychological and sociological studies of any kind is to risk complete self-contradiction. It is this descriptive side, as opposed to the therapeutic side of conceptual analysis that I want to emphasise generally in my account. This is not, of course, to argue that the former aspect is more important than the latter in the general structure of conceptual analytic philosophy.

So Wittgenstein cannot be opposed to all and every study of the social and experiential world, and indeed, his own approach precludes this blanket condemnation. But he is opposed to the attempt to mould such studies on the model of the natural sciences. This is the area of greatest 'conceptual confusion' as far as he is concerned. We have already noted his condemnation of the experimental method in psychology, made in the *Philosophical Investigations.* The empirical method, refined in experiments, cannot deliver the goods in psychology as it has done in physics.

In his *Conversations on Freud* Wittgenstein again criticised the use, allegedly by Freud, of physics as a model. Only in this case Wittgenstein complains that Freud is not empirical enough, and his theories are not backed up by sufficient evidence. Against Freud, introspectionist psychologists of a positivistic bent like Gestaltists, and psychologists in general, Wittgenstein claims that the very notion of theoretical or lawful explanation on the model of physics is a waste of time (1966, p. 42):

> When we are studying psychology we may feel that there is something unsatisfactory, some difficulty about the whole subject or study—because we are taking physics as our ideal science. We think of formulating laws as in physics. And then we find that we cannot use the same sort of 'metric', the same ideas of measurement as in physics, This is especially clear when we try to describe appearances: the least noticeable differences of colours: the least noticeable differences of length, and so on. Here it seems that we cannot say 'If A B, and B C, then A C', for instance. And this sort of trouble goes all through the subject.

He also notes the 'misleading parallel: psychology treats of processes in the psychical sphere, as does physics in the physical' (1963, p. 151).

Wittgenstein is saying that neither precise measurement nor lawful theorising is possible where a study has to rely on a subject's report of his experience. The 'least noticeable' difference is a subjective experience, a phenomenological datum; it is also the application of criteria and standards, the use of a conceptual scheme. The way that phenomenological description and description of the uses and application of concepts, advocated by phenomenology and conceptual analysis respectively, come together will be discussed later, (chapter 5 below). Wittgenstein might have had Gestalt theories of perception in mind when he made this remark, for Hamlyn has developed Wittgenstein's criticisms of psychology precisely in the direction of Gestalt psychology. And when we come to discuss Gestalt psychology it will be seen that Hamlyn's conceptual analysis of perceiving concepts involves necessarily a kind of phenomenological description of perceptual experience. For the moment it is sufficient merely to recognise that conceptual analysis involves some kind of descriptive study (and therefore cannot be anti-study) and also that the main area of conceptual muddles and confusions, as far as it is concerned, in psychology is the reductionist idea of modelling psychology on physics.

Conceptual analysis is not explicitly committed to a dualistic picture (ignoring, for a moment, the very important contributions of Strawson and Hampshire to the school). Yet when writing of psychology and sociology, it does tend to find the major conceptual confusion requiring therapy in the area where humanistic and reductionist conceptual schemas overlap. That is, most of the alleged confusions are said to occur when the conceptual schemes relating to the movement or behaviour of physical things are applied to the conceptual schemes relating to human action. The basis for this dualism was discussed in chapter 2, when it was seen that the conceptual analytic school, in spite of Wittgenstein's obscurities and Ryle's disingenuous 'rejection' of dualism, became more and more concerned with the nature of action concepts. Analysis of action concepts, always proceeded on the assumption that (or, at least, always happened to reach the conclusion that) such concepts were of a very different kind than those which applied to the movement of bodies and physical things. Usually it was asserted that purposes, reasons, intentions and motives came into the analysis and explanation of human actions, and that this class of concepts did not enter into the analysis or explanation of non-human behaviour. In this general perspective, conceptual analysts from Wittgenstein onwards (with the ambiguous exception of Ryle) criticised behaviourist psychology. This is because behaviourism committed itself to the conceptual confusions inherent in treating human behaviour as if it were merely reactive bodily movement, and in accepting the reductionist idea that psychology ought to be physics-like.

In the final chapter of *The Concept of Mind* Ryle, for all his flirtation with behaviouristic kind of approach, does in fact state his antipathy to the reductionist idea in just as stringent terms as Wittgenstein. He criticises the idea of a mechanics of the mind or of action which takes its inspiration from Hobbes and Newton and its cue from physics. Wittgenstein's feeling of the 'barrenness' of this attitude in psychology has its counterpart in Ryle's view that there is a great disparity between the 'para-Newtonian' programme and the performance of psychology.

He voices serious doubts about the behaviourist revolt in psychology, and its attack on the 'ghost in the machine' dualistic myth. Although the behaviourists might have been said to be practising in psychology more or less the same thing as Ryle was preaching in philosophy, Ryle in his concluding remarks turns the tables completely on his erstwhile comrades. Despite his own arguments against dualism, Ryle thinks that the 'good effects' of dualism may have outweighed its 'bad effects' in psychology. He thinks that the 'Cartesian story' has been 'more productive' than the Hobbesian story: that dualism has been 'more fruitful' in philosophy and psychology than monistic and mechanistic determinism; we could go on (1963, pp. 310-11).

Ryle's successors have overcome his own doubts, ambiguities and changes of mind. They simply assert a dualism where he had insinuated one. One half of the dualism is the same as it has always been, i.e. the concepts and explanations relating to physical things and their determined behaviour. The other half is a revised variation of man as a free being, i.e. the concepts and explanations relating to man as a purposive rule-following actor. Behaviourist psychology, which denies any dualism and which would reduce the latter to the former, must, necessarily, stand condemned by conceptual analysis.

However, Ryle has bequeathed to the school, a more explicit antipathy to theory than that present in Wittgenstein's writings, and this is worth a closer look, since it also contributes to the critique of behaviourist psychology and the reductionist idea by the school. In Ryle's view, to call psychology a fully fledged science leads us to expect it to have an explanatory theory for all human doings. But he believes that in fact psychology can only explain what people themselves cannot explain about their own actions, perceptions and states of mind. It is only where the subject is at a loss to understand his own behaviour, according to Ryle, that the psychologist is justified in appealing to 'hidden' facts, 'hidden' causes in his explanations. It is only in these circumstances that the psychologist can invoke, in his explanatory theory or account, phenomena and processes that are 'hidden', or not present to the ordinary person's experience. It is only in the case of illusion, deception and abnormality in general that Ryle would countenance extra-experiential and extra-ordinary explanations. The background to this serious limitation on theory and explanation is partly due to the commitment Ryle makes to the sufficiency of the subject's own account of what he is doing. This is part and parcel of the dualism and the humanism that was stressed already as major features of the conceptual analytic school, and which is a topic we will return to later. But the anti-theoretic limitation can be approached from a different angle.

In chapter 2 it was seen that conceptual analysis in so far as it stemmed from Wittgenstein, arose partly in the form of a rejection of the unitary *Tractatus* theory of the nature of language and meaning. Instead there was to be an appreciation of the diversity of uses and forms of meaning in a natural language. And Austin's connoisseur's approach was a rather extreme development of this concern for the distinctive nature of every little bit of language and communication. Any general theory of the nature of language, which says, for instance, that it is the job of all sentences that are meaningful to refer to some state of affairs, as the early Wittgenstein and Russell had believed, necessarily cannot appreciate the many different jobs that different kinds of sentence do in different situations. Antipathy to theory, then, derives from the cultivation of diversity.

It is the same cast of mind that is revealed in the antipathy of conceptual analysis to any over-all, explain-all, theory of action. Behaviourist psychology provides such a theory, as indeed does Freudian psychology, and Gestalt psychology. But to hold that all action can be explained as some kind of conditioned response to some kind of stimulus is simply to stop confronting the actual diverse nature of action as we all know it in our own lives. The behaviourist picture is a round hole into which every variety of square, rectangular and triangular peg must be fitted, but into which, in the nature of things, they cannot be fitted. It is a picture which takes a hold on our imaginations, which takes a grip on our minds which we must shake off by simply confronting the actual phenomena of acting. And one way of confronting such phenomena is to look at the ways we describe, conceive of, and talk about actions.

According to conceptual analysis there can be no single bewitching picture of action any more than there can be of the uses of language. Behaviourism must be wrong. We do all sorts of things for all sorts of different reasons, in all sorts of different social games. We can only describe the diverse world of ordinary experience. We cannot explain this diversity and this experience, we can only testify to it. We must appreciate the diversity of actions, we must not explain them by showing how they were caused by phenomena and processess that are beyond our experience, and hidden behind what we know to be the case.

Only where things happen to a person, and where he does not see them or understand them or do them himself, can the psychologist step in with causal, theoretical and extra-experiential explanations. Here we can usefully anticipate our discussion of Gestalt psychology, and particularly Hamlyn's conceptual analytic critique of such an overall theory of perception. Hamlyn takes his anti-theoretical cue from a remark by Ryle, in the *Concept of Mind*. Ryle (ibid., p. 308) says:

> We feel that the wrong sort of promise is being made when we are offered ... psychological explanations for our correct estimations of shape, size, illumination and speed. Let the psychologist tell us why we are deceived; but we can tell him ourselves why we are not.

We may assume that we are not deceived in our visual perceptions most of the time, otherwise life would be impossible, so deception and illusion are abnormal and marginal phenomena that happen to a person. According to Ryle and, following him, Hamlyn, only these marginal phenomena of perceiving can be explained by the psychologist's theories. The greater part of perceiving must receive a very different account than a theoretical explanation; it must receive our own account, our own explanations of how we saw something in the way that we saw it. And here we are getting back into the field of diverse conceptual and classificatory schemes, diverse criteria of application, and diverse perceptual skills performed by human beings, whose distinctive nature is guaranteed by the possession of these concepts and these skills (see chapter 5 below).

It may also be noted that the same kind of argument can be made relevant to Freudian psychological explanations. We can usefully anticipate our later discussion of this area also (chapter 6 below). Both MacIntyre's and Peters's critiques of Freud stem from Ryle's and Wittgenstein's opinions, particularly their antipathy to over-all explanations of human actions. As far as the latter two philosophers are concerned, Freud's ideas could be seen as useful explanations of marginal and abnormal phenomena like neuroses, phobias, twitches, obsessions and other things that happen to a person rather than can be said to be produced by him. However, Freud's ideas are rejected by Ryle, Wittgenstein and the ensuing school if they are formulated as an over-all explanatory theory covering normal actions, which can receive an agent's own explanations as well as abnormal ones.

So psychological explanation must eat off the floor—it can only apply to the marginal and abnormal, never to the ordinary and the normal. The normal, according to Ryle, is defined as that which a person does, produces or brings about. The abnormal, conversely, is defined as that which happens to a person and which mystifies him.

Peters, in his monograph on *The Concept of Motivation* (1958), develops this line of argument in relation to Freudian and 'drive' theories. His discussions of the former will be dealt with later (see chapter 6 below). The latter 'drive' theories are most relevant to our discussion of behaviourist psychology. Earlier, when outlining the main ideas of behaviourism, the point was made that more than one type of stimulus was envisaged by this psychology. Besides 'outer' environmental stimuli, there were also held to be 'inner' stimuli within the organism. It is these 'inner' stimuli, the needs of the organism, the drives for food and sex and so on, which in the first place impel it to behave and move. It is through the rewarding and punishing aspects of the environment, outer stimuli, that various modes of behaviour become established in the organism. Peters shows that the concepts of drive and of drive-reduction are central hypotheses for most of the important behaviourist psychologists, and that the notion of 'inner' stimulation is as important to their approaches as that of 'outer' stimulation. It is the coincidence of the two that is held to produce the conditioning and the performance of a certain repertoire of behaviour by the animal. Of the major behaviourists, Hull (1943), in particular, made great use of hypotheses about drives, the organism's needs and need-reduction, as 'intervening variables' to fill out the classical stimulus-response framework inherited from Pavlov and Watson.

Peters notes how psychologists have become more and more dissatisfied with the limitations of explaining behaviour in terms of a limited sort of inner stimulation such as hunger, and how they have extended the notion of drive to include 'drives to know', 'to explore', etc. And the concept has been stretched even further by the introduction of learnt or acquired drives, that is drives that are no longer simply expressions of the genetically inherited physiological structure of any given animal. Whatever confusions there may have always been in the use of the term drive, and its occasional unwitting conflation with the term's conscious purpose, Peters holds, with much justification, that these confusions have now been multiplied. The term drive might once have had a fairly specific definition, but if it is to be used to accommodate spontaneous quests for knowledge as well as conditioned quests for food (and in the case of the human animal perhaps also acquired needs for reading T. S. Eliot, for playing chess, or for arguing with one's wife), then the term is simply a confusion. If it must cover all, then it can cover nothing well.

This acceptable line of criticism by Peters is, however, flawed by the limitations on explanatory theory (which, as we have already seen, Ryle advocates) with which he accompanies his argument. The limitation on explanatory theory in psychology was that it may only apply in marginal and abnormal cases where something happens to a man which he cannot explain or understand. Thus Peters thinks that if drive theories are to apply at all, then they may only apply to cases where something happens to a man and he is driven to act in ways he cannot himself understand. He asks whether or not it would be better for 'psychologists to confine a concept like that of "drive" to cases where, in ordinary language, a man could properly be said to be "driven" to act' (1958, p. 155), and his implication is that it would be.

Peters is doing two things with this limitation, he is giving some sense to the application of deterministic and physiologically based theories on the one hand, but on the other he is restricting the application to an area which he presumes is marginal and unimportant.

We can deal with the former point first. Peters's substantive demonstration of the confusion of drive theories cannot have any bearing upon the imposition of a formal limitation upon theories in general, drive theories included, at least from a positivist point of view. This view has it that it must be up to the scientist to state what types of facts his theory applies to, it is not up to the material under observation (i.e. human beings) to stipulate when his theory applies and when it does not. Thus the states of affairs that a theory explains must be 'objectively definable', and 'observable'. The subject's testimony, 'now I feel driven', and 'now I don't feel driven' provides only a subjective definition of only a subjectively 'observable' state of affairs. A scientist could not accept such a phenomenological limitation on the applicability of his theory. He would want to define 'drive' in terms of the 'operations' required to measure it, or in terms of its effects and symptoms apparent to an observer but not necessarily to the subject. Having given the positivist objection a run for its money, we can now turn to more humanistic and phenomenological objections to Peters's second point. This was the presumption that the feeling of 'being driven' must necessarily be an unimportant and abnormal phenomenon.

Peters presumes that, for the most part, man is a purposive rule-following entity, 'a chess-player writ large' (ibid., p. 7). Extraneous factors sometimes intrude upon a man's chess-playing; he may have a cold, a migraine, or his opponent's pipe smoke might get in his eyes, but most of the time he simply plays the game and exhibits what skill he has without any such thing happening to him. Most of the time he simply does what he wants within the boundaries of the rules of the game, and he is not forced into doing anything he does not want to do. Peters, and conceptual analysts in general, would like to believe that the nature of man as a social being is much like this, and that the notion of being driven to act only applies to cases of compulsive repetition, or extreme hunger and so on (ibid., p. 155).

But we should not accept this rather glib restatement of the free will versus determinism debate and its over-easy commitment to the free will side. It is not that the chess-player analogy is wrong, but rather that Peters does not take it far enough. The purpose of both players in chess is to win, and yet one loses, one is 'forced' into a bad position, and 'feels driven' to resign. And all this 'happens to' a player whose free will is given ample opportunity to procure what it wants, a win, but which 'is coerced' eventually into procuring what it does not want, a loss. The analogy with social games is not at all frivolous, for these kinds of things regularly, as a matter of course, go on between people in society and between people and their social institutions, structures and processes.

In the final chapter a more realistic humanistic position will be investigated further. Important sociological and psychiatric theories rely on such a position. But what must be noted here, in criticism of Peters and the conceptual analytic version of this position, is that their version is not realistic enough. 'Being driven', 'feeling compelled' and so on, are not marginal and abnormal features of the experience of the average social actor. They are central and everyday features. Gross compulsions are the very stuff of social life.

The humanistic element in Peters's work, as in the work of most conceptual analysts, is usually entwined with a conservative-liberal ideological element which is at once politically naive and sociologically unperceptive (see, for example, Gellner's 1959 and Cornforth's 1965 critiques). This element can be found clearest in their works on political philosophy with which I will not be specifically dealing, but can also be traced in the works under discussion here. Authority, and behind it power, and behind that physical violence, is arguably what social order is all about. And coercion of the individual to do what he otherwise would not want to do, in gross ways and in subtle ways, is a most commonplace feature of social life. If chess is to be the analogy, it would do conceptual analysis a lot of good to look long and hard at the concept of 'losing', and to stop insinuating that every man who has free will is a winner. Man has free will, even in his defeats, even when he is 'being driven'.

In a paper with H. Tajfel, Peters made further criticisms of behaviourist psychology and its philosophical background. With Hull cast as the psychologist, and with Hobbes cast as the philosophical stage-designer, the paper was entitled, *Hobbes and Hull: Metaphysicians of Behaviour* (1957). The juxtaposition is a fair one. Hobbes fathered much of the individualistic utilitarian and empiricist thinking in the British tradition of philosophy, but he always assumed that all human behaviour could be understood if man were viewed as a physiological mechanism, which operated 'to continue its own motion', and whose 'appetites' and 'aversions' were functional for this survival goal. Hull similarly based his psychology on the concepts of organic needs, environmental stimulation which was either pleasurable or painful for the organism, and consequent conditioning of certain ways of behaving and responding in the organism.

Hull's aim was largely to realise the project of turning the study of human behaviour into a natural science by setting up a deductive system in which statements about behaviour could be deduced from more general laws, which would ultimately be physiological laws (Peters and Tajfel, 1957, p. 38). Peters and Tajfel claim that both Hobbes and Hull were deluded by the undoubted relevance of physiology to human behaviour, into thinking that human actions could be deduced from, and therefore explained in the terms of, physiological theories alone. Physiology is a *sine qua non* of behaviour, but not an explanation of it; walking is not explained merely by the possession of legs. On the contrary, as far as Peters and Tajfel and indeed conceptual analysis in general are concerned, there is a logical gulf between, on the one hand, either intra-organic 'movements' and gross bodily movements, and on the other hand, purposive and rational action.

This logical, or rather ontological, dualism is asserted in the interests of a humanistic position, the main lines of which have been outlined here and in chapter 2. Behaviourism stands criticised by conceptual analysis because of its attempt to override this dualism in the interests explicitly of the reductionist unification of all science, and implicitly of a monistic and materialist ontology. It is criticised for proposing an explain-all theory which cannot take account of the diversity of ordinary experience, and which attempts to explain in alien terms what is richly explanatory as it stands. That is, behaviourism wants to go behind ordinary experience, whereas conceptual analysis wants to consult, describe and analyse the everyday facts of this experience, if only as a necessary technique for philosophical therapy.

Finally, an important work on behaviourist psychology which might also be mentioned as stemming from a more or less conceptual analytic point of view, is C. Taylor's *The Explanation of Behaviour* (1967) (see also a development of Taylor's position for the logic of the social sciences, Wright, 1971). Taylor does not really fit the normal requirements for consideration as a member of the conceptual analytic school, but rather represents a development of the school's general humanistic position. Earlier, Taylor had contributed a paper to an Aristotelian Society meeting on the similarities between linguistic analysis and phenomenology (Taylor and Ayer, 1959). And he is one of the few Anglo-American philosophers to have discussed, however briefly, the kind of convergences with which we are concerned in this book. Broadly speaking, his position in *The Explanation of Behaviour* is very similar on the nature of human action as purposive and rule-following to that of Peters and other conceptual analysts. However, Taylor does not have the ultimate commitment to therapy, and to the dissolution of conceptual confusions that members of this school have. He discusses the difference between the behaviourist and the humanist conceptions of action for its own sake, rather than as a means of scoring points in the therapeutic game.

His commitment, like that of the conceptual analysts, is to the idea that the behaviour of animate organisms can only be understood in a teleological framework, that is in terms of some sort of purpose or the other. Human reasons, intentions and motives are a special class of teleological data relating to a special class of animal. But all animals are in some sense purposive (1967, pt 1, ch. 3 in particular). And he has no difficulty in demonstrating, along with Peters, that the behaviourists failed to exclude anthropomorphic and purposive terms and descriptions, even from their accounts of the behaviour of rats and pigeons, let alone in their extrapolation from these accounts to the behaviour of humans.

Where Taylor's discussion differs greatly from those of conceptual analysts is in his attitude to theories and laws, and explanation by means of them. Taylor defends theories, where commentators such as Peters attack them. Taylor discusses Hamlyn's, Ryle's and Peters's belief that physiological causes can only provide the necessary and never the sufficient conditions for the explanation of human action, except in cases of abnormal breakdowns of human skill. Taylor's reinterpretation takes the general and nomothetic form that Ryle *et al.* shy away from, which is that 'the normal operation of the organism follows teleological laws' (ibid., pp. 24-5).

But Taylor does not defend reductionist theories which must be expressed in physicalist terms and be deductively unifiable with physical theories. He does not defend truth-functional requirements, and the exclusion of intentional propositions from the theoretical or empirical language, as a logical empiricist point of view would have it (see for instance Körner, 1966, ch. 13). Quite the reverse, Taylor argues that the laws and theories from which behaviour and actions may one day be deduced could be teleological laws and theories. He does not think that there is anything confusing or unscientific in conceiving of this possibility. On the contrary, he believes that it has been unscientific of behaviourism and logical empiricist philosophy to have excluded this possibility by fiat. However, Taylor's thesis is very cautiously proposed throughout and he concedes the possibility, ultimately, of reductionism, that is, of the deduction of laws relating to human purposive action from laws relating to the purpose-like behaviour of animate organisms, and the deduction of these teleological laws, ultimately, from non-teleological physical laws (1966, p. 71). So his humanism, unlike that of conceptual analysis, is guarded and of a singular type. He keeps the reductionist option open. Conceptual analysis has continually, and perhaps more consistently rejected this option.

With the main features of the conceptual analytic critique of behaviourist and reductionist psychology now before us we can turn to the phenomenological critique of the same family of ideas.

Phenomenology

In chapter 1 two species of phenomenology were identified, pure and existential. The main critiques of behaviourist and reductionist psychology have been written from the existential point of view. If anything pure phenomenology, as an idealistic form of philosophy, would be even more opposed to the deterministic picture of man, and monistic picture of the world that behaviourism presents, than existential phenomenology. But there has been little written from this angle; behaviourism is so remote from pure phenomenology that their paths have never crossed in criticism.

As against this, two weak points might be made to close the gap between behaviourism and pure phenomenology. One is that behaviourism might be said to practise a kind of epoche when it looks at human action. It removes all our ordinary presuppositions about action, that it is purposeful, thoughtful and so on, and it leaves us with the alleged skeletal framework of our observations of other men. It leaves us with pure physical movement from which all presuppositions have been removed, and which is a kind of eidetic intuition, a capturing of the essence of action. There is little to be said about this, it is simply a wrong interpretation, and a badly misleading line of thought. We can be sure that if a pure phenomenological reduction was performed on an observation of experience or another's action, the most essential feature which would be revealed would be that of purposiveness and not that of pure physical movement. In any case, behaviourism would attempt to measure its 'eidetic intuition', its pure physical responses; enough to make Husserl turn in his grave. The second weak point that might be made is to play on the kind of structural similarity we have already noticed in chapter 3, between pure phenomenology and logical empiricism. They both attempt to reduce all concepts to a common basis and reconstruct the various levels of concepts and the realities to which they refer from this base. In this sense pure phenomenology is as reductionist minded as is logical empiricism and, its handmaiden, behaviourist psychology. Once again there is little to be said about this apart from saying that it is wrong. The structural similarity of two doctrines in no way guarantees that the doctrines have the same or even similar things to say. Two buckets may look alike but one may hold earth and the other water; in this case one holds a doctrine of transcendental ideas, and the other holds a doctrine of mundane sensations.

So our focus of attention will be on the relationship of existential, rather than pure, phenomenology to behaviourism. The major discussions of behaviourism and physiological reductionist psychology by existential phenomenologists are contained in Merleau-Ponty's *The Structure of Behaviour* (1965) and *Phenomenology of Perception* (1962), particularly the former. Sartre's short critique of psychological theories of emotion and imagination are also relevant (see also Wahn, 1964).

Both Sartre and Merleau-Ponty believe that man and his actions can only be understood in terms of his concrete existence in the world. The situation as man sees it, other people as he sees them, social facts as he sees them, the physical world as he sees it, these are what 'determine' a man's actions. It is in terms of these realities that a man lives his life, his thought and his action. In chapter 1 it was suggested that this emphasis on existence and being-in-the-world, present in Sartre and Merleau-Ponty's writings, is present also (if only in the para-theological guise of a description of man's inauthenticity and fallenness) in Heidegger's preliminary ontological speculations in *Being and Time* (1962). But the emphasis derives, to quite a significant extent, ultimately from Husserl's concept of the intersubjective taken-for-granted world of ordinary life, the natural attitude and its presuppositions about reality which the pure phenomenologist must duly seek to 'bracket off' and to minimise in the epoche.

At the risk of trivialising the whole existential perspective, I have suggested that such an approach to the understanding of man's thoughts and actions bears a comparison with the conceptual analytic humanist position. The existential perspective is sometimes developed by its practitioners in rather theatrical gestures of profundity. The conceptual analytic perspective, in contrast, is often developed as a non-serious, and rather aimless ramble through the commonplace of everyday communication. But in spite of sometimes almost unbridgeable differences in style, the two schools are by no means saying very different things. Both propose that men must be understood as acting in terms of what they believe to be the case, and in terms of some purpose or intention. Both reject deterministic accounts of behaviour which refer to phenomena and processes outside the experience of the actor. Behavourism is such an account. A man may believe that he is writing a poem, for instance, or inventing a machine, or speaking his mind, whereas 'in fact' the behaviourist would assure him that he 'really' is not doing any of these things in quite the way he thinks he is. Rather he is responding to stimuli of some kind, his reactions are controlled by certain balances reached between environmental stimuli and his organic needs and drives. Both conceptual analysis and phenomenology reject this kind of account.

Merleau-Ponty wrote *The Structures of Behaviour* before he embarked upon his major statement of his version of the existentialist perspective in the *Phenomenology of Perception*. Thus, while it contains the seeds of the later work, these seeds of existential phenomenology are not very thoroughly developed and are incidental to the main theme. This theme was a critique of behaviourist psychological theories, and an investigation of ways of understanding behaviour and mind which allegedly transcended determinism, like Gestalt psychology. His conclusion on Gestalt psychology is also ultimately critical. Merleau-Ponty tries to demonstrate that a new principle, that of structure, and not determination, underlies the relation of man's body, his physiology, to his behaviour and thought. And further he tries to show that this principle underlies the relationship of man's thought and behaviour to the world he lives in.

Merleau-Ponty's critique and his concept of structure will be outlined in this and the following chapter, when the attitudes of the two schools to Gestaltism are discussed. So Merleau-Ponty's general thesis in the book will be taken up again in a later section, as well as being discussed here. His work on behaviourism will be discussed here, and that on Gestalt psychology will be discussed in chapter 5. But it must be borne in mind that this procedure is somewhat artificial, as Merleau-Ponty comes to his discussion of Gestalt psychology by utilising the critique that this psychology developed of behaviourist psychology.

We have seen already that there are two types of stimuli present in the behaviourist schema; there is environmental stimulation, and there is intra-organic drive stimulation. Watson and the early Behaviourists tended to stress the former and to ignore the latter, but later practitioners like Hull tried to achieve a theoretical balance between the two. However, their hypotheses and speculations about intra-organic goings-on were always of a rather primitive kind and, for most of them, the activity of the human brain was not considered to be a very important topic. As long as assumptions could be made about the nervous system, about the mechanics of the muscle system, and about the various drives to be reduced and needs to be satiated, the brain need not come into the account at all.

The Gestalt rejection of behaviourism centred around this topic, the importance and the nature of brain activities. The rejection began as a dissatisfaction with the way behaviourism ignored experimentally testable phenomena of human perception. It culminated in a critique by the Gestaltists of the naivety of the behaviourist physiological and particularly neurological assumptions. Merleau-Ponty's discussion of behaviourism tends to follow, part of the way at least, these kinds of Gestaltist criticisms.

Merleau-Ponty's argument is therefore somewhat more technical than that of Peters, for instance, in being more concerned with experimental and neurological disproofs of behaviourist assumptions. He deals specifically with Pavlov's experiments on the conditioning of animals, and with the physiological assumptions Pavlov can be accredited with. He calls Pavlov's approach 'reflexology', since it dealt mainly with the acquisition by animals of conditioned reflexes. Pavlov's dogs, which produced saliva when presented with food, were conditioned to salivate at the sound of a bell, by the continual association of the bell with the presentation of food. Eventually no food was required, and they would automatically salivate at the sound of the bell. A conditioned reflex had been produced (1965, pp. 51 and 65).

Both Pavlov, and following him, Hull, made conditioned reflexes the cornerstone of their work. Reflexive responses are evoked from an organism by unconditioned stimuli like hunger, i.e. inherited 'inner' drive stimulation. The mechanism of the conditioned reflex is association. All elements of an environmental stimulus complex playing upon an animal's sensory receptors at, or near, the time that a response is evoked can themselves acquire the capacity to evoke substantially the same response, so the theory goes. Thus Pavlov conditioned his dogs to salivate at the sound of the bell by continually associating it with the provision of food, with the consequent satiation of the dogs' hunger drive, and with general reduction of nervous tension in the animal's body.

Reflexology, as far as Merleau-Ponty is concerned, relies on atomistic assumptions about physiology. It holds that the stimuli can be isolated in some ultimate and objective way. The area of sensitisation of nerve ends must be isolable, and so must be the discrete nerve impulse to the brain, and the discrete nerve pathway it follows. And finally it is presumed that a specifiable local area of the brain receives the nerve impulse and initiates the response sequence. Thus all of the more complex processes can be broken down into the singular processes and elements which make them up. Merleau-Ponty calls this sort of physiological speculation 'physiological atomism'.

As against this Merleau-Ponty cites research into brain functions and into the nature of the nervous system which imply that the whole cannot be reduced to the sum of its parts (ibid., p. 62). In fact he relies here upon the same kind of evidence that the Gestalt psychologists relied upon, which in this period was mainly associated with the neurophysiological work of Gelb, Goldstein and Lashley (Schutz discusses the former two (1962, pp. 260-86)).

The backing for holistic, or Gestaltist, arguments rather than atomistic ones, then, relies in part at least upon investigations of brain function. One main point is that the same nerve pathways carry many different kinds of information to the brain from stimulation of nerve ends. As against atomism, then, it is not the case that each nerve pathway has a distinct and singular function. Similarly, the same general areas of the brain have been found to do many diverse kinds of jobs for the rest of the organism. Surgical removal of, or accidental damage to parts of the brain have been found to have consequences inconsistent with the atomist's hypothesis about the specificity of functions in local areas of the brain. For instance, the functions performed by a removed or damaged part may be taken over and performed by another part of the brain. Or, alternatively, many more functions may be affected by such removal or damage than were thought to be related to the part; the whole nature of a person's behaviour or of his personality may be affected by a small, local lesion, for instance. These two possibilities are not self-contradictory, and neither of them provides support for the atomist's 'one area, one function' view.

The human brain at least has organisations, structures, capacities and functions which cannot be accounted for in terms of an atomistic view. And these functions are a great deal more important and autonomous than merely mediations between stimulations and responses. The brain is more than merely a half-way house in stimulus-response circuits. At the very least the brain's mediation between experiential 'inputs' into the organism and behavioural 'outputs' from the organism is of an important and qualitative nature. The brain is more a qualitatively different organ within the human body than merely some kind of reflexive cerebral muscle which twitches out responses when stimulated.

Behaviourism, on the other hand, seems to presume that the human brain is not at all a qualitatively distinct physiological feature. It seems to presume that its contribution to behaviour is minimal. Merleau-Ponty, following the Gestaltists, rejects this behaviouristic avoidance of neurology, and of the special features of brain function. Even if the behaviourists could get away with the abolition of mind and consciousness, it is difficult, in terms of their own avowed commitment to physiological reductionism, to see how they could get away with abolishing the importance of the brain. Thus Merleau-Ponty concludes: 'Pavlov's conceptions are irreconcilable with modern pathology and physiology' (1965, p. 88).

Of course, for Merleau-Ponty, and originally for the Gestalt psychologists also, emphasis on the brain and its qualitative contributions to human behaviour was a way of reintroducing consciousness and purposiveness into any account of man. When we come to further consideration of Gestalt psychology, it will be seen that it became preoccupied with neurophysiology at the expense of its analysis of consciousness. And because of this, Merleau-Ponty turned on Gestalt psychology with as much fervour as he had criticised behaviourism and reflexology. In fact, he rejected it, ultimately, for being 'a simple antithesis or counterpart of atomism' (ibid., p. 76). Ultimately, it just seemed to settle for filling out the, admittedly very large, gaps in the behaviourists' deterministic physiological account of man. Consciousness, for the Gestaltists, became just as much of an epiphenomenon of brain processes as it had become an epiphenomenon (in fact a non-phenomenon) of stimulus-response processes.

Merleau-Ponty wanted to retain some conception of brain processes together with an analysis of consciousness. He wanted, in his account of man's nature, to supersede the materialistic and deterministic implications of neurophysiology, on the one hand, and to supersede the idealistic implications of an analysis of consciousness on the other. He thought that the Gestalt psychologists may have begun with some similar idea in mind, and there is no doubt that they were influenced originally by Husserlian phenomenology. However, Merleau-Ponty thought they had failed to radically supersede behaviourism and its physiologically reductionist, and ultimately materialist conception of man. Whether Merleau-Ponty himself succeeded in uniting the fire and water of materialism and idealism, in defiance of the Cartesian dualistic heritage of French intellectual life, is debatable. It seems to me that he failed. Whatever the virtues of his philosophical position, and there are many, it is not one of them that he provided some neo-Hegelian ontological synthesis superseding the thesis of materialism and the antithesis of idealism.

One of the ways Merleau-Ponty suggested of bringing brain processes and descriptions of consciousness together, and hopefully of superseding the materialist implications of the one and the idealist implications of the other, was as follows. He proposed that neurology should use concepts derived from visual experience in the characterisation of brain processes and brain functions. In particular, it ought to take the concepts of 'figure' and 'ground' from ordinary perceptual experience. When we see something, we distinguish it as a figure against a background. This distinction is one that the viewer creates and which he sets up, so as to speak; it is a subjective achievement and not an objective feature of the world. Seeing is, in part, a focusing of attention and interest, and is in this respect like shining a spotlight on objects otherwise in the dark. The spotlit circle and the encircling darkness, like the figure and the ground, are in one sense objective; they are 'out there' in the world. But in another sense the spotlit circle and the encircling darkness, like the figure and ground, are subjective; they are achieved and directed by a subject. The figure-ground structure of all visual experience ought to be very relevant to the way we conceptualise the processes at work in the brain during a seeing experience. The brain processes crucial to seeing something, according to Merleau-Ponty, could be called the 'figure' of which all the supporting processes in the rest of the brain may be called the essential 'ground'.

Believing that he has shown that this neurological application of concepts relating to the structure of experience is both viable and valid, Merleau-Ponty writes (ibid., pp. 92-3):

> Since [the] structure of behaviour and the cerebral functioning which supports it can only be conceived in terms borrowed from the perceived world, this latter no longer appears as an order of phenomena parallel to the order of physiological phenomena but as one that is richer than it. Physiology cannot be completely conceptualised without borrowing from psychology ...

Here Merleau-Ponty means descriptive or phenomenological psychology.

It is in this fashion that Merleau-Ponty attempted to reject deterministic and physiologically reductionist psychologies and philosophies of man. Rather than merely avoid them, he attempted to see how they could be integrated into an overall picture of man which was essentially humanistic, in the sense in which that term has been used in this book. Rather than be informed by the reductionists in neurology that specific brain processes and states determine specific experiential states, and that consciousness is thereby made epiphenomenal, Merleau-Ponty would turn the tables. He would inform *them* that brain states and processes could not be conceptualised properly without using experiential concepts, without analysing, that is, the structure of consciousness and states of mind. This was not an attempt to reverse the determinism and to demand that brain states be thought of as epiphenomena of experiential states, but rather it was an attempt to supercede the deterministic principles relating Body and Mind altogether. As an anti-Cartesian exercise it is as interesting as Ryle's but, unfortunately, it is also as unclear and as ultimately unsuccessful.

Merleau-Ponty, the existential phenomenologist, the student of man's consciousness, could not seriously have hoped to co-opt, in the service of this study, neurology, which in its nature must provide a deterministic account of the phenomena it studies, and which in any case is still virtually in its infancy as a branch of knowledge. For the humanistic position such co-option of deterministic physiological approaches is an impractical and a lost cause. Fortunately the criticism and rejection of such approaches from the humanistic position is an altogether more straightforward business. Behaviourism is a fairly crudely reductionist approach, and has been met with criticism by both conceptual analysts and phenomenologists like Merleau-Ponty. Such criticism is a straightforward rejection of the stimulus-response frame of reference of behaviourism. Conceptual analysis, however, has rarely taken on, in critical discussion, more neurologically based approaches, with the important exception of its critique of Gestalt psychology, so it has not become as entangled as Merleau-Ponty became in the attractions of the more ennobling forms of materialism, the forms that accredit man with a brain

Merleau-Ponty's critique of behaviourist and physiologically reductionist psychology, then, is based ultimately on his humanistic commitment to the idea that it is man's being-in-the-world, his conscious existence, that 'determines' his action. Behaviourism, with its deterministic and reductionist perspectives, would undermine the importance and the relevance of man's conscious existence, so it must stand criticised by Merleau-Ponty.

However, Merleau-Ponty's zeal for co-opting and integrating his enemies' view with his own creeps back in, in a footnote in *The Structure of Behaviour* (1965, p. 226), even with regard to such a demonstrably anti-humanistic school of thought as behaviourist psychology. But since Merleau-Ponty, in this aside, strikes a chord in behaviourism similar to that developed by the social theorist, G. H. Mead, the point is worth looking at. Merleau-Ponty suggests that Watson's original brand of behaviourism anticipated the existential approach to the understanding of man by discussing behaviour as a product of man's interaction with and adaptation to his environment. He agrees that the framework of Watson's behaviourism was a mechanistic and deterministic one, but he thought that in spite of this, and apart from this, the approach contained intimations of existentialism. It must be borne in mind here that Merleau-Ponty interpreted Watson's approach as a purely environmental version of stimulus response thinking. To some extent this is correct; Watson certainly did not stress intra-organic versions of stimulation to the same extent as Pavlov and Hull. But even so, it may still be hard to see how the theories of a psychologist who abolished consciousness can possibly be invoked as supporting, in any way, the theories of a philosopher who relied so heavily on some concept of consciousness. The link, tenuous as it is, is through the concept of consciousness as an existential state, that is, as a mode of existing in the midst of the world.

Watson held that there is nothing other than the organism and the environment which stimulates it. Consciousness is no special thing, and is not required as a hypothesis to explain the way the organism and the environment interact. Merleau-Ponty for his part held that there is nothing other than the perceiving subject and the world that it perceives. As against the Cartesians, he held that consciousness is not a special thing, distinct from the objects that men are conscious of; to reiterate Brentano's dictum on the intentionality of consciousness, consciousness is always 'consciousness of' something. That is, for Merleau-Ponty, it would be impossible to conceive of a mental state which would not also be an existential state; it would be impossible to conceive of a state of mind or consciousness which was not also an awareness of some kind of objective existence. (By 'objective existence' we do not necessarily mean 'actual physical presence in the world', we simply mean that states of mind must be *about* something, whether those somethings are fictional things like dragons, future things like goals a man wants to achieve, or more mundane physical things a man perceives around him.) If we simplify the comparison, it appears that Watson dissolved mind or consciousness into environmental stimulation of the human organism, and he portrayed human behaviour as an evoked response to the stimulating environment. Merleau-Ponty, in a superficially similar vein, dissolved mind or consciousness into the environment that the human subject sees about it, and believes it sees about it. And he portrayed human behaviour as a reasoned response to the perceived environment.

The similarities here are superficial because the 'stimulating environment of an organism' need not at all be the same as the 'environment that the subject sees, wants to see and believes it sees around it'. It is possible that Watson may be interpreted in this way, but subsequent revisions of his position by his followers certainly cannot be. Furthermore, Watson's 'evoked response' is not at all the same as Merleau-Ponty's 'reasoned response'. For the former behaviour is determined, for the latter behaviour is rational.

But Watson's position was modified by the social theorist, G. H. Mead, to a point where a comparison with Merleau-Ponty would reveal some very basic areas of similarity, more or less along the lines that Merleau-Ponty suggested. Unlike most of Watson's psychological followers and interpreters, Mead, from the point of view of social psychology and sociology, made behaviourism more humanistic and less deterministic. In developing his 'social behaviourism', Mead criticised the physiological orientation of behaviourism and its concern for man only in respect of his animal nature. Mead, like Merleau-Ponty, and like Schutz whom he influenced (see for example, Schutz, 1962, p. 216) and unlike Watson, was concerned with man as a social being, and as a being which experiences the world it lives in, which is conscious of it, and which acts in terms of this experience.

Mead demonstrated that Watson had ignored the social and symbolic (linguistic) environment of man, and therefore that his conceptions of man as a being which reacted and responded to its environment must be inadequate (1967, pp. 10-11 and 100-9). The social and symbolic environment, in any case, as far as Mead was concerned, required the introduction of a different principle than that of determinism in order to characterise its relationship with the individual human being. And much in the same way as Merleau-Ponty attempts to supersede determinism, so Mead developed the notion of 'interaction'. For both of them, some such notion is required, as against purely behaviourist frames of reference, to explain how it is that man arises as a social agent, influenced but not totally conditioned by the social environment, and lives as a purposive agent in relation to this environment.

Both for Mead, the social behaviourist, and for Merleau-Ponty, the existential phenomenologist, a simple-minded determinism, such as that of behaviourism, reflexology and physiologically reductionist psychology in general, is not good enough. It does not help us understand the nature of men as a purposive agency in a social environment, or the nature of that social environment, its structures and processes. It is in confrontation with these general types of problems that the concerns of humanistic schools of thought, like conceptual analysis but more particularly existential phenomenology, converge in interesting and important ways with the concerns of social theorists and sociologists. But further consideration of this sort of convergence must wait until the last chapter.

The development of existential phenomenology has generally been over the bodies of psychological theories of the nature of man. Merleau-Ponty's work developed in this way as did Sartre's before him. Merleau-Ponty's approach in any case was somewhat of a considered response to Sartre's more sketchy critiques of psychology. Merleau-Ponty's detailed discussions of physiological assumptions in psychology, and his criticism of them, could be seen as an expansion of criticisms and opinions which Sartre had voiced more boldly, but with less substantiation.

Sartre's main criticisms of behaviourist and physiological psychology were stated in two short books, *The Imagination: A Psychological Critique* (1962a) and *A Sketch for a Theory of the Emotions* (1962b), first published in 1936 and 1939 respectively.

Merleau-Ponty attempted to explicitly oppose his existentialist position to the more traditional Cartesian dualism of French philosophy. But Sartre, on the other hand, developed his existentialism, not by opposing but by exploiting this dualism. The general features of his position have already been discussed in chapter 1, as they were set out in *Being and Nothingness*. The two critiques of psychology which preceded this major work represented an attempt to put his newly found commitment to phenomenology to work. And it also represented a dawning of the need to expand the existential and ontological analyses of man, the philosophical anthropology that Husserl had only hinted at.

So although Sartre's critiques are substantially similar to those of Merleau-Ponty, they have their differences also, mainly differences of emphasis. For instance, on a crude level of analysis, Sartre simply writes a lot more about 'consciousness' than Merleau-Ponty, and a lot less about 'behaviour'. Both criticise behaviourism but Merleau-Ponty expressed his criticisms in terms of alternative ways of understanding the 'structure of behaviour'. Sartre, on the other hand, expressed his criticisms in terms of alternative ways of understanding the structures of consciousness. In the final analysis, existentialism meant for both philosophers that states and structures of behaviour were the same as states and structures of consciousness. They are, for both philosophers, simply two different ways of talking about states and structures of existence, that is, of experienced life.

Initially the superficial distinction between these two existential phenomenologists was that Sartre concerned himself with understanding states of consciousness (imagination and emotions), while Merleau-Ponty concerned himself with understanding behaviour and action. But eventually, in parts of *Being and Nothingness*, and in fact in parts of his account of emotions, Sartre became as interested in action as Merleau-Ponty. Indeed, it would have been hard for a philosopher who was also a novelist to have long ignored behaviour and action. And, conversely, Merleau-Ponty integrated his account of man acting in terms of his perceived world, with an account of that perceived world, and of perception and visual states of consciousness in general, in his later work the *Phenomenology of Perception*. So the differences of emphasis between them were not of an ultimately important kind at this stage of their respective intellectual developments, although such differences did subsequently arise.

The main point that Sartre wanted to establish in his critique of theories of imagination was that an image was not something 'in' the mind, but a state of mind. That is, it was not some object 'in' consciousness, but a certain mode of consciousness, a certain way that a subject relates to a type of objectivity. He wanted to establish the relevance of the phenomenological view of consciousness, the view which stressed the intentionality of consciousness. The basic feature of this view, the different forms in which it was stated by

Brentano and Husserl, have already been examined in chapter 1, and there is no need to examine them further here. Sartre was therefore objecting both to psychologies which relied on a non-intentional and thus—from his point of view—inadequate notion of consciousness, and to psychologies like behaviourism and physiological reductionism, which relied on no notion of consciousness at all. Sartre felt that this latter class of psychologies stemmed from Hume's sensationalistic theory of knowledge. He felt that they reduced all experiences to sensory experiences, and explained these in terms of internal or external stimulations. Images and memories were for Hume, as has been seen in chapter 3, but pale after-images of originally vivid sense impressions. Structures of ideas are built up over time and by the association of 'similar' and proximate sense impressions with one another. The association mechanism remained a mysterious and unconscious process, determining the structure of conscious ideas on Hume's account, and ideas and images were determined facts or things somehow 'in' one's mind (1962a, p. 13).

Reviewing French exponents of sensationalism in psychology, followers of Hume and J. S. Mill like Taine, Ribot and others, Sartre concluded that their main frame of reference was that of materialism; every phenomenon is some kind of thing, and consciousness is no different. Thus he held that their attitude was: 'Man is a thing alive: an image is a thing: and a thought, likewise, is a thing' (ibid., p. 34). And equally boldly Sartre asserted the basis of his opposition to this materialism in Cartesian-like terms that Merleau-Ponty, for instance, would never have used. He writes: 'That there are only two types of existence, as a thing in the world and as consciousness, is an ontological law' (ibid., p. 166). Consciousness is not some kind of thing, and an image is not some kind of thing in the mind, for Sartre. Thus he concludes by asserting that 'an image is a certain type of consciousness. An image is an act, not some thing. An image is a consciousness *of* some thing' (ibid., p. 146). In passing, we may note a comparison here with Wittgenstein's view that: 'The concept of imagining is rather like one of doing than receiving. Imagining may be called a creative act' (1967, p. 111).

In his earlier work, Sartre's frame of reference for his rejection of behaviourist and physiological forms of psychology was the same rejection of materialism implied by the Cartesian dualistic ontology. To be more specific, his arguments were cast almost entirely in terms of Husserl's pure phenomenology, a family relative of Cartesianism. There is very little of the existentialist perspective, that was growing in his thoughts at this time, present in this work, a point which Merleau-Ponty noted in criticism (1964a, p. 73).

In *A Sketch for a Theory of the Emotions*, however, written three years later, the existentialist perspective is distinctly present. There are a number of references in the monograph to Heidegger, and his concept of being-in-the-world, in particular (1962b, p. 18, 23, 25 and 91). Sartre also mentions the psychologist Kurt Lewin's 'hodological' (experienced field) concept, which is similar to Heidegger's *Umwelt*. Sartre has retained the concept in his more recent work (1963b, p. 79). Thus Sartre was becoming aware of the break that had occurred between Husserl and Heidegger, between the pure phenomenological epistemologist and the descriptive phenomenological ontologist. Henceforth Sartre's rejection of materialism and of the materialistic and deterministic psychological approaches such as behaviourism, would be couched in terms of man's being-in-the-world, the existentialist terms we have become familiar with in Merleau-Ponty's work (which itself came soon after Sartre's).

In the monograph on emotion Sartre examines four psychological theories of emotion, those of William James, Pierre Janet, T. Dembo and Freud. Each is seen as progressively less inadequate than the former. But even the most adequate, Freud's, is fatally flawed, from Sartre's point of view, by Freud's use of the concept of the unconscious. We will reserve discussion of Sartre's critique of Freud for a later chapter (chapter 6), but in any case Sartre was most critical of James in this monograph, since James's theory of emotion was most demonstrably reductionist.

Sartre in fact wasted few words on James, merely pinning the label of physiological reductionism on him and having done with him. While this certainly is a fair characterisation of James's theory of emotions, it is not a fair characterisation of other aspects of his psychological thinking, which, as we have already indicated were in part influenced by Brentano. It was James, for instance, who provided the basis for Mead's humanistic conception of man as both a social self, a 'me', and an active agency, an 'I'. Thus, like Freud, James provides the basis for either a humanistic or a reductionist interpretation. Sartre chooses the latter.

According to the reductionist interpretation of his major work, *The Principles of Psychology* (1890), James stressed the importance of genetically inherited instincts and drives. Behaviour was 'inner' determined. A generation later Watson founded behaviourism in part on an attempted refutation of James's theory of anxiety and emotion. Behaviour was not 'inner' determined, rather it was 'outer' determined. This appeared at the time more of a contradiction than it eventually turned out to be; we have seen that behaviourists like Hull have tried to achieve a theoretical and experimental balance between 'inner' and 'outer' stimulations of the organism. James thus has his place within and not outside of the development of behaviourist psychology, on this interpretation.

Basically he believed that anxiety was an instinctive reaction to certain objects or situations, some of which would in fact be threats to the survival of the human being. Thus some anxiety reactions had a biological utility, produced by the evolutionary struggle for survival. The important part of the theory for Sartre was not this Darwinian gloss, but the following point. Instinctive reaction to danger was viewed as a bodily reflex which was not the product of an awareness in the animal of danger. The experience of fear or anxiety was seen as a *consequence* of the instinctive physiological changes and reflexes in the body, and not as the *cause* of such changes. Normally we would tend to believe the opposite. We would tend to believe that when a man sees a wild lion, for instance, he feels scared and takes to his heels. But James (and Karl Lange who developed the same theory independently at the same time) would have us believe that the man sees the lion, takes to his heels, and consequently starts to feel scared.

Thus James and Lange present emotional states of mind as being caused by physiological states of innervation in the body. James's theory (1890, vol. 1, p. 449), is 'that the bodily changes follow directly the perception of the exciting fact, and that our feeling of the same changes as they occur *is* the emotion'. In the example above, the fear is caused by the running, the consciousness of fear is somehow primarily a consciousness of changes in one's body. Sartre (1962b, p. 33) says that: 'The essence of (James's) thesis is that the states of consciousness called joy, anger, and so forth, are nothing but the consciousness *of* physiological manifestations—or, if you will, their projection into consciousness'. As against this, Sartre tries to show that emotional states of mind contain *more* elements than a mere consciousness of bodily changes, if indeed they can be shown to contain them. But also they contain very *different* elements than that proposed by this account, principally the element of organisation or structure. Sartre (ibid.) asks: 'can a physiological disturbance, *whatever it may be*, render an account of the *organised* character of an emotion', and as far as he is concerned the answer is, plainly not. Emotional feelings and actions which people would call 'irrational', have, according to Sartre, a rationale, and in fact have their own rationality. They are not chaotic and meaningless, they are organised and meaningful ways of thinking and being in the world. Once again, note in passing the comparison with Wittgenstein (1967, p. 90):

> It is quite possible that the glands of a sad person secrete differently from those of someone who is glad; and also that their secretion is the or a cause of sadness. But does it follow that the sadness is a *sensation* produced by this secretion? (1967, p. 90).

The organised and meaningful character of emotions is an intrinsic property of them, for Sartre, because, in the final analysis it is an intrinsic part of all states of mind and of all conscious actions. He regards emotion in the explicitly rationalistic and teleological terms of being 'an organised pattern of means directed to an end' (1962b, p. 41). There is thus need, in his view, for phenomenological descriptions of emotional states of mind and emotional behaviour in their existential setting (compare with Wittgenstein, 1967, pp. 86-7). And he hoped, by pointing the way, to influence others to produce a series of monographic studies of joy, sadness and other emotions (1962b, p. 92). The stress he placed on pure phenomenology in his earlier work on the imagination is considerably and explicitly reduced relative to this new stress on existential phenomenological description (ibid., p. 94). The sphere of the pure ego is avoided, and the new stress is on being-in-the-world, the concept originated by Heidegger, and developed, after Sartre, by Merleau-Ponty in his concept of being-in-the-midst-of-the-world (*être au monde*).

It is in this frame of reference that Sartre asserts that 'Emotion is not an accident, it is a mode of our conscious existence, one of the ways in which consciousness understands (in Heidegger's sense of *Verstehen*) its being-in-the-world' (ibid., p. 91). According to James's theory, Sartre believes that an emotion would have to be experienced as some 'ineffable quality; like brick-red or the pure feeling of pain' (ibid., p. 91). But emotional consciousness is nothing like this, it is a way of being and hence acting in the world. It is not a thing in consciousness, it is a mode of consciousness.

Enough has now been said for the antipathy of existential phenomenology to behaviourist and physiological reductionist psychologies to be seen fairly clearly. What is also clear is that the existential phenomenological antipathy has an underlying similarity to the conceptual analytic antipathy discussed previously. We can at this point recap on this similarity.

Conclusion

Conceptual analysts on the one hand and existential phenomenologists on the other are both equally critical of the notion of psychology as a natural science. Both reject the reductionist idea that the proper aim of psychology is for deductive unification with, or reduction to, neuro-physiological and even lower level theories and axioms, such as those of physics. Broadly speaking, both schools voice a humanistic objection to the materialistic and deterministic implications of such an approach. Conceptual analytic objections tend to be couched in terms of the logical discontinuities between concepts relating to human actions and concepts relating to the more physical movement of bodies and things. This logical dualism very often takes on the role of an ontological dualism between man and things, a dualism which Ryle failed to scuttle, implicitly endorsed and which has been explicitly stated by successive conceptual analysts such as Strawson.

Phenomenology more straightforwardly asserts the same kind of ontological discontinuity between the concepts and explanations proper to man and those proper to things. Both schools also rely on a descriptive approach to man's experiences of acting and interacting with other men and they both view man's experience in an intersubjective or social frame of reference. This descriptive approach is a primary feature of existential phenomenology, but conceptual analysts would make it a secondary feature of their philosophy, the primary aim of which, allegedly, is the therapeutic dissolution of conceptual confusions. These are the areas of similarity between the two humanistic schools that will be pursued in the following sections.

5 Gestalt psychology

Gestalt psychology, as its name implies, is a psychology which uses the concept of whole or form as a primary concept. In a sense it is an anti-reductionist psychology because it emphasises the irreducible 'emergent' features of organised wholes and structured forms, the fact that their properties cannot be reduced to the sum of the parts that make them up. Much as the sociologist might say that society cannot be reduced to an association of individuals, or the biologist might say that an animate organism cannot be reduced to an association of inanimate molecules, so the Gestalt psychologist holds that the wholes and forms of both brain functions and of perceptual experience cannot be reduced to a mere association of elements which make them up. Thus perceptual experience cannot be atomistically reduced to a bundle of sensations, for instance. And neither can brain functions be reduced to mere localisable mediations of specific stimulus-response circuits. According to Gestalt psychology both the empirical/experiential account of behaviourist and reductionist psychology is wrong, and so is its implied neuro-physiological account.

Before we go into the nature of Gestalt psychology any further some indication may be given of why both existential phenomenologists and conceptual analysts would be interested in discussing it. One reason is that, although Gestalt psychology had pretensions at going beyond a deterministic and reductionist account of man's experience, ultimately it did not do so, and it ended up offering a very similar kind of approach. It certainly began as a humanistic type of psychology, but it became a reductionist and naturalistic type within a fairly short space of time, in the inter-war years. Phenomenologists in particular, out of the humanistic philosophers, felt somewhat let down over this development, as the original Gestalt psychologists, Koffka and Kohler, had named Husserl as one of their main influences.[1] Both Aron Gurwitch's and Merleau-Ponty's philosophies are, to a great extent, attempts to retain the original humanistic inspiration of Gestalt psychology, and to develop its analysis of the structured nature of perceptual experience into a general philosophy of man. Merleau-Ponty's existential phenomenological critique of the way that Gestalt psychology developed was therefore consistent with, and indeed required by, his commitment to its original phenomenological inspiration.

The two conceptual analytic commentaries on Gestalt psychology, those of Kurtz (1969) and Hamlyn (1951; 1961a) which we will also discuss, are more roundly critical of it. Conceptual analysts generally do not show nearly as much interest in Gestalt psychology as do phenomenologists such as Merleau-Ponty. But it serves as a chopping block for Kurtz and Hamlyn to exhibit some of the respectively naive and subtle features of conceptual analysis. Hamlyn, like Merleau-Ponty, discusses perception as an activity, an achievement. In this and other respects they present a similar critique of the ultimately deterministic account of perception presented by Gestalt psychology.

But before the critiques of the two schools, and their similarities, are investigated further, a brief account must be given of the development of Gestalt psychological concepts.

In 1912 Max Wertheimer investigated the phi-phenomenon. This is the illusion of movement that occurs when two spots of light are projected on to a screen, in succession, a certain distance from one another. Thus two discrete stimuli impinge upon the retina but under certain conditions regarding the intensity of light, the speed of succession, the distance between them and so on—the subject will not report two impressions but will report the one movement of a single spot. Movie films are in many ways 'more real' than say still photographs, yet their reality is based on the same kind of illusion that Wertheimer and others investigated.

At the time, this investigation was the beginning of a new movement in psychology, because it appeared to overthrow the long established presumption that all experience could be broken down and analysed into ultimate atomic sensations. We have already seen how the physiological thinking behind sensory atomism was also atomistic. It was presumed that each sensation had its isolable area of sensitisation of the organism's receptors, its isolable nerve-pathway, and its isolable effector centre in the brain and spinal cord. Further, it was presumed that all of the neuro-physiological processes relevant to behaviour could be analysed into such isolated stimulus-response circuits. Wertheimer, having cast doubt on the atomistic theory of experience, proceeded to cast doubt on the associated atomistic theory of physiology and sensitisation.

Wertheimer's idea of what goes on in the brain of a subject seeing the illusory movement was a deceptively simple one. The subject sees as a whole things that are close to one another, that are similar, that have a common movement and so on, according to Wertheimer's laws of Gestalt forms. Similarly, excitation and activity in the brain irradiate a local area and, if two sources of excitation produce irradiation in quick succession and close to one another, then an irreducible emergent whole of brain excitation occurs which is in some way identical with the perceived whole. This is the thesis of 'psychological isomorphism', which was developed at greater length by W. Kohler (1947).

Kohler stated this thesis as follows: experienced order in space and time 'is always structurally identical with a functional order in the distribution of underlying brain processes ... [and in the] sequence of correlated brain processes', respectively (ibid., p. 39). Thus the experienced order is supposed to be 'a true representation of a corresponding order in the processes upon which experience depends' (ibid.). Kohler conceives of brain processes on analogy with field theory in physics. When a person perceives an object Kohler believes that 'there is actually a field of force in the brain, which extends from the processes corresponding to the self to those corresponding to the object' (ibid., p. 177). Or another analogy might be the field of forces on a chess board where experience is part of the field, say a corner, and where brain processes are the rest of the field (ibid., p. 147). These are some of the ways he tries to explicate the notion of isomorphism, and they are less than clear.

One obscurity concerns the degree of organisation of the impinging stimuli. Kohler says that a stimulus-response model is wrong. Although it is allegedly an empirical approach, it does not take into account the 'empirical fact' (ibid., p. 40) of sensory organisation which is a characteristic and distinctive achievement of the nervous system. Thus Kohler thinks that a far better formula than stimulus-response is the following: 'pattern of stimulation—organisation—response to the products of organisation' (ibid., p. 97). Patterns are stimuli, experienced wholes are the response, and the brain mediates in between with its organising function.

But this is equivocal. At least in the stimulus-response model we knew what was supposed to be causing what and why; this cannot be said of Kohler's formula. Is he saying that the world is made up of segregated wholes which impose an organised pattern of stimulation on the organism? Is brain organisation therefore a reflexive type of response to this patterned stimulation? Kohler would want to deny this. Is the structured and meaningful nature of perceptual experience some kind of reflexive response to nerve and brain organisation? Kohler would want to deny this also. He would not want to assert that nerve and brain organisations are reflexive epiphenomena of the independent organisation of the world. He would not want to say that the brain simply registers the world's organisation, rather the reverse, the brain's organising produces our experience of an organised world. According to the thesis of 'psycho-physical parallelism', however, this reverse causation cannot be right either, for the experienced organisation of the world is somehow 'one with' and 'the same as' nerve and brain organisation, and not an epiphenomenal product of it.

In the stimulus-response schema the mechanics of the whole process are clear and simple, even if they are useless for actually understanding human thought and action as we know them. With Gestalt psychology, on the other hand, the actual processes at work, and the principles they exemplify, are rather difficult to excavate. But this failure is balanced by the suspicion that Gestalt psychology, when clarified and philosophically explicated, *might* be of great importance for understanding human thought and action as we know them. Merleau-Ponty, at least, is gripped by such a suspicion. But the conceptual analysts, to whom we turn first, are not quite so fascinated by the possible importance of Gestalt psychology. They are far more interested in its equivocations and conceptual confusions, and even invent some that the Gestaltists probably never dreamed that they possessed.

Conceptual analysis

Kohler, like William James and Freud, is one of the few psychologists to have found his way into the text of Wittgenstein's later philosophical notes and writings (1963, p. 203). And although there is a reverential suspicion abroad that Wittgenstein never read any other thinker's work barring his own, it is clear that he was well acquainted at least with Gestalt psychology. Some of his remarks on seeing and seeing things as something, and seeing an aspect of something in the *Philosophical Investigations* (ibid., pp. 193-230) are quite subtle attempts to remind one, and to draw one's attention to, both the intricacies of visual experience and the way we communicate and conceptualise it. This descriptive phenomenology and this conceptual analysis of perception, however, is something of a preliminary to the main point. This point, stated in *Zettel* (1967, p. 106) is Wittgenstein's straightforward objection to the possibility of accounting for visual experience purely in terms of neuro-physiological causal explanations. While not attributing the concept to Kohler, he criticises the concept which Kohler introduced of 'psycho-physical parallelism'. Wittgenstein's argument is that it may be the case that there is no parallel or corresponding physiological phenomenon for any given psychological or mental phenomenon.

Wittgenstein gives the example of memory, of recognising a man who one had not seen for years, and of instantly remembering his name. He asks why we should presume that some 'trace', originally registered in our nervous system, had been reactivated. And he asserts that nothing need have been stored up in any way for reactivation, that no original 'trace' need have been left behind in some form in the nervous system. He asks (ibid.):

> Why should there not be a psycholgical regularity to which *no* physiological regularity corresponds? If this upsets our concept of causality then it is high time that this was upset .... It is perfectly possible that certain psychological phenomena *cannot* be investigated physiologically, because physiologically nothing corresponds to them.

This simple antipathy to extra-experiential explanations of experience, by Wittgenstein and subsequent conceptual analysts, can be returned to later, after we have first made a more complex point.

Conceptual analysis can be interpreted as largely a philosophy which stresses learning, it is a philosophy of social nurture. By contrast, Gestalt psychology, in its explicit opposition to behaviourism, developed a psychology of the inherited natural features of human physiology and human visual experience. It opposed a psychology of 'learning' (conditioning). Thus it is to be expected that a philosophy which endorses the concept of learning and of social nurture (conceptual analysis) would be very critical of a psychology which rejected theories of learning (albeit crude and misleading ones) and which espoused a theory of inherited and unalterable human nature.

One of the recurrent themes throughout Wittgensteins' *Philosophical Investigations* is his concern, for the purposes of argument, to reveal how things are learned. This is exemplified in the great number of questions he asks like 'how would this be taught?', 'how would this concept be learned?', and 'how do we acquire a rule of this kind?' Invariably Wittgenstein then outlines the kind of things one would point to, the kind of concrete examples one would use: to enable a person to 'go on in the same way'; to teach them the correct and the incorrect way of doing something; to give them a sense of the the criteria of good and bad, of skilful and inept standards of performance, either with spoken concepts or with actions; to socialise them into acceptable and unacceptable rule-governed behaviour, as regards their most abstract and innermost thinking as much as their simple public performances.

At the very least every man learns a languages from birth. Without any choice on his part he becomes an entity which cannot do much else except communicate. That is, he becomes an entity which would have to go to great lengths if it *did not* want to communicate, and all this through social learning, socialisation into language use. All men, without much obvious effort, acquire linguistic skills, they become *freely* able to express themselves because they have been (deterministically?) socialised. In the field of language, and in every other field also, a man becomes an intentional performer because of (in terms of) social conventions.

One consequence for the theory of knowledge of this picture of man in a state of language has already been discussed in the analysis of the work of Strawson and Hampshire It is that the physical (and social) objective world comes to be understood and described by men in terms of socially learned systems of classification. Such systems of classification allow meaningful reference to re-identifiable particulars: one cannot differentiate indefinitely all the features of the world, one must be able to re-identify something as the 'same as before', and classify things together: and even the naming of something as 'different', or 'unique', means 'not the same as', or 'different from' some class of similar things, and implies classificatory systems.

All this has many implications; let us look at three of them. First, no sense can be given to the idea that the world is somehow already divided up into atoms or wholes before a human classification is imposed upon it. (To deny *pre-social* naive realism in this way is not, of course, to deny *social* naive realism: it is not to deny that in the natural attitude, according to everyday taken-for-granted conceptual schemes, the world appears as divided objectively, somehow independent of human classification.) Second, any identifiable element of reality can, in principle, be classified in all sorts of ways, according to different schemas. And third, a judgement, or the adoption of a point of view, within and in terms of some conceptual schema, is due directly to the voluntary exercise, by the individual, of a socially learnt skill and ability. Also, necessarily, but more distantly, it is due to the less voluntary background of cultural and social saturation with a particular set of conceptual schemes and classificatory systems.

Gestalt psychology, however, in various ways, contradicts all these three points. With regard to the first point, it sometimes takes a pre-social naively realistic view of the independence of organised features of the world. That is, it reifies wholes, or Gestalten. With regard to the second point, while accepting that conceptual schemes can be confusing in perception by overlapping, Gestalt psychology does seem to hold that conceptual/perceptual sets are constants of human organic constitution, and not socio-culturally variable. (Whether they are invariable because the world is invariable or because the brain is invariable is never made quite clear.) And finally, with regard to the third point, it would hold that a perception, whether it is something received in one's mind/consciousness/experience from the outside world, or from brain activity, is essentially a *reception:* it is not an *achievement*, something that one can learn how to get or that one can strive for well or badly.

Gestalt psychology avoids such phenomena of social learning, partly because it arose out of a critique of behaviourist ideas about a special type of 'learning', sensory conditioning. By working on a black and white distinction between nature and nurture, between genetic inheritance as opposed to learning, Gestalt psychology could distinguish itself clearly and boldly from behaviourism. Behaviourism concentrated (so it could be said) on the determined development of the individual's nature by his sensory environment, to the exclusion of all but the most superficial considerations of his physiology, and to the particular exclusion of neurological considerations. Gestalt psychology, in contrast, could be said to concentrate on the physiological nature of the individual, his genetic inheritance, particularly his neurological inheritance. In development from infancy, the human being does not acquire neurological structures and processes that he did not already have, in order to be able to think and act in the developing ways that he does. Rather these capacities and their neurological foundations are inborn and simply revealed progressively as the human grows up. Gestalt psychology has tended to engrave its distinction from behaviourism in this commitment to nature as opposed to nurture. As Kohler says: 'it seems to be the natural fate of Gestalt psychology to become Gestalt Biology' (1947, p. 210).

It is true that some Gestalt-inspired psychologists, particularly those in America, like M. Sherif (1956; see also Koffka, 1928; Lewin, 1942), attempt to represent, if not learning, then at least the influence of social norms on perception, but this remains rather exceptional. Sherif, for instance, shows experimentally how the autokinetic phenomenon can be socially influenced. This phenomenon is the illusion that a fixed point of light appears to move to a subject who views it in a totally dark room which provides no visual frame of reference in terms of which the position of the light can be fixed. In experiments Sherif found that subjects' estimations of the 'movement' of the light after a succession of inquiries by the experimenter, tended to become stabilised. In the absence of any visual frame of reference, the subjects would invariably attempt to establish some regular frame of reference, even if it was only the allegedly 'regular movements' of the light. However, if other people are introduced to the experimental situation, and each give their estimation of the light's 'movements', their estimations tend to be very similar to one another's (1956, p. 257). Thus a social norm, a social classification of the 'objective' world, arises; a reality that is in its essence social, and not physically objective, arises.

However, in spite of fascinating developments of this nature by social psychologists like Sherif, the old school of Gestalt psychology, Koffka, Kohler and others cannot be said to be very interested, either in the influence of society and social pressures on perception, or in the way in which perceiving is an activity that has to be taught and learned in a social setting.

Generally speaking, Gestalt psychologists opt for neuro-physiological explanations of the perception that, say, this object is the 'same one' that one saw 'then' or 'over there', the perception, that is, of the constancy of objects over time and space. Object constancy, for Kohler, is the result of sensory organisation which 'appears as a primary fact which arises from the elementary dynamics of the nervous system' (1947, p. 118). It is not somehow a learned fact, rather it is a primitive neuro-physiological fact; it is not nurture, it is nature. One does not learn forms and shapes and classifications; the nervous system automatically produced them. But Kohler cannot make up his mind whether form and organised wholes are produced by the immutable nature of the brain and nervous systems, and is hence unlearned, or whether it is produced by the immutable nature of the physical world, and is hence unlearned. For although he has stated the former, he hedges his bets by stating the latter also (ibid., p. 114):

> We do, of course, admit that given specific entities with their shapes, readily acquire meanings. But when this happens, the entities are given first, and the meanings attach themselves to such shaped things later. I am not acquainted with any facts to show that, conversely, learning *builds* things and shapes.

Whatever visual perception is about, from what Kohler says, it is not primarily a matter of exercising learnt classificatory skills as the conceptual analysts propose.

Despite Kohler's equivocation, in the notion of 'psycho-physical isomorphism', about exactly what causes what and how, his viewpoint is ultimately deterministic and physiological; it is not an experiential viewpoint, but an extra-experiential one. It is not you or I who sees, but it is our brain and nervous system which does various things we know nothing about and which thereby produces in us our experience of seeing.

Earlier it was seen that Wittgenstein rejected the deterministic implications of psycho-physical parallelism. Hamlyn, in his account of Gestalt psychology, is no less critical. He too believes that visual perception, for Gestalt psychology, is 'merely the experience which is the end product of a process of stimulation and neural excitation'

(1961a, p. 112). The account is ultimately extra-experiential and deterministic; as opposed to this both Hamlyn and Wittgenstein rely on descriptions of perceptual experiences and description of the uses of perceptual concepts, and also on a non-deterministic account of how people come to have such experiences and use such concepts.

But an important qualification must be entered here. In this as in other fields, Wittgenstein and his followers seem to be as antagonistic to the term 'experience' as they are to the term 'causal explanation'. While they definitely hold that the way we communicate and our uses of concepts is in no way determined by our neuro-physiological structures as organisms, they seem to be equally critical of the relevance of 'experience' to concepts and their uses. This belief in the independence of the world of concepts from the world of experience, as odd as it seems, can have subtle and crude interpretations. Wittgenstein and Hamlyn present subtle arguments and complex positions upon which it would be wrong to pronounce too quickly. First, we can look at a crude presentation of this feature of the conceptual analytic position, on which it would be wrong *not* to pronounce too quickly.

R. M. Kurtz presented his critique of Gestalt-inspired psychology in a short paper entitled 'A conceptual investigation of Witkin's notion of perceptual style' (*Mind*, 1969). H. Witkin had aroused Kurtz's professional interest in conceptual confusions by, allegedly, confusing some ordinary language concepts with a cavalier disregard for the sacrosanct occupations to which the said concepts may normally be put. The said concepts were 'perception' and 'style'. The cavalier disregard or, more satisfyingly, *gauche* blunder, was to use the said concepts to describe the differences between individuals' reported visual experience in an experimental situation. Witkin was interested in the degree of dependence or independence of different people, in their perceptions of things, on some frame of reference; rather like Sherif's experiments on the auto-kinetic phenomenon already mentioned. In estimating the vertical position of objects, or of themselves, for instance, people rely on comparisons with other objects in the field of original object.

Witkin, following many others in this field, used a subject sitting in a seat which could be tilted, facing a realistic looking mock-up of a room, which could also be tilted and moved. By getting people to estimate when things are vertical and horizontal under different conditions, when the room and themselves are slightly out of true, etc., differences between people as to their 'field-dependence' can be demonstrated. Some people rely a lot more in making such estimations, on comparison with other features of the field, and are hence more field dependent than others. As a simple fact about people, Witkin called the difference one of 'perceptual style', and like other simple facts about the differences between people's personality and intelligence, the fact is not in itself particularly explanatory. It was not an inflated theory needing immediate philosophic deflation; it was on the contrary a reasonably lowly and unpretentious piece of research, although Witkin went on to use differences in 'perceptual style' to characterise different forms of pathology and mental illness.

Kurtz, however, was somewhat affronted by the implication that both 'perception' and 'style' could be used as if they were characterising some activity or the other. Did not Ryle, in the *Concept of Mind* give us the last word on the meaning of these concepts? He showed us that 'perception' is not a process-naming concept, and it is not an activity-naming concept, rather, it is a terminus indication; it indicates that something has been achieved. Because 'perception' is an achievement which one can try successfully or unsuccessfully to accomplish, the use of the term in adjectival form to characterise 'style' is grossly inappropriate, as far as Kurtz is concerned. One simply does something with style, one does not succeed or fail to do something with style. Thus Kurtz writes (1969, p. 527): 'There are, in short, no perceptual styles since "perceive" is a detection-verb. One sees the bird or one doesn't, but one cannot call either the seeing or the not seeing of it a style, any more than hitting or missing the bird is a style'. There is more than a hint of nominalist legislation in this piece of superior grammar; is Kurtz suggesting that there is no such phenomenon as field dependence in visual perception, and that the facts of the differences between people as to their field dependence are spurious non-facts? If he is not suggesting this, then why did he waste so much effort to argue that a phenomenon which has simply been casually and loosely described ought to be re-described? It may be more clear to speak of perceptual achievements, and of perceptual skills, rather than perceptual style, but the gain in clarity is only marginal. It was hardly worth Kurtz's effort, and it would certainly not be worth distracting Witkin from his research to inform him.

But perhaps Kurtz was trying to make the point mentioned previously in regard to Wittgenstein, that study of experience, whether experimental, as with the Gestalt psychologists, or less formal description, as with the phenomenologists, can have no bearing on the understanding of our concepts. It is almost as if conceptual analysis were some technique in a limbo between grammatical analysis and semantic description, destined to be only the shadow of a study and never substantial because of its self-imposed prohibition about describing experience. When discussing perception Wittgenstein wrote: 'Do not try to analyse your own inner experience'.[2] While this appears to be a prohibition against phenmenological analysis, in effect it is an argument against the interpretation of experience by empiricists as purely sensational. Wittgenstein is warning against fishing in the mind for 'impressions' and sensations. But all of the examples he gives are otherwise descriptive of his own experience or of what he believes his own and other people's experience would be in specific circumstances. In fact, one of the arguments which he uses to counter the notions that there are visual impressions in the mind which somehow cause seeing, on the empiricist model, is descriptive in some senses (ibid., p. 202): 'When I see the picture of a galloping horse—do I merely *know* that this is the kind of movement meant? Is it superstition to think I *see* the horse galloping in the picture?—And does my visual impression gallop too?' The inner experience, the introspectable black box, wherein visual impressions gallop, seems as daft to the phenomenologist describing visual experiences as it does to the conceptual analyst describing the uses of visual concepts and the contexts and criteria of their applicability. In as much as the Gestalt psychologists were working on the black box model they too must stand criticised. Wittgenstein tries to show, in fact, that if the quality of organisation of an object, if its nature as a structured whole, is put on a par as a visual impression, with the colour and the shape of the object, then this Gestalt analysis of experience fails in just the same way as does the sensationalist analysis. Thus he writes (ibid., p. 196): 'If you put the "organisation" of a visual impression on a level with colours and shapes, you are proceeding from the idea of the visual impression as an inner object. Of course this makes the object into a chimera; a queerly shifting construction.'

Hamlyn tries to be just as critical about experience. He, like Wittgenstein, Ryle, Austin and all of the others, relies on various forms of description of potential conceptual uses, and of experiences that are communicable when they are not actually about communication. So we must return to the theme of the ambiguous relationship that conceptual analysis has with some concept of description of experience. But first Ryle's particular influence on Hamlyn may be noted.

It has already been noted that Ryle was opposed to overall explanations, in the *Concept of Mind*, and in favour of piecemeal explanations of failures and mistakes in the performance of skills. He thought that whatever account is given of the presumed majority of skilful performances of which humans are capable, it cannot be an overall deterministic one. This kind of account would only apply to the cases where things 'happen to' a person, where they did not make them come about. It was also seen how this limitation on deterministic theory was accepted in Peters's examination of drive theories. Thus Peters thought that drive explanations should only apply to cases where a person, through no doing of their own, felt 'driven' to do something.

Ryle, it may be recalled, asserted that psychologists should not try and explain our correct estimations of shape, size, illumination and speed: 'Let the psychologists tell us why we are deceived; but we can tell ourselves and him why we are not deceived' (ibid., p. 308). Thus psychological explanations of perception must only be concerned with the occasional and abnormal facts of illusion and deception which happen to a person, and where his perceptual skills break down in spite of his efforts.

Hamlyn, in his monograph, *The Psychology of Perception* (1961a), follows Ryle's lead, and he makes its antipathy to deterministic theory very explicit: He writes (ibid., p. 16):

> But what could be said in a general way about correct perceivings? As I have attempted to make clear, we can say that people see things correctly under normal conditions, but what conditions are normal can be determined only negatively by contrast with the abnormal conditions which produce illusions. This means that there is a definite limitation to the application of the phrase 'law of perception'. Indeed it might be said that a better phrase would be 'law of illusory perception'.

And (ibid., p. 97):

> And Hayek says, rightly I think, that psychology must concern itself with cases where what we claim to see does not correspond to what is actually to be seen; that is to say, it must proceed by a study of illusions.

He believes that if theories explain laws by providing the conditions sufficient for the laws to hold, then: 'there is no room for theories of this sort in the psychology of perception' (ibid., p. 115). This is because the psychologist would be trying to explain skills, and the whole point about skills is not that they have invariable law-like relationships with certain stimulus conditions, which can be discovered and theoretically stated, but precisely the opposite. The whole point about skills is that they can be performed in response to various different kinds of conditions, and are not determined by, or controlled by, the occurrence of any particular set of stimulus conditions.

To explain this point further we can refer to Chomsky's concept, in linguistics, of 'linguistic competence'.[3] By the use of this example we in no way want to suggest that the rest of Chomsky's theoretical framework, from which it has been plucked, in any way exemplifies either a phenomenological or a conceptual analytic approach, because it does not. But, taken completely out of context, the concept of 'linguistic competence' is like and is relevant to conceptual analysts' accounts of linguistic and conceptual skills. 'Linguistic competence' is the ability that any speaker of a language possesses to generate sentence and word combinations he has never heard before. This competence or general linguistic skill is 'stimulus free', that is it can be evoked by, or rather performed in terms of, many different stimulus situations. Chomsky, like the Gestalt psychologists, tends to regard such a general competence as being inborn, genetically inherited, and ultimately capable of neurological specification, and like the Gestalt psychologists his critique of behaviourism is very thoroughgoing: the assertion of the natural distinctiveness of human neuro-physiology as against the behaviourists' assertion of the homogeneity of all organisms, conditioning by the nurturing of the environment.

Ryle, an anti-behaviourist, but a proponent of learning, reaches similar conclusions about skills and competence to Chomsky, an anti-behaviourist, but a proponent of genetic inheritance. For Chomsky (as for the Gestaltists whom he sometimes resembles) a general competence is inborn; for competence is stimulus-free. Ryle believes that learning is becoming capable of doing 'some correct or suitable thing' in any situation of general sorts (1963, p. 141). Perceiving then, for Ryle, is a general area of many learnt skills. And following him, Hamlyn asserts that in the psychological investigation of perception we must basically be concerned with 'a skill and its breakdown' (1961a, p. 114).

Now at first hearing it may seem odd to say that perceiving an object is an activity that is stimulus-free, as if the object seen somehow need not be there to stimulate the seeing of it. But things are not as simple as that. I do claim to see things that on later inspection may be discovered not to be there at all. Conversely, most of the time I do not see even a fraction of the vast number of objects that confront me in easily visible positions. And then there is the use of the concept seen in relation to no visible objects at all, that is when it is used to assert comprehension of an argument, or the solution of a problem, when we say 'Now I see it' or 'Now I see what you are getting at'. Of course, some object must be there to be seen, but not every object that is there is seen, and such things as 'aspects of an object', 'features of a situation' and 'the gist of an argument' can be seen also.

Given that perception is then some kind of human activity, we can return to the problem of whether the understanding of perception can avoid being some kind of description of the experience of perceiving and the experience of conceptualising and communicating perceptions. Conceptual analysis, having outlawed overall deterministic theories, and physiological theories in particular, also seems to outlaw any consultation of any kind of experience. But while the former outlawing is consistent with their humanistic approach, the latter outlawing is not consistent, even with their stress on philosophic therapy for conceptual confusions. This point has been argued previously in the discussion of conceptual analytic attitudes to behaviourism; it can now be argued in terms of Hamlyn's conceptual analytic approach to perception.

In the field of perception Hamlyn argues that there should be description and analysis of the ordinary perceptual concepts that we use, their appropriate contexts and situations of use, and the purposes behind their use. We must analyse the family of concepts, situations and purposive uses which includes glimpsing, observing, discerning, attending, focusing, recognising, identifying, classifying and so on. And if we do not consult *some* areas of our experience when we are engaged in such analysis it is hard to see exactly what else we would have to analyse. Concepts are experienced; to describe concepts is therefore to describe some form and some areas of one's experience and one's consciousness, i.e. it is to describe what one knows about and what one knows how to perform. Conceptual analysts take the sensationalistic empiricist's analysis of experience and of meaning too seriously. He may well establish, against the empiricist, that private and incommunicable 'raw-feels' for instance, are irrelevant to the meaning of a speech-act. But this does not establish, against the descriptive phenomenologist who simply wants to report experience and not to impose presuppositions on it, that the speech-act is not in some sense experienced. It is experienced as a generative act, at least, by the speaker, and as a received message by the hearer. The conceptual analytic notion of experience is phenomenologically myopic. The point is whether we can avoid considering our experience of uses and situations, whether we can avoid what we know and claim to be aware of, when we are investigating conceptual distinctions. Surely the conceptual analyst, far from avoiding this type of experience, precisely has recourse to it. The point is *not* whether we can avoid the (alleged) experience of raw-feels, sense-data, and the rest of the sensational empiricist's paraphenalia in a conceptual analysis. For it is quite clear that conceptual analysis, in the company of existential phenomenology, can and does avoid this type of experience.

The curious consequences of conceptual analysts' restrictive definition of experience, which is the empiricist definition, is that they have to claim that many self-evidently experiential and experience phenomena like willing, intending, doing, remembering and so on, have 'no experiential content', etc., in order to be consistent. It is fair enough that if experience of consciousness is merely made up of received sensations, then willing or doing or intending, not being any kind of received sensation, can thereby be said not be to an experiential phenomenon, not to be experienced and not to be conscious. It is then easy to see how the conceptual analysts' rejection of the relevance of a sensory interpretation of experience, consciousness or mind could have appeared as very similar to the behaviourists' rejection of mind, when in fact it was not at all similar. The behaviourists, following their rejection of mind, studied animal reflexes. The conceptual analysts, following *their* rejection of the empiricist interpretation of mind (see note 3, p. 152) found other ways of studying and of talking about the phenomena we normally associated with mind, willing, intending, imagining and the host of other areas that Wittgenstein, for instance, discussed in the *Philosophical Investigations*.

When Hamlyn asserts that description of experience is irrelevant to the examination of perceptual concepts, he is simply objecting to the myopic sensationalistic conception, and to that conception alone. Talking of the figure-ground structure of perception he writes (1961a, p. 56): 'if we are to see an object at all, it is a logical necessity that we must distinguish it from a background. This is not contingent and therefore not a matter of experience.' The Humean anachronistic equation of experience or consciousness with contingent sensory impingements is a characteristic weakness of conceptual analytic discussions. Whether they like it or not, they are implying that logical necessity is not something that can be experienced. And if this is not possible, then their major pit-prop, the concept of man as a conscious-rule-follower, simply falls. Their doctrinal myopia over experience undermines their doctrinal humanism. Existential phenomenological descriptions of experience could not possibly come within the frame of reference of Hamlyn's objection. It too is opposed to the sensationalist conception, and in any case conceptual analysis itself exhibits a similar kind of detailed investigation and description of the concrete possibilities of social and communicative experience as does existential phenomenology. It could not object to the latter without chancing self-contradiction. However, Hamlyn, while he is not critical of the existential branch, is very critical of the pure Husserlian branch of phenomenology. In particular, he criticises Husserl's influence on the early Gestalt psychologists (1961a, pp. 14, 46 and 58). Of this we will have more to say in the ensuing section discussing phenomenological critiques of Gestalt psychology, particularly those of Merleau-Ponty. For the moment it may just be noted that Hamlyn's objection to pure phenomenology has no implications whatsoever for the similarity we are trying to uncover between his own conceptual analytic views and those of existential phenomenology. It could at most only affect a comparison between conceptual analysis and pure phenomenology and that is not a topic under consideration in this book.

In any case Hamlyn's definition of phenomenology, whatever branch it is supposed to refer to, has a perhaps unwitting application to his own approach. In his earlier work, *Sensation and Perception*, Hamlyn makes the following point: 'Any attempt to give an exact account of what is given in perception may be described as "phenomenological"' (1961b, p. 173). All that remains to be demonstrated, in order to show that Hamlyn's own approach is phenomenological in this sense, is that he himself tries to give 'an exact account of what is given in perception'.

Consider, for example, the way that conceptual distinctions appear as 'the given' in Hamlyn's comments on the 'figure-ground' structure of perceptions. For Gestalt psychology, the visual field of any perceiver is structured. There is the whole or patterned object that the perceiver pays attention to, the 'figure', and there is the background, the 'ground'. The perceiver does not pay explicit attention to the 'ground', but he uses it to provide the boundaries of the 'figure', and to provide a general frame of reference for locating the size and position of the 'figure'. In some cases figure and ground can be ambiguous and interchangeable. Such is the case for instance where the perceiver is presented with a black and white drawing, which can at one moment be seen as a white vase on a black background, and at another can be seen as two black faces, in profile, facing one another, and separated by a white background (formerly the vase figure).

If we try to see both figures at the same time, then we find it confusing and difficult, because every figure in our perception requires its field, and here there would be no field, only a doomed attempt to see two shapes simultaneously as figures. It cannot be done; the figure-ground structure of perception is a given. When we report our difficulty to someone, or when the subject reports his confusion to the experimental investigator, then we would describe the picture in one of three ways: as 'of a vase'; as 'of two faces'; or as 'ambiguous'. We would be unable to describe the picture as simultaneously one or two faces and a vase, but if we did we would not also be able to describe it as ambiguous. We would be unlikely to describe things in this way because if we did we would not make sense, and we want to make sense. Hamlyn says: 'We cannot see the figure in both ways at the same time, and this "cannot" is a logical "cannot", not an empirical one' (1961a, p. 27). Here he seems to be saying that it is a logical matter and not a matter of contingent experience. He wants to stress that this is the way things necessarily are, and not the way they just happen to crop up. This is the way experience is structured, not in a contingent and haphazard way, but conceptually organised. As Wittgenstein wrote about the same figure-ground problem: 'A *concept* forces itself on one' (1963, p. 204).

In writing this Wittgenstein italicised 'concept'; he might just as well have italicised 'forces' also. Both he and Hamlyn are concerned with the givens of experience, the way it is conceptually organised, and in the process they have to criticise recourse to 'inner experience' (Wittgenstein) and 'empirical matters' (Hamlyn). But in the ultimate analysis they make assertions about the basic nature of experience in different fields, here the perceptual field, in much the same way as do the phenomenologists. The conceptual structure of our experience is a phenomenological given, something necessary to experience, and without which our experience would not be what it is. Phenomenologists, as much as conceptual analysts, are interested in the meaningful structure of perception and other 'mental states'; and as much as conceptual analysts they reject the sensationalist's meaningless and structureless portrayal of experience.

But a word of criticism against Hamlyn, and conceptual analysts in general, may be mentioned in respect of their contrast of 'logical' and 'empirical'. This is the contrast between a 'necessary' structure of meaning and experience on the one hand, and merely a 'contingent' feature of experience on the other. Gestalt psychology asserts that the figure-ground structure of perceptions is a necessary and not a contingent feature of perceptions. But Hamlyn criticises it, as we have seen, on the basis that an empirical science like Gestalt psychology must ultimately base itself on contingent facts, it cannot base itself on the (allegedly) unempirical concept of necessary facts. As opposed to this, Hamlyn believes that the necessity of, for instance, the figure-ground structure in perception can be demonstrated as a consequence of our conceptual scheme and our language.

Hamlyn is right; there is contingency deep below the Gestaltists' assertion of the necessity of the figure-ground phenomenon. But there is contingency deep below his assertion also. If the Gestalt psychologists rely on standard facts of ordinary human neurophysiology, then all that has to be seen is that there is nothing ultimately immutable and invariable about such neurophysiology. Evolution from ape-like animals could just as well have produced a three-eyed human with a brain of three or twenty-three frontal lobes instead of two. We might still be evolving, and man a million years from now could well be a very different creature, whose perception may not have a figure-ground structure. But exactly the same undercutting of necessity applies to Hamlyn and to conceptual analysis in general. In fact we need no imagination and consideration of biological possibilities to place linguistic and conceptual schemes under a higher contingency. We merely have to consult anthropological facts about different societies, cultures, languages and conceptual systems to realise that there is nothing ultimately 'logical', 'necessary', and 'non-contingent' about the way we happen to structure our experience, and the way we happen to slice up the world into comprehensible chunks. It is conceivable, for instance, that in languages which do not have a subject-predicate structure, and which isolate and reidentify processes rather than material objects (such as the language of the North American Hopi Indians, see Whorf, 1956), the differentiation of figure from ground would take, at least, a very different form from that given by the very different linguistic and conceptual structures of European languages. There is nothing ultimately necessary about our own parochial conceptual schemes, they are ultimately contingent social facts like any other facts.

Conceptual analytic opposition to the sensationalistic picture of the mind and its contingent picture of empirical experience is something that both Gestalt psychology and, in a different vein, phenomenology, support. Rather, all agree that experience, particularly perceptual experience, has some necessary non-contingent structural features. But conceptual analysis can occasionally get very holy and sanctimonious about the logical and structured nature of meaning systems, and forget that meaning systems are, in the final analysis, contingent features of the world.

But we must look further at the phenomenological, descriptive and experiential nature of Hamlyn's conceptual analytic approach to perception. He discussed whether a nervous system could be said to 'classify' incoming stimuli by responding differentially to them, and further whether this could be an explanation of perception. Thus he is led to a discussion of the ordinary uses of concepts like classifying and perceiving, and the relations that hold between them in everyday talk. He says (1961a, p. 100): 'If in perceiving we are classifying, we cannot be said to be classifying any of those things which we should ordinarily be said to perceive; yet we are not ordinarily aware of stimuli or of ourselves as classifying them'. This is an argument from what we are ordinarily aware of doing; from the experience of the use of concepts, not from some more abstract 'logic of concepts'. Similarly, 'we are not classifying *when* we are perceiving' (ibid., p. 99). The stress on the temporal (and, dare I say it, contingent and empirical?) distinction, as opposed to the logical distinction, here is Hamlyn's own.

The same experiential approach surfaces through his criticism of what he calls the transactional theory of perception. This is the theory that perception is a transaction in which the perceiver brings his past experience to bear on what is offered by the environment. As against this Hamlyn says: 'In perceiving something are we interpreting impingements from the environment on the basis of past experience?' (ibid., p. 105). What is Hamlyn asking his readers? He is asking them, is this what we are doing when we perceive something? Is this what we are aware of doing? However 'abstract' and 'philosophical' such questions may seem to be, they are addressed to the reader's concrete experience, his knowledge of the application and uses of concepts and criteria. They may not be addressed to the reader's awareness of impinging sensations; such a concept of experience, in any case, although it looks superficially clear-headed, is in reality a mare's nest of confusions and best rejected, as Hamlyn does reject it. But this is not to say that his questions are not addressed to experience interpreted in a non-sensationalistic way; for they clearly are addressed to some interpretation of experience.

Enough has now been said about the descriptive approach required by conceptual analysis to man's experience seen as in a state of language. This complements the more explicit critiques that conceptual analysts present of deterministic explanations of experience and meanings, in terms of causal processes that are themselves beyond the actor's experience and meaningless. We have examined their critiques of behaviourism and now Gestalt psychology, and in both cases the reduction by these psychologies of thought and action to neurophysiological terms, theories and processes was particularly criticised.

The attitude of existential phenomenology to behaviourism has been examined, and we must now turn to its attitude to Gestalt psychology. It has been seen in the former case, and it remains to be seen in the latter case, that the existential phenomenological position, like the conceptual analytic one, relies on description of experience and on critique of extra-experiential and deterministic psychological explanations of thought and action.

Phenomenology

Although Merleau-Ponty is the chief source of discussion and criticism of Gestalt psychology from the point of view of existential phenomenology, the influence of Husserl and pure phenomenology on the Gestalt psychologists must first be mentioned. (Space prevents me from discussing Aron Gurwitsch's work in this field, but see his *Studies in Phenomenology and Psychology*, 1966, chs 1 and 10).

Hamlyn, in the monograph discussed above, was at pains to point out the relationship between pure phenomenology and Gestalt psychology. He thereby wanted to implicate the one in his distaste for, and criticism of, the other. There is no doubt that both the Wurzburg school of introspectionist psychologists and the early Gestalt psychologists, like Koffka, acknowledged Husserl as one of the main influences upon them (see note 1, p. 142). But the fact remains that this affection was not reciprocated. Husserl did not regard Gestalt psychology as embodying the main themes of his own philosophy at all. In the preface to his major work, *Ideas*, Husserl explicitly criticised Gestalt psychology. He stated that, in trying to become a natural science of mind it was falling into the same kind of irrelevance to philosophy and particularly to phenomenological analysis of mind that sensationalistic theories of knowledge and theories of psychology had fallen into. He wrote: 'atomistic and Gestalt psychology alike participate in that intrinsic meaning of psychological "naturalism" [which] may also be termed "sensationalism"' (1967, p. 24).

Therefore Hamlyn's criticisms of Gestalt psychology cannot be allowed to rub off on pure phenomenology. In some ways these psychologists simply misinterpreted Husserl. For instance, as Hamlyn points out, Koffka and his colleagues were inspired by Husserl's conception of 'pure presuppositionless experience', and of the 'absolute naivety of transcendental subjectivity'. But instead of applying Husserl's epoche procedure, the bracketing-off of all presuppositions, the Gestalt psychologists seemed to Hamlyn to want to achieve the same goal of pure untainted experience from another angle and by other, more experimental, procedures. What they did was to study the perceptions and other experiences of people, like uneducated adults and very young children, who (allegedly) had fewer presuppositions and were more naive than older and more educated people (1961a pp. 14, 43-4 and 46). That is, Husserl's concept of 'pure ego' was grossly misinterpreted as meaning *tabula rasa*. Hamlyn only mentions the influence of Husserl's concept, he does not mention that it was a completely misrepresented influence. Hamlyn's association of Husserl's concept of the 'pure ego' with a psychology of the *tabula rasa* variety is quite misguided. (For Husserl's own position—as opposed to Hamlyn's misrepresentation of his position see Husserl, 1966). For instance, speaking of Western man's development of rational self-examination Husserl (ibid., p. 189) writes:

> Now, how did the beginning of such a self-examination come about? A beginning was impossible so long as sensualism, or better, a psychology of data, a *tabula rasa* psychology, held the field. Only when Brentano promoted psychology to being a science of vital intentional experience, was an impulse given that could lead further.

Obviously Husserl's pure phenomenology can be criticised, and in chapter 1 we outlined the criticisms of it that led to the development of existential phenomenology, but not on the grounds of its superficial associations with some eminently criticisable features of Gestalt psychology. Clearly a *tabula rasa* has nothing whatever to do with the concept of a 'pure ego', and the experimental investigation of the former could have no consequences or relevance to the philosophical investigation of the latter. The 'pure-ego' is an achievement of a meditative and reflective technique; the *tabula rasa*, best exemplified by the experience of a child in the womb perhaps, is no kind of achievement, it is simply a fact. The 'pure ego' is a presuppositionless state because (in principle) a person has made a supreme intellectual effort to suspend and bracket-off his presuppositions about the world: the *tabula rasa* is a presuppositionless state because it knows nothing of the world, it is pure and naive through ignorance and not through intellectual effort.

In fact, Hamlyn is wrong to overemphasise the role of the 'pure ego' concept in the Gestalt psychologists' *tabula rasa* approach. It is far more likely and consistent that this approach was inspired by the desire to demonstrate the genetically inherited organising functions of the brain and nervous system. This demonstration of the capacities nature has given us would have been all the more forceful if the environmental effects and 'distortions' of conditioning, learning and of nurturing in general could have been minimised. Thus it would have been reasonable to investigate experimentally the perceptual experience of young and uneducated subjects rather than older and more educated ones because the former would have been less exposed to the effects of environmental nurture than the latter.

Thus Gestalt psychologists may well have believed that, if perceptual experience could be examined in a relatively un-nurtured primeval state, it would be found to be organised in terms of forms and shapes. We could then be sure that these features were not learned, but rather were produced by (or rather, in some unanalysable 'isomorphic' relationship with) the natural organising functions of the brain and nervous system. So it is far more likely that the *tabula rasa* approach was inspired by (pure?) neurological considerations than by pure phenomenological ones. It is consistent with the Gestalt psychologists' emphasis on nature as opposed to nurture, while it does not seem to be at all consistent with whatever inspiration they may have derived from Husserl. Hamlyn's justified criticism of the approach cannot really be held to rub off on pure phenomenology as he wants to imply. If pure phenomenology can be criticised it certainly is not for an association with Gestalt psychology, which itself is not precisely demonstrable, and which in any case Husserl disowned.

Merleau-Ponty was a lot more interested in Gestalt psychology than Husserl seems to have been, and took it a lot more seriously. But in the final analysis his judgement on it is virtually identical with Husserl's, and very similar to the conclusions reached by conceptual analysts like Hamlyn. Hamlyn's portrayal of the relationship between pure phenomenology and Gestalt psychology is misleading because ultimately Husserl is as critical of the latter as Hamlyn is. However, it is with existential phenomenology that

Hamlyn's conceptual analytic approach really stands comparison. Pure phenomenology investigates man's experience or consciousness in its transcendental aspects, where existential and other presuppositions about the objects of consciousness are deliberately ignored and minimised. It would not be correct to say that conceptual analysis bore much comparison with this brand of philosophy. However, existential phenomenology investigate's man's experience or consciousness in its existential situation, placed among realities which exist for oneself and for others, confronting and interacting with such realities and such others. Conceptual analysis, investigating man's experience, and his experiential or mental concepts, in a state of language and communication, does bear comparison with this version of phenomenology. And this is a comparison we can return to after consideration of Merleau-Ponty's existential phenomenological discussion and critique of Gestalt psychology.

Merleau-Ponty discussed or commented upon Gestalt psychology in at least four pieces of work: from the early major statements of *The Structure of Behaviour* (1965, written in 1942), and the *Phenomenology of Perception* (1962, written in 1945), and the early paper *The Primacy of Perception* (1964a, written in 1945) to one of the last papers he wrote *Phenomenology and the Sciences of Man* (1964a, written in 1961). But throughout his writings there is a concern, if not for the psychology of perception, then for the philosophy of perception and for phenomenological description of perceptual experience. Thus his interests were never very far from those of Gestalt psychology of perception, and in a sense his whole position owed as much to his critical development of Gestalt psychology as it owed to his critical development of Husserl's philosophy.

In his earlier work, *The Structure of Behaviour*, Merleau-Ponty, as has already been seen, used Gestaltist theories and experimental findings to demolish behaviourism and reflexology. And he used the Gestaltists' study of the brain to underline the behaviourists' avoidance of neurological facts. But in the final analysis he did not think that they went far enough in their objections; perhaps ultimately Gestalt psychology only represented a 'simple antithesis or counterpart of atomism' (1965, p. 76).

On the one hand Gestalt psychology did not go far enough in its critique of behaviourism and physiological reductionism in psychology, but on the other hand it went too far. It could have stayed at the level of investigation and description of perceptual experience, its organisations and structures and meanings, thus refuting the sensationalistic analysis of concrete experience experientially. But it chose to go on into the more abstract realm of physiological theoretical assumptions, things that are not experientially concrete, to refute sensationalism's naive physiological foundations. And that is where it stayed, beyond the realm of concrete perceptual experience where, according to Merleau-Ponty, it should rather have been.

In *The Structure of Behaviour* Merleau-Ponty states the problem as almost an ontological one. There are, as far as he is concerned, different orders of being; an inanimate physical or material order; an animate, or life order; and finally, a human order which involves consciousness and rational purpose (ibid., part 3). Each level is irreducible to the other and has 'emergent' features. Gestalt psychology, however, by its neurophysiological investigations, must appear ultimately as a reductionist approach; one that does not respect the irreducibility of the higher levels of being; one that is ultimately a materialistic approach. Thus he asks; 'But can the originality of biological and mental structures be really conserved, as Gestalt theory tries to do, while at the same time founding them on physical structures?' (ibid., p. 136). His answer to this question was in the negative in all of the four books and papers which were referred to above.

His most explicit portrayal of Gestalt psychology as a materialistic and deterministic theory occurred in the paper summarising the main theses of the *Phenomenology of Perception* called *The Primacy of Perception* (1964a). There he stated that, although Gestalt psychologists described the perceived world as he did, they had never drawn the philosophical conclusions that they could have done from this. Instead he thought that (ibid., pp. 23-4):

> Ultimately they consider the structures of the perceived as the simple result of certain physical and physiological processes which take place in the nervous system and completely determine the gestalten and the experience of the gestalten... When ... Gestalt psychology tried to explain itself—in spite of its own discoveries—in terms of scientistic or positivistic ontology, it was at the price of an internal contradiction which we have to reject.

Thus 'psycho-physical isomorphism' or 'parallelism' is interpreted by Merleau-Ponty ultimately as physiological determinism of consciousness and of experiential or mental states, which is how Wittgenstein and Hamlyn interpreted it also (ibid., pp. 76-7).

At first Gestalt theory appeared to be reintroducing the human level of consciousness back into psychology from whence it had been kicked by behaviourism, but with its ensuing neurophysiological interest the Gestaltists came to be seen as defending, not the conscious order of being, but, less ambitiously, the merely animate order of being. Perhaps this is what Kohler had in mind with his remark, mentioned previously, about the 'natural fate' of Gestalt psychology being 'Gestalt biology'. It can be argued that biology deals with an irreducible life level of being, that of animate organisms, to which perhaps some 'unscientific' teleological type of explanation is appropriate. And perhaps this is what is implied in Kohler's otherwise rather mysterious concept of 'psycho-physical isomorphism'.

Merleau-Ponty, in *The Structure of Behaviour*, considered this kind of interpretation at some length. This possibility was weighed during his discussions of Kohler's field theory of nerve and brain functioning, and Goldstein's and others' observations of the structured nature of brain-functioning even in pathological conditions. But ultimately he decided against it. Rather than credit Gestalt psychology with some original version of vitalism or animism, he decided to discredit it by interpreting it as some unorthodox and rogue form of materialism. Thus the different orders of 'matter, life and mind' are 'reduced' by the 'common denominator of physical forms' in Gestalt theory. It is no longer consciousness that defines man, Merleau-Ponty alleges, because Gestalt psychology makes consciousness an epiphenomena of 'particularly complex physical structures, an effect determined by physiological causes (1965, pp. 135-6).

So, for Merleau-Ponty, the distinct reality that man is, is defined by consciousness. But as we have already pointed out in our discussion of his views on behaviourism, this consciousness is not a rationalist or idealistic kind. It is not some inner reality populated with inner mental things which can be fished up by introspection and intuition. Both Husserl and Descartes removed themselves too far in their analysis of consciousness from ordinary and everyday experience. Merleau-Ponty's conception of consciousness was an attempt to bring these other conceptions down to earth.

But on the other hand, it was not an attempt to provide a sensationalistic analysis of experience, like the empiricists and materialists provided. They not only brought consciousness down to earth, they buried it as well. Merleau-Ponty always tried to present his approach to consciousness and experience as some kind of midway between these two opposing positions of idealism on the one hand and sensationalistic materialism on the other. Perhaps, since he had a penchant for Hegelian dialectics, the term 'midway' could also be rendered as a 'synthesis', surpassing and yet incorporating two anti-thetical positions. But perhaps not, because Merleau-Ponty was also a very commonsensical philosopher whose main area of investigation and analysis was common sense, and whose main concern was to reveal and to remind us of the nature of our everyday experience and existence.

Merleau-Ponty's development of Husserl's thinking, and his own original philosophy, was based on a return to the world that is given to us in ordinary perception, hence the title of one of his papers:

The Primacy of Perception. It was here that he saw the idealist/rationalist emphasis on consciousness or experience (he uses the latter term as an unexceptionable version of the former) converge with the empiricist/materialist emphasis on existence and contingent facts. Or rather it is from the concrete world of perceptual experience that each of these abstract positions diverge.

In one's ordinary perception of the realities of a surrounding world, the consciousness which the idealist and rationalist positions abstracted as some kind of extra-terrestial ingredient of man, is pitched into the world of facts, realities and existents. It is brought down to earth, and to existential considerations from which it should never have been parted. Perceptual consciousness is suffused with existence; suffused with the factual organic existence of the perceiver, who is confronted with, and interacts with, other existent organisms and physical things. Perception is integrated totally with existence; according to Merleau-Ponty perception is better called an existential state than a mental state; and all mental states are, or are analysable as, existential states of a human being in its relations with the realities it sees about it.

Part of what we are perceptually conscious of, and in the midst of, is the purely material and 'tangible' world, the world exalted by the materialists and empiricists. But this exaltation is an abstraction from the concrete phenomena of ordinary perceptual consciousness, because the conception that it has of the perceiver is that of a receptacle determined by features of the world. It has no conception of how features of the world are determined by the perceiving subject; how their aspects are selected and chosen for attention; how we actively and bodily try to see the world, try to achieve certain standpoints from which to view it, try to grasp it and to use it for our purposes, and so on. Materialism and empiricism reify consciousness, and therefore are just as abstract as idealism and rationalism which deify consciousness.

Only perceptual experience is concrete, and the philosopher, if he is to base himself anywhere, must base himself here, on description and investigation of perceptual consciousness. This was Merleau-Ponty's credo, and one which he tried to implement in his own career. In *The Structure of Behaviour* he concluded on the theme that it is consciousness which structures and determines the organised nature of behaviour. But this was a consciousness which he had, through his analysis of Gestaltist neurology, demonstrated as embedded in the world, and embodied in a perceiving organism, which has a situation, an environment and an horizon in the world.

In the *Phenomenology of Perception* Merleau-Ponty tried to build on this theme, examining all forms that the human organism has of knowingly relating to the world that it knows about. In doing this, one of Merleau-Ponty's chief aims was to demolish the wedge that Descartes had driven through man's self-conception in the divorcing of Mind and Body, the Ghost in the Machine. Merleau-Ponty was attempting to re-establish man's integrated nature. The way to do this was to see man as a living being, existing in a world that he knows about and that he expresses himself in. This ordinary perceptual knowledge and this expression can be investigated by the philosopher. It is a concrete phenomenon. We do not investigate visual experience by introspective fishing in the depths of some consciousness; we investigate it by describing the world that is seen, *that* is the visual experience. We do not describe what is 'inside'; we describe what is 'outside' the perceiver. We are not so much interested in the subjective pole of man's consciousness—we take it for granted *that* he wills, that he intends, that he sees and so on—rather we are interested in the objective pole of his consciousness, *what* he wills, what he intends, and what he sees, according to Merleau-Ponty.

How he deals with embodiment and the problem of how to understand the body is probably the best test of how to differentiate the idealistic pure phenomenological philosopher from the existential phenomenological philosopher. The former, following Husserl following Descartes, will try to avoid considering the body in its conception of man's consciousness and mind. The latter, following Merleau-Ponty refuting Descartes, will place it in the centre of his picture of man's conscious nature.

The human body, for Merleau-Ponty, 'is our expression in the world; the visible form of our intentions' (1964a, p. 5). The perceiving subject is not some rationalistic absolute thinker, 'rather, it functions according to a natal pact between our body and the world between ourselves and our body' (ibid., p. 6). The body is not some machine under the watchful gaze of some ghostly controlling mind, rather 'It is on the side of the subject; it is our point of view on the world, the place where the spirit takes on a certain physical and historical situation' (ibid., p. 5). And all of its functions contribute to perception in as much as they contribute to behaviour. A man perceives *by* behaving, because he behaves; and equally a man behaves *by* perceiving, because he perceives. That is man's situation; that is the circle that Merleau-Ponty traces. A man does not passively receive perception, or receive the world as he sees it; he must act if he is alive; he actively tries to see and understand and grasp features of the world, and actively means, with his body, behaviourally.

For instance, our ideas of space and spatial relations between things are not passively received in passive perceptions. Rather (ibid.):

> We grasp external space through our bodily situation. A 'corporeal or postural scheme' gives us at every moment a

> global, practical and implicit notion of the relation between our body and things, of our hold on them. A system of possible movements, or 'motor projects', radiates from us to our environment. Our body is not in space like things; it inhabits or haunts space. It applies itself to space like a hand to an instrument.

It is this kind of knowledge of the world that Merleau-Ponty wanted to reveal in his investigations of perceptual experience or consciousness.

But of course men are embodied, and embedded actively, in social and historical realities, as well as in a world of tangible realities. And they see, hear and perceive their social world just as they perceive the allegedly more tangible physical world. Men are born into language, an historical period, a certain place in a certain society, but they can achieve changes in their social position, in the roles that they play, in the expectations they are required to conform to and so on, with greater or lesser difficulty, depending on a great number of factors, none of which we need to elaborate upon at this point. Whether man is ascribed to a social position, or whether he achieves it, is not as important as the simple fact that either way, a man discriminates the world, classifies it, and attends to it, in ways heavily influenced by his existence as a social actor in a social world. To take a very simple example, the manager of a supermarket looks at the crowd milling in his store through different eyes, with a different standpoint, attending to different things, than the store detective he employs. The detective sees, discriminates and attends to the crowd, and to individuals' actions in the crowd in terms of his role as thief-catcher. The manager sees consumers, not potential thieves, he sees a different crowd and different actions, in this sense, than his detective does.

The extent to which social existence reaches into man's nature, and into what he experiences, perceives and thinks, is an important topic which will be discussed further in the last chapter which deals with the general humanistic conception of man. For the moment the point must be emphasised that both conceptual analysis and existential phenomenology provide a social analysis of man's nature. This has been seen before, in their common rejection of any concept of solipsism. Sartre and Merleau-Ponty, no less than Strawson and Hampshire, reject the preoccupations of traditional philosophy with the doubts that a man can entertain about the reality of other men, conscious like himself. On the contrary, the representatives of both schools are concerned to reveal and investigate not man's doubts about reality, but his commitments to reality. Man accepts that certain things exist and other things do not, that certain things are good and others are bad, which ultimately derive from social existence and the acceptance of social rules and criteria, and from the social fact of language.

These general points can be seen in greater magnification when perception and the psycholgy of perception are looked at. We have seen that for the conceptual analysts perception is a socially learnt skill, a socially acquired ability to classify the world basically, in the same way as everybody else does, a socially communicable achievement and so on. Existential phenomenology has no less of a social position on man's perception; man not only is an entity which perceives, but it is an entity which *is* perceived, and which can be aware that it is so perceived. Man is not only embedded in the world in his body, he is embedded in the world as 'that which Others see'. He is not only a physically defined and physically real existence, he is a socially defined and socially real existence.

This concrete refutation of solipsism was behind Sartre's analysis, in *Being and Nothingness* (1966) of the gaze of the Other (see chapter 1 above). We cannot be in doubt that others exist, for we see them looking at us, defining us, and making us into an 'external object or reality' for themselves. And, of course, we do the same to them as far as they are concerned. They see this image of themselves as external realities in our eyes also, and cannot doubt that we exist seeing and defining them. Sartre waxed a little too eloquent on this particular theme, as he then went on to talk of the inevitability of total conflict between any two people who recognise one another's existence. This was based on the difficulty that each of the two would have in reconciling his own opinion of himself as a subject with the Other's (presumed) perception of him as an object. This 'hell is others' anti-social philosophy, however, is clearly founded on a more primary philosophical consideration of intersubjective and social existence.

It is with this kind of consideration that Merleau-Ponty was very preoccupied with in part of the *Phenomenology of Perception*, and in some of his later psychological and political writings also. He asserts that experience of the Other, social experience that is, is primordial in the sense of being developed very early in the infant stage, in the relationship between the child and its mother and significant others' (1962 p. 352). Merleau-Ponty was originally a child psychologist, so it is natural that he should rely on information and theories about infant development such as those of Piaget and Freud (1964a, pp. 96-155). Because man is fundamentally social, reared by other men, and destined to live among other men all its life, it is provided with the ability to communicate, and to see a world that is the same for everybody in the sense of being communicable in a common language and common conceptual structures of meaning.

From what he considers to be the facts of social existence, given in socialisation into language use, and in the general ability we learn to distinguish 'self' from 'others' in infancy, Merleau-Ponty chipped away at Sartre's 'hell is others' theme until the intersubjective base upon which it rested became clear. This is the theme that 'there are others' irrespective of whether subsequently we must conclude that such social coexistence is heaven or hell. Thus he writes (1962, p. 360): 'It is said that I must choose between others and myself. But we choose one *against* the other, and thus assert both.' And further (ibid., p. 362): 'The social is already there when we come to know or judge it. An individualistic or a sociological philosophy is a certain perception of coexistence systematised and made explicit.' That is, whether we take a very individualistic line, even amounting to a solipsistic philosophy (ibid., p. 360), or a very sociological line, even amounting to an idealistic 'group mind' philosophy, both of these extremes and all of the more moderate intermediate positions presume and rely on a philosophy of *social coexistence*. From the beginning we see and perceive and hear other people, purposes, physical instruments constructed for a purpose, cultural and symbolic objects like books that embody ideas. From the beginning our perception is of a social world and what we see is communicable. On the basis of our certainties we may later intellectualise and construct doubts, such as solipsistic doubts, which are artificial and not existentially real. An existentialist can easily be a moral cynic, hard-headed and 'realistic' about men's nature; but he cannot be an ontological sceptic in the empiricist fashion, or a solipsistic doubter in the rationalist fashion. In the analysis of perceptual consciousness he must analyse physical and social worlds-as-perceived, the existing realities and certainties surrounding and situating man's conscious existence.

In broad terms this is the positive side of Merleau-Ponty's discussion of Gestalt psychology. It was in defence of this position, and this kind of analysis, that he criticised the non-phenomenological and neuro-physiological direction of Gestalt psychology. Similarly with the conceptual analysts; in defence of a return to analysis of man's perceiving activity, and the social/linguistic origin, nature and context of this activity, they criticise the Gestalt account. Both schools point out that neurophysiological deterministic theories, even ultimately including Kohler's 'psycho-physical isomorphism', cannot explain either the nature of perceptual experience, the world-as-perceived (existential phenomenology), or the stimulus-free performance of perceptual and conceptual skills (conceptual analysis).

Conclusion

Both schools have been seen to reject a physiologically reductionist account of perceptual experience and behaviour, preferring to rely on some kind of descriptive and analytical investigation of this experience and behaviour. As pointed out previously, this descriptive approach is, however, a primary feature of existential phenomenology, and only a secondary and sometimes even disavowed feature of conceptual analysis.

Thus both schools rely on some forms of humanist position as regards the description and explanation of human thought and action, in this field of perception as in other fields. Not only are both opposed to reductionist and determinist accounts, but there is some similarity in the way both allow such causal accounts a limited area of valid application. When discussing Peters's analysis of behaviourism, and Hamlyn's analysis of Gestalt psychology, it was pointed out that these two conceptual analysts followed Ryle on the application of causal explanations. Peters would only see drive theories applicable where a man felt driven to act, and was incapable of himself giving an account or reasonable justification of his behaviour. Similarly Hamlyn (and earlier Ryle) thought that causal theories of perception should only be applicable where a person was mistaken, confused or deceived, and where he could not explain why he had failed to be able to discriminate and see something. Something akin to this restriction of deterministic explanation, as opposed to rational and more humanistic explanations, in terms of reasons, skills, purposes and so on, is implied also in Merleau-Ponty's comment: 'The possibility of constructing a causal explanation of behaviour is exactly proportional to the inadequacy of the structurations accomplished by the subject' (1965, p. 179). This comment, however, was evoked by a consideration of Freud's theories, and it is to the similarities between conceptual analysis and existential phenomenology in this area of psychology and psychiatry that we now turn.

6 Freudian psychology

Introduction: reductionism and humanism, psychology and sociology

In the two preceding chapters the attitudes of the two humanistic schools of philosophy under investigation, conceptual analysis and existential phenomenology, to behaviourist and Gestalt psychology were found to be ultimately very critical. And the same is to be expected of their respective attitudes to Freudian psychology, which has figured very prominently as a topic in various writings by important philosophers in both schools.

The main target of their criticisms is the reductionist idea of a science of mind and action which was discussed in general terms in chapter 3. In the preceding two sections, however, the reductionist idea was seen in more specific and concrete terms, embodied in the aspirations of behaviourist and Gestalt psychology. Both psychologies proposed deterministic and extra-experiential explanations of what a person does, what he sees and what he thinks. The former built its theories on simplistic physiological assumptions about the needs and drives of human and other organisms, their cortico-nervous systems, and the interrelationship of the organism with the stimulating, rewarding and punishing environment. The latter built its theories on more sophisticated neurophysiological assumptions and facts about the organised functioning of the brain and nervous system. Conceptual analysis and existential phenomenology, nevertheless, objected to both on the grounds of reductionism. And this is the same line that they take with Freud's theories, which were related to, if not based upon, the simple kind of drive hypotheses found in the behaviourist tradition.

As opposed to the reductionist idea, both conceptual analysis and existential phenomenology proposed types of humanistic positions. For instance, both proposed that man's actions can only be understood in terms of his intentions, purposes and reasons. Thus both were found to be committed to some kind of rationalistic or personalistic teleology as regards the explanation of human behaviour.

Complementary with this, both proposed that experiential and conscious phenomena can only be understood in terms of man's active, behavioural, relationship to his perceived world, a world he uses and in which he expresses himself. A prime feature of man's active relationship with this world, of course, is his active communication with his fellow men. Both schools, in different ways, made the point that man's consciousness and his experience can only be analysed in terms of his relationship with his social world. Thus, on the one hand, Merleau-Ponty renamed 'mental states' such as perceptions, 'existential states'. He held that perceptual states are not 'in' any mind but must be seen as states of a relationship, the existential relationship between a man and the world-as-he-sees-it. On the other hand, conceptual analysts asserted a parallel thesis. They analysed mental states such as perceptions in terms of action concepts, which is not the mere reduction of behavioural phenomena as some critics mistakenly presume. Perception then became understandable as a skilful and communicable performance and achievement. It appears to us in the way that it does, and not in some other way, because of our immersion in a specifiable social world of linguistic and conceptual structures of meaning.

Thus both schools take humanistic positions which have some important common elements: (a) man is a purposive actor; and (b) man is a social animal—he exists and acts in the social world, and his consciousness is largely integrated with the structures of meaning and of communication in the social world. This common position, upon which we must elaborate in the final chapter, is diametrically opposed to the reductionist position which has been excavated from behaviourist and Gestalt psychology, and which remains to be discovered in Freudian psychology also.

The rest of the argument in this thesis is less preoccupied with psychology, and more preoccupied with sociology. The point is that the reductionist position, opposed by the two schools of philosophy we are interested in, is not too hard to find in the various branches of psychology, but it is difficult to find in sociology. Conversely, the humanistic position (broadly, (a) and (b) above) can at times be extremely difficult to find in the various forms of psychology, whereas it is easily found in many different types of sociology.

It is easier for psychology to accept some form of reductionism than it is for sociology. This is because, to oversimplify, psychology deals with a-social individuals, and with a-social characteristics of individuals. Psychology deals with an abstract conception of man, because it makes man out of context, out of society. Biologists can take fish out of water and, when they are dead, investigate them to explain how they live. The same is not true of psychology; it cannot abstract man from society—outside of meanings, purposes and life—and expect to understand his life. But psychologists have rarely accepted this, and their 'fish out of water' abstraction has always had someone to justify it in psychology. Given this, it is not hard to see how psychology could feel that it had nothing to lose and everything to gain from committing itself, as it has done in the notorious case of behaviourism, to the reductionist ideal. It could gain the prestige of being a 'true' science and with it the explanatory power of being able to account for many phenomena with rigorous deductive theories. For this possibility the portrayal of man as a determined organism, whose consciousness and experience is epiphenomenal and unimportant, is a small price to pay.

Not only is man a-social, but he is also non-purposive; this completely contradicts the two humanistic points mentioned earlier; but this anti-humanism has to be swallowed 'in the interests of science'. In any case, the psychologist could ask—surely it is weak thinking to presume that man is 'rational' when, in many instances, he is demonstrably 'irrational'? It is far better, more hard-headed and altogether more 'scientific' to presume that man is determined by extra-experiential processes, and therefore ultimately totally irrational. On this issue of rationality, humanism and reductionism are completely at loggerheads. Reductionists hold that even 'rational' man is ultimately irrational. And humanistic psychiatrists would hold that the most 'demonstrably irrational' of all of us, people who are 'stark raving mad' and 'mentally ill' are in fact comprehensible. That is, there is reason in their madness, and purpose in their purposelessness. We will discuss this humanistic psychiatric pole of the arguments further in chapter 7.

The situation is very different with sociology; reductionism in this field has nothing like the attraction it possesses in the psychological field. For a start, the humanist assertion of the social nature of man could hardly be contradicted by sociology, and is obviously endorsed in different ways by the different types of sociology. Similarly the humanist assertion of the purposive nature of man is also endorsed, sometimes as an axiom, by the different types of sociology.

Sociology, no less than our two schools of philosophy, is bound up with humanistic ontological and other presuppositions. This theme must be pursued later, in the final chapter, chapter 9. But we may introduce this theme, in the discussion of Freud here and in the ensuing discussion of psychiatric and sociological accounts of mental illness. It is in this field of mental illness that the relationship of existential phenomenology (but not conceptual analysis) to sociology can usefully be illustrated. And further the division between their humanistically oriented theories and the reductively oriented theories of psychology, even Freudian psychology, can also be illustrated.

Freud could well be called the founding father of modern psychiatry. But a great gap has arisen, in present day psychiatry between humanistic and reductionist theories and therapies. Many of Freud's theories, plus all behaviouristic and genetic theories of mental illness, can be called reductionist. As against this, some of Freud's interpretations of his own theories, and certainly many of the later revisions of his theories by such as Adler, Stekel, Fromm, Horney, Sullivan and others, can be called humanistic, or interpretive, or hermeneutic. Most significant in this category, however, are existential phenomenological forms of psycho-analysis, such as those of Binswanger, Jaspers and the English school of Laing, Cooper and others (see chapter 7 below).

Now it is of great importance, from the point of view of what we have been saying, that sociological theories of mental illness, those of Scheff, Szasz and others, fall most naturally and readily into the humanistic and not into the reductionist category. The link-up which has occurred in this field between existential phenomenological theories and sociological theories is quite extensive, and must be discussed in chapter 7.

Unfortunately for the purposes of symmetry of presentation, it cannot be said that conceptual analysis has any theory of mental illness on a par with that of existential phenomenology and therefore comparable with sociological theories. In fact, mental illness is a decided affront to their conceptual analytic complacement form of humanism. Conceptual analysts could not be said to be at all happy about the fact that there are reasonably large numbers of people who cannot, or who will not, communicate and respect criteria of meaningfulness in speech, who do not appear to be conceptual rule-followers, who misuse language, break rules and invent 'private languages'. This last point must almost be painful to any member of the school who had taken Wittgenstein's demonstration of the impossibility of private languages seriously. But, albeit unbeknown to the school, humanistically oriented psychiatry and sociology of deviance is aware of conceptual analytic philosophy (see Szasz, 1962, on Peters; Blum, 1970, on Wittgenstein; and McHugh, 1970). And, in any case whether they like it or not, some aspects of the conceptual analytic approach, in so far as it shares in the common humanistic position we have indicated with existential phenomenology, must be of use to this type of psychiatry.

Following the pattern of the previous sections on behaviourist and Gestalt psychology, the main concepts in Freudian psychology will be introduced first. Then the respective attitudes of conceptual analysis and existential phenomenology will be reviewed. The focus, as before, will be their common critique of the reductionist idea, in so far as Freud endorses it.

In the main, the Freudian concept which most preoccupies writers in both schools, Sartre and Merleau-Ponty on the one hand and Peters and MacIntyre on the other, is that of the Unconscious. This is to be expected when due consideration is given to the commitments of both schools to some conception of man as a conscious and purposive actor. Freud subverted this humanistic picture by the portrayal of man as determined by unconscious desires and needs that were ultimately based on sexual physiology, and that were ultimately beyond his conscious experience. Freud made the extra-experiential nature of his deterministic conclusions explicit, in his concept of the Unconscious. Both schools of philosophy have devoted time and effort to refuting the concept and to rejecting the conclusions. And these are the same conclusions they have rejected in the cases of behaviourist and Gestalt psychology also.

Freud

Freudian psychology consists of two distinguishable sets of ideas, those related to theory and those related to therapy. The theory of mental functioning, and of the development of neuroticism in particular, can be interpreted as a kind of reductionist and scientistic theory. The therapeutic methods and procedures, talk therapy, the patient-doctor discussion of the patient's memories and experiences, and so on, when unhitched from the theory, can be presented as a humanistic method. The development of humanistic psychiatry has been precisely in this direction of liberating the therapeutic encounter with the patient from the presuppositions of Freudian theory.

This theory-therapy division in Freudian psychology is the same kind of division that exists in the field designated by the term 'medicine'. In this field also there are theories of normal and abnormal functioning, on the one hand, and therapeutic procedures and methods for curing or alleviating malfunctions of the body, on the other. Freud, true to his training as a research neurologist and as a medical practitioner, stayed within the framework of these ideas. Medicine involves theories about and therapy for, the body; Freudian psychology involves theories about, and therapy for, the mind. Freud's revolutionary impact in psychology was never an attempt to overthrow the concept of a science of the mind, and was never intended to be other than ultimately compatible with scientific medicine. This latter point has always been exemplified in the initiation procedures into the psycho-analytic profession, which stipulate that, before becoming psycho-analysts aspirants must first qualify as ordinary medical practitioners.

It is a little ironic that abuse has been heaped on Freudian psychology, not only from the humanistic side of the two cultures, but also from the scientific side. Freudian psychology, which once flourished because of its ambiguity between the two cultures of humanistic and scientific knowledge, is now suffering because of this ambiguity, at least in the specific field of psychiatry. Freudian concepts have spread in this century far beyond the confines of academic psychiatry, however, and the concept of the Unconscious has become part of everyday conventional wisdom. Humanistic intellectuals may not know one end of Einstein's energy equation from the other, but woe betide them if they cannot spot the workings of their Unconscious in its mental deep. It is attractive and gratifying to 'know' that one has a mental deep, and that there are profound patterns behind every mindless, boring and trivial thing that one does. Einstein's theories are not nearly so complimentary. However, within psychiatry, Freud's theories have probably passed their peak of influence. From one direction they have been subjected to criticism and to erosion of influence by explicitly scientistic theories and forms of therapy, such as behaviourist 'aversion' therapy, and from the opposite direction explicitly humanistic theories and forms of therapy, such as 'existential psycho-analysis' have also chipped away at Freudian theories and therapeutic influence.

The behaviourists simply do not accept that there is such a thing as a conscious mind, within and 'underneath' which an Unconscious mind may be discovered. They accuse Freud's theories of being irrefutable and thus unscientific (see Eysenck, 1965, chs 3-5; Skinner, 1965; Hilgard, 1965). Other scientistic and reductionist commentators would hold that Freud should have stuck with his research into the neurological conditions of neurotic behaviour, upon which he was occupied early in his career (see Grunbaum, Nagel and others in Hook, 1959).

The humanists also do not accept the concept of an Unconscious mind, but for opposite reasons to those of the behaviourists. They want to investigate consciousness, not legislate it into non-existence. Thus they would hold that when Freud's thinking took its major turn, in 1895, in his study of hysteria with Breuer, he should have gone all the way with it. But instead, according to them, he allowed his revolution in the theory of hysteria to be put into jeopardy. He had succeeded in explaining hysteria in terms of the sexual experiences of the subject. But this success was put in jeopardy by the manoeuvre of making the experiential processes unconscious. Freud thereby kept open the door of compatibility between unconscious processes and neuro-physiological processes. This compatibility, and the possibility of ultimate translation into neurophysiological theories, has made Freud's approach suspect in the eyes of humanistic critics.

Freud summarised his main achievements once in the following manner: 'It seems to be my fate to discover only the obvious; that children have sexual feelings, which every nursemaid knows; and that night dreams are just as much wish fulfilments as day dreams' (quoted in Jones, 1964, p. 299). This offhand remark pinpoints the two areas in which Freud developed his theories to the greatest degree; those of infantile sexuality and the interpretation of dreams. Although whether his analysis of these areas was merely an elaboration of the obvious is certainly arguable; there is nothing obvious about Freud's account of the workings of the Unconscious.

His analysis of infantile sexuality and dreams developed as a concomitant of his work with Breuer in the 1890s on hysteria. The main theme of this work, as we have mentioned, was that hysterical behaviour expressed an abnormal state of anxiety, tension and fear in the subject. And this in turn was caused by thwarted sexuality; some damming up and inhibition of the normal sexual needs and desires of the subject. Sexual needs and desires, or 'libido', were conceived of by Freud and Breuer as physiological drives, 'internal' stimulation which the organism had to act to satiate. Drives were tensions in the organism which had to be reduced. Thus, like the desire to eat, conscious sexual desires, thoughts and emotions were held to arise naturally and spontaneously from the needs of the body. However, if this discharging of energy, this reduction of internal excitation, is checked for any reason, then the subject's consciousness begins to reflect the growing level of tension in his physiology. He becomes anxious, ultimately to the point of serious neurosis and mental breakdown.

The specific blocking and interfering force, according to Freud, was invariably some inhibition erected in the subject's personality early in his life. His sexual development, instead of passing through various stages up to the adult stage, gets halted at some infantile level, possible due to some traumatic seduction before the age of puberty. In adult life the subject still lives his sexual life in terms of the stage at which his development was interfered with. He is frustrated and inhibited from expressing his sexuality as his physiological nature requires. Sooner or later this anxiety bursts through his rational control of his behaviour. He becomes hysterical or, on a lesser scale, neurotically obsessional in his interests and actions. On the basis of what his patients told him, Freud supposed that hysteria was associated with a passive and unpleasurable sexual trauma or seduction in infancy, and that obsession was associated with pleasurable and aggressively active collusion in such a trauma by the subject. But to his dismay at the time, Freud discovered that most of what his patients told him about their early memories of sexual seduction by their parents and others were not true. They were phantasies and fiction invented for his consumption.

In this work the seeds of his later theories about infantile sexuality and dreams were clearly present. So too was the concept of the Unconscious. This concept was that the infantile sexual thoughts and memories of people were repressed in the course of their childhood socialisation. Those repressed or 'dynamically unconscious' thoughts and memories nevertheless exercised an effective and causal role in relation to neurotic behaviour. Freud's discovery that his patients' 'memories' were fictions and phantasies simply inspired him to treat these also as behavioural symptoms of an underlying neurosis. Instead of accepting them as true, and thus basing his own account on fictions and falsehoods, he accepted them precisely as false, and used the true fact of their falsity as evidence in his explanation. The patient's fictions were facts explained by Freud's sexual account and were not self-explanatory. The patients' accounts of their own sexual history was not to be accepted as self-explanatory, but rather as a symptom requiring a deeper and different sexual explanation.

The patients' fictional accounts of their infantile sexual experiences were wish fulfilments, Freud decided. This is what they would *like* to have happened, but which probably did not happen. If these were phantasies, and phantasies were fulfilments of otherwise sublimated and repressed wishes, then why not investigate that great reservoir of phantasy experience—dreams? This line of thinking, and Freud's need to get to the bottom of his own neurosis and depression in the 1890–1900 period, led to his own self-analysis. This in turn issued in one of his major works *The Interpretation of Dreams* (1899) where Freud presented a sexual interpretation of a selection of his own dreams. He wanted to demonstrate how the symbols and meanings of phantasy experiences are in fact caused and generated by sexual frustrations hidden from any kind of consciousness.

Dreams provided Freud with a 'royal road to the Unconscious' (Jones 1964, p. 300). He believed that in dreams the subject has an experience that is determined directly by repressed memories of infancy, particularly the 'prehistoric period' from the age of one to three years, that is normally virtually beyond recall. Dreams are universal phenomena; everybody can report experiencing them at some time or another, but not everybody is neurotic or hysterical. Thus Freud summarised his position by saying that what was seen in the prehistoric period by the infant gives rise to dreams in the normal adult; what was heard gives rise to phantasies that the neurotic adult tells his analyst about; and what was sexually experienced in this period of infancy gives rise to psychoneurosis and other mental abnormalities in the adult. Freud thought that the repeating of what had been experienced in that period was in itself the fulfilment of an unconscious wish or libidinal desire (ibid., p. 304).

Freud was later able to bring his various low and high level theories and insights under the one concept of the Unconscious, interpreted as an instinctual, pleasure-seeking, excitation-discharging 'id', 'it' or 'thing' in English. He seems to have got this concept from a contemporary, Georg Groddeck (1961), who in turn probably found it in the well-known writings of Friederich Nietzsche.

Goddeck's belief was that 'we are "lived" by unknown and uncontrollable forces' according to Freud who endorsed it as follows: 'we need feel no hesitation in finding a place for Groddeck's discovery in the structure of science' (1962, p. 13). Thus every individual conscious 'ego' is largely determined in what he thinks and does by the workings of his unconscious 'id' which to use Freud's words, 'lives' him.

Freud portrayed the conscious ego as a controlling Reality Principle engaged in a life-long losing battle with the id, the uncontrollable force of the Pleasure Principle. This particular statement of his ideas came late in his career (*The Ego and the Id*, 1962, first published in 1923), when his ideas were already established and his intellectual influence on the psychological and psychiatric world was considerable. In this mature statement of his general position Freud drew attention to weakness of the Ego and to the fallacy of merely investigating consciousness, as others in the contemporary German philosophical and psychological community, like Husserl and Jaspers, were advocating. Thus: 'The ego represents what may be called reason and common sense, in contrast to the id, which contains the passions' (ibid., p. 15). And like a rider on a stubborn horse, the ego is obliged to guide the id in the direction that the id wants to go, according to Freud. This is a universal assertion of the basic irrationality of man. Further, special concepts like the Unconscious Id and special kinds of investigations are supposed to be required in order to explain the depths of his irrationality and the shallowness of his rationality. It is to be expected that both conceptual analysis and phenomenology are critical, at least of this feature of Freud's psychology.

Conceptual analysis

The most important statements by conceptual analytic philosophers on Freudian psychology occur in Wittgenstein's *Lectures and Conversations on Aesthetics, Psychology and Religious Belief* (1966), Peters' *The Concept of Motivation* (1958) and MacIntyre's *The Unconscious: A Conceptual Analysis* (1960). It is with these three works that we shall be mainly concerned. However, it is worth pointing out that the number of brief discussions about Freud to be found in the work of many other conceptual analytic philosophers is quite large. Among these Hampshire's comments in *Thought and Action* (1959), Alexander (1955; 1962), Beck (1966), Toulmin (1949) and Wisdom (1957) ought to be mentioned. Wittgenstein, Peters and MacIntyre, broadly speaking, all criticise Freud for not being humanistic and for encouraging reductionist interpretations of his theories. But before we describe and analyse these criticisms it must be pointed out that Freud's ambiguous two-culture fence-sitting results in some ambiguity of interpretation by conceptual analysts. For instance, Hampshire and Beck portray Freud as a theorist who extended the use of humanistic and teleological terms like 'purpose', 'desire' and 'wish', albeit 'unconscious' varieties, to cover a lot more phenomena of human action and behaviour than would otherwise have been able to be conceptualised in this way.

Thus, for the major conceptual analytic commentators, Freudian psychology presents a deterministic picture of man. But for commentators such as Hampshire and Beck, Freudian psychology, while demonstrating that man is determined and hence unfree, also contributes to man's freedom by giving him this knowledge, so that he may act to minimise the effectiveness of the things that determine him.

Hampshire accepts that Freud's theories of the workings of the unconscious mind apply to all men, normal, neurotic or mad. And he accepts that they do not merely apply in a piecemeal and limited fashion to a clearly marked range of abnormal behaviour such as neuroticism. This is a point, as will be seen, upon which other commentators like Peters tend to equivocate. However, the universality of the Unconscious and the universality of its effectiveness, does not mean, as far as Hampshire is concerned, that people cannot know what they are doing and why they are doing it. It does not mean that people's conscious intentions and purposes are always and necessarily ineffective with regard to their actions and behaviour (Hampshire, 1959, pp. 133 and 179). Rather it means that we are not as free as we like to think we are; we are certainly not absolutely free. And further it means that we can increase our degree of freedom by increasing our knowledge about the extent and nature of the determining factors that affect us, and then by taking action to minimise these factors.

Hampshire seems to be implying here that Freudian therapy is a conscious form of liberation from the Unconscious. But Freudians could well object that this is not the case at all. Mere apprehension by the subject of the alleged existence and workings of unconscious wishes, and the subsequent New Year's resolution not to be affected by them ever again, is just too rational for Freudians. This may be relevant to Catholic confessionals but it is not how psycho-analytic therapy is envisaged at all. Man's conscious ego is too weak to overcome the irrational forces within him with one rational decision and at one sitting. Rather he must engage in a long association with his analyst, during which he unconsciously internalises the analyst's account. He reconditions himself to accept the previously unacceptable sexual wishes as his own. And this is an acceptance of a new way of living in the world, seeing the relationship between himself and significant others, like his parents perhaps, in a new way.

It is not a particularly conscious and intellectual re-evaluation of his life, it is more of an unconscious conditioning. The patient must, whether he knows it or not, identify with the analyst's interpretation. His own story and interpretation, as Freud had found, are not to be trusted as accurate information, but as fictional reconstructions. In overcoming the patient's account of his experiences and of his own nature, and in superimposing the psycho-analytic account, the analyst must be prepared to overcome the 'resistance' of the patient. The patient may become depressed, surly, evasive, deceitful, not forthcoming and so on, in this long subtle struggle. But according to Freud, unless this resistance by the patient to the largely unconscious process of identification with the analyst's account is overcome, then the patient will not be cured.

The analysis, far from being seen as a form of conscious and free liberation from determinism, can easily be seen as quite the opposite kind of operation. Rather, it can be seen as an effective 'cure' for neurosis only when the patient's self-conception is redetermined and reconstructed by the enlightened psycho-analytic craftsman in ways that the patient need not be aware. If therapy is effective it is not because it releases man from determinism and allows him to be more rational. The 'cured' man is just as irrationally and unconsciously determined as before, only now in more acceptable 'normal' ways rather than in unacceptable 'neurotic' ones.

Hampshire is right that *some* forms of psycho-analysis can be liberating in the humanistic direction he is thinking of, but it would be a misrepresentation of Freudian theory and therapy to portray *it* in this fashion. But, within conceptual analysis, Hampshire and those who think like him, are in a minority compared with those who think like Wittgenstein, Peters and MacIntyre. Both sub-divisions are humanists, but the former recruit Freud to their humanism, while the latter exile him from theirs.

Wittgenstein, in his conversations and lectures on Freud, was a good deal more suspicious of the liberating nature of Freud's theories and of his therapeutic method in particular. One of the main points he felt obliged to make against Freud was that the analyst's interpretation need not be true in order to effect a 'cure'. It does not matter whether the analyst's account, which is couched in terms of the unconscious, accurately documents the infantile sexual biography of the patient. It is effective as a cure over the long period of analysis, not because it is true and rationally acceptable, but because it is persuasive and emotionally acceptable. Wittgenstein comments that it is easy to see how persuasive and effective the analyst's interpretation can be. It is easy to see how great a relief it must be to an anxious and worried person to be shown how their life has the pattern of a tragedy; 'the tragic working out and repetition of a pattern determined by the primal scene' (1966, p. 51).

But Freud based the truth of his theories on the basis of the effectiveness of his therapy, which meant that the success of the therapy was held to indicate the truth of theory. But if the success of the therapy could also be interpreted as showing the persuasiveness, rather than the truth of the theoretically oriented analyst's interpretation of the patient's early life, then Freud's 'science' is built on sand. Perhaps the same persuasive integration of the patient's early experiences could be provided by an astrologer, or a priest, or a magician; and perhaps the same cure of the neurosis might be produced. Nobody would then argue that this proved the truth of astrological theories, or of theological theories, or of magic. All the more so if, in order to get the patient to accept the astrological account, the astrologist/analyst had to overcome the patient's 'resistance', and win the patient over from the patient's own memories and explanations, to an acceptance of the astrological account.

Yet this is precisely what Freud does. In *The Ego and the Id* he bases the truth of his theory on the therapeutic success it has. This success hinges on overcoming the 'resistance' of the patients, and his reluctance to recognise the existence of buried memories. Or is this resistance merely the patient's dislike of being subtly intimidated and indoctrinated? Freud does not consider this latter possibility, but rather asserts that the phenomenon of resistance, and its therapeutic overthrow, renders his theory 'irrefutable' (1962, p. 4). In view of the fact that resistance and therapeutic success can be interpreted in at least two ways, one endorsing, the other undermining Freud, it was premature of him even to say that his theory was corroborated, as if therapy tested its validity. But to go further and to say that it is 'irrefutable' is to go beyond the pale of science completely. How could his theory remain a scientific one, capable of empirical tests, if it was presumed to be incapable of empirical refutation? Perhaps we should not make too much of this 'Freudian slip' from enthusiastic scientist into unwitting metaphysician. But this is certainly the direction that Wittgenstein felt Freud had drifted. He concluded, in line with what we have been discussing, that therapeutic success was not, in itself, corroboration of Freudian theory. Thus Wittgenstein asserted: 'But there is no way of showing that the whole result of analysis may not be delusion' (1966, p. 44).

The delusion of sanity perhaps? The delusion that one's life fits a certain astrological, or theological, or ideological, or physical, or Freudian pattern (see Blum's Wittgensteinian analysis of therapist—client talk and interaction in Blum, 1970).

Wittgenstein, as we have already seen, was very concerned with the persuasiveness of general theories and patterns, both in philosophical thinking and in everyday thinking. Such theories and patterns get a hold on one's mind and 'bewitch' one's intelligence. Thus it is the duty of the philosopher to fragment the general theory, to smash the unitary model, and to exorcise the malevolent influence of any overall pattern from the inquiring intelligence. The unitary theory of language which he himself presented in the *Tractatus* was the first general theory he dissolved in his later philosophy. And Freud's theory of the mind was another such general theory which required dissolution. Why? Because general theories distort and simply overlook concrete and specific things that we otherwise know to be true in our experience. They run a steam roller over the infinitely diverse humps and bumps of our ordinary knowledge; they simplify it by flattening it all to the same level and reducing it all to the same terms.

The *Tractatus* theory of language flattened all the diverse uses to which language is and can be put. Similarly, Freudian psychology flattens all of the diverse kinds of actions we perform, and the diverse kinds of thoughts, reasons and intentions which go into them. For the author of the *Tractatus*, all meaning is reference, all sentences and concepts do one job of asserting or denying states of affairs. Similarly, for Freud, all actions and thoughts exhibit the paramount influence of the Unconscious; they have only one correct mode of interpretation.

Thus we find Wittgenstein objecting in fairly strong terms to Freud's interpretation of dreams. Freud's interpretation may well hold for this or that dream, but it does not hold for all dreams. Some dreams are quite possibly hallucinated wish fulfilments, but Wittgenstein thinks that it is 'muddled' to oversimplify the picture and say that *all* dreams are of this nature. Freud, he thinks, wanted to find the 'essence' of dreams, and asserted that he had done so. One cannot discover that then the 'essence' of all is merely the fortuitous similarity of some (1966, p. 48).

In any case, according to Wittgenstein, it is hard to see even on Freud's own theory how dreams could be wish-fulfilments of unconscious wishes. They are, after all, hallucinatory diversions, and substitutes for the real enactment of the repressed wish. So the wish is cheated after all, and not fulfilled. Or perhaps it is the repressive censor in the mind, in the customs post between the conscious and the Unconscious, which is cheated and deceived.

Wittgenstein asserts that Freud does not make it very clear. And he concludes: 'the dream is not an hallucinated satisfaction of anything' (ibid., p. 47). Further, he makes the telling point that there are numerous dreams in the experience of all of us that are straightforward sexual phantasies, in which case there is no diversionary hallucinating going on. Here it is not necessary for the analyst to reveal the sexual nature of the symbolism, as for instance in dreams about umbrellas and other allegedly 'phallic symbols'. In a sexual dream, *ipso facto*, there is no hidden sexual meaning. But Wittgenstein points out that Freud rarely, if ever, described and analysed this common type of dream. Perhaps it was because in such dreams no wish is cheated, no censor is avoided, nothing is symbolised, no hidden meanings require interpretation, and no support is given to Freud's theory at all.

Wittgenstein concluded by airing the possibility that there are many types of dreams and no overall, over-simple theory could explain all of them. What goes for dreams goes for actions too. For Wittgenstein and subsequent conceptual analysts there can be no overall deterministic theory of action. There can be no theory, of the behaviourist type, which avoids any consideration of consciousness and meaning. Nor can there be a theory, of the Freudian type, which flirts with an analysis of consciousness and meaning, only to demonstrate how they are determined by forces and processes beyond all consciousness, beyond all meaning, and beyond all reason.

Dreams are self-explanatory, they do not symbolise or mean or refer to anything beyond themselves. Their meaning, such as it is, like that of an absent-minded doodle, is contained within them. Sexual dreams are but one example of this, they are directly self-explanatory. Actions too, like dreams, are self-explanatory, only more obviously so in the sense that they are consciously generated, and do not merely 'happen' to a passive and slumbering consciousness. The meaning of actions, and their explanation, is contained within them, so as to speak. There is no need to look elsewhere, or beyond, or below, for hidden meaning or for hidden causes, according to conceptual analysis.

The conceptual analytic position on action and its explanation has already been discussed in a number of places in this book, and we need not go much further into it here. The position is a very rationalistic one. Thus if a person announces an intention to do something, and then goes ahead and does it, Wittgenstein, Ryle and subsequent exponents of the position would hold that the explanation, or meaning of the action stands revealed in our comprehension of the intention, or of the reason for which it was performed. This would be an ideal case. Many actions may be a lot more confusing than this to the observer, if the intention is not announced by the actor and if the observer has to guess or interpret it. Actions may be confusing to the actor himself; he may be trying to do a number of different things with the one action; or he may be acting in terms of a situation which he cannot fully grasp and make up his mind about. There are infinite gradations in the classification of actions from the clear-headed to the absent-minded, from the purposeful to the 'purpose-less'. The point about them all is that they have their explanation and their meaning in whatever purposes and reasons the actor may be credited with. Thus different actions have different explanations, because they are performed for infinitely diverse reasons. No one theory, particularly a theory of extra-experiential determinism of thought and action like Freud's, can be right.

Wittgenstein's objections to Freud tended to be more in the sphere of thoughts—dreams, wishes, etc.—than in the sphere of actions. But exactly the same kind of argument has been applied in the sphere of actions, by subsequent conceptual analysts like Peters, who, following Wittgenstein and Ryle, has objected to Freud's explanation of behaviour.

Peters's thesis in *The Concept of Motivation* has already been referred to in respect of his discussion of physiological drive theories and behaviourist psychology. Although he ultimately discusses Freud in more or less the same terms, that is as a physiological drive theorist, he at first equivocates and tries to recruit Freud to the kind of conception of explanation that Ryle proposed. This, it will be recalled, was the conception that only phenomena which can be said to 'happen to' the actor and which confuse him, can be explained by a deterministic theory which cites processes and mechanisms beyond the experience and consciousness of the actor. Hamlyn applied this piecemeal conception of deterministic explanation of human thought and action in the sphere of perception. Peters attempts to apply it in the sphere of behaviour. But before damning Freud for producing an overall rather than a piecemeal theory of behaviour, he first tried the opposite tack, portraying Freud's theory as a piecemeal one.

Freud provided some basis for this kind of analysis in one of his major works *The Psychopathology of Everyday Life* (1965). Here he explained piecemeal, abnormal and pathological features of everyday experience, things like making mistakes, forgetting things, making slips on the tongue and so on, as caused by unconscious repressions and processes. Thus Peters recruited Freud to Ryle's piecemeal and humanistic conception of explanation of behaviour in the following way. He states (1958, p. 11; see also 1956-7) that Freud:

> only intended to explain by reference to unconscious mental processes cases where the purposive rule-following model breaks down. He did not think—and often explicitly denied—that

this sort of explanation can be appropriately given for everything—for cases where a man acts as well as for cases where something happens to a man.

The other evidence that Peters cites for this piecemeal interpretation of Freud's theories is the dualism that Freud erected between the Ego and the Id, or the Reality Principle and the Pleasure Principle, respectively. These are, in effect, two totally distinct explanatory principles which Freud could have invoked depending on circumstances. Thus, where ordinary rational and purposive actions are involved, Freud could talk of the triumph of the Ego and its Reality Principle over the unconscious and irrational forces bubbling within. However, where abnormalities and pathological forms of behaviour such as neuroticism and hysteria are involved, Freud could talk of the triumph of the Pleasure Principle, the irrational and unruly Id driving us from deep within our Unconscious (ibid., pp. 71 and 74).

But the evidence that Freud proposed his theory on the Unconscious mind as an overall deterministic theory, ultimately based on physiological factors which are present in every person, is overwhelming. And Peters ultimately comes around to this interpretation of Freud, abandoning the pragmatic, piecemeal and humanist interpretation. The difference between the neurotic and the normal person, even given that it is easy to make such a distinction which it certainly is not, can only be one of degrees and not of kind. It is thus reasonable that a theory formed to account for neuroticism, like Freud's, was generalised to apply to all people, normal and neurotic.

For instance, Freud believed that 'ordinary' and 'reasonable' and 'everyday' character traits of, let us say, cleanliness, orderliness and obstinacy, which are not at all abnormal, pathological or neurotic, were caused by infantile anal eroticism. That is, the infant's delight in holding back faeces, disapproved of by the parents, would be, according to Freud, sublimated in later life by personality characteristics such as the holding back of compliance with the wishes and arguments of others' obstinacy. Or the infant's delight in playing with, hoarding of and counting of his faeces would be sublimated in later life in an interest in hoarding, counting and dealing with money, which on this account would be a 'substitute object'.

Obstinacy is an everyday and 'normal' character trait, as is an interest in money in any but the most primitive tribal societies. In our industrialised market society 'money-grabbing' may not only be socially tolerated, it may be socially approved and encouraged. That is, it may be 'normal' in the sense of socially accepted, while at the same time being 'abnormal' and pathologically obsessive on the other criteria, such as the ultimate stability of those personalities involved.

In any case, even if a difference between neuroticism and normality can be precisely drawn, it cannot exclude the possibility that a large minority of any given population, even a majority, could be classified as neurotic.

Normality is more of a standard than a fact. The existence of a standard of 'good car-driving' is consistent with the fact that most of the time most drivers break the law in small ways and drive badly. Similarly, but more generally, the existence of standards of normal behaviour is consistent with the fact, or the possibility, that most people most of the time ignore the standard in small ways and act in neurotic ways. This is not an abstract hypothesis; in present day America and England the numbers of diagnosed neurotics and people who are 'mentally ill' in one way and another form a significant proportion of the population. Add to this the fact that, like crimes, most neurotic activity (or rather activity reportable and label-able as 'criminal', 'neurotic', etc.) actually goes undiagnosed and unreported and the concept of a large minority of the population being neurotic and mentally ill, all or part of the time, can be seen in its true light, not as an abstract hypothesis but as a concrete and current social phenomenon and social problem. Whether Freud's theories are relevant to this social problem is a topic we must discuss in chapter 7.

But the point at the moment is that Freud's theories, good or bad, are universalist and not piecemeal. One cannot single out a type of personality or a type of action about which a Freudian explanation cannot be given. Far from his theories only applying to the mentally ill, and not to more normal people and phenomena, as Peters at first implied, it is far more interesting to interpret Freud's theories as applying the other way round. That is, some modern psychiatrists would say that Freud's theories only apply to normal, and paranormal phenomena like neuroticism, and that they do not apply to real mental illnesses like schizophrenia and other types of psychosis.

Clinical categories, particularly the division of abnormal mental and behavioural states into the extreme types, psychoses, and the less extreme types, neuroses, are descriptive categories. They are applied loosely according to the phenomenological criteria of whether the patient appears to share our common world or not. The neurotic does, and the psychotic does not. At this point we may recall Merleau-Ponty's equation of subjective mental state with the subject's existential state of living in and perceiving an intersubjective world; the equation of subjective mind with intersubjective world. Crowcroft, who is in no sense a phenomenological psychiatrist, relies on some kind of equation like this when he attempts to distinguish neuroses from psychoses. The neurotic can be said to be 'in' his mind and in our common world; the psychotic, on the other hand, is 'not only out of his mind, but also out of our world' (1967, p. 21). Freud concentrated almost exclusively on the para-normal states of neurosis when developing his explanatory concepts. He rarely applied his ideas to psychotic states like schizophrenia and his subsequent followers have not had much success in this direction either. Fenichel (1945), although optimistic about the possibilities of psycho-analysing psychoses like schizophrenia, admits some of the differences and difficulties in contrast with the analysis of neurosis (e.g. p. 416). There is a simple and obvious reason for this. Freudian psycho-analytic therapy can only take place within a 'normal' frame of reference. The patient must be willing to talk, to perform free associations, and to recall memories for his analyst. This is easy to achieve with a neurotic, but it may be virtually impossible to achieve with a psychotic, who may be violent, who may choose not to talk or co-operate at all, and so on.

Far then, from being a piecemeal theory of oddities and abnormalities, Freudian theory could well be seen as an explanation of everything *except* the oddities and abnormalities of psychosis. It is wrong to confine Freud's deterministic and non-humanistic account to peripheral and pathological forms of behaviour, and to say that Freud never meant to explain the vast majority of normal conscious and purposeful forms of behaviour. It is arguable that the reverse is the case, and that Freud's theory only applies to rational and purposeful forms of behaviour, within which one could include mild neuroses. His deterministic theory competes with rational explanations over the vast majority of normal and para-normal actions. But it has to opt out of explaining uncommon and fringe types of behaviour such as psychotic behaviour. However, it would not be correct to say that Freudians present no theoretical account of psychoses; they do, but it is not 'backed up' by therapeutic success (whatever such success is worth and whatever 'cure' means).

Peters might think that Freud's theory cannot be applied to normal purposeful behaviour, and psychiatrists might think that his theory cannot be applied to psychoses, but there seems little reason to doubt that Freud meant his theory to apply to all men, whether they are normal, neurotic or psychotic. His theory was a universal one. All men have an unconscious; all men pass through various stages in their sexual development in infancy, and so on. Ultimately the Id's drive is an instinctual one, deriving from the biological sexual constitution of human beings. Similarly the various Ego-functions, which censure and repress the workings of the Id, also ultimately have their basis in facts about human neurological and nerve systems, according to Freud. And it is to this interpretation that Peters finally comes around. He comes around in this way in order to put Freud's theory in the same anti-humanist reductionist category as behaviourism; to criticise it, and to reject it in favour of a humanistic approach.

Peters and, as we shall see, MacIntyre both try to demonstrate that Freud's theory of the primary processes of the mind was couched in the form of, and evolved in the light of, his earlier attempt to provide an explanatory theory of the nervous system. In this line of theory and research, at the beginning of his career, he conceived of the nervous system in mechanistic and even hydraulic terms (Jones, 1964, p. 10). He postulated the existence of basic nerve entities called 'neurones, which carried information and energy to and from the brain, from drives within the organism and from stimulation outside of the organism. The theory he evolved later pictured the continuous flow of subconscious wishes coming up to encounter consciousness, and to express themselves in consciousness in a camouflaged and symbolic manner. This later theory was a kind of decoration of his earlier theory of energy flow. It was merely the statement, in psychological terms, of an energy and excitation flow which, in principle, could be pinned down primarily in neurophysiological terms. 'Instinctual wishes' of the Unconscious that are never known as such, that are caused by physiology and never actually wished by the person, is really a concept that can only be describing matter in motion. Thus Peters believes that Freud 'never really abandoned Hobbes' hoary hypothesis ... that psychical states were reflections of material elements subject to the laws of motion' (1958, p. 65). Rather, such overall causal explanations are 'otiose when we know the point of a person's action' (ibid., p. 11). That is, our ordinary understanding of another's action as purposive, reasonable and intentional ought to be sufficient for us. Humanistic knowledge ought to be sufficient; we should not think that we can gain any more understanding by resorting to the para-scientific metaphysics of materialism and determinism with regard to human action, as did the behaviourists, and now, it appears, Freud also. This is Peters's blandly asserted, but not on that account false or unattractive, humanistic thesis.

MacIntyre, in *The Unconscious—A Conceptual Analysis* (1960), takes more or less the same line as Peters, but more consistently. Throughout he portrays Freud's theory as universal and deterministic, and he never dallies with the idea that it is some kind of Rylean piecemeal humanism. MacIntyre writes: 'It is my contention that Freud preserved the view of the mind as a piece of machinery and merely wrote up in psychological terms what had originally been intended as a neurological theory' (ibid., p. 22; see also 1955; 1971, ch. 3). Freudian psychology is thus mechanistic, physiologically based and universally deterministic: 'The whole structure of his theory leads him to see an omnipresent causation exerted upon conscious life by the unconscious' (1960, p. 90).

MacIntyre is therefore critical of the concepts of the unconscious and of repression when used in a theoretical explanation which is extra-experiential and deterministic. However, he is prepared to accept that these concepts can have a purely descriptive, as opposed to explanatory, role. That is, like the concepts 'neurosis' and 'psychosis', the terms 'unconscious' and 'repression' may be used in causal or in clinical descriptions without implying any explanatory theory. When we come to discuss psychiatric theorists influenced by existential phenomenology it will be seen that they take the same line as this, and agree to a descriptive use of terms like 'unconscious' but not to a theoretical explanation in such terms.

The explanation of thought and action proposed by Freud stands condemned by Peters and MacIntyre as much as by Wittgenstein, as a 'bewitching' general theory which must be undermined and opposed. And yet both commentators oppose this general theory with an equally general and universalist theory, what amounts to an ontological theory asserting that man has a different kind of being than things. For instance, Peters opposed a deterministic explanation of man's behaviour by asserting that man is, on the contrary, a purposeful, rule-following animal, whose action should be understood in terms of this general consideration. Man in society, he wrote 'is like a chess-player writ large' (1958, p. 7). Clearly he does not believe that all general theories, or all ontological commitments, 'bewitch'; some do, some do not: materialistic, determinist and reductionist ones do, humanist and teleological ones do not.

MacIntyre is no less explicitly committed to a general type of humanism. For instance, he compares 'the specifically human', and explanations in terms of the 'specifically human' phenomena of purposes, reasons and so on, with explanations which only invoke 'nervous system plus muscles' (1960, p. 98), or some other category of physical facts. The 'specifically human' resides in the ordinary language concepts with which we talk about human intentions and actions. When we describe actions in ordinary conversation, we are also accounting for them, interpreting and explaining them. The only trouble with this conceptual analytic approach to the explanation and description of action is the complacent presumption that often accompanies it that we always explain and describe our own and others' actions well and sufficiently, when we most often do not, and do not want to.

Our ordinary conversational descriptions and explanations do not aspire to any insights. They are not inspired by any serious or therapeutic concern, for instance, and are for the most part superficial, and acknowledged to be so. But interpersonal understanding, and explanations and descriptions of actions as purposeful and intentional, can be deepened beyond the level of off-hand gossip. Given this, then the conceptual analytic approach falls into the same kind of category as does existential phenomenology. The difference between their respective types of humanism is one of style. The self image of the one is that of toying wittily with problems of thought and action, whereas the self image of the other is that of wrestling profoundly with the same sort of problems. But this is an over-simplification. Wittgenstein's style was always that of the worried thinker, encouraged by the profundity of his questions and depressed by the superficiality of his answers.

However, superficial or not, all that need be noted for the moment is that MacIntyre's and Peters's conceptual analytic objections to Freudian concepts and explanations spring from and invoke a single and simple theory of the nature of man, to wit, that man is a purposive, reason-giving social actor. Their conceptual analytic endorsement of the diversity of actions and intentions is based on this theory. And further, their conceptual analytic objections to general theories, merely because they are general theories, are shown up as disingenuous since they rely on a general humanistic theory.

Phenomenology

If one had to point to a major difference between the humanistic philosophies of conceptual analysis and existential phenomenology in the area of Freudian psychology it would not merely be one of style. The fact is that the critiques offered by the former have had only an intellectual and philosophical influence, whereas the critiques offered by the latter have had practical influences. That is, forms of psychotherapy, and psychiatric theories have arisen acknowledging the influence of existential phenomenology, and attempting to put this conception of man to work in the field of mental illness. No such therapeutic and theoretical developments have occurred in psychotherapy as a result of the work of conceptual analytic philosophers.

Sartre's outline of 'existential psycho-analysis' in *Being and Nothingness* found a response among psychiatrists and the work of Laing and Cooper might be mentioned in particular (see chapter 7 below). Karl Jaspers, himself both an existentialist philosopher and psychotherapist, developed a similar theory of hermeneutic, interpretive and humanistic psycho-analysis in his *General Psychopathology* (1963). Jaspers and Sartre both had criticised Freud. Heidegger, who has never written on Freud, and who has never explicitly proposed a programme for a therapeutic alternative, nevertheless has been most influential in psychotherapy. This influence may be seen in the work of Binswanger and Minkowski, among others (see chapter 7 below). Conceptual analysis, by contrast, has had up to now a virtually negligible influence on psychotherapy with its critique of Freud. Partly this is because it does not explicitly propose a therapeutic alternative, and partly it is also due to the fact that conceptual analysis is a more recent school than existential phenomenology. The latter had had its humanising influence in psychotherapy in the inter-war years, when conceptual analysis was still a seed being tended in its Oxbridge hothouse, primarily by Wittgenstein along with Wisdom and Ryle and others. Psychotherapy was one area it could not claim to have revolutionised in its post-war development as a philosophical school.

The main phenomenological critique of Freudian psychology which rationalised some developments in psychotherapy, and which generated others, are to be found in the work of Sartre and Merleau-Ponty. Merleau-Ponty's *The Structure of Behaviour*, Sartre's *Being and Nothingness*, and *A Sketch for a Theory of the Emotions*, all contain discussions of Freud's concepts, and particularly of the concept of the Unconscious (see also Husserl (1970a) pp. 385-7).

Both Sartre and Merleau-Ponty's criticisms focus on the idea that what is conscious can be caused and determined by what is not. They dislike the idea that experience and purposes can be determined by processes beyond the knowledge, and beyond the possibility of knowledge, of the subject of them. For existential phenomenology it is a confusion even to talk of an Unconscious, let alone to say that it could exist in a causal relationship to consciousness. Rather, the human being decides what he will do, and decides what he will make of himself on the basis of what he believes to be the case about the realities he is surrounded by, his perceived world; he is freely active and conscious, respectively. To accept Freudian concepts would be to reject this. The existential phenomenologist believes that the universal and distinctive feature of man is his freedom and his consciousness. The Freudian believes that, on the contrary, man's universal and distinguishing feature is his Unconscious and his lack of freedom in respect of it. We must look at Freud's concept of the Unconscious a little more closely, and then we can turn to Sartre's rather convoluted critique of it.

Freud sometimes presented the concept of consciousness and the unconsciousness on the model of Kant's concepts of 'phenomena' and 'noumena'. At the risk of parodying Kant's extremely complicated and internally rather inconsistent background to the two concepts (i.e. his attempt to reconcile a doctrine of 'transcendental idealism' with a position of 'empirical realism'), his idea is as follows. We do not experience the external world neat, as it were. Our sensory experience of it is always and everywhere structured in terms of the categories of space and time, which are not themselves derived from experience. Categorical-sensory knowledge is thus limited and bounded, it is not capable of direct access to the external world as it is in itself. Man only ever knows the appearances of things, never the things in themselves: that is to say, he can only ever know 'phenomena' and never 'noumena'. Distinctions between what were essentially regulative principles of knowledge in Kant, become, in Freud, distinctions between substantial modes of reality. Thus Freud (1938, p. 542) stated, for instance: 'The unconscious is the true psychic reality, in its inner nature it is just as much unknown to us as the reality of the external world, as it is just as imperfectly communicated to us by the reports of our sense organs.'

In Freud's two main statements on the Unconscious (1962; 1953, pp. 54-63), he introduced this concept by examining the phenomena of hypnotism and dreams. He compared our lack of consciousness in these cases with our lack of consciousness, our lack of awareness, in other sorts of cases. These latter cases would be, for instance, when we think of something, then it drifts, 'out of our minds', away from our attention, and suddenly we think of it again. As far as Freud is concerned, this sort of case illustrates that at least some application of the term 'unconscious' is appropriate. For he could say that what we were thinking of became unconscious for a few moments. It was not gone completely, but lay around ready to be spotlighted again; it rested in the wings, off-stage in the mind, together with virtually all of our knowledge, memories, skills, etc. Only a few thoughts occupy the spotlight of consciousness at any one time. The rest of what we know, and of what we have thought of before, must be waiting in the wings, in the 'latent' sphere of the mind which Freud called the 'pre-conscious' (see also Dunlap, 1965; Ellenberger; 1970; Martin, 1964; Machotka, 1964; Siegler, 1967; Whallon, 1964-5; Laplanche and Pontalis, 1968; on the Unconscious).

Freud compared the kind of unconscious mind which we can infer, or so he thought, from these sorts of mental goings-on, with the unconscious mind we can infer the existence of from dreams and hypnosis. This is far less straightforward, and altogether more devious. Here the term 'unconscious' ceases to have an innocuous descriptive role, and it begins to take on a more arguable explanatory role. It is a well known phenomenon that a person can be ordered to do a specific action while under an hypnotic trance, to be performed when he has been brought out of the trance. When, subsequently, the subject, now fully conscious, performs the action he was instructed to perform, he cannot explain why and may appear puzzled by it all. Or perhaps he may invent some justification for it on the spot, and hence 'rationalise' it. What attracted Freud about the phenomenon of post-hypnotic suggestion was the model of mental processes it suggested. The subject's action is caused, but he is unaware of the causation, and may even rationalise it away with his own demonstrably weak reasons, which get nowhere near the real underlying cause.

This is precisely the model that Freud appropriated for the workings of the sexually and physiologically based Unconscious. It too could be portrayed as causing a person's action in a way that the person may be completely confused and otherwise ignorant about. In order to justify and rationalise his action, the person may invent some reason and purpose to satisfy both himself and anybody else involved. Thus he would unwittingly be dressing up the sexual drives of the Unconscious, the wolf in the sheep's clothing of acceptable reasons, or obsessions, or ultimately unacceptable hysteria. That is, he would do anything but call the wolf a wolf; he is condemned to call it a sheep because he is simply ignorant of its real nature, unless, so the story goes, he sees a Freudian psycho-analyst who will let him in on the secret.

The attraction of this model of mental processes for Freud allowed him to invoke the phenomenon of 'resistance' which we already mentioned as arising during the course of therapeutic analysis, as evidence for his theory rather than as evidence against it. Resistance is simply the patient's commitment to his false rationalisations and self-justifications being overcome. That these need to be purged from the patient's mind with some effort on the part of the analyst, convinced Freud of the dynamic and deep-rooted nature of the unconscious processes. We have seen that Wittgenstein was suspicious that the overcoming of the patient's resistance was simply the triumph of persuasion and not of truth, the supplanting of the 'delusion' of purpose and consciousness, with the delusion of determinism and of the Unconscious. But Freud took the opposite view; for him, in overcoming resistance, the analyst is diminishing the repression which conceals the workings of the Unconscious from the patient's unconsciousness.

There are, then, at least two senses of the term 'unconscious' in Freud's writings (1962, pp. 50-2). One is explanatory and the other is descriptive. Laing in *The Self and Others* (1961, p. 7) writes in a similar vein:

> It becomes imperative at this point to make a phenomenological distinction between two quite different usages of 'unconscious': 1) The term 'unconscious' may connote dynamic structures, functions, mechanisms, processes, etc. postulated to account for (explain) a person's actions and/or his experiences. Concepts of such meta-experiential structures, functions, mechanisms or processes can be used to 'explain' what experientially is either conscious or unconscious. These concepts are outside the realm

> of phenomenology, but depend upon a correct phenomenology for their starting point; 2) 'Unconscious' may refer to a mode of primary awareness of which the person is not usually reflectively aware [see also Laing's reformulation of this analysis in the revised edition of this book, 1969, p. 7].

The latter sense is used in causal or clinical descriptions of the latent and preconscious aspects of a person's state of mind. In this respect even terms like 'unconscious wish' and 'repressed wish' have a fairly straightforward meaning, and can be used without further commitments to theories being implied. Thus a repressed or unconscious wish could be said to be one that we have entertained, in some form or another, but which now we have forgotten about. More than this, we may have purposefully decided to forget about it. However, it may haunt us from the 'back of our minds', in the same way that conscience, or knowledge of right and wrong, or knowledge of how to breathe, haunts us.

But the former explanatory sense invokes a theory about the activity of the dynamically repressed areas of the mind (1962, p. 5), and it is this theory which MacIntyre for conceptual analysis, and Sartre and Laing for existential phenomenology, all object to. On the other hand, they all accept the validity of descriptive, as opposed to explanatory, uses of the concept 'unconscious'.

Sartre is very critical of the confusions that arise out of Freud's venture in the back-stage explanatory mechanics of the mind (see also Schutz, 1962, p. 241; 1970, pp. 14-15). And yet he is amenable to the more loose and non-committal descriptive applications of a term like 'unconscious'. As regards the unconscious mechanics of the mind, Sartre simply asserts that Freud must be wrong on this. Relying on a Cartesian-type of argument, Sartre asserts that consciousness is the distinctive feature of man, not the possession of an unconscious, and further, that consciousness is always potential self-consciousness. That is, in principle, if a person is conscious of something they must be capable of being conscious that they are conscious of it. If I know something, it is a criterion of whether I really know it or not, that I can know, by a self-conscious reflection, that I know it, or at least I can be self-consciously aware that I am claiming, or assuming, or presuming something to be the case. As far as Sartre is concerned, there is no sense in pre-fixing the term 'conscious' with 'un-' in the way that Freud did; it is like calling something 'not-water', when what is really being specified is 'fire'.

Freud, of course, was the complete anti-Cartesian. He did not think that a conscious mind was the distinguishing feature of man, in terms of which man must be understood. He thought that an *unconscious* mind was man's distinguishing feature through which he could be understood. Neither did he think that man's distinguishing consciousness must imply self-consciousness. On the contrary, man's distinguishing feature of his unconscious mind implied no self-consciousness at all (apart from an intensive, extensive and expensive resort to psycho-analysis, that is).

Sartre held the idea of a type of consciousness which is ignorant of itself, such as Freud's idea of the Unconscious, to be 'absurd' (1966, p. lxi). It involves the idea of intentions and purposes which are not known about by the agencies allegedly pursuing them. This is most obviously the case with the concept of 'unconscious wishes'. These are alleged to come from an Id which cannot be said to have wished them, and to determine an Ego which cannot be said to know them as wishes, or to know them at all, under any description. The Id is not self-conscious; the Ego is not self-conscious. How about the censor function? This was appointed by Freud as the agency which 'represses' the stream of inner stimulation from the Id, which attempts to censor its explicitly sexual content, and to restrain its pleasure-seeking influence. Occasionally Freud also represented this censor function as a Super-ego, like a conscience, an internalised Father/God figure and morality-giver to the subject. But this is a rather different sort of concept, and one which sociologists like Parsons have resorted to in order to explain how society controls the behaviour of the individual. The censor function, however, came to be portrayed by Freud as part of the biologically based Unconscious, and not as part of the sociologically influenced conscious Ego. It may even be said to be located in the Ego, according to Freud, but the subject cannot be said to be aware of it.

Sartre discussed the concept of the censor when he dealt with the notion of 'bad-faith', or 'self-deception', in *Being and Nothingness* (1966, pp. 56-86). The censor, for Sartre, exemplifies bad-faith. It is a kind of consciousness. After all, it must be discerning and know what it is that it is repressing, and also what it is that it is allowing through to full consciousness. And yet the other aspect of its purpose is to hide what it is doing from full consciousness. And this, for Sartre, must involve the censor function hiding what it is doing from itself. Sartre expresses this point in a somewhat convoluted reply to the hypothetical question as to what kind of self-consciousness the censor can possibly have. He wrote that 'It must be the consciousness (of) being conscious of the drive to be repressed, but precisely *in order not to be conscious of it*' (ibid., p. 64).

Sartre held that self-deception is a comprehensible project of the whole human personality. It is something that one does to oneself. There is no need, on the contrary, as Freud did, to 'cut the psychic whole into two' (ibid., p. 61). So that I am the Ego but I am not the Id. Nor is there any need, according to Sartre, to theorise about repression and censoring as completely unthinking mechanisms by which one half of the divided whole, unconscious Id, produces its effects in the other half, the conscious Ego.

Rather, there is a need for simply attending to a person's consciousness, which, for an existential phenomenologist, is the same as attending to the person's existence, his life in his world. There is a need, in psychotherapy in particular, to attend to the strategies, plans and purposes, jumbled or clear, lying behind people's actions. We must consult a consciousness, not an Unconscious. We must attend to the way in which each of us chooses the kind of person we are in the way that we project ourselves into our thoughts and actions, and in the way that we channel our life into roles and shapes which have a social significance for others. For we may even choose madness, and we may easily choose neurosis. There is need, in short, as Sartre states, for an 'existential psycho-analysis' which 'rejects the hypothesis of the unconscious' (ibid., p. 699) and which, rather, is an analysis of consciousness, which is to say, an analysis of a man's existence.

This is not a replacement of one piece of naivety with another. The axiom that man is irrationally determined is certainly being replaced, here, by the axiom that man is rational and free. But this is merely a recognition that man can act purposefully, can think what he wants, and can act on the basis of what he thinks. Freedom is not a good, it is a necessity; and rationality does not guarantee that man will give soundly judged reasons for his actions; he may give very unsound or confused reasons, and he may even give terrible reasons (i.e. be 'irrational'). The necessity of viewing man as free is only a reminder that he generates his own action, but he may do this in response to coercion and the threat of death, therefore this concept of freedom is compatible with slavery, to take the most extreme example. Even the slave is a free man on this definition, for ultimately it is *he* who submits and *he* who produces the action called 'submission'. Similarly, to regard man as rational is simply to acknowledge that what he does, and what he makes of himself, whatever that may be, he does so with his eyes at least partly open, and for reasons. Thus on this definition, even the most irrational among us, those who are raving mad, are rational. People who are called 'mad' have their reasons for thinking what they think and for acting the way that they do. These may or may not have been very good reasons to start with. They may have got progressively more flimsy and strange as the person got further into his mad existence, his mad role and his mad world. They may be hidden deliberately in life and phantasies, or they may be lost beneath confusions and uncertainties. But they remain reasons nonetheless.

Existential psycho-analysis operates on this presumption of the ultimately reasoned, and hence comprehensible, nature of 'mental illness', and can claim some success (see for example, Cooper, 1968). Its therapy is therefore oriented at eliminating the 'causes' of illness only in the precisely humanistic sense of eliminating the reasons for going mad. The intolerable situation which makes madness the only rational way out for the trapped person is the main point of attack for the therapist. The patient's world is made more tolerable. The threatening nature of the patient's social world, embodied in the interference with his life and personality by significant others such as members of his family, perhaps, is minimised.

We will discuss this therapeutic approach in relation to sociological theories of the social generation of mental illness in the following chapter, but it might be noted here that Sartre, despite the changes in his philosophic interests and standpoints since *Being and Nothingness*, still holds to the same conception of existential psycho-analysis and of mental illness. For example, introducing a study of his own writings by Laing and Cooper (1968), two English psychotherapists, Sartre endorsed their work and defined mental illness as 'the outcome which the free organism, in its total unity, contrives in order to be able to live an intolerable situation'.

Previous to the critique of Freud and the statement of the existential alternative in *Being and Nothingness*, Sartre had given a preview of these ideas in his discussion of emotions, This piece of work has already been examined in respect of Sartre's criticisms of William James's physiologically reductionist theory of emotion (see chapter 4 above). It was pointed out then that Sartre, in this work, was beginning to revise his conception of consciousness in line with Heidegger's concept of 'being-in-the-world', or existence. Thus emotional consciousness was asserted by Sartre (1962b, p. 91) to be a mode of existence, or of 'being-in-the-world'. Emotion thus is not an accident that 'happens to' a person of which there is a physical cause, but an organised and meaningful way of looking at, and acting in, the world, which has a reason. Ordinary emotional thought and action, as much as extraordinary 'mentally ill' emotional thought and action, is a rational production by the actor and is rationally comprehensible by others. That which we normally call 'irrational', like fits of anger, periods of depression, fears, pleasure and joy are all rational. They are meaningful to the subject, and can be meaningfully communicated—or rather, irrespective of whether or not we intend to communicate them, something is seen, interpretations are made of our bodily and facial expressions and states of mind by other people. Emotions have a point, a reason, an intentional object. Wittgenstein (1967, pp. 86-7) took a similar line to Sartre when he pointed out: 'Among emotions the directed might be distinguished from the undirected. Fear *at* something, joy *over* something. This something is the object, not the cause of the emotion'. Emotions, for both of them, are *about* something. A person is angry at this, is overjoyed at that, feels pleased 'because ...', loves this, hates that, and so on. And this, to Sartre, is because emotion is a form of consciousness, it is a way of being aware; and to be conscious or to be aware, as Brentano and Husserl had asserted, means to be conscious *of* something, and to be aware *of* something. Whether that something can be said to exist for other people besides the subject is a different matter.

'Somethings', like ghosts or centaurs, exist 'in the minds' of the people who think about them mostly in the mode of 'imaginary somethings', not as intersubjectively and tangibly real somethings. But then God and the Devil are really existent for a large proportion of the Earth's population, and a ghost may be real enough to cause heart attacks among the nervous among us. The existential reality of God, the Devil and ghosts, their meaning for people, is only tangentially related to their physical existence or non-existence, their material presence or absence. It is with meaningful intentional objectivity that existential psycho-analysis is concerned, not meaningless and mute material objectivity. It is with the human world, a world we are conscious of, and not the sensorily and theoretically abstract world of physics, that the existential phenomenologist is concerned.

Freudian psychology, however, leads us away from the human world. It leads us away from the world we are conscious of, away from our conscious being in the world, and away from the intentional objectivities of consciousness. Freud leads us instead to the world of the Unconscious; and Sartre, with the existentialist, phenomenologist and Cartesian in him protesting, will not be led. According to Sartre (1962b, p. 51):

> The psychoanalytic interpretation conceives the conscious phenomenon as the symbolic realisation of a desire repressed by the censor. Note that, for consciousness, the desire is *not implicated in its symbolic realisation.*

That is, there is, on the one hand, an Unconscious wish, such as the son's Oedipal wish to have sex with his mother, and there is, on the other hand, the conscious wish that the son may have, for instance, to please his mother by running errands for her. On the Freudian account the former desire causes the latter desire, and the latter desire symbolises the former. Like a hunter reading trails in the forest, or an archaeologist deciphering hieroglyphics, the psychoanalyst can 'read off', so as to speak, the Unconscious wish from the conscious one. The subject who, allegedly, has both wishes cannot read off the one from the other, because he is not a trained psychoanalyst.

Sartre is prepared to admit that, to use our example, the errand running desire may 'stand for' or symbolise some other desire or wish in the depths or in the confusions of the subject's consciousness, but he refused to accept that a conscious desire could stand for an unconscious one. Thus 'it would be better to recognise frankly that whatever is going on in consciousness can receive its explanation nowhere but from consciousness itself' (ibid., p. 55). He believed that, while Freudian analysts denied this in theory, they proceeded on this basis in their analysis. Existential psycho-analysis is thus merely a development from what Sartre sees as the inherent contradictions in Freudian psychology, bringing the theoretical rationale into line with the therapeutic practice. If the practice is 'flexible research into the intra-conscious relation between symbolisation and symbol' (ibid., p. 54), it is self-contradictory to go on insisting in theory that the symbolisation goes on in the Unconscious and the symbol is thus caused to occur in consciousness. This makes the relation between them extra-conscious. To get back to the example, if the subject has Oedipal wishes, why must we presume that he has not conscious knowledge of them, and that the only relevant knowledge that he does have is of desires that he does not even realise are camouflages? Could he not suspect his own motives in doing certain things, and be frightened or confused about them? Why must repression be presumed to be unconscious? Is it not more reasonable to relate a subject's neurotic thoughts and actions to his own attempts actively to repress some repugnant thought and some perverse suspicion than to relate his neurosis to a wish and a repression that are both totally unconscious? And what is gained by burying all relevant sexual and other information not only in the Unconscious, but also in the prehistoric period of earliest infancy? Must everything that a patient says in analysis have a theoretical interpretation as standing for something else and never standing for itself?

These are the kinds of questions which Sartre's critique of Freud involves, and which can only be tackled by revising Freudian theory as generations of Freud's erstwhile disciples have also discovered. One such disciple was Wilheim Stekel, who was with Freud from the very beginning of psycho-analysis, and was supposed to have encouraged Freud to found the first psycho-analytical society in 1902. A decade later Stekel had split from Freud, as Adler had done, and as Jung and many others were soon to do (see Jones, 1964).

Stekel, like Sartre, could not accept the overwhelming importance Freud attached to the notion of the Unconscious. Thus Stekel is a Freudian revisionist often referred to by both Sartre and Merleau-Ponty. Stekel's main conceptual break (1937) was embodied in his use of the term 'scotomisation', while his main area of research and therapy was frigidity in women. To take the former first, 'scotomisation' is a term borrowed from opthalmology which refers to the process whereby part of a person's field of vision becomes obscured, the person becomes partly blind. Stekel applied this term, somewhat metaphorically, to the way people 'turn a blind eye' to things that they do not want to see and, more important, to things that they do not want to take responsibility for. This is thus a process of repression, and the term 'unconscious' can then be used to designate all of those things that a person has avoided responsibility for, all things that he has repressed and turned a blind eye to.

This, of course, dovetailed nicely with the humanistic concerns of the existential phenomenologists, as did Stekel's analysis of frigidity. He showed that the phenomenon is rarely related to some physiological genital and sexual malfunction. Rather he viewed it in the straightforward terms of a refusal by the woman to achieve orgasm in sexual relations with her husband. Perhaps the reason for this refusal might be the husband's infidelity and his interest in other women. But whether this, or some other situation, provides the woman with a motive to refuse orgasm, the point is that her frigidity is a project which she more or less consciously embarks upon herself, it is not something that can be said to happen to her, like a cancer might be said to happen to her.

Sartre (1966) discussed this approach to frigidity in the development of his concepts of bad-faith or self-deception. He observes that, whatever the original situation was that provided the woman with a motive and reason to refuse orgasm, this situation and her reasons may subsequently be presumed to become more complex. Eventually one of the main features of her project, and one of her main reasons for refusing orgasm, becomes her need to prove to herself that she is 'frigid', and that frigidity is something that has 'happened to' her. That is, her project becomes twisted; she becomes involved in actively denying responsibility for something which she more or less actively and more or less consciously pursued in the first place. The agonising twists and turns involved in trying to repress and subjugate one's consciousness and responsibilities for one's actions in this way are accessible through ordinary communication, and therapy does not require any invocation of the Unconscious with its causal relationship to meaningful and conscious phenomena. To discuss repression in the Freudian terms of the Unconscious is, for Sartre, to reify the phenomenon. It is far more true to life to examine neurotic problems, such as frigidity, in terms of a dynamic and humanistic conception of repression, one which sees that repression is self-inflicted, it is self-deception, it is living in bad-faith. Existential psycho-analysis must, therefore, according to Sartre, be oriented to understanding the way the frigid woman, or neurotic and psychotic people in general, takes on the world and projects herself in it. Existential psycho-analysis leads to the understanding of a person's being-in-the-world, Freudian psycho-analysis leads only to the understanding of a myth of its own creation, the person's alleged Unconscious. The former could be called humanistic knowledge because it is knowledge of a human being; but it is not clear what kind of knowledge Freudian psychology permits, or even if it is knowledge at all.

Merleau-Ponty referred to the same study by Stekel on frigidity (1962, p. 158) to endorse its critical differences from the Freudian position in the same way that Sartre had. We have noted before the stylistic difference between Merleau-Ponty and Sartre, the former shying away from the latter's Cartesian-like adherence to the term 'consciousness'. Both men presented philosophical analyses based on the concept of man's being-in-the-world. But Sartre often used the term 'unconsciousness' to designate this, and was not sensitive, as was Merleau-Ponty, to the Mind-Body Cartesian dualism tangentially implied in such use. Merleau-Ponty thus referred to Stekel on frigidity to demonstrate the fallacy of any Mind-Body dualism, whereas Sartre's reference to the same piece of work was a demonstration of the sense and value of existential psycho-analysis. However, this is merely a difference of emphasis, and Merleau-Ponty's comments can easily be seen as complementary to Sartre's.

Merleau-Ponty wanted to drive home the fact that man exists in the world as, among other things, a sexual body. Man is not a disembodied and unsituated intelligence, he is an embodied and situated actor. Man's sexuality, to which Freud drew attention, cannot just be a physiological kind of fact, as far as Merleau-Ponty is concerned. Rather it is also, and primarily for the philosopher, an existential fact. Sexuality is a conscious mode of existing and acting. It is not the be all and end all of everything, as Freud presumed, but nonetheless it is a vitally important dimension of existence in terms of which people think, act and relate to each other. Sex is an existential fact as well as being a physiological fact, and therefore, according to Merleau-Ponty, it is wrong to import the explanations relevant to the latter in order to understand the former. Stekel's demonstration that frigidity is an existential phenomenon which has no physiological basis, and therefore no physiological explanation, thus supports Merleau-Ponty's point.

What is required is not physiological explanation but phenomenological descriptions of existential states and facts. And this is something that Freud failed fully to understand, according to the existential phenomenologists. Faced with the choice, Freud tended to opt for the physiology of sex rather than for the phenomenology of sexuality. He tended to opt for extra-conscious, and extra-experiential explanations, which, if they were not explicitly conceived in physiological terms, were only one step removed from them. The Unconscious is ultimately related to the sexual instincts and drives; it is a para-physiological mechanism which determines consciousness from 'outside'.

In *The Structure of Behaviour*, Merleau-Ponty discussed Freud's choice as a mistaken choice of language and concepts; Freud chose reductionist rather than humanistic language in which to discuss man's sexuality. Thus he wrote (1965, p. 177):

> Without calling into question the role which Freud assigns to the erotic infrastructure and to social regulations, what we should like to ask is whether the conflicts themselves of which he speaks and the physiological mechanisms which he has described—the formation of complexes, repression, regression, resistance, transfer, compensation and sublimation really require the system of causal notions by which he interprets them. . . . For it is easy to see that causal thinking is not indispensable here and that one can use another language.

Merleau-Ponty here rejects the deterministic and extra-experiential perspective that Freud adopted, and his alternative, which is to remain *within* experience or consciousness, and to retain some conception of man as a free thinker and actor, takes virtually the same line as Sartre took in his discussion of emotions. Thus Merleau-Ponty concludes (ibid., p. 220):

> We have rejected Freud's causal categories and replaced his energic metaphors with structural metaphors ... the complex is not a thing outside of consciousness, which would produce its effects in it ... it is only a structure of consciousness.

Merleau-Ponty later, in the *Phenomenology of Perception*, reined in the possible Cartesian implications, the possible Mind-Body dualism of this emphasis on consciousness. Unconscious complexes and sexual drives cannot be seen as outside of man's conscious *existence*, his conscious being-in-the-world. Freud was wrong to locate sexuality in the Body, but it is not on that account in the Mind, for this Cartesian dualism is wrong. Sexuality, if it is 'in' anywhere, is in existence, it is in that Body-Mind fusion that is a man's being-in-the-world. This is still basically the same line that Sartre took but, in his later work, Merleau-Ponty, going to some lengths to get out of Sartre's shadow, tried to recruit Freud's theories to existential phenomenology. That is, Merleau-Ponty appeared to reverse his earlier critique of Freud, which was easily integrated with Sartre's critique. In his later work he minimised Freud's reductionism (1962, p. 158), and played up his humanism, thus implicitly questioning the originality of Sartre's alternative, existential psycho-analysis.

But these differences between Sartre and Merleau-Ponty are superficial and unimportant. Such differences of emphasis do not affect the point that both philosophers are critical of Freudian theory in its reductionist and physiological interpretation, and of the para-reductionist concept of the Unconscious. Neither do they affect the point that both philosophers criticise such reductionism in terms of the same humanistic perspective on man's thought and action, that of the existential concept of man's being-in-the-world.

Conclusion

Generally speaking, the attitudes of philosophers of both schools which have been reviewed here, regarding Freudian psychology, have been seen to have some important similarities. Freud is seen by both schools to have proposed a theory of thought and action which is deterministic, materialistic and extra-experiential. But some philosophers in both schools think that Freud's therapy relies on more humanistic assumptions. Either way, whether Freud is rejected or recruited, the positions, in terms of which his psychology is judged by both schools, are what we have called humanistic, as opposed to reductionist, positions. These involve such assumptions as that man is a rational and purposive actor, and also that man is a social animal.

Given these overall similarities, the main differences between conceptual analysis and existential phenomenology in regard to Freudian psychology has been over the explanation of mental illness, the neuroses and the psychoses. Mental illness is an abnormality, and we have seen that Ryle believed that a causal, deterministic and extra-experiential explanation *can* be given of abnormalities in thought, perception and action. In the, presumed, majority of normal thoughts, perceptions and actions, however, we can rely on specific reasons and justifications given by the subject. In both abnormality and normality—cases where respectively something 'happens to' one, and where one does something—explanations are piecemeal and have no general foundation or general implications.

Thus Ryle makes two points which appear to be very different from anything that Sartre and Merleau-Ponty would assert. First, he asserts that humanistic explanations, although covering the majority, do not cover all types of thoughts and actions; piecemeal reductionism has a place in the explanation of abnormal thoughts and actions like those involved in mental illness. Second, he asserts that humanistic explanations do not imply or spring from any general theory of the nature of man; they are *ad hoc* and piecemeal. Before we make the point that conceptual analysts like Peters, and indeed Ryle himself, have a general theory of the nature of man, the differences between these assertions and those of existential phenomenology may be noted.

First, existential phenomenology does not accord any place at all to reductionist explanations, piecemeal or not, and particularly so in the case of mental illness. Here, more than anywhere else, the method of phenomenological description of the subject's existential situation, and of the subject's reasons for doing what he does, have been successfully applied. And second, existential phenomenology does present its humanistic explanations as springing from and implying a general theory of the nature of man. On both of these points there is a contradiction with Ryle's conceptual analytic assertions.

But the contradiction on at least one of the points is illusory. That is, Ryle's denial of proposing a general humanistic theory of man, and a general humanistic theory of the rational nature of explanation of men's thoughts and actions, is simply bogus. This allegation has been argued at length elsewhere in this book already. In this chapter it has also been substantiated in the case of Peters and his critique of Freudian and behaviourist reductionism in psychology. His alternative conception of man to the one given by these forms of psychology is that of 'a chess-player writ large'. That is, man is a reason-giving, rule-following animal, and so on. And this is a general theory in terms of which every specific subjectively rational explanation of a thought or action has its justification and acceptability. Stated with intimations of complacency and common sense, rather than with the intimations of profundity and melodrama with which Sartre states it, the position is, none the less, very similar to the general existential phenomenological position.

However, this very complacency traps conceptual analysis into limiting the generality of its humanism. Ryle, Peters and others allow reductionism to explain abnormalities like mental illness, and this established a distinct and specific difference between conceptual analysis and existential phenomenology. There is no reason at all why the conceptual analytic notion of man as a chess-player writ large, etc., should not have an application in the field of psychotherapy and psychiatry, providing one treats the game context as problematic and evolving. In fact, Szasz has used Peters's concept and Blum has applied Wittgenstein's concept in the sociology of mental illness but, unfortunately, such applications are not even entertained by conceptual analysts, and they might even be disowned. Existential phenomenology, on the other hand, has established an important relationship with modern psychiatry and psychotherapy, and has found its general humanistic concepts applied in therapeutic practice.

In the final chapter, chapter 9, we discuss the relationship of humanistic philosophy with sociology. Sociology, like humanistic philosophy, generally speaking, takes as axiomatic both that men are rational and purposive actors, and that they are social animals. Thus, like humanistic philosophy, it is equally committed to rejection of psychological and further physical reductionism in the explanation of thought and action. As an introduction to this theme, in the next chapter, we can look at one of a number of areas where sociology and humanistic philosophy meet one another. This area is that of mental illness. Here sociology, like humanistic psychotherapy, rejects the explanatory value and therapeutic significance of Freudian behaviourist, genetic and other reductionist theories. Instead, the sociology of deviant behaviour comes to a similar conclusion to that of humanistic psychotherapy. Life would be simple if conceptual analysis and existential phenomenology, as two humanistic schools of philosophy, had made equal contributions to the post-Freudian humanisation of psychotherapy. Unfortunately, in spite of the similarity of their critiques of Freud, we have seen in this chapter that conceptual analysis has established no relation to the theory and therapy of mental illness, whereas existential phenomenology has done so. So, in introducing the topic of the similarity between the axioms of social theory and those of humanistic philosophy, through the specific area of mental illness, we must necessarily be forced to consider only existential phenomenology out of our two schools at this stage. However, in chapter 8 the attitudes and relationships of *both* schools to sociology is taken up, with specific reference to Weber's sociological concepts. In chapter 9, the kind of humanistic positions that both schools adopt is related in more general terms to sociology, in order to establish that sociology, whatever kind of discipline it is, does not comply with the reductionist idea of a social science.

7 Humanistic psychiatry and sociology

The most important distinction which has been the subject of our dogged attentions in this book so far is that between reductionist and humanistic principles of explanation of men's thoughts and actions. At the risk of giving this simple and useful distinction too much work to do we have used it to characterise psychology and sociology. Psychology, or at least the psychological theories examined in the preceding chapters, appears to be oriented towards reductionist principles. That is, in spite of psychology being one of the 'humanities', it is not the case that it is primarily oriented towards humanistic principles of explanation. Sociology on the other hand, in the form that its major theorists have given it, has consistently rejected psychological and other further reductions of the phenomena of social structures, processes and actions. More positively, there are numerous explicit axioms in most of the major sociological theories, sufficient to justify our picture of sociology as oriented to humanistic principles of explanation. In this and the following two chapters we will be concerned to elaborate this picture and to reveal its justifications.

While justification for this humanistic interpretation of sociology is not hard to find at the level of sociological theory, still it is better to begin from a concrete problem area. Hence the attention we will give to the area of 'mental illness', and to differing explanations of the phenomena grouped under that largely misleading name. It is in the field of mental illness that a definite convergence can be observed between explanations that are explicitly humanistic and explanations that are only called 'sociological'. On the one hand there is a humanistic branch of psychiatry, and on the other there is the sociology of deviant behaviour, and they both provide similar sorts of explanations. The former, existential psychotherapy, is, as we have already indicated, a practical implementation of key existential phenomenological ideas. The latter, the sociology of deviance, is a speciality that has arisen from a number of sources in sociological theory, notably from symbolic interactionism and from various 'system' theories. To tie up humanistic psychiatry with the sociology of deviance is thus, in effect, to tie up the teachings of a humanistic school of philosophy, like existential phenomenology, with major areas of sociological theory.

This kind of tie up and convergence is in marked contrast to the divergence between humanistic philosophy and the reductionist orientation of psychological theories. Freudian psychology, behaviourism, together with neurology and genetics have all proposed explanations of the phenomena of abnormality covered by the term 'mental illness'. But these explanations have been criticised in theory by humanistic philosophy, and ignored in practice by humanistic psychiatry, for being reductionist. As against this, it has recently been the case that sociological theories of mental illness have been accepted as relevant to humanistic psychiatry and psychotherapy.

The field of mental illness, then, serves as a basis for the argument that humanistic philosophy has an intrinsic significance for sociology that it does not have for psychology. It has this significance because sociology utilises humanistic principles of explanation, and psychology utilises reductionist principles. That is, broadly speaking, psychologists are prepared to use explanations of men's thoughts and actions which refer to deterministic processes that go on beyond the actor's awareness. And furthermore, the men whose thought and action is thus determined are differentiated ultimately as physical and biological individuals; they are not seen to be socially differentiated individuals. The reductionist explanations of psychology do not refer to men's consciousness, to men's purposes, or to men's social nature and situation. Humanistic explanations, on the other hand, refer precisely to consciousness, purpose and society. This is the case, it will be argued in this chapter, for both existential psychotherapy and for the sociology of deviance. It is in terms of these three features of humanistic explanations that humanistic psychiatry and sociology will be seen to converge. The immediate task, in order to demonstrate this convergence, then, is to examine and review first the psychiatric and then the sociological attempts to explain and understand mental illness.

Humanistic psychiatry

Freud revolutionised psychiatric theories of mental illness, first, because he emphasised the importance of sex, and second, because he advocated talking to the mentally ill subject. But Freud's influence in psychiatry stems as much from the revision of these ideas as it does from the acceptance of them. Freudian revisionists, like Adler, Jung and Stekel pointed out that Freud had over-emphasised the importance of sex in the analysis of human personality compared with other things such as inferiority/superiority (Adler), introversion/extroversion (Jung) and responsibility/rejection of responsibility (Stekel). And Freud, in any case, even misinterpreted sexuality and the need for sex as a purely physiologically based energy flow, rather than in more interpersonal and humanistic terms, according to most of his revisionists.

But what could be wrong with talking with the patient? This was indeed something of an advance over the prevailing late nineteenth-century concern purely for the physiological abnormalities presumed to be underlying the mental and behavioural abnormalities. But, the revisionists objected, the Freudian therapist did not talk *with* the patient, he talked *to* him about a third party, the patient's Unconscious. It was rather like a marriage where the only topic of conversation was the mother-in-law, out of sight, but a threatening presence none the less. Talking with the patient was a form of therapy which developed almost in spite of Freudian psycho-analysis, and not because of it.

Virtually all of Freud's critics and revisers, even hybrids like Jung, objected to what we discussed in the previous chapter as the reductionist features of Freud's approach. All of them substituted different theories and approaches which were more or less humanistic. In particular, virtually all of them reduced the importance that Freud attached to the concept of the Unconscious, parallel with their reduction of the importance that Freud attached to physiologically based sexual drives (Jung was alone in maximising the Unconscious at the same time as minimising sex drive). Later revisionists, like Horney, Fromm and Sullivan, not only concentrated their therapeutic attentions on a conscious ego behind which no sexual Unconscious sat, but tried to understand this ego as a social self. That is, they maximised to relevance of the social and cultural environment in the development of personality, going far beyond Freud's grudging and minimal acknowledgment of parent-infant interaction.

The field of Freud's followers, revisers and critics is a vast and complex one, and in a sense all non-medical psychiatrists take their cue one way or another from Freud (see Brown, 1961; Ellenberger, 1970). But there were some who also took their cue from Husserl and Heidegger, and later from Sartre (see Friedman, 1964). It is on to these existential psychotherapists that we must turn the main spotlight of attention, for they embodied more clearly than any others the humanistic nature of the break from Freud.

Existential psychotherapy began in the writings and work of Minkowski and Binswanger in the inter-war period. Previous to this

Dilthey's humanistic conception of 'understanding', which he held to be a distinctive feature of the humanistic disciplines, had been applied in psychiatry by Jaspers. But Freud's expanding reputation and influence in the early decades of this century cast a shadow over this development which could only be lifted with the backing of thinkers of equal weight and importance to Freud. In Husserl and Heidegger, Minkowski and Binswanger found their respective backers. They found here their intellectual justifications for taking what Freud said with a pinch of salt, as less than gospel.

Minkowski's first important piece of work, a paper called 'A psychological study and phenomenological analysis of a case of schizophrenic depression' (1958) was first published in 1923. In it Minkowski applied the analysis of the experience or consciousness of time, which he found in the philosophical writings of both Bergson and Husserl, to a particular case study. The philosophers discussed time as a central feature of ordinary human consciousness. Parallel with Einstein's presentation of time in physical theory as relative to such things as the velocity of movement of the observer, so Husserl and Bergson, in phenomenological philosophy, stressed the relativity of subjective time. Time, as a person experiences it, is thus relative to his present situation, his interpretation of his past, and his expectations about the future. Man is aware that he lives in temporal terms; he lives in a vanishing present, informed by the past and oriented to the future. Man's time is not clock-time, although the temporal terms in which he lives and projects himself are patterns which also take account of clock-time, as a social fact if not as an absolute standard.

This was relevant to the understanding of a case of schizophrenic depression in the following way. Minkowski's patient was possessed of some very exotic and imaginative guilt feelings, fears about the imminent punishment awaiting him, and various other delusions of persecution. Besides this, his experience of time was abnormal and fragmented. He did not experience the normal person's continual flow from one's personal present towards one's personal future. Like a gramophone needle stuck on a crack in a record he would repeat morning after morning that he was to be tortured to death that evening, despite the continuing demonstration of the falsity of this belief by his continued ability to state it. His experienced time was fragmented into identical days, the same day repeating and repeating itself. There was no change or flow towards the future: 'the future was blocked' in this man's experience of time, according to Minkowski (1958, p. 133).

Traditional and Freudian psychiatry would have held that the delusion of imminent execution produced the distortion of experienced time. Thus the job for the psychiatrist would be to discover the causes of the delusion, be they located in the patient's physiological abnormalities or in the patient's sexual Unconscious. As against this, Minkowski held that there was no need to go behind or beyond the execution delusion and the distortion of experienced time to explanatory processes in the organism or in the Unconscious. All that was required in order to explain and understand the execution delusion was a rearrangement of its relation to the distortion of experienced time. Thus it is wrong to picture the latter as an epiphenomenon of the former, rather the contrary is true. 'Could we not suppose', he asks, 'that the more basic disorder is the distorted attitudes towards the future, whereas the (execution MR) delusion is only one of its manifestations?' (ibid., p. 132). Thus the schizophrenic illness, if illness it be, is understood as an abnormality in the patient's way of experiencing his present and future. Mental 'illness' is an abnormality in a man's mode of being-in-the-world. Although this latter term was only introduced by Heidegger three years later, in 1926, and adopted by Binswanger in the early 1930s, it is implicit in Minkowski's account. The exotic delusions of the schizophrenic do not require a causal explanation in terms of 'outside' physiological or Unconscious facts. Rather they can be understood from 'inside' in terms of the way the subject has his being. Delusions are not thought 'disorders' causally determined; they are organised systems of meaning produced by the subject to balance and disguise the disorder of his being-in-the-world, and the disintegration of his personality. We must describe delusional thought 'disorders' as ordered products of more down to earth existential disorders, disorders in a man's being-in-the-world. Minkowski, and to a much lesser extent, Binswanger also, tended to leave things up in the air like this. Thought 'disorders' are a comprehensible product of existential disorders. But how is it that people's mode of existence, their mode of being in the world, can come to be so tragically disturbed? Minkowski is enlightening when he informs us that his patient's execution delusions, a major 'symptom' of his 'illness', are a product of the patient's conviction that his 'future' is blocked', and that he cannot go forward in his life. But what is the reason for this existential impasse? Why is his future blocked? Binswanger is somewhat more enlightening on the principles involved in such issues than Minkowski. But, as we will see, it is the recent English development of existential psychotherapy by Laing and his associates which goes furthest in answering these questions.

Binswanger was one of Freud's earliest followers, first attending the embryonic Vienna Psycho-Analytical Society with Jung in 1907. But whereas Jung made a distinct break with Freud, Binswanger remained on friendly terms with him until the latter's death (1939), despite the fact that he had long since given up Freud's theories for existential ones. Although Heidegger's *Being and Time* came to be the most important influence on Binswanger's psychiatric thinking, Buber's book *I and Thou* (1923) also had an influence on him. Heidegger's concepts of *Dasein* and *Mitwelt* (which are but marginal preliminaries to his, as yet unwritten, grand ontology, but which are his main legacy to existential phenomenology) we have already examined in chapter 1. *Dasein* refers to man's being-there-in-the-world, and *Mitwelt* refers to the fact that man coexists with man, that his world is a social one to its deepest roots. Binswanger took over these two concepts for psychiatry and elaborated the latter in terms of Buber's simple and poetic assertions in *I and Thou* about the nature of man and the nature of his interpersonal communication with his fellow man. Buber differentiated man's possible relationships to his objective world into an 'I—Thou' type, where communication between two human beings is established, and an 'I—It' type, which is simply a relationship between man and non-man, between man and things or objects. Binswanger further differentiated the *Mitwelt* or 'I—Thou' existential mode into (a) dual modes (such as love, friendship and so on); (b) plural modes (such as competition, formal and contractual relations); (c) singular modes (relationships that man has with himself, modelled on competitive and formal criteria, rather than dual criteria, such as in autism or schizophrenia); (d) and anonymous modes (such as men in a crowd, or a soldier killing an enemy soldier). Thus the way was clear for Binswanger to analyse and interpret mental illnesses as various deformations of a person's being in the world, particularly their being in the social world of other people. He was able to view 'insanity as a life-historical phenomenon' (1945b, p. 214).

Although later existential psychotherapists developed the analysis of the social world of the 'mentally ill' person a good deal further and with greater clarity than Binswanger did, his discussions of one aspect of that world remain important. That aspect was the patient-therapist relationship. For Binswanger the therapeutic relationship must be a genuine dialogue and communication between two people, an I—Thou relationship. Social ostracism, turning the patient into an object of avoidance, pity and judgement, cancels out 'the possibility of a purely loving encounter (ibid., p. 228) with this strange and alien entity. In this way people in the social world of the 'mentally ill' subject exclude the possibility of an I—Thou relationship, as well as the possibility of everyday, let alone deep, communication with him. They relate to him in an I—It mode. This is bad for the subject; it is non- and in fact anti-therapeutic. And yet both classical and Freudian psychiatry hardly improves on this form of relationship at all. The subject is 'sick' and 'ill', the prevailing model being the medical one of organic disease. His illness must be diagnosed, and its symptoms properly categorised according to a standardised set of criteria. The 'therapy' that follows upon this adoption of an I—It relationship between the psychiatrist and the patient can do the patient as little good as less well-intentioned social ostracism does, according to Binswanger (ibid.; see also Rogers, 1951; 1967).

Minkowski, Binswanger, Storch (1924), Boss (1949), and the numerous other existential analysts and *Dasein* analysts of the later inter-war years, were feeling their way slowly up from a purely phenomenological and descriptive approach to a more dynamic conception of neurotic and psychotic 'illnesses' (see Sonneman, 1954; Van den Berg, 1955; Macnab, 1965; Ruitenbeek, 1962; Friedman, 1964). They had demonstrated well enough, to return to the point mentioned in regard to Minkowski's case study, that delusional thought 'disorders' were in fact ordered. That is, they had shown that such 'meaningless' disorders of thought and action as those encountered in the psychotic conditions like schizophrenia were in fact comprehensible projects that the person embarked upon in response to disorders and disruptions in his existence, his being-in-the-world. The task now indicated was to investigate the patient's being-in-the-world, and the disruptions that occurred in his existential situation. This implied, fundamentally, an investigation of the social world of the patient. The focus of investigation must come to be the interpersonal networks of relationships in which the patient was involved, and the influence of the people in his world on the patient.

Such investigations might even reveal, not only the comprehensibility, rationality and meaningfulness of delusions, but, in the case of delusions of persecution, they might even reveal the truth of such 'delusions'. In the later development of existential psychotherapy the possibility came to be seriously entertained, not only that delusions are more comprehensible projects of the patient rather than disorders that happened to him, but also that some delusions are not delusions.

In passing it might be mentioned that humanistic psychiatrists in America, while not adopting the concepts of existential phenomenological philosophy, came to the same kind of conclusions as their European colleagues in the later inter-war and early post-war period. Rogers (1951) called his therapeutic approach 'client-centred', echoing Binswanger's commitment to therapy as the genuine communication of an I—Thou encounter. Similarly Sullivan (1947; 1955; 1962) discussed schizophrenia in more explicitly interpersonal and social terms than did Binswanger, despite the latter's emphasis on the importance of analysing the patient's *Mitwelt*. In fact a considerable body of theory and research couched in terms of interpersonal self-others relationships has since grown up in American humanistic psychiatry (see Berne, 1961; 1964; Moustakas, 1966;

E. Becker, 1962; 1964; Farber, 1966; May, 1967; 1970). And these developments are even more consonant with the recent developments of existential psychotherapy in Europe than the earlier work of Sullivan and Rogers was with the work of Binswanger and Minkowski. For two examples of the more recent direction in American psychiatry we can look at the respective work of Szasz and of Bateson and his associates. We can look then at the consonance, and in fact utilisation of this work by recent European (British) existential psychotherapists such as Laing and Cooper.

Szasz, in *The Myth of Mental Illness*, launched a wide ranging attack on medical metaphors and disease-process habits of thinking in psychiatry (see also Szasz, 1971). Szasz thus argued for a humanist as against a reductionist case. Reductionist psychiatry viewed mental illness, if not as an effect of presumed neurophysiological abnormalities, then as on a par with physical illness. Freud was as steeped in this medical metaphor of the unfolding of a disease process within an individual's body, or here, mind, as was orthodox physiological psychiatry, according to Szasz (1962, ch. 4). In his view Freud portrayed neuroticism, particularly hysteria, precisely in this misleading medical metaphor of intra-organic, or here intra-psychic illness. But the phenomena covered by the term mental illness could be conceptualised in far more therapeutically revealing and relevant ways. They can be understood and explained in humanistic terms which refer to the subject's consciousness, his purposes and responsibility for his actions, and to the social world in which he acts. The reductionist conceptual framework of mental illness is not necessary to understand the phenomena covered by the term, and thus mental illness is in this sense a 'myth', according to Szasz.

Drawing from many sources Szasz then attempted to present a number of alternative humanistic conceptual frameworks which could be used to understand hysteria in particular. All behaviour, but hysterical behaviour in particular, can be analysed as a form of language or sign-using communication; or it can be analysed as a form of rule-following; or finally it can be analysed as a form of game-playing. Szasz thinks that the game-playing model, which he accredits to G. H. Mead and Piaget, encompasses the other two (ibid., Book 2).

Hysteria denotes the imitation of organic diseases and afflictions by the subject. The hysterical person is subject to anaesthesia of parts of the body, paralysis, tremors, vomiting and even seizures resembling epileptic fits. Thus it can be appropriate, argues Szasz, to analyse hysterical behaviour as a species of 'body-language', as a form of non-verbal communication making use of a special set of signs (ibid., p. 115). The hysteric , in his body-language of apparently physical illness, communicates to other people who are important to him, 'Look, I am physically sick', and so 'Help me', or 'Stop making me sick'. He wants to communicate the straits he feels himself in, to avoid the question of his responsibility for himself, since he is 'at the end of his tether', 'can do no more' etc., and to ask for help or for a change in the attitudes of those around him.

Related to this linguistic interpretation is the rule-following interpretation. This is the only point in the present chapter in which a conceptual analyst could conceivably squeeze into the discussion. So we duly record here that Szasz (ibid., p. 168) accredits the main development of the rule-following framework to Peters, whose thesis we have already examined in chapters 4 and 6. Hysteria, then, can be interpreted as a system of behaviour which makes special use of rules related to helplessness, illness and coercion of others. But whether Peters had this kind of relatively exotic game in mind when he called man a 'chess-player writ large' is debatable.

In any case the final conceptual framework Szasz presents, the game-playing framework, encompasses these other two. This framework simply makes quite explicit the interpersonal context of behaviour, and of hysterical behaviour in particular. In a game players communicate with one another and they follow rules. The hysteria game, says Szasz (ibid., p. 279), 'is characterised by the goal of dominance and interpersonal control. The typical strategies employed in pursuing this goal are coercion by disability and illness. Deceitful gambits of various types, especially lies, also play a significant part in this game.' As admirable as this analysis is, it does little to differentiate the specific hysteria game from games played between nations, such as the world war game, or within them, such as the civil war game or the employers versus employees game. No matter, perhaps these games are all hysterical.

Szasz's humanistic analyses, like the Freudian ones they criticised, pertained only to hysteria and neurosis. Bateson and his associates, in their paper 'Toward a theory of schizophrenia', went further than this by extending the humanistic terms of reference such as games, communications and rules, specifically to cover the psychotic condition, that of schizophrenia (see also Haley, 1963; Jackson, 1960; 1964; Weakland, 1960). Freud had hardly dealt at all with psychosis, which meant that Minkowski, Binswanger and the other early existential psychotherapists virtually had the field to themselves. Humanistic psychiatry founded itself in an almost unexplored area, which orthodox psychiatry, as much as the ordinary man in the street, avoided as being completely incomprehensible. The early existential psychotherapists revealed the shallowness of this attribution in demonstrating the comprehensibility of the 'mad' world of delusions and hallucinations. Bateson's paper is but one example in more recent American psychiatry of an approach which belongs in the same tradition as this existentialist approach.

Bateson and his colleagues tried to show how schizophrenia develops as an apparent distortion of a person's thoughts and actions, because of distortions, and indeed contortions, of communication in the person's social milieu. This milieu must be an interpersonal network of communications and relationships which the person participates in intimately. Thus they could have made their point about the mental illnesses that arise from distortions of communication in the army milieu of a soldier, or in the prison milieu of a prisoner, or in the asylum milieu of a mental patient, and so on. However, they chose to make the point about a more common and general social milieu than these, the family. And it is true that this milieu is different from the others in that, generally speaking, more social learning and personality formation goes on in it for a longer time than in any other.

The central argument of Bateson and his colleagues was that the kind of communication-distortion likely to result in schizophrenic personality disorders was a 'double-bind' situation. The subject is placed in a double-bind situation when he feels that he must correctly interpret the messages and communications of significant others, but where these messages are more or less deliberately presented in an ambiguous way. The most critical kind of double-bind situation occurs when there are two distinct messages being presented for the subject's responses at the same time, one of which negates the other. Thus an affirmation may be expressed verbally, while its negation may be expressed non-verbally, in bodily posture, gestures, facial expressions, and so on, by the same person. For instance, a mother may say to her son, 'Come here and kiss me', while indicating in other ways her anxiety and fear should he dare do what she asks him to do. Clearly here it is the mother and not the son who has the problem, but she is foisting it upon the son. And while his initial responses to this may be relatively harmless ones of confusion, the procedure, if kept up long enough and engaged in by other family members, it is argued, can result in the son in this example becoming schizophrenic.

Laing, Cooper and others of the recently developed British movement of existential psychotherapy have made much use of the work of Szasz, Bateson *et al.* and American interpersonal and social psychiatrists. Thus Cooper (1968; 1971) does not believe that the term 'schizophrenia' denotes an isolable disturbed pattern of behaviour 'in' one person at all. Rather, he believes that it denotes a disturbed pattern of communication and of mutual influences between the members of a community of people such as a family. He holds that the person called 'schizophrenic' has been in some sense 'elected and identified' as such by members of the family, friends, neighbours and others. And, furthermore, this election has been confirmed by 'official' medical and judicial agencies and labelling processes. If we must use the term at all, then 'schizophrenia' ought to mean for the psychiatrist a disturbed group, and not a disturbed individual (1968, p. 2).

At this point the bridge between humanistic psychiatry and the sociology of deviance is beginning to come into view. But before we reach it there is time to recap on the main themes of existential psychotherapy through an examination, however brief, of Laing's arguments. His first, and possibly most important, work was *The Divided Self: An Existential Study in Sanity and Madness* (1965a). Here he drew on Heidegger and Sartre's philosophy, and Binswanger, Minkowski and others' psychiatric applications of existential phenomenological philosophy, and he tried to show how schizophrenia is best understood both as the experience of 'primary ontological insecurity', and as the efforts of the subject to deal with, and come to terms with, this experience (ibid., p. 39).

'Primary ontological insecurity' was Laing's identification of the existential disorders which earlier psychotherapists, like Binswanger, had suspected to be the basis of the delusional thought disorders. The fear of death breaks through into the life of every human at one time or another, and it can be distinguished from the fear of the unknown, and from fear of physical mutilation during death. It is quite simply the apprehension of non-existence, and of the fact that ultimately one's self, one's being-in-the-world, will cease to be. Ontologically secure humans locate their non-existence in their physical death, and leave it at that. Ontologically insecure humans fear their non-existence, their spiritual extinction, the death of their soul and self, as a possibility in life as well as in physical death. The living death of the self is a possibility because the self swims in a social sea, and it can drown or be engulfed by that sea, without consequent death of the self's body. Death of the body and continuing life of the spiritual self is a theological hypothesis; on the other hand, death of the spiritual self and continuing life of the body is an all too common and tragic psychiatric fact.

Thus Laing identified the key existential problem as one of the preservation or loss of one's sense of self, one's identity. And he further located the genesis of self, its preservation and its possible mutilation or loss, in self-other relations (see Laing, 1965b; 1965c; 1967; 1969a; 1969b; 1971). If man sinks or swims in a social sea, then we must investigate the nature of the sea as much as that of the swimmer. That way we can understand better the relationship between both and the swimmer's consequent progress. Thus we must understand the intimate social milieu of the subject at least, and for

Laing and Cooper this means the family milieu. But both are aware that wider social institutions, structures and processes are also relevant, further consideration of which we leave for the next section.

When Laing and Cooper wrote their study (1964) of Sartre's philosophy and writings of the 1950–60 period, Sartre prefaced the work with remarks that are relevant to our discussion, He wrote:

> I believe that we are not able to study or restore a neurosis to health, without a primordial regard for the person of the patient; without a constant effort to grasp the basic situation, to relive it; without taking a step to rediscover the person's responsibility in this situation—And I hold, as you do, mental illness to be the outcome which the free organism in its total unity, contrives in order to be able to live an intolerable situation.

The important phrases here are 'person's responsibility' and 'intolerable situation'. It is precisely the juxtaposition between these two things that modern existential psychotherapy has been concerned with.

Ontological insecurity, like more superficial forms of insecurity such as embarrassment, being ill at ease, and so on, is a product of the relation between a person and his social milieu of other people. It is this relationship which existential analysts, following existential philosophers, have tried to capture in the concept of being-in-the-world. Man is a social being, his existential situation is a social one. His self-identity coexists in a field of other self-identities. And it is continually validated or invalidated, renewed or lost, partly through his own efforts and partly through the efforts of others. The psychiatrist is concerned with the relatively abnormal phenomena of total invalidation. And to understand this he must understand both the subject's responsibility for his mental disorder, and also the responsibility of other people for the subject's situation which the subject experiences as an intolerable one. The balance between the two poles of self and others, in the subject's existential situation, is a fine and subtle one to grasp in the abstract. But for Laing, Cooper and their colleagues, gross overbalances of responsibility can often occur in concrete cases. They point to the communicator's responsibility for deliberate ambiguities in 'double-bind' situations. They point, following Searles (1959) to the importance of 'the effort to drive the other person crazy', in the development of a diagnosed schizophrenic in disturbed families (see Esterson, 1970; Laing and Esterson, 1964; Morris and Wynne, 1965; Spiegel and Bell, 1959; Bickford, 1968).

Thus the line of analysis is as follows. The subject is wholly responsible for his 'disordered' thoughts and actions. But mad and strange thoughts and actions are only superficially disordered, incomprehensible, meaningless and so on. In relation to the intolerable social situation in which the subject exists they may be seen as quite comprehensible, ordered and meaningful ways of dealing with the situation. The subject has some responsibility for his social situation, but necessarily, other people have a responsibility for that situation too, since they largely comprise it. Both modern European existential psychiatry and modern American interpersonal psychiatry are very concerned to demonstrate, in fact, the magnitude of the responsibilities of others for the social situation experienced and defined by the subject as intolerable. And this is a bridge to more manifestly sociological theories and perspectives. For the sociology of deviance, in the area of mental illness, is precisely interested in understanding the social genesis of the social fact of an intolerable situation, which has the consequence of generating the social fact, or problem of the mental patient.

Sociology and mental illness

A preliminary distinction must be made between the relationship of sociology to psychiatry and to psychology. This is in order to forestall the suspicion that sociological theories of mental illness are inherently psychologically reductionist. Psychology competes with sociology over wide ranges of human thought and action; why a man believes something or why he does something may be explained in either sociological or psychological terms. We have already seen the extent to which psychological explanation is reductionist, in that it explains thoughts or actions as determined epiphenomena of intra-organic, or intra-psychic, processes which are not themselves experienced. Sociological explanation, it will be argued in the ensuing chapters, is humanistic in comparison with this. Men's thinking and acting is accepted as explanatory and as axiomatic in much sociological theory, and not as epiphenomena that are explained and that themselves have no explanatory value, as in reductionist psychology.

Humanistic psychiatry, which we have been discussing in the previous section, is far more of a complementary study of sociology than a competitive one. If it were a competitor it could not be a very important one, for it has a limited focus in mental illness. Competition with sociological explanations in this field would be irrelevant to the vast number of phenomena and explanations which sociology is concerned with apart from mental illness. However, humanistic psychiatry has a commitment to the explanatory value of thoughts and actions in explaining why even madmen do what they do. And this is a family relative of the same kind of commitments which can be seen in sociological theories, consequently the relation between the two disciplines is complementary and not competitive.

So it is not the case that sociology, by dealing with the (disturbed) 'individual' and trying to explain how he comes to be what he is, is necessarily engaging in psychological reduction and forsaking the study of 'society'. The alleged clash of interests between study of the individual and study of society is in the category of 'great red herrings of our time'. It serves simply to obscure far more important clashes of interest such as those between humanistic and reductionist explanatory principles. Mental illness is at once a personal problem which also has a wide social distribution, and is thus a 'social problem'. And, furthermore, the typical mentally ill person is the product of typical social processes, or so the sociologists of deviance we examine below argue. Sociology is hardly selling its birthright and succumbing to the allure of psychological reductionism by studying typical social processes. Its convergence with humanistic psychiatry on a number of issues in this field says more about the sociological nature of psychiatry than it does about the psychological leanings of sociology. As Eliot (1956) writes, 'psychiatry is intimate sociology'; and there would be just as little reductionism implied by reversing that, and saying that sociology is a kind of distant, anonymous and gross psychiatry.

Having cleared the stage of the villains of the piece, psychology and reductionism, we can now get on with the play. The sociology of mental illness has probably always had its practitioners in various countries, but the most influential work, generally speaking, has gone on in the U.S.A. Most of this work has been done in the post-war period, and it is upon this that we must focus attention. However, this work was foreshadowed by, and in some cases founded upon, the association that developed in American sociology of the inter-war years between psychiatry and sociology (see Rose, 1956).

Although there were undoubtedly numerous sources of inspiration for such an association, not least from the Boy Scout 'mental hygiene' values of small-town America, two main sources must be identified. One was Freud and the other was the Depression. From the early days of psycho-analysis Freud had sent representatives to America to spread the word. And the word became all the more influential when, Nazism having uprooted the mainly Jewish psycho-analytic movement in Germany, the main body of migrant Freudians settled in America in the 1930s. As the importance of Freudian concepts grew, the importance of criticising and revising them also grew. The Freudian revisionists Fromm, Horney, Sullivan and others, by stressing social, cultural and interpersonal factors in the development, maintenance and breakdown of personality, founded humanistic psychiatry in America. And in doing so they established professional and theoretical links with sociologists, who for their part acknowledged an interest in using some Freudian concepts while discarding others.

Sociological interest in psychiatric problems and answers also stemmed from the experience of the Depression. In the massive unemployment of the 1930s, with its consequent assault on people's earnings and status, with its arbitrary enforcement of poverty, downward social mobility, and general social degradation, the effect of society on the individual personality was an unavoidable fact of life. People went crazy because society had gone crazy, and social disintegration precipitated increases in the rates of personality disintegration. The social causes of personality problems which had social dimensions stood clearly revealed. And the link which had always existed between academic social studies and ameliorative welfare work deepened into a link with more intimate and detailed psychiatric work.

Sociological interest in the two main categories of 'deviant behaviour', crime and mental illness, flourished in the inter-war years in America in this climate of social dislocation and theoretical stimulation. But not all of the theoretical stimulation came from Freud and his critics. Such sociological interest was a natural concomitant of the symbolic interactionist social theories of such men as Cooley, Thomas and Mead in this period. There is no need to go into detail here about theories which have become so much taken for granted in sociology that their status as theories has largely been forgotten. Basically they are assertions, in one form or another, of the social nature of the self. In fact the analysis of humanism that we have presented throughout this book is, in a number of respects, similar to a symbolic interactionist one.

Symbolic interactionism asserts that man is a purposive actor and that he is a social animal, developed socially, who acts mainly in the social world on the basis of what he believes to be the case. Cooley's (1922) contribution has been summed up as the analysis of the 'looking-glass self'. People see themselves as they believe others see them; the further extension of this is that people act in the ways that they believe others expect them to act. Man's self image is a social one, and his actions are socially conforming.

Mead (1967, ch. 22), differentiated man's social self image, his 'me', from his ability to spontaneously bring himself to act, his 'I', thus taking the teeth out of Cooley's social conformism. For Mead, as for related European thinkers like Piaget, man is certainly a social product, but unless this 'product' achieves a degree of rational autonomy from all influences and determinations, including social ones, then it is not a man. It must be able to represent to itself society's reactions to its actions, a man must be able to take the position of the other, or else he could not successfully talk, play or interact with others at all. But this 'me', this sense of the 'generalised other', this awareness of society and of oneself in society's terms, is one pole of the human equation. The other is the ability to generate an action which knowingly conforms to, or which knowingly deviates from, social expectations and rules.

Finally, Thomas may be mentioned for his attack on the reductionist instinct theories of his period in the concept of 'definition of the situation'. Thus 'if men define situations as real, they are real in their consequences' (1928, p. 584; see also McHugh, 1968). Men act, he believed, not because of the blind workings of instincts within them, but because they see social situations in certain ways. Thus society and social situations 'determine' man, unlike instincts, through man's thoughts and through his rationality.

Thus symbolic interactionism with its emphasis of the social formation and maintenance of the self, and its view of society as networks of interacting selves, provided a climate within which it was reasonable to study the breakdown and invalidation of selves also. It was not by complete chance that the social theorist, Mead, and the social student, Thomas, worked in the same institution, Chicago University, as did some of the most important and influential sociological students of crime and mental illness in this period (see Rose, 1956).

Having looked into the reasons why American sociology developed and has maintained, an interest in psychiatric problems, one distinction between inter-war and recent post-war theories must be pointed out. The distinction, to state it in terms which are at once too black and too white, is this. Inter-war sociology viewed mental illness as the consequence of social illness, so to speak. Thus it is where there are social 'abnormalities' and 'undesirable' phenomena like unemployment, poverty, downward social mobility, slum conditions, and so on, that psychiatric personal 'abnormalities' and 'undesirable' phenomena like neuroses, psychoses and crime occur. The assumption seemed to be that in a society where no gross and undesirable social phenomena occurred (admittedly a utopian ideal, but one perhaps inspired by the concept of scientific and technological 'progress'), then no strange and undesirable personal thinking and action would occur. The post-war theorists, on the other hand, rejected both the analysis and its optimistic assumption.

They argued that on the contrary it was not societal 'illness', disorganisation, abnormality, disintegration and suchlike which generates so-called mental illness. Rather, it was precisely the opposite: it was societal 'health', organisation, normality and integration which generated mental illness. Thus the assumption was that even if this societal equilibrium and 'health' could be achieved at the utopian level where the running sores of poverty, unemployment and so on had been eliminated, and not just patched over, then *still* crime and mental illness would occur.

The difference between the pre- and post-war view is not quite that of optimism and pessimism respectively. Rather, it is more a question of tolerance. Must the sociologist implicitly condemn crime and mental illness as 'bad' and as socially 'undesirable'? Can he not simply have the anthropologist's interest in the strange, and the sea-shell collector's interest in the diverse? This almost aesthetic appreciation of actions, without any interest in their classification as crime, as mental illness, or generally as social deviance, has been proposed by Matza (1969). In order to understand his thesis (and further reaches of it which cross the border of mere tolerance, and which 'take the side of' the criminal and the psychotic), we must take a closer look at the post-war sociology of deviance.

Although the field is an extensive one, the main landmarks are not hard to see. One such landmark was Lemert's paper 'Paranoia and the dynamics of exclusion' (1967). Lemert's work has had vital significance in the more recent post-war sociology of deviance. Many of the veins now being mined, such as labelling, societal reaction, deviance amplification and so on, largely originated in his work in the late 1940s, which culminated in his *Social Pathology* (1951).

Other major landmarks occur in the work of Becker, Goffman and Scheff, and we will come to these after a look at Lemert's paper. One feature that they all share is an emphasis on the importance of the 'audience reaction' to an initially 'deviant' act. That is, they emphasise a person's action is only deviant because other people recognise it and define it as such. The suspicion that recent theorists have articulated into a theory is that it is the social recognition, definition and labelling of the deviant act and of the deviant, that generates further deviant acts by a person who now believes himself to be what everybody says he is.

Lemert stated this most forcefully in his paper as a critique of a previous paper by Cameron (1943). Cameron had argued that paranoid persons are people whose deficient social learning, combined with social conditions of stress, leads to an inability to interact successfully and skilfully with others. The person thus projects the responsibility for his incompetence on to a social world around him which he then suspects and fears as 'out to get him', etc. That is, the person avoids responsibility for his own failings by putting the blame on what Cameron called 'the paranoid pseudo-community'. The important point about this community is that it is pseudo, the person's fiction, not corresponding with any reality which outside and independent observers would be able to see. Lemert questions this and asserts that while it is true that the paranoid person acts in terms of a social world he experiences as threatening him, there is no reason to assume that the threats are figments of his imagination. Thus Lemert believes that the 'paranoid community' is real and not pseudo, basing this on an empirical investigation of how paranoics come to be defined and committed to a mental institution.

The process that results in committal and exclusion from the community begins in the interpersonal disturbances that arise between an individual and either his family, employers, work associates or neighbours, over a real and apparently inevitable threat of loss of status. This threat may occur for any of a number of reasons; getting old and 'past it', accidents resulting in stigmatising mutilations, infringement of professional ethics and loss of a professional qualification, being passed over in the promotion stakes, or simply being sacked, etc. For whatever reason the process begins with a person thinking of himself as a failure, being irritable and anxious, and being 'difficult to get on with', and thus being made quite distinctly 'a stranger on trial' in each new occupational and other group he joins.

These groups' treatment of such a stranger is not uniformly hostile. It is ambiguous, now friendly now suspicious, because the group believes him to be an ambiguous figure, now friendly now untrustworthy. Thus communication between the person and members of the group is subject to rapid and unsettled Gestalt switches, with the subject getting emotional and upset and the group members keeping emotionally controlled by putting themselves in the position of watching him, judging him and humouring him. It is this kind of 'spurious interaction', as Lemert calls it, that is the main factor in precipitating a formal crisis and formal exclusion of the subject from his work group and, further, from his family and community. During both the informal and more formal phases of the process, members of the work group have become conspiratorial and secretive in relation to the subject. Their only interactions with him are of the spurious humouring kind. They talk 'behind his back', and make contingency plans of the kind 'if he does this, then we'll ...'. And finally, depending upon the power of the work group (the conspirators may be an intimate group or a large one, may or may not officially hold power in the organisation), then the subject can be kicked out or, with the collaboration of his 'friends' and family, official proceedings can be entered into to get him put away.

Like all conspirators, those attempting to exclude the subject fear him, spy on him, misrepresent him, and finally betray him before the courts. In the case of the paranoid the conspiracy against him *has* to be an exceedingly well organised and well planned one, unlike the situation with schizophrenic adolescents for instance. This is because the paranoic is old enough and wise enough to contest the court proceedings and sue for damages, according to Lemert. As with the other workers in this field, Lemert, to resort to canine metaphors, (a) supports the underdog, and (b) believes in the truth of what is expressed in the saying 'give a dog a bad name'.

Goffman, in his work on mental institutions (1968b), and on the characteristic of what he calls 'total institutions' in general, takes up the same theme as Lemert where the latter leaves off. That is, Goffman is concerned most with the patient-phase of a mentally ill person's 'career', whereas Lemert's paper dealt with the pre-patient phase. The use of the term 'career' with its implication of apprenticeship and initiation into a craftsman group, or of training and initiation into a profession, is a common one in this field of the sociology of deviance (see Becker, 1966, ch. 2). The usage may appear to be ironic because 'career' implies social enhancement and a way of life that is socially respectable, whereas in mental illness we are dealing with social degradation and a way of life that is feared and shunned by conventional society. But the irony is in fact superficial and marginal, as the term is apt and fully justifiable in this context. Like all careers, mental illness usually means life-long involvement with social institutions and organisations which determine central and not peripheral aspects of one's actions.

As a user of public transport services my involvement with such organisations will probably be life-long, but it is peripheral to the determination of my actions by the organisation in which I pursue my career. On the other hand, the transport organisation is a centrally important influence on the actions of its bus drivers. Their involvement with it, which may be as life-long as mine, is thus different from mine by being a career involvement. Mental illness thus is a career in the specific sense of implying an important and longstanding involvement of the subject with an institution. The institution determines his actions and the roles he must play, not in a peripheral or transient way but in a way that is central to him. A career takes up most of one's time, most of one's effort and most of one's personality; thus mental illness is a career.

But while some careers are *merely central* to a person's life, others, like mental illness, can be said to *monopolise* it. Goffman brings out this difference in his concept of the 'total institution'. A career in the ordinary open institutions of society does not preoccupy the subject to the exclusion of *all* else; he can still be a husband, a father, a lover, a football/golf/etc. fanatic, a churchgoer and so on, besides and apart from his career of bus driving, dentistry or whatever. But a career in a total institution virtually monopolises every waking minute of a person's life.

Armies, prisons, monasteries and mental asylums are examples of total institutions; and a career as a soldier, a prisoner, a monk or a lunatic in such institutions does not leave much room for anything else. To overstate the point, the soldier and the monk, the prisoner and the lunatic *are* nothing else than their career role. Total institutions do not permit their members to be or do anything else, or much spare time in which to be or to do it. It makes no difference that the soldier and the monk voluntarily allowed themselves to be limited and monopolised in this way, and that usually prisoners and lunatics became part of the institution against their will. The point is that once in, the person conforms to the institution's definition of what he is and what he must do, at all times. Otherwise pressure of a more or less violent sort can be applied to make him conform.

At the less violent end of the scale is the monk's guilt and penance for 'sins' that he is helped to 'acknowledge' by his confessor, normally a monk of higher rank, of more authority in the monastic community. At the more violent end of the scale is solitary confinement, and withdrawal of privileges for soldier, prisoner and lunatic alike. In the latter's case there are also a growing range of techniques he can be subjected to 'for his own good'. Leucotomy and brain surgery, fashionable in the early post-war period, have gone out of fashion in the last decade, being inspired by the same overbalance of technique over knowledge, and having the same unpredictable results as cracking nuts with sledgehammers. But the 'bull in a china shop' mentality in asylum 'therapy' is served equally well by electro-convulsive therapy, which is the calculated production in the patient of something resembling an epileptic fit. Behaviourist techniques of deconditioning and reconditioning also involve electric shocks, besides drugs to produce vomiting and so on.

Sociologists and humanistic psychiatrists tend to concur on their attitudes to this at least. They both believe that such techniques are used in the closed social system of the asylum by people in authority on people under authority to assert this authority structure. 'Therapy' and the effort to 'cure', where it exists, has an organisational role as a means of social control and manipulation. It is used to discipline and not to help the patient. They believe, further, that it is used to enforce the patient's career as a mentally ill person, which is an anti-therapeutic function.

Thus the possibility exists that 'therapeutic' discipline may be used on the patient, not only when he exhibits gross and violent behaviour, and when he is endangering his own and others' physical life, but also when he *refuses* to exhibit any such 'symptomatic behaviour' at all. There is a symbolic value in the ritual struggles between madman and orderlies in 'violent' wards, for the authorities, for instance. So it is reasonable to suspect that incidents may be provoked by the representatives of authority, just as they are in prisons, in the army or in classrooms, in order to 'set an example' and 'show them who's boss', etc. Violence by the patient is a display of the 'symptoms' of mental illness, and as such confirms the diagnosis. But this is a gross and usually minimal form of 'symptomatic behaviour' in any asylum, since there are many other kinds of symptoms which the authorities can encourage, and which are a lot more easy to deal with.

Like armaments' manufacturers, who may have vested interests in encouraging war, the 'staff' of mental asylums have vested interests in encouraging their 'inmates' displays of insanity. Thus patients may be encouraged to 'remember' when their symptoms first appeared, what they were like, whether they have appeared recently, if so how often and when. They may be encouraged to 'act out' their troubles, and to acknowledge that they are sick and in need of treatment. They are a broken-down machine that needs servicing; they are infected with a disease that must be isolated from the outside world, and treated; they are invalid, in both the medical and legal interpretations of this term, and they must be made aware of all this, if they are not already, which is unlikely. They must be confirmed in this way of looking at themselves; they must accept that they are mental patients, that that is their career, and that that is what they are. The staff may use talk or the violent techniques we have referred to in order to enforce their diagnosis on the subject, and in order to get them to conform to their expected role in the total institution, the role of madness.

The mental institution is a classroom where inmates learn, both from the staff and from other inmates, how to play the limited number of roles, and the restricted repertoire of actions required of a mentally ill patient. Goffman discusses all of this in terms of his concept of 'primary adjustment' (1968b, p. 171), virtually taking it for granted in order to highlight his main interest in 'secondary adjustments'. Primary adjustment is the basic adjustment that an individual makes in his concept of himself, of what he is and what he must do, which fits in with the roles and expectations that the organisation he has joined has for him. The descriptions of this kind of subjugation of the self in the interests of acquiring the self that the organisation wants from the person, gives many of Goffman's descriptions a touch of tragedy, particularly in the sphere of mental illness. But his descriptions of what he calls secondary adjustments that the self makes, given the primary ones, gives his descriptions and analyses their colour. Secondary adjustments 'represent the ways in which the individual stands apart from the role and the self that were taken for granted for him by the institution'. They represent the ways in which, within the confines of the specific social system, the individual 'makes out', 'gets by', 'plays the system', etc.

Even total systems have their members who conform, not only because they fear the consequences and certainly because they believe that it is the right thing to do, but because they know how to extract rewards and fringe benefits from their situation. Unofficial and informal arrangements can arise among the inmates, and between the staff and the inmates, in any given asylum, for instance. Just as in prisons or army barracks, so in asylums there exist unofficial information 'grape-vines', unofficial distribution of and even creation of rewards and privileges by the staff in return for equally unofficial services by the inmates. This is even more the case where the staff have to live in the institution with the inmates; Goffman gives the example of inmates being used as gardeners, handymen and even babysitters by the staff. But generally the phenomenon of secondary adjustments, and the recognition that it occurs to a greater or lesser extent in all social institutions, is important as a reminder that social conformism is usually reasoned and not blind.

There is considerable evidence, for instance, that in the Southern States of the U.S.A., before the recent changes in black attitudes and social power, a black man would play at being a 'nigger' for the white men who controlled and oppressed him. By confirming their definition of him, and by apparently conforming to it, he was able to receive rewards and privileges that he might not otherwise have got, at the same time having the grim satisfaction that he was not the creature that he was play-acting. By conforming he benefited materially and spiritually, but the latter was most important: if he could play-act at being a 'nigger' then he could believe that he must be something else than a 'nigger', he might even be a man. The same kind of processes may account for some of the conformist behaviour that goes on in total institutions. If a man can play-act at being 'a soldier', 'a prisoner/criminal' or, in our case, 'a madman', that is, if he can 'fool them', then he has a reason for believing that 'in reality' or 'essentially' he is not only, not merely, 'a soldier', 'a prisoner/criminal', or 'a madman' (see also Goffman, 1961 for his analysis of role-distance). This kind of reasoning from the depths of despair would only occur in the oppressive and suffocating regime of a total institution, such as prisons, asylums and American slave-worked plantations. In a more open situation, such as in the pre-patient phase of the career of the mentally ill subject, then social definitions, labelling, role-expectations, 'diagnosis' and categorisation may all be fought by the subject. In the more open situation, therefore, the mentally ill person may be said to be sane enough to fight against his labelling and commitment to an asylum by the others in his social world. While in the total institution situation he may be said to be sane enough to conform to his insane role, even sane enough to play-act it.

The final landmark in the sociology of deviance that must be referred to is Scheff's attempt in *Being Mentally Ill* to present a sociological theory of the genesis of 'career-deviance'. His theory is couched in terms of a 'deviance-amplifying' social system, which, he believes, reverberates around the allegedly mentally ill subject before his commital to an asylum. So, in a sense, Scheff (1966) fills out Lemert's analysis of the pre-patient phase, and takes for granted Goffman's extension of the analysis into the patient phase. Scheff's systematic approach was influenced by Buckley (1967), and is similar to that of Wilkins (1964). But before we look at this approach further, Scheff's indebtedness to Becker's (1963) analysis of deviance and rule-breaking must first be noted. Scheff views most symptoms of mental illness as instances of 'residual rule-breaking', utilising Becker's concept of 'residual rules'. This concept applies to those rules, and taken-for-granted assumptions about thought and behaviour which remain the boundary of even deviant acts like crime, perversion, drunkenness and bad manners. These latter concepts are all norm-violation concepts, referring to the breaking of social rules. But beyond these rules there lies the boundary of meaning. All of the deviations and norm-violations that terms like bad manners and perversion refer to are, so to speak, 'within the pale', they are odd but not alien. But residual rules are broken when behaviour becomes 'meaningless', when it is bizarre, alien and 'beyond the pale'. Behaviour that is labelled as mentally ill breaks such residual rules.

Such unspoken rules are the stuff of the 'natural attitude' (phenomenology) or of the 'basic conceptual structure' (Strawsonish conceptual analysis). There are residual rules relating to speech production, criteria of well-formed utterances and sentence organisation and so on at the boundaries of meaning in any given society and culture. The prospective mentally ill person breaks such rules; he speaks to himself loudly in public, or his utterances are topsy-turvy and ungrammatical, for example (see McHugh, 1970; Blum, 1970).

But, like Lemert, Kitsuse (1968) and others before him (see for example, Rose, 1962; Gough, 1968; Mechanic, 1962; Sampson, Messinger and Towne, 1968), and like Scheff after him, Becker believes that 'audience reaction' is the most important factor in the understanding of deviance. For, apart from situational and more gross social 'causes' of deviance, Becker believes that 'social groups create deviance by making the rules whose infraction constitutes deviance, and by applying those rules to particular people and labelling them as outsiders' (1966, p. 9). This is as true and as self-evident (after it has been pointed out) as saying that the 'box office success' or 'failure' of a film is not a somehow intrinsic quality of the film, but rather is constituted by the audience reaction to it. They define it a 'box office success' or 'failure'. Similarly 'deviance' is not a quality intrinsic to an act; it is the product of an audience, or social definition. No legal code?—no criminal act; no social rule?—no deviant act; no defining social audience?—then equally no such thing as a man or an act defined as 'insane' or 'deviant' (see the work on this approach in Becker (ed.), 1964; Douglas (ed.), 1970b; Rubington and Weinberg (eds.), 1968; and Scheff (ed.), 1967a).

Scheff's theory then, is that the social act of labelling a man or an action as 'mentally ill', that is, as breaking a residual rule, 'is the single most important cause of careers of residual deviance' (1966, p. 93). Various studies have shown that most actors and acts that could be labelled as residual rule-breaking in fact pass unnoticed and unlabelled for one reason or another, and that only a small percentage get labelled. Scheff's main fieldwork investigation was a study of the psychiatric and legal decision-making procedures in an American state, particularly with regard to committal proceedings against prospective mental patients. He found that the influence of medical norms and disease process thinking among the psychiatrists predisposed them to diagnose illness rather than health. This predisposition is in the patient's best interests in the case of suspected organic ailments but it is an unthinking and unjustified one when taken out of context to apply to 'mental illnesses'. Commitment to an asylum, and the public labelling that it results from, may not only intensify the 'symptoms' but may in fact create them, according to Scheff. He argues that labelled deviants may be rewarded for playing the stereotyped deviant role, which he and the labelling community has learned about in childhood and had had continually reaffirmed in everyday gossip, T.V., Press and other channels of 'information'. And conversely, labelled deviants are punished when they attempt to return to more conventional, 'sane', roles. Ex-convicts and ex-mental patients find it very difficult to get employment after they leave their respective total institutions, for instance.

The crisis associated with public labelling (psychiatric examinations, court proceedings, neighbours gossiping, family ashamed, etc.) may lead, Scheff thinks, to the residual rule-breaker becoming highly suggestible in his confusion, shame and guilt. He is placed in a stressful situation, the only way out of which is to accept the role of insanity offered to him by all concerned. And this is like a person having their first heroin 'fix'. Once the subject begins to organise and reorganise his behaviour and his perspective of the world in terms of being insane (or in the other example, of being a 'junkie'), then 'he is "hooked", and will proceed on a career of chronic deviance' (ibid., p. 88; see also Matza, ch. 5-7).

Lemert has offered a conceptual distinction between 'primary' and 'secondary' deviation which complements and clarifies this kind of analysis (1967, ch. 3). Primary deviation refers to rule-breaking which has unimportant consequences for the status, identity and self-system of the actor. It may occur for any number of different reasons and causes, including genetic and physiological ones. But it is (seen to be) managed and handled within the field of interaction of the performances. If it is recurrent it is normalised and accepted by all concerned. We may think here of actions of the mentally handicapped and retarded child or adult, the blind person, or the stutterer. Although such actions are rule-breaking, they *can* be managed and allowed for in most social contexts. On the other hand, where they are continually stigmatised, pointed out, ridiculed or whatever, the concept of secondary deviation comes into play. A deviation remains primary in so far as the actor experiences his act as ultimately acceptable to and accepted by others, as ultimately manageable and managed by others. It becomes secondary in so far as the actor experiences his act as ultimately unacceptable to others. Of course, the societal or audience reaction is crucial here in making this distinction for the actor to experience. In secondary deviation the audience reaction to the actor's performance, and his experience of this reaction, is destructive and negative for him. He is stigmatised, and he experiences being stigmatised. His status, identity and self-system are consequently affected profoundly and traumatically. His audience imposes a new role upon him and he has no choice but to 'make out' or 'get by' in it.

Scheff and Buckley view these processes as a deviation-amplifying feed-back loop. This reverberates originally from the audience (family, friends, police, etc.), in the definition of the act and actor as deviant—to the subject's self image. He begins to think that he is what people say he is, and thus begins to act more deviantly to fit the social stereotype. Further acts produce further definitions and labellings by the audience, until finally the spiral culminates in the public and official labelling processes with their attendant crises and stress for all concerned. The career of mental illness is then well and truly launched by committal to an asylum, with its attendant socialising machinery and systems. And the society that made the subject an outsider will not welcome him back to normality and sanity after his sojourn in an asylum. These are the kinds of conclusions to which the whole modern tradition of sociology of deviance and of mental illness tend to arrive at. Lemert, Scheff, Goffman, Becker, Matza and the many others, whose work we have not the space to discuss, can all be viewed in the doggy terms we mentioned earlier. They are *for* the labelled individual as an 'underdog', in a process which involves 'giving a dog a bad name'.

They are for the deviant, in the sense of redressing the previous overbalance in favour of what Matza calls the 'correctional perspective' in sociology (1969, ch. 2). They are not interested in the morality or lack of it of the deviant, of his acts or of the society he deviates from. Like anthropologists, they seem to see their main job as that of fieldwork and empirical description of the strange practices and processes that go on within 'normal' society. And as against their pre-war predecessors, they hold that it is not a society out of control, and disorganised such as in the Depression, which creates mental disorders. But rather it is the reverse, social order and social control, and even the organisation of psychiatric 'therapy' in asylums, creates the mentally ill career or a person. And, furthermore, this career, and the actions expected of the role-player, are far from 'disordered'. Certain types of social order can be seen to produce certain types of personality order called mental illness.

Therefore the recent tradition thinks that we should look again at the older presumption that social disorder produces personality disorders. Social degradation and invalidation of an individual can occur in organised and stable social contexts as well as in unstable and disorganised ones. Furthermore, the mental illness of individuals is less the determined effect of blind social causes; rather, it is the responsibility, partly of the subject, but also of the social agencies and agents who define, label, commit and treat the individual (see also Szasz, 1971; Foucault, 1967; G. Rosen, 1968). It may be, as Scheff points out that the individual's responsibility for his condition is small, and thus that mental illness is 'largely ascribed rather than achieved' (1966, p. 168). But it is equally the case that, as Lemert has pointed out, the social world of the paranoid, at least, is a really conspiring and motivated world and not at all a 'pseudo-community', or the subject's delusion. It is with this in mind that we must note the convergence between the recent sociology of deviance and the humanistic and existential psychotherapy we discussed in the previous section.

Conclusion

The fact of a certain degree of cross-reference between the sociologists of deviance and the humanistic psychiatrists we have discussed suggests a *prima facie* consonance between their respective views. To take some examples of this almost wholly laudatory and complimentary cross-reference, it might be noted that Scheff referred to Laing's work, in *Being Mentally Ill* (1966, p. 17), and Laing returned the compliment by referring to Scheff's and Lemert's work in the second edition of *The Self and Others* (1969, p. 116). In a related vein Matza acknowledged Sartre's existential phenomenological influence on his own conception of sociology of deviance (1969, p. 93n).

The most blatant convergence between the view of these two

superficially distinct areas of study is that over the social nature of mental illness. Both propose that mental illness is the result of a social process; it results from the actions of other people in their own right and, acting on behalf of various social institutions, in the social world of the individual. The psychiatrists complement the sociologists, who are only interested in the original rule-breaking acts of the subject as a kind of 'input' into a social process, by revealing the interpersonal reasons even for these initial acts. But beyond this both concur that it is the social process which is of paramount importance.

But some attention must be given to the possible objection that the sociologists conceive of the social process in very different terms from the psychiatrists. The former, it may be argued, speak of a blind and purposeless, almost mechanical, process, while the latter speak in terms of responsibility and purposes. The sociologists speak of deterministic systems in which the subject is processed. While, on the other hand, the psychiatrists speak of collusions and conspiracies in the family and beyond which are humanly responsible for the labelling and commitment of the individual. And they also speak of the responsibility of the individual himself for what he does, and that his insanity is a course of action and a project, which he chooses and which he makes in the face of a situation that offers little else. Thus the psychiatrists conceive of the whole process as an interaction, in fact a struggle, of purposes. There are the people around the individual, on the one hand, whose definitions and purposes constitute an 'intolerable situation', and there is the individual, on the other hand, who is ultimately responsible for what he is and what he does in the face of a situation he sees as intolerable.

But to say that these complexities and, further, these humanistic concepts of responsibility, consciousness-of-the-situation, purposes and so on are excluded from the sociological approach simply misrepresents this approach. Lemert was convinced, as we have seen, that his evidence showed that the progress of a paranoic into a mental patient was the responsibility of the real conspirators around him. A conspiracy is not a blind and purposeless social mechanism, it comes complete with purposes, intentional actions, consciousness and all of the other distinctively human phenomena. Scheff's 'deviation amplifying system' similarly works only through the changes in the subject's self image, due to the purposive actions of labelling and excluding carried on knowingly by people interacting with the subject. Similarly Goffman's mental patient is not thoroughly and blindly determined by the total institution of which he is a member. On the contrary, he is capable of 'playing the system', and of rationally distancing himself from the mentally ill role expected of him.

There are sociological concepts which have been invented specifically to avoid and get around questions of responsibility and purpose in social life. Thus Merton, for instance, urges the sociologist to attend to the 'latent' rather than the 'manifest' functions of social phenomena. That is, he urges attention to the unconscious, unforeseen and unintended aspects of social life as against the conscious, foreseen and intentional aspects. So it might be possible to understand the social genesis of mental illness and of individual mentally ill careers as completely unwitting, unforeseen and unintended consequences of actions which have other more laudable intentions perhaps. But once again this is simply to misrepresent the phenomena that investigators, both sociological and psychiatric, have discovered in this particular field. The manifest function of a family may be said to be the care and protection of its offspring; and the manifest function of an asylum may be said to be the care, therapy and cure of the patient. But families can knowingly make an offspring a scapegoat for their own inadequacies, guilt and mental troubles. Similarly, asylum staff can knowingly enforce the mental patient role on asylum inmates. Public committal proceedings to get the subject into an asylum are quite knowing and purposeful; it is hard to see what else they could be. And similarly the paranoid person is surrounded by a real conspiracy, a real attempt to exclude him, and not a fictional or delusional conspiracy. Nothing would be gained, and much would be lost by trying to call these processes and actions 'latent' functions, or 'unintended consequences'. As unpalatable as they are, nonetheless, they are as manifest and as intentional as are any of the more palatable and official functions of the family, asylum or other relevant institutions. The sociologist, in this field at least, has tried to come to terms with complexities and depths and contradictions of purposes; quite rightly he has not resorted to concepts which exclude this humanistic perspective.

A more marginal and acceptable objection might well be that too little is made of the subject's responsibility for his actions, granted that something is made of it. Thus it might be said that humanistic psychiatrists and sociologists of deviance make too much of the responsibility of actors other than the subject, some representing social institutions and agencies, for the subject's problems (see Spitzer and Denzin, 1968, p. 462). They overdo their support for the underdog. But this is a matter that can only be decided by further investigation, and it is one that must vary considerably from case to case. Problems in the accurate weighting of personal as against social responsibility in any given case do not affect the general thesis that both of these factors contribute in important ways. Their interaction constitutes the phenomenon of mental illness as a social one. It could not be otherwise, for man, whether sane or insane, is a social animal. His sense of self and identity is a social product of the interaction between himself and others around him. Thus everyman, besides believing that he is wholly responsible for himself, is partly responsible for the nature of others, just as they are partly responsible for his nature. Sociology from the early days of symbolic interactionism and Weberian 'interpretive sociology' (see chapter 8 below) has never completely lost its feel for the subtleties and complexities of man's social existence. And in spite of the flights from understanding social existence, that C. Wright Mills (1959) has called 'abstracted empiricism' and 'grand theory', sociology has returned to such themes in the sociology of deviance. We can only mention here in passing, that there have been corresponding movements in this direction in the sociology of religion (Berger, 1967), the sociology of knowledge (Berger and Luckmann, 1967), the sociology of economic organisations (Silverman, 1970) and the sociology of education (Young, 1971). Phenomenological sociology, in Schutz's work, forms part of our discussion of Weber in the next chapter, and these topics will be returned to in a general way in the final chapter, when ethnomethodology will also be considered.

Humanistic psychiatry and the sociology of deviance can be said to converge on a very similar, and in some cases identical, understanding and explanation of mental illness. In demonstrating this convergence hopefully the more general background consonances between existential phenomenology (which inspired much of the psychiatry) and sociological assumptions (particularly about the social and purposive nature of the self) may have been indicated.

This consonance must be compared with the dissonance that exists between existential phenomenology and psychology, and which we have tracked through preceding chapters. Psychology is committed to reductionist principles of explanation of human thought and action. Sociology is committed, whether it likes it or not, to one version or another of humanistic and teleological explanation of human thought and action.

In the following chapter we return to the less specific and concrete problems of sociological theory and method, as expressed in Weber's work. And, as with the preceding chapters on psychology, the main point will be to discover whatever similarities exist between the attitudes of, on the one hand, conceptual analysis, and on the other, phenomenology, to a general area of the humanities. In the present chapter conceptual analysis has, of needs, been ignored; its explicit contributions to the specific area of understanding mental illness are minimal, although limited use of its concepts has occurred. However, in so far as it has been seen to share a common humanistic position with existential phenomenology, then it has been implicated in the comparisons and convergences that have been noted in this chapter.

In particular it is implicated in the consonance noted between one variety of humanistic philosophy and the humanistic assumptions and background theories of sociology.

8 Weber's sociology

Humanistic philosophy, downright censorious in its discussions of psychology, is merely irritable with sociology. In the reductionist commitments of psychology it finds an enemy which appears to have the heroic dimensions that any worthwhile enemy ought to have. But in the humanistic commitments of sociology it merely finds a wife to grouse at. In the philosophical literature there is much more heroic battling to choose from than there is familial grousing, as might be expected. But it is still possible to track down a sociological topic which both types of humanistic philosophy in which we are interested (conceptual analysis and phenomenology) have had a grouse about. That topic is Weber's sociology.

In this chapter then, as in previous chapters concerning psychology, the focus of attention is on the similarities between the discussions offered by both humanistic schools of philosophy. The sociological topic here is Weber's sociology, but we could have chosen Marxist sociology. Sartre and Merleau-Ponty on the one hand, and MacIntyre, Winch and others on the other hand, have devoted sufficient attention to Marxism to provide material for a comparison. But partly because that material is only barely sufficient, partly for reasons of space, and partly because the example of Weber serves our sociological interest just as well as that of Marx, the discussion is confined to Weber's theories.

Weber's approach to sociology (see Stammer, 1971; Freund, 1968; Bendix, 1960; Bendix and Roth, 1971; Parsons, 1937; Hughes, 1959), as to other disciplines such as law, economic history, politics and so on, was broadly humanistic, and not at all reductionist or positivistic. And we must enlarge upon this aspect of his approach before investigating the philosophers' discussions of him. However, it is well to indicate at this point that both schools of philosophy, in spite of Weber's humanism, grouse about certain features of his approach which could, at a stretch, receive a reductionist interpretation. These features are not all ones that Weber intended, indeed some are unwitting inconsistencies. Weber, no less than Freud or any of the other great thinkers of our century, was quite capable of inconsistency. But the main feature that has pained his humanistic philosophical commentators was certainly a deliberate one, whether or not it was inconsistent.

This feature was Weber's simultaneous endorsement of two types of explanation of individuals' social behaviour. On the one hand there was the explanation in terms of causality and statistical correlations, while on the other hand there was the explanation by means of the construction of ideal types of actions, action sequences and action systems, together with the attempt to understand the motivation of actors, or *Verstehen*. Both types of explanation were subjected to critical analyses by humanistic philosophers, but naturally the former was regarded with a good deal more suspicion that the latter. The latter was an explicitly humanistic form of explanation, the former was not. It is necessary now to take a closer look at Weber's analysis of sociological explanation in order to provide a basis from which to examine the fraternal criticisms offered by the schools of philosophy in which we are interested.

Following the interests of his philosophical commentators, our discussion of Weber can be confined to the ideas contained in two specific pieces of his work. One is the collection of essays which make up *The Protestant Ethic and the Spirit of Capitalism* (1930). This first saw the light of day in 1904-5, but was considerably revised in 1920, the year of Weber's death (see also Weber on sects in Gerth and Mills, 1967). The other is the methodological essay called 'Basic sociological terms', which was first published in 1913, later to be revised and published posthumously as an introduction to a larger work on the theory of social and economic organisation called *Economy and Society* in 1922 (see Weber, 1968, vol. 1; 'Basic sociological terms' is the first chapter of this volume).

It is notable that although both pieces of work were revised at the same time shortly before Weber's death, the more empirical of the two preceded the more theoretical of the two. Thus some care has to be taken over interpreting the relationship between the two works. The casual implication that the more empirical work embodied the concepts and direction of thought of the more theoretical work, for instance, is clearly a little *too* casual. Weber proceeded with his empirical explanations and his attempts to understand historical and social phenomena *before* he pronounced on what was the nature of social scientific explanation and understanding. And while it is probable that the empirical work was written with the explanatory criteria he later developed systematically in mind, it is not clear that such work can automatically be pointed to as demonstrating such criteria in action.

But, given this, undeveloped forms of 'ideal-type' explanation together with undeveloped explanatory criteria of causality and of *Verstehen* do appear in the *Protestant Ethic* essays.

In the two pieces of work at issue here, as in all of the rest of his work, Weber was influenced in his general approach by what he called the 'historical school' (1949, p. 106). This referred specifically to the analysis of the difference between the natural sciences and the humanities proposed by his colleague Rickert (1962). But the background of German intellectual life in the late nineteenth century and early twentieth century included variations on this distinction between the natural sciences and the humanities by others such as Dilthey and Windelband (see Rickman, 1961; Hodges, 1969; Hughes, 1959; Parsons, 1937). And, as we have already noted (in chapter 1) Dilthey came to influence Husserl's later thinking, while Heidegger studied under Rickert. Phenomenology in fact grew out of these turn-of-the-century discussions, with its head firmly turned towards recognising the distinction which we have called here that between reductionist and humanistic explanations of human thought and action. Weber was associated with this early discussion, and was directly influenced by Rickert, and also by Dilthey more indirectly, through his acknowledgment of the concept of *Verstehen* in the writings of Jaspers, among others.

Dilthey believed that the natural sciences and the humanities, specifically history, dealt with two distinct areas of being, more or less corresponding respectively to Matter and Mind. Rickert, on the other hand, believed that the natural sciences and the humanities both dealt with the same range of objects but by different methods and from different points of view.

Weber accepted Rickert's methodological distinction between the social sciences, specifically history and the natural sciences. He agreed with Rickert that the nature of historical knowledge was very different from the nature of natural scientific knowledge, but no less trustworthy because of that. Historical and humanistic knowledge was not to be contrasted with natural scientific knowledge as an anti-rational and anti-scientific form. If this implication could be derived from Dilthey's position, then Weber did not want anything to do with it. Weber thought that Dilthey was right to say that the historian 'understands' his field of interest because it consists mainly of other men's actions, whereas the natural scientist does not 'understand' his data in the same way. But he thought further, irrespective of Dilthey's views, that *Verstehen* was a rational method. It was capable of systematic examination, and the elements of which it was comprised could be rationally understood; it was not an irrational and mysterious method. If history used it, then, this did not make history non-scientific in Weber's eyes.

Historical knowledge was scientific knowledge even though it differed from natural scientific knowledge in so far as it was arrived at, and stated in terms of, *Verstehen*, and even though it gave knowledge of the unique and the individual rather than of the universal and the lawful. This latter point was Rickert's main one. It is the argument that scientific knowledge is not all of a unity; some sciences are law and theory oriented (nomothetic), and others are interested in individual phenomena for their own sake, and not as exemplifying some law or theory (idiographic).

Of course, this idiographic orientation was just as possible in the sphere of physical objects and phenomena as it was in the sphere of human thoughts and actions. Parts of geology and of astronomy, most of zoology and other such natural scientific disciplines all exhibit idiographic features, i.e. an interest in specific and concrete phenomena for the sake of it. Logical empiricist philosophy has always tried to demonstrate that idiographic knowledge depends upon, and gets whatever validity it has, from nomothetic, knowledge in any given particular field. This has been reasonably successful in the sphere of natural scientific studies like geology, astronomy, zoology and so on. Explanations and descriptions in these fields do, often wittingly and equally often unwittingly, invoke laws and theories about the structure and processes of rocks, planetary movements and animal physiology respectively. But the case still has to be proved for human history, particularly social, economic and political history. If Weber were alive today to take part in the 'covering-law' (nomothetic, see Hempel, 1959) versus 'rational interpretations of motives' (idiographic humanism, see Dray, 1957) argument in the modern philosophy of history, the chances are that he would support the latter case.

Thus Weber's support for the 'historical school' meant that his consequent analysis of the nature and methods of sociology was made almost completely in terms of the nature and methods of history. His support for causal explanation, particularly, must be seen in this light. As will be seen, it is sometimes taken as implying that Weber was in favour of causal generalisations and laws, when in fact nothing of the sort was intended. We can at this point usefully take a look at the main themes of *The Protestant Ethic and the Spirit of Capitalism*, which was distinctly historical in its approach to the understanding of modern capitalist economic organisation and rationalistic social organisation. The approach was also one which Weber thought of as a causalist one. At the same time it used undeveloped *Verstehen* and ideal-typical methods, which Weber only fully analysed and developed later, in his *Basic Concepts of Sociology* essay.

In *The Protestant Ethic and the Spirit of Capitalism* Weber did not believe that he had demonstrated that Calvinist and Puritan aspects of the Reformation determined the subsequent Industrial Revolution and the growth of modern capitalistic economics. For one thing he was more modest about his essays, considering them preparatory to more detailed work which would have to be done; they were not a 'demonstration', in the sense of definitive 'proof' of anything. And for another thing the relationship he hoped to demonstrate, in this less formal sense, was between an 'ethic' and a 'spirit', between a religion and an 'ethos'. Of course the presumption was that men acted on the basis of the prevailing ethos, and on the basis of maxims that were connected with religious beliefs. But Weber hedged this presumption cautiously and with a subtlety at times amounting to deviousness. For instance at one point he argued that his position did *not* amount to anything so gross as a 'one-sided spiritualistic causal interpretation of culture and of history' (1930, p. 183). He was not attempting to stand Marx on his head, to stand Hegel back on his feet, or to engage in any of the other contortions European academics fancied themselves getting up to. To investigate, as he did, the influences of certain factors on the *ethos* of an economic system, was not self-evidently and immediately to demonstrate conclusively the direct causal efficacy and causal monopoly of those factors of the economic system, which he did not do in any case.

Weber even calls the thesis that the spirit of capitalism could only have arisen as the result of certain effects of the Reformation, and further the thesis that capitalism as an economic system is a creation of the Reformation 'foolish and doctrinaire' (ibid., p. 91). As against this he admits the importance of economic factors and conditions in understanding and explaining Western rationalistic and capitalistic culture (ibid., p. 26) and accepts that it is necessary to understand the economic and social influence on Protestantism (ibid., p. 183). There are so many hedged bets and qualifications in the final version of his thesis, written in 1919, that it is difficult to understand the controversy that the original 1904-5 version, and variations on the theme in Weber's other works, apparently aroused. It is the scope more than the substance of his arguments which still excite interest; Weber's encyclopaedic mind had tried to grasp the essence of modern culture and civilisation and rationalism, and relate it, through the economic ethos, to a religious ethic. It was an interpretation, a 'one-sided accentuation', a picture drawn from a certain explicit perspective; and the topic was the essential nature of modern civilisation. As an interpretation it came within the scope of aesthetic criteria such as simplicity, coherence and plausibility, as well as within the scope of more empirical criteria of its testability. And as a topic it was on a sufficiently grand scale to appear to upset all of the other grand designs in the market-place, including both theological and Marxist ones, at the same time.

Calvin and the English Puritans exemplified the Protestant Ethic most clearly for Weber. While on the other hand Benjamin Franklin's eighteenth-century economic maxims such as 'time is money', which made hard work and the constant accumulation of capital the main ends of life, exemplified the 'spirit of capitalism'. Weber was mainly preoccupied with showing how the former mutated into the latter, how the ethic of 'idleness is sinful' transformed itself into the maxim 'time is money'. Weber found the link in the Calvinist concepts of 'calling' and 'predestination'.

According to this doctrine man could not acquire salvation by amassing grace or 'indulgences' as Catholicism taught. Rather his status as a 'saint' or one of the 'elect' on the one hand, or one of the damned on the other, was an immutable fact ordained at his conception by God. No lax social institution stood between a 'saint' and his God, as it did between the Catholic and his. No confessional system cosseted his human weaknesses. He stood, all of his life and all of his waking moments, in the psychological cell of his predestination; he lived in total transparency to God, in a servile solitude that was at once the paradox of being totally personal and totally impersonal. It was a personal relationship with God, in that it appeared to be on a par with a man-to-man relationship; it was an impersonal relationship because it was experienced without any human warmth, as a relationship between a machine and its creator.

The clinching factor for Weber was that Catholic Christianity had always ordered man *out* of society if he hoped to practise his religion ascetically. The monk, like the hermit, had to renounce the world and live apart. The saint, on the other hand, was called to utilise his abilities to the maximum in the service of God *within* society. It was, as Weber put it, a 'worldly asceticism'. Like the strictest monastic code the saint must renounce the pleasures of the flesh, possessions, mammon, and so on, but within society and not without it. Numerous critics of Weber (see essays in Green, 1959; Eisenstadt, 1968) have pointed out the anti-mammon bias of many of the Calvinists' writings as if that argues against their more unwitting influence on the capitalist mentality. Of course it does nothing of the kind, as Weber points out in his discussion of the ethical writings of Richard Baxter, a politically important Puritan both in Cromwell's and the Restoration Parliament (1930, ch. 5). Money and possessions of themselves were morally neutral. Rather, it was the attitude of their possessor to them, his decision to relax and to enjoy himself by means of them and so 'waste' his time, that constituted the evil. The evil of mammon lay in man's weakness towards it, not in the stuff itself. Man could thus possess money and great wealth so long as he did not use it to enjoy himself, consume lavishly and live in leisure and luxury on the basis of it.

Man must work hard and dutifully at his calling, while at the same time he must live frugally. The accumulation of wealth for the pleasures it can buy was sinful; but to accumulate it, and save it, as a fruit of one's labour in a calling was a sign of God's blessing, a demonstration of one's election. Thus restless and continuous labour in the acquisition of wealth that would be saved and not spent derived from a religious ethic which reached into the deepest well of the soul. Reaching into the deepest spiritual and not materialistic motivations of man this 'must have been' says Weber 'the most powerful conceivable lever' for the expansion of the spirit of capitalism (ibid., p. 172).

Thus Weber held that the Protestant Ethic was captured in the phrase 'idleness is sinful' and its attendant implications, and he felt that the phrase 'time is money' captured the essence of the spirit of capitalism. Weber, in his essays on this subject, showed first how it was plausible and rationally comprehensible that the former attitude should have produced, or mutated into, the latter attitude. And secondly, he went some way towards showing that this rational connection was also probable, or empirical, or that things had actually and historically happened more or less in that way.

He recognised that the flow of history, like one's own stream of consciousness, is literally meaningless and chaotic until some categorisation and abstraction of features is applied to it. Thus he considered his approach to be 'ideal typical' in that he consciously attempted to construct typical courses and contexts of meaningful actions. He imposed frameworks upon the empirical reality. Although he modified his position later, in *The Protestant Ethic* he did not proceed by discovering empirical generalisations. Neither did he subject his hypothesis of the connection between Protestantism and capitalism to empirical test in the normal sense of the word 'test'. It is true, however, that his studies in comparative religions undertaken at the same time were designed to investigate the importance of the *absence* of such a factor as Protestantism in Oriental religions to economic attitudes and life in Oriental societies. And this could be said to be an extremely preliminary form of assessment of the causal significance of this factor in Western economic development. But the whole tenor of Weber's argument, and also the assurance he made that no overweighted mono-causal account could do justice to the complexities of historical development, leads one away from a causal-law (or causal-generalisation) view of Weber's thesis. This element is undoubtedly latent in his thesis, but he himself did not stress it.

Critics since have subjected Weber's thesis to close scrutiny, pointing out, for instance, how Catholics and Lutherans were more represented among the early capitalists than were Calvinists: how Calvinist Geneva was an authoritarian, anti-materialist and thus anti-capitalist society; how Catholic Belgium industrialised before Protestant Holland and so on. But lack of empirical support for the thesis has not in fact demonstrated the falsity or the uselessness of it in most sociologists' eyes. That would have been so only if the thesis had been explicitly and unequivocally based on empirical generalisations, which it was not.

Weber's resort to social statistics throughout the whole of his thesis was minimal. Those that he did use related to a study of the religion of entrepreneurs in the German city of Baden made in the late nineteenth century. This would have been rather a narrow base, and rather distant historically and geographically from Puritan England, which was his main reference point, had he wanted to more than merely sketch in the empirical relevance of his thesis. Without denying such empirical relevance, nevertheless, Weber was concerned with sketches and diagrams drawn from different perspectives which focused on the rationality and the meaningfulness of social actions. He was not so much concerned with the photographs that empirical generalisations allegedly constitute. These are taken from no explicit perspective and take no heed of the meaningfulness of social actions. His method in this early thesis, and even more so in his later analytical and theoretical work, was far more that of the ideal-type sketch than that of the empiricist's photograph (even granting, as Weber following Rickert might not have done, that such undiscriminating empiricist reproduction of reality was a comprehensible alternative in principle).

In his *Protestant Ethic* thesis, and in many of his other studies in comparative religion, Weber used historical and empirical material to construct a coherent relationship, a grand over-all picture, between them. His picture or ideal type of the capitalist economic system included such elements as continuous organised pursuit of profit through peaceful exchange, rational book-keeping and calculations of the effects of actions, and the organisation of formally free labour. No economic system we would ordinarily call a capitalist one manifests all of these features to the same extent. And more important, these are never the *only* features that such a system manifests. It is the same with Weber's ideal-type bureaucracy, which he saw as an attendant aspect of the progressive and fateful rationalisation of modern social and economic life (1968, vol. 1). No organisation which we would ordinarily call a bureaucracy manifests all of the features of Weber's ideal type to the same extent, and once again, it is imperative to understand that these are never the *only* features that such an organisation manifests. Organisations may display so many 'red-tape', informal and 'dysfunctional' features that these may, in any empirical instance, outweigh the formal functional and efficient features that Weber chose to stress.

The purpose of such ideal types or pictures or sketches was not necessarily to reproduce the real world truly or accurately, although *parts* might be reproduced in the context of the whole abstraction and construction of the ideal type. But rather their purpose was to provide some standard *against which* the real world could be compared and, in some sense, measured. So at the same time in many of Weber's writings, particularly his historical studies, he is involved in two projects. On the one hand, he is constructing ideal types out of historical, biographical and other material, and on the other hand, he is comparing real historical developments with the relevant ideal types, and with their constructed relationship. It is possibly this dual orientation that gives Weber's work, not least in studies such as *The Protestant Ethic*, its ambiguous quality, where every position seems to be qualified almost out of existence somewhere else in the work. These ambiguities and changes of position were made somewhat more explicit in Weber's methodological writings, at which we can now take a closer look.

In the methodological works, which Weber wrote around the time that he was writing the first version of *The Protestant Ethic* (1930), he used history as the central discipline of the humanistic studies, or 'cultural sciences'. In the later methodological work, 'Basic sociological terms', Weber forced himself to consider the differences between sociology and history, rather than go on implying that sociology was some unspecified kind of history. Thus, in this essay, he found that he had to take the general and lawful study of social actions and social institutions far more seriously than he had ever done before. Previously his emphasis had always been, following Rickert, on the individual and historically specific nature of ideal-type knowledge. Similarly, his emphasis had been on the understanding of historically specific causal linkages and sequences. Now he had to consider ideal-type knowledge in a more general and abstract light and, similarly, he had to give some account of the possibility of causal laws in sociology. Whereas in his earlier methodological essays he had always been able to divorce historical knowledge from (natural scientific) theoretical knowledge, he now had to consider the unavoidably theoretical nature of sociology. His analysis, like his economic and social history, was a major achievement, but not one completely free from ambiguities and from difficulties of interpretation.

Weber differentiated history and sociology in the following way. History deals with culturally significant individual actions, personalities, institutions and social structures which it attempts to analyse and explain causally. Sociology, on the other hand, 'seeks to formulate type concepts and generalised uniformities of empirical process' (1968, vol. I, p. 19). In the rest of his essay Weber contributes to the first part of this definition of sociology by formulating types related to social action, social relationships, legitimate authority, conflict and competition, voluntary and compulsory social organisations, religious and political organisations, social power and domination and so on. The rest of the work, *Economy and Society*, which the essay introduces, is also concerned with the formulation of types and the construction of concepts relating to various forms of economic action and various forms of authority. This is the theoretical half of sociology as Weber saw it. The other half must be empirical, and must necessarily involve the production and examination of statistics about society to establish uniformities of process and associations between factors which may be called a causal relation.

There are two points to be made about this apparent acceptance by Weber of the relevance of causal laws for sociology and, furthermore, its relevance as explanatory. The first point is that a causal law is an observed regular association between two factors which has been universalised. Thus, instead of saying 'every observed human who smoked *n* cigarettes per day developed lung cancer', we may feel justified in universalising this as follows 'all humans who smoke *n* cigarettes per day develop lung cancer'. This is a causal law, based on evidence, and from which we may predict fairly accurately, let us assume. But we are still at liberty to say that it simply states a problem, about the causes of cancer, and does not solve it. We look at such a causal law as a *fact*, of some unspecified kind, to be further explained; we do not look upon it as explanatory in relation to cancer except in the most superficial way. We need a physiological theory which reveals the micro-processes at work and which explains the macro-associations of such causal laws. To assert therefore a causal uniformity, such as 'poverty breeds crime', and to universalise this into a causal law, such as '*x* degree of poverty always breeds *x* degree of crime', is not necessarily to *explain* anything. Rather it may be to set up the fact of various associations between large scale factors more vividly so that work may be encouraged on the micro-processes upon which these associations rest and which must ultimately figure in the theoretical explanation of the law. But, as we saw in the previous chapter, where such 'micro-processes' as family interactions were examined in relation to the causation of mental illness, sociology can choose to rely on humanistic axioms at this level.

Micro-process theory in physiology, which would explain macro-associations like that of smoking and cancer, would quite naturally and rightly resort to physical, chemical and bio-chemical theories. Micro-process theory in sociology, in contrast, is not reducible in the same way to, say, psychology, for instance. In the particular instance of mental illness, and possibly also that of crime and criminal actions in general, sociology is unifiable with theories of psychiatry that are explicitly humanistic, but not with psychological theories that may be deterministic and reductionist.

Sociological theories of deviance, partly inspired by wider theories such as symbolic interactionism, assert the responsibility of the actor for his own actions. They assert his purposiveness and rationality, and they provide a rational interpretation of his actions and of the actions of relevant social institutions. Weber's 'Basic sociological terms', his theoretical analyses, were framed in very similar terms to such theories.

The second point that may be made about 'empirical uniformities' and 'causal laws' in relation to Weber's definition of sociology, then, concerns the way he stipulated what kinds of empirical uniformities could be called 'sociological'. He asserted that statistical uniformities must be about meaningful/intelligible/rational human action of one kind or another in order to qualify as a sociological generalisation (1968, p. 12). Statistics about rainfall, the productivity of machines and (a rather borderline example) human deaths, did not, in his opinion, qualify. Statistics about crime rates, prices, the number of acres that farmers devoted to crops and the distribution of the population according to occupation, in his opinion, were the sort of empirical uniformities that did qualify as sociological.

As to the associations between such uniformities in meaningful action, which might amount to causal laws, he did not think that they needed to be quantifiable or even precisely calculable. Perhaps a causal association, unembellished, and as unpretentious and as true as any proverb, such as 'poverty causes/breeds crime', would have fitted Weber's bill. Nothing that Weber wrote about causal analysis and explanation in sociology, and about the use of sociological statistics, would in any way license a blindly deterministic conception of social causation, neither would it license what Sorokin (1956) has called 'quantophrenia' in sociology. Sociological interpretations must be 'adequate' not only on the level of cause, but on the level of meaning also (1968, vol. 1, p. 11). We must be fairly sure, and be able to predict from our empirical knowledge and experience, that something will follow upon something else in society. That is, our knowledge must be 'causally adequate'. But the 'somethings' that follow on one another must be meaningful actions, that is, must give us knowledge that is adequate on the level of meaning. To assert, for instance, that the command of a legitimate political authority will be followed by an action complying with the command would be, according to Weber, to state a more or less calculable probability, and also to provide a rational connection. It would be causally and meaningfully adequate. Weber synthesised these two criteria in another definition of sociology, which was that sociology is a 'science concerning itself with the interpretative understanding of social action and thereby with a causal explanation of its course and consequences' (ibid., p. 4).

This synthesis, which can appear so ambiguous at times, and which has appeared to some commentators to confound two distinct explanatory principles, can be seen in a clearer light, if we bear in mind Weber's original legal training. In law, the demonstration of a man's guilt and responsibility (or lack of it) for actions and their consequences synthesises an account of the man's motives and intentions with an account of his causal efficacy in a specific sequence of events. Weber merely makes this synthesis explicit for the sociologist also.

Conceptual analysis

In general there is a consonance between Weber's *Verstehen* approach, which emphasised the interpretation and understanding of the purposive, rational and intentional nature of human action, with conceptual analytic views on this issue. But everybody differentiates themselves most strongly from those they are most like, in order to assert the marginal distinctiveness of their own identity, and conceptual analytic philosophers are no exception to this rule. They find plenty to grouse about in the style of Weber's humanism, without seriously challenging the substance of it.

The main grouse concerns Weber's liking for the concept of causality, and his use of it both in the *Protestant Ethic* and in the 'Basic sociological terms' essay. The two main grousers have been Winch and MacIntyre. However, it must be said here that MacIntyre now disowns (1966; 1967) the views that he expressed in the paper 'A mistake about causality in social science' (1962), where he was critical of Weber. None the less we will examine the thesis of this paper (even though it may be a mistake about a mistake about social science), together with Winch's similar thesis in *The Idea of a Social Science* (1958), which has not been disowned in the same way by its author (see also Louch, 1966; Apel, 1967).

Winch's thesis has been most influential, and it is to this that we turn first. His criticisms of Weber are woven into his more broad attack on the idea of a social science in general. In so far as this is an attack on what I have called the 'reductionist idea' and in so far as its point is to establish a closer relationship between humanistic philosophy and sociological theory than has usually been acknowledged, then my argument is consonant with his.

My analysis of his thesis will be on the whole, fairly critical, particularly with regard to his treatment of concepts like causality and observation. But Winch's advice to the sociologist to get back to the problem of the actor's meanings and rules of action is consonant in a broad sense with both Schutz's position (discussed below in this chapter), and Cicourel's and Garfinkel's position (discussed in chapter 9). Further, and consonant with more conventional sociology, Winch states that the concepts we use to understand a society need *not* necessarily be those of the actors involved. It is just that the sociologist must proceed through an analysis of and understanding of the latter concepts in order to provide a basis for the former concepts.

Winch summarises his qualifying remarks in the following (1958, p. 89):

> I do not wish to maintain that we must stop at the unreflective kind of understanding of which I gave as an instance the engineer's understanding of the activity of his colleagues. But I do not want to say that any more reflective understanding must necessarily presuppose, if it is to count as genuine understanding at all, the participants unreflective understanding. And this in itself makes it misleading to compare it with the natural scientist's understanding of his scientific data. Similarly, although the reflective student of society, or of a particular mode of social life, may find it necessary to use concepts which are not taken from the forms of activity which which he is investigating, but which are taken rather from the context of his own investigation, still these technical concepts of his will imply a previous understanding of those other concepts which belong to the activities under investigation.

Such qualifications, by Winch, of his general position are not often noted or pointed out by his critics; but, having been noted here, they will now largely be ignored.

Generally he seems to imply a complacency about the need continually to confront social phenomena, and a belief that somehow we already know most of what there is to be known about society that is of theoretical interest. In this respect Winch's thesis is dissonant, not only with the approach in this book, but also with the descriptive features of the conceptual analytic school from which it stems.

It is one thing to have humanistic axioms which are applied to the investigation of social phenomena, such as that of mental illness which we discussed in the previous chapter, and in terms of which our knowledge about such phenomena can be organised. What Winch does is very different. First, he seems to hold to such axioms with the attitude of discouraging their relevance to the *investigation* of social phenomena. And second, he seems to hold to such axioms with the attitude of discouraging the *organisation* of our social knowledge in terms of them. That is, it is a very different thing to withdraw them completely from relevance to sociological theorising. This withdrawal is possible, under the guise of making philosophy appear *closer* and more relevant to sociology, by the rather crude expedient to which Winch resorts, in an otherwise subtly argued thesis, of dissolving and conflating sociology *into* conceptual analysis.

Winch conflates 'the central problem of sociology, that of giving an account of the nature of social phenomena in general' (ibid., p. 43) into being one of the things that the epistemological branch of conceptual analysis, that concerned with analysing everyday concepts relating to knowledge, deals with on its leisurely strolls through Everyman's language. Observation he believes to be irrelevant to this problem (ibid., p. 110). Thus, whatever unification sociological students strive for in sociology, between social investigation and theoretical organisation of knowledge, would be dissolved in Winch's conflation. Social investigation is cut adrift to go to the dogs, and sociological knowledge, organised theoretically, is to be dismantled and disorganised by the piecemeal approach of the conceptual analytic philosopher.

The price of buying Winch's critique of the idea of a social science, in support of our general humanistic repudiation of reductionism, is almost too high. The price is the integrity, viability and, more important, the vitality, of sociology as (some kind of) a discipline. It is not in the interests of academic rigour that I haggle, it is in the interests of intellectual vigour. It does not matter whether one is called a philosopher, a sociologist or whatever so long as one does, as Winch says, 'give an account of the nature of social phenomena in general'. If this phrase means anything at all, then is it fair to ask of conceptual analysis, where is its account of modern capitalism, of racialism and so on? It has no account, either at the highly general level at which these phenomena operate in modern societies, or at the experiential level of (the concepts of) modern man's everyday knowledge of his social world. Conceptual analysis provide a fairly thorough analysis of the action, and the concepts relating to the action, of raising one's arm (see Wittgenstein, 1963, p. 161; Melden, 1967, ch. 4). Unfortunately their analyses have not yet happened across the concepts of acting and of knowing in areas like 'being employed', 'being black', 'being mentally ill' or simply 'being in modern society'. In the (pirated) words of the old proverb—'There are "language-games" and "forms of life" not dreamed of in your philosophy, sir'.

What Winch threatens sociology with is not so much conflation into philosophy or dissolution, but paralysis. But, after his projected amputation of social observation and investigation from the body of sociology, after his excision of the need to confront the world and to discover the existence of and the nature of the social phenomena it contains, the rest of the body is useless anyway. If it can be said to collapse naturally into philosophy, then so much the worse for philosophy.

To put this point in the terms of conceptual analysis, it is difficult to see how 'the concept of a form of life' (which Winch equates with 'the nature of social phenomena in general') (1958, p. 42) can be 'elucidated' without a continual (even if only Austinian) recourse to specific forms of life and to the concrete facts concerning types of communication and interaction in any given society and culture. (On 'forms of life' see Specht, 1969, and also the sociological work of Blum and McHugh, 1971.) Assume that Winch accepts, which he does not seem to, that his 'a priorist' and axiomatic elucidations ought to be continually informed by studies of particular forms of life. This leaves the problems that such elucidation would not be systematic (contrast Strawson), that the relation between basic elucidation and analyses of particular forms of life would be obscure, and that these particular analyses themselves would, in the best traditions of conceptual analytic procedure, be pursued in a piecemeal and unsystematic fashion.

It is in the light of these kinds of objections to Winch's conclusions even interpreted in their best light, that the attractions of his otherwise interesting humanistic attack on the reductionist idea of social science must be viewed. (For further discussions of his thesis see B. Wilson, 1970.) His attack on J. S. Mill's and Pareto's reductionist interpretation of psychology and sociology (1958, chs 3 and 4), for instance, is perfectly consonant with discussions of them from within sociology by such as Weber and Parsons. But in his general thesis, and in some of his remarks on Weber, Winch throws out the baby of social study with the bath-water of the reductionist idea of a social science. Attempted infanticide, metaphorical or otherwise, is a sorry last resort for anyone to come to, let alone a philosopher committed to 'leaving the world as it is'.

We have jumped on Winch's conclusions first, partly because they are designed to be controversial, and thus to be jumped on, and partly because they arise from premises and a line of argument which is by now well trodden ground in this thesis. However, to tread it once more, the basic premise is that concerning the rule-governed nature of our concepts and hence of our thought and action. Winch proceeds from Wittgenstein's analysis of the rule-governed nature of concepts and the social nature of meaning of language and of language-use. Our understanding of other men, what they do and what they say, is only possible because of our socialisation into the uses and concepts of language. Hence, what we do and think can be described in language, by us or, better, it can be stated in language.

The neo-behaviourist implications of this are that if we cannot describe and state what we are thinking and doing, then we cannot meaningfully be said to be thinking or doing anything. Similarly, others can tell me what they are thinking or doing, and it is this possibility that guarantees that they are, in fact (?), thinking and acting. Of course most of the time others do not tell me what they are thinking and doing, and I interpret their behaviour in terms of some rule or concept that they may or may not be following. Thus I can be wrong about people, and they about me, but this does not lead to solipsistic scepticism, as it has done in both empiricist and rationalist philosophies at one time or another. For I can know for certain about the 'mind' of another person, and what it is they are thinking under a certain condition. And this condition is that they tell me truthfully what it is that they are thinking. Similarly, I am not destined to remain for ever in doubt about why people behave in the way that they do. For I can know for certain why a man behaves in a particular way when he tells me truthfully what it is that he is trying to do, what his purpose, motive or reason is, and what rule he is following.

These are not ideal limiting cases. It would be hard to envisage a social world where everybody lied always about their thoughts and purposes. It is within this arena of meaning, that we can and do understand one another's thoughts and actions. The arena is language, and is our common socialisation into conceptual schemes and language uses which hold for everybody. The arena is the community of rules of meaning that everybody implicitly accepts in order to be able to communicate at all. The understanding of men's thoughts and actions goes on in this arena, or it does not go on at all. We have a member's understanding of fellow members or we have none at all (see also Garfinkel, 1967). We understand men's thoughts and actions through the concepts that they are using and the rules that they are following, or we do not understand at all. This is Winch's case just as it had been Wittgenstein's and, in more idiosyncratic form, Ryle's. Peters, Hamlyn and the other conceptual analysts we have already discussed all take this general line also, and it is echoed in the work of the ethnomethodologists in sociology (see chapter 9 below).

Two main points are involved in the case; one is that one understands a man's actions by noting the describable rule-governed intention or purpose from which it springs and which it embodies. The other is that one further understands rule-governed intentions as related to their context, the sets of rules, the schemas, the 'language-games' and social 'forms of life' that they occur within, and in the terms of which they occur. Both points are, of course, intimately related, and both points automatically exclude any relevant use of the term 'cause', according to Winch and to most, but not all, conceptual analysts. They like to call the relation between an action and its intention, and between an intention and its context of rules, a 'logical' one and not a causal one.

Thus the understanding of an action in terms of its intention and its context is a logical elucidation, and not an assertion of causal sequence. An example of this might be taken from our understanding of a player's manoeuvre in a football game, or a player's move in a chess game. The ultimate authority in such cases is the player himself, and his account of his reasons for doing something would give us, in conceptual analytic eyes, as good an account of his behaviour as we could hope to get. But spectators at a football or chess game do not continuously interrupt play to ask why players did such and such, nor do they come away at the end feeling that they have not understood anything that they have witnessed. Certain moves may puzzle them, but they could provide some kind of rational reconstruction of most of the important features and moves of the particular games that they saw. Given that there would be vast differences in degrees and types of understanding, we can say that they understood most of what they saw; they will make social and communicable sense out of what they saw.

Conceptual analysis would argue that such understanding of actions involves figuring out the reason why a certain pass was made in front of goal, or a certain pawn was sacrificed, in terms of the player's purposes and the game-situation which confronted him at that particular time. Furthermore, the understanding of game-situations requires both knowledge of the rules of play, the ultimate point of play, typical strategies, action sequences and manoeuvres and so on.

Thus to understand any particular action, a person would have to both know, or make a guess at, the player's reasons, intentions or purposes, and also he would have to 'know the game'. Players' actions have an 'internal' or 'logical' relation to their intentions and to the game in which they are playing. And, to round off the circle, intentions have an internal or logical relation to the game in which they are played. Actions that have a physical description, like raising one's arm, are understood differently if the game is 'asking teacher to go to the toilet', than if it is 'starting a race'. Similarly, the utterance-action 'I've had enough' must be understood differently if the game is 'eating up a meal' than if the game is 'boxing'.

Winch, like most other conceptual analysts, makes a total distinction between physical behaviour and events on the one hand, and human actions on the other. And he restricts the valid use of the term 'cause' to the former, excluding it completely from the latter (1958, pp. 75-80). Therefore, if sociology attempts to understand human action, as it must, it cannot have recourse to the term 'cause' according to Winch. Rather, like the football or chess spectator, the sociologist or anthropologist studying a society or sub-group of a society must learn the language and the rules and he must get to know the game. The actions of individuals or of organisations of individuals are only comprehensible from within the fabric of the rules and assumptions they are acting in terms of.

A sociologist who has got 'inside' of social games in this way will understand social phenomena as well as he can ever expect to, according to Winch (see also Winch, 1964, but note his qualifying remarks quoted earlier). He will have about as much use for information on statistical uniformities in the society as a person who has learned a language has for information on the frequency of occurrence of certain phenomes in the spoken language. Such information could not contribute to his understanding of the language; he either knows what people are talking about or he does not. Statistical regularities and possible causal sequences of word production in the language are irrelevant to this understanding, or so Winch would argue.

Winch therefore objects to Weber's argument that the understanding of social action must meet both the criterion of being 'meaningfully adequate', and the criterion of being 'causally adequate' also. From what we have seen of his views it is clear that he would reject the relevance of the latter criterion. Rather, he would have the social student offer explanations and an understanding of social phenomena to which only the criterion of adequacy of meaning, if any criterion at all, would be relevant. Before we deal more specifically with Winch's criticisms of Weber's endorsement of some form of causal explanation, it is worth mentioning that Winch is also dissatisfied with Weber's conception of meaningful behaviour, and consequently with his concept of interpretative understanding, or *Verstehen*.

Winch's basic objection on this point is that Weber roots meaning in the *individual's* subjective intention and not in the *social* meaning structures of language. In the early paragraphs of his 'Basic sociological terms' essay, Weber distinguishes 'social action' as a sub-type of meaningful action in general. An action is meaningful if it has a 'subjective sense' of meaning 'associated' with it by an actor. But only some such meaningful actions are social, and those are actions which are oriented towards other actors and which take them into account in some way. Thus he excludes, for instance, religious behaviour such as solitary prayer, and the behaviour of individuals in a crowd, when they act like sheep and not like men. Weber even excludes what he calls 'mere "imitation" of the action of others' from the category of 'social actions', and from the realm open to interpretative sociology. Definitional log-chopping can be taken too far, and Weber admits that crowd behaviour and imitation 'stand on the indefinite borderline of social action' (1968, vol. 1, pp. 23-4).

But the possibility of making any distinction at all between meaningful action that is social and meaningful action that is not is seriously questioned by the whole of Winch's approach. Thus he writes 'all behaviour must be social, since it can be meaningful only if governed by rules, and rules presuppose a social setting' (1958, p. 116). Orientation of action towards others is not the criterion of whether a meaningful action is social or not; according to Winch, if it is meaningful then it is automatically social. The most solitary prayer is still couched in socially learned concepts; the most solitary relationship between a man and a physical object is only meaningful for the man in terms of socially learned abilities to classify, differentiate and perhaps put to use the physical objects. Nobody would have been more distant and solitary in respect of society than the first man on the moon but, equally, few people have been so socially trained as actors, one might even say socially programmed, as he was.

Every man's every moment of thought and action is socially filtered through the structures and networks of concepts and skills that his social interaction with other people, from earliest infancy, has provided him with. If there are not distinctively social actions then, Winch concludes, there can be no distinctive sociological study, particularly theoretical study. Philosophy can make a reasonable claim to give an account of the nature of all and every type of action. Thus if, on the one hand, sociologists like Weber provide a stipulative definition of what counts as a social action and what does not, then they necessarily miss out on the infinity of actions outside of the definitions that are social because they are meaningful. If, on the other hand, sociology tries to encompass everything, it may do no worse, but it is unlikely to do any better than philosophy, which in any case has a prior claim to this field. At least, this is the way that Winch sets up the dilemma for sociology in order to make his dissolution of sociological theory into conceptual analysis easier to swallow. Sociology may, against Weber, choose the latter course, equating social action with all meaningful action and extending the sociological realm to cover all forms of action. This may indeed lead sociological theory into a close liaison with philosophy; but a liaison is not a dissolution, and the type of philosophy does not automatically have to be conceptual analysis.

Weber's restriction of the sociologist's interpretive understanding, or *Verstehen*, to other-oriented acts is an unnecessary and artificial restriction. Sociologists influenced by Weber, like Parsons, have, for instance, found the more general notion of 'value-oriented' or 'goal-oriented' action to be more useful in denoting the area sociology covers, than Weber's definition of the area in terms of other-oriented action. Winch's conclusions and the style of his argument along this line of thinking are relatively original, but also they are unacceptable for the sociologist. However, this line of thinking itself is not particularly original, having been anticipated by, and therefore being acceptable to, sociologists. Winch voices a dissatisfaction with the scope of *Verstehen* and rational or interpretative understanding that has been felt already, without his assistance, in sociology. Winch is merely dissatisfied with Weber's concept of *Verstehen*, but he is positively antagonistic to his concept of judging the worth of a prospective explanation in terms of its 'causal adequacy' as well as its *Verstehen*/meaning adequacy. In so far as Winch's antagonism expresses an objection to any kind of causal explanation in sociology, then it does not harmonise with similar feelings within sociology. No sociologist has as many scruples about causal explanation, and its alleged inapplicability to human actions, as most conceptual analysts have.

Discussing Weber's assertion that *Verstehen* explanations by themselves can only ever be 'plausible' and never 'causally valid' (1968, vol. 1, p. 11), Winch (1958, p. 113) states:

> I want to question Weber's implied suggestion that *Verstehen* is something which is logically incomplete and needs supplementing by a different method altogether, namely the collection of statistics. The compatability of an interpretation with the statistics does not prove its validity.

It must be borne in mind here that Winch is not chiding Weber's lack of rigour, and the laxity of his concept of validity or verification; rather he is criticising whatever rigour, and whatever empirical relevance and backing, Weber tried to support *Verstehen* with.

The context of Winch's remark is his intolerant, and ultimately sublimely idealistic, aversion to empiricism and to the worth of 'observation' in social study. The context of Weber's advocacy of the criterion of causal adequacy was a precisely opposite attempt to ground *Verstehen* in empirical observation of the social world. However, this is not to say that Winch retreats wholly into some other-worldly realm of concepts. He believes, though less obviously than many conceptual analysts, that the everyday concepts of language are 'in' the world in some sense. But because he also believes that such concepts 'are' the world, in some sense (ibid., pp, 14-15), Winch meets himself coming the other way in his traffic between idealism and embryonic empiricism. Neither may it be assumed that

Weber's conceptions of empirical verification, causal explanation and validity have any remote connection with logical empiricist conceptions. Weber was trying to ground *Verstehen;* logical empiricism has tried to bury it. Winch is therefore wrong to tar Weber with the logical empiricist brush in his critique of him.

Weber is by no means free from ambiguity on this matter of causal explanation, as was indicated earlier. For instance, his position changed from an acceptance of Rickert's thesis of the idiographic rather than nomothetic nature of the humanities, to a conviction that sociology, at least among the humanities, must 'formulate type concepts and generalised uniformities of empirical processes' (1968, vol. 1, p. 19). Thus he changed from emphasising the more singular historical type of causal sequence, as in the *Protestant Ethic* thesis, to a consideration of the more general and recurrent sociological type of causal sequence.

But this was not a turnabout, it was rather a change of emphasis. Weber always thought that to establish even singular historical sequences of factors as a truly causal sequence (that is to be able to say that one factor 'probably' caused another), thought experiments and comparisons were necessary for the historian. The historian must consider 'what would have happened if' a certain factor had not occurred, or was not operating. And to help him with this thought experiment he must compare the sequence he is interested in with sequences in other countries, other cultures and other times, where such a factor was absent; the historian must resort to comparative sociology (ibid., p. 10). This kind of reasoning which he later made explicit underlay Weber's earlier comparative sociology of religion, within which the *Protestant Ethic* thesis had its place.

But still, the most useful example, considering Weber's legal training, of the interaction of *Verstehen* and causal types of explanation can be taken from the field of law. The important point about the establishment of the guilt or innocence of a person for a certain act is that it incorporates both showing that the person was, or was not, responsible for his action, and also that he was, or was not, the sufficient cause of a specific sequence of events. It is true that the motive for the crime, which establishes the person's responsibility, must be a kind of final cause. If his motive can be shown to have been caused by genetic or other factors, then his responsibility cannot be established. The causal sequence must be reconstructed by the prosecution back to the defendant's motive, and no further, in order to establish his guilt. But it can, and must be traced back that far, as a *causal sequence*. The crime must be shown to be motivated, and thus both as rationally comprehensible and also as actually caused by a man.

Thus, in legal procedure, there is a synthesis of causal and rational explanations of specific sequences of actions and events. Perhaps this gives sleepless nights to conceptual analytic philosophers sensitive enough to worry about the worth of their arguments against such a synthesis, but it is also noteworthy that the goal and the termination of legal procedure is a judgement; 'truth' and 'falsity' here, as in the court of science, is established by human fallible decision, and not by some communion with Infallibility and with Truth.

This synthesis is not only of interest to the historian interested in demonstrating both the rationality and the fact of singular historical sequences of events and actions. For the aim of sociology also is to gain a rational understanding (*Verstehen*) of social actions, and of the uniformities of social actions expressed in sociological generalisations. Such generalisations, it will be recalled, are restricted, by Weber, to intelligible actions. And though they issue as crime statistics, or whatever, nevertheless they are still merely statistical expressions of the dimensions and incidence of certain types of intelligible action. Further, to establish a causal law, or law-like assertion, associating two statistical uniformities, does not establish that the intelligible actions thus related are subject to some subliminal determinism. In the general sociological account, just as in the singular historical and legal accounts, the use of causal terms in explanations merely links intelligible actions to their social context and their social consequences. Irrespective of how the term is used in the natural sciences, in the humanities, the social sciences, the term is used to situate intelligible actions in time and space, and in social time and space.

Statistical laws, generalisations, regularities, uniformities and so on have this empirical situating function in sociology. It is in this sense that they validate, or verify, or 'logically complete' (Winch) *Verstehen.* Causal adequacy, for Weber, meant simply the empirical situating, and reconstruction of the context and consequences, of intelligible actions and types of actions. Weber intended the criterion of meaning adequacy to guarantee that sociological knowledge was primarily of intelligible actions. And he intended the criterion of causal adequacy to guarantee that sociological knowledge was also of, and about, the real world. Objections to the first criterion are conceivable, objections to the second are virtually inconceivable.

Winch (credit where credit is due) has conceived of the virtually inconceivable. He seems to think that there can be knowledge which is *about* nothing. Motivated actions, intelligible behaviour, rules, games, forms of life are either part of the real world or they are not. If they are, then information can be gathered about them, and any information can be codified in terms of when, where, how much, for how long and so on. Any information about the real world can be codified quantitatively and statistically. Whether such codification should be undertaken with pretentious seriousness, or with tongue in cheek, is another matter altogether. For the moment it is not the value, but the very possibility of statistics that is being looked at. Statistics seen in this light, no matter how crude, rule of thumb, 'imprecise', etc., are simply an index of the existence of phenomena. We need not be led into the excesses of quantophrenia by acknowledging that Winch's distaste for social statistics is an expression of his distaste for study of the social world. And since I have already argued previously in this book a number of times that conceptual analysis *requires* some kind of study of the social world, it must be said that Winch is an atypical conceptual analyst in this respect.

If we qualify this judgement and say that, as a more typical conceptual analyst, Winch *is* oriented towards reality, towards the social world of language games, forms of life and so on, then he cannot maintain an absolute ban against the relevance of statistics. Social statistics of what people regularly do, and hence of what they are likely to do on various occasions, may well be the only way for the sociologist to orient himself in a preliminary way, in whatever culture or sub-culture he is studying. It may be the only way to discover the existence of a social game. The discovery of a certain statistical uniformity may well be the only tangible proof of the existence of a normative uniformity. It is all very well to believe that the sociologist's informants are going immediately to tell him the truth, the whole truth and nothing but the truth, but of course this is pie-in-the-sky; it is an ideal limiting case. Even then the duty of the sociologist to provide an accurate descriptive and theoretical account of the systems and organisations involved in his study area automatically require him to 'logically complete' his interpretative understanding of the social goings-on with data of some kind; who, what, when, where, how often, etc. But most often the sociologist, like the anthropologist and the psychiatrist, may get lied-to and deceived by the subjects whose action is under the spotlight.

If the sociologist is studying a criminal organisation, or a 'deviant sub-culture' of any kind, then it may be in the interests of the subjects to refuse him information, mislead him and so on. Then, instead of being able to tie up the statistical regularity of, let us say, a certain rate of petty thefts in surburban shops at certain times of the day, with rule-governed actions of middle-class housewives contained in the phrase 'I'm bored, so I steal', the sociologist must base his interpretation solely on the statistics. And what is wrong with this? He would, in any case, have to give an account *of* some social phenomena, and therefore present facts, interpretations and explanations *about* it. Thus it is inconceivable that the sociologist could avoid statistical material, no matter how crude, about the extensiveness, etc., of the phenomenon. To avoid this he would have to avoid the phenomenon.

So, statistical regularities can indicate that a game is being played, that rules are being followed and so on. They can be used to demonstrate not only the existence of the game, but also its nature as well, in as much as the regularities of behaviour are interpreted as expressing norms of action. If Winch would object to this then he must also object to the notion that social forms of life and language games are social realities that exist in that culture, over a certain period of time, and that involve certain regular and repeated aspects. Winch's distinction between understanding rules on the one hand, and appreciating empirical uniformities or statistical regularities on the other, cuts not only through the fabric of sociology, but also, arguably, through the fabric of conceptual analysis.

A conceptual analyst who, while employing the same general type of argument against sociology, and Weber's concepts in particular, tries to give more significance to social statistics, is MacIntyre in his paper 'A mistake about causality in social science'. He is just as opposed as Winch is to any notion of causal explanation in sociology, but he manages to find a place, nonetheless, for actual social study, and therefore social statistics.

Winch's conception of social study was simply that of learning the rules of new social games, getting 'inside the skin' of foreign and exotic cultures and societies, like the anthropologist has to do. Winch's model was that of learning a language, once that had been done then the social student had learned all that was important, he had acquired a 'native's-eye view' and his work was complete. Cross-cultural comparisons and the importation of standards alien to the society, such as those of scientific and empirical testing, to evaluate the standards and types of beliefs of the society, were severely frowned upon by Winch. The position of the sociologist as anthropologist in his *own* society; the fact of cultural and sub-cultural overlap within and between societies; the blatantly international and inter-cultural nature of the modern world which not only makes comparative sociology a possibility, but makes it an unavoidable fact (industrialisation means very similar things in America, Russia, Japan, etc., starvation means very similar things in India, Brazil, etc.); all of these kinds of considerations are overlooked in what passes for social study in Winch's eyes (see 'Understanding a primitive society,' 1964). MacIntyre, however, even when most in agreement with Winch, still manages to take a more realistic look at social study, and hence at Weber's emphasis on social statistics and cross-cultural comparisons.

MacIntyre has now withdrawn the pro-Winch arguments he put

forward in 'A mistake about causality...', in more recent papers (1966; 1967). But in spite of this the original paper and its views are worthy of comment, if only as museum pieces.

While Winch was most concerned to analyse Weber's methodological points of view, MacIntyre supplemented this analysis with a critique of Weber's thesis in *The Protestant Ethic and the Spirit of Capitalism.* MacIntyre took exactly the same line against causality as Winch, and the founding fathers of the school before him, had taken. Intentions, purposes, motives, reasons and so on can only be said to have 'logical' or 'internal' relations with men's actions, and never 'causal' or 'contingent' or 'external' relations, he maintained. Using Hume's notion of causality—the constant conjunction of contingent events—as a chopping block, MacIntyre argued that intentions, etc. could not be said to cause actions because they were not mental events, which could be said to 'occur' before an action. Neither could they be said to be contingently related to an action. Rather an action cannot be described except by reference to its intention, neither can an intention be described except by reference to the action which would fulfil it.

As Daveney pointed out (1966-7), intentions and actions are linked through 'identity of description', and cannot be said to have a contingent relationship. They do not just happen to be associated; it would be inconceivable for them not to be. The humanistic nature of this thesis has already been pointed out, as has the fact that the apparent reversal of it, which McIntyre ultimately allowed himself, of saying that intentions or the will, or whatever, can be said to cause actions, is no less humanistic (see chapter 2 above).

However, in his comments on Weber, MacIntyre used the older, anti-causalist formulation. Thus he held that the relationship Weber asserted between a religious ethic and economic maxims could not be a causal one. Rather it was a logical and internal kind of relationship between a set of beliefs and the actions they implied. MacIntyre thus rejected Weber's concept of the 'spirit' of capitalism, in favour of the more straightforward concept of capitalistic economic actions. *The Protestant Ethic*, as a set of beliefs, could then be shown to be logically related to these actions. He writes that 'Weber in fact presents us with capitalist actions as the conclusion of a practical syllogism which has Protestant premises' (1962, p. 55). But it must be mentioned that since the 'premises' necessarily contained among them an imperative, for example, 'You must do what God commands', the actual logic of the syllogism is of the relatively uncharted 'deontic' type, and the deduction is not as easy and as rational as MacIntyre seems to presume (see for example, Rescher, 1967).

Whereas Winch held that epistemology, the analysis of the ordinary concepts of knowledge in society, was central for sociology, so MacIntyre offered the theory of ideology as central, in the same way, for sociology. In order to understand men's actions you must understand their own descriptions of them, and their beliefs and ideas. Winch integrated men's ideas and beliefs with the forms of life, language games and so on of their social context. MacIntyre integrated men's ideas and beliefs with the 'stock of descriptions of actions', with the stock of justifications and beliefs, and generally with the ideologies current in any given society. From similar kinds of reasoning Winch concludes with a washed-out prospectus for sociology, with idealist overtones, while MacIntyre concludes with a prospectus for sociology as an ongoing rational critique of ideology—a marginally more lively outlook, with Marxist undertones. This awareness that sociology might actually be a going concern also filters through MacIntyre's comments on the use of sociological statistics (which have the appearance of morning-after sobrieties which nearly missed the boat).

But, afterthoughts or not, MacIntyre's acceptance of the relevance of sociological investigation, and hence statistics, is a welcome change from Winch's intransigent objections to them. Giving the *Protestant Ethic* thesis as an example, he states that statistical work done before and since on Weber's thesis, correlating Protestant beliefs and capitalist practice in Europe, is not made irrelevant by the interpretation of the connection as a logical and not a causal one. Rather such material establishes that 'enough' people were both Protestants and were gripped by the 'time is money' attitude and by the attitude that 'money is to save, accumulate and reinvest and not to spend'.

Of course, MacIntyre's assumption that the subsequent historical research and statistical evidence has endorsed Weber's thesis is entirely gratuitous. We have already pointed out above that it is possible that the reverse is true. In spite of MacIntyre's conceptual analytic neo-behaviourism, there is enough distinction between beliefs and actions to be able to say that people hold beliefs they do not act upon. Given that the connection when they do is logico-meaningful, how many do so act, how many do not, and why the latter class do not are all relevant problems in any sociological account. Also relevant, regarding Weber's thesis, is the possibility that the number of Protestant capitalists was actually insignificant. What *does* MacIntyre mean in this context by saying that: 'What the statistical material shows is that enough of the same people were Protestants and engaged in the relevant kinds of activity'? How does the possibility that 'enough' were not, affect the logico-meaningful connection? It is not good enough for him, just as it was not for Winch, ultimately to ignore the methodological problems of evidence in the social sciences. This failing not only limits their sociological relevance, it also diminishes the philosophical significance of their analyses.

Whether the assertion is true or not, what MacIntyre ultimately must be interpreted as saying is that enough people were both Protestants and capitalists to validate that the logical and meaningful connection was actually historically causally effective. Unfortunately MacIntyre could not, in this paper at least, screw his courage up to the mark to use the phrase 'causally effective'. Indeed, *had* he been able to use it, he could not have gone through with his allegation that sociology had made a 'mistake' about causality—but at least he might have got around to his eventual change of heart on this issue a little sooner. MacIntyre proposes that Winch's 'mistaken thesis' (which was substantially similar to MacIntyre's own original thesis, 'A mistake about causality in social science' (1962)) is that 'we cannot go beyond a society's own self-description'. But he thinks that Winch's 'true thesis' is that 'we must not do this except and until we have grasped the criteria embodied in that self-description' (1967, pp. 129-30). MacIntyre's change of heart on causality is basically the assertion that motive, intentions, reasons, rules and so on are causal factors as well as meaningful requirements of social action. His change of heart is *not* to accept the dichotomy between causes and reasons, to decide in favour of the former, and to ignore the latter.

Thus MacIntyre and Winch both proposed objections to the notion of causal explanation in relation to Weber's sociology which sociologists can safely ignore. Otherwise they both supported, with modifications, Weber's notion of *Verstehen* explanation, and his emphasis on the necessity to understand the rationale and meaning of action. In this basically humanistic interpretation of Weber's sociology they bear comparison with existential phenomenologists.

Phenomenology

The question of whether the humanities are proto-natural sciences, or whether they are distinctive bodies of knowledge using distinctive methods, was one that deeply concerned German intellectuals in the early decades of this century. Dilthey and Rickert were among the most important figures to set the question and to attempt to answer it in favour of the distinctiveness of the humanities. Weber's historical and sociological work grew up in the atmosphere of this question and of the debate around it, and so did Husserl's philosophy. But although they were contemporaries, and can be said to have taken the same side (in different ways) in this debate, there are no direct references in the work of either to the work of the other. Weber, in any case, died (1920) before Husserl's philosophy changed its emphasis and direction, in the 1920s and 1930s partly under the influence of Dilthey and Heidegger, which brought it closer to the methodological concerns of the humanities.

However, a close link between Husserl's phenomenology and Weber's sociology was established by Alfred Schutz in *The Phenomenology of the Social World* (1967), first published in 1932. Merleau-Ponty, in various essays written in the mid-1950s, also came to recognise a link between his own existential interpretation of phenomenology and Weber's work. It is with the attitudes of these two phenomenologists to Weber that we must mainly be concerned in this section. However, a mention must also be made of Jasper's influence on Weber, and vice versa. Although he claimed to be influenced by Husserl, Jaspers's existentialism was not indebted to Husserl's phenomenology to the same extent as was Heidegger's, Sartre's and Merleau-Ponty's. He was more directly influenced by the writings of Kierkegaard and Dilthey, and by the personality of Weber, with whom he was deeeply impressed. On the concept of *Verstehen*, in particular, there seems to have been some give and take between Jaspers and Weber (see Manasse, and Weber, 1968, p. 3). Jaspers, besides influencing Weber, was himself deeply impressed, as was Merleau-Ponty, with Weber's personality. Manasse writes: '[Weber] is the spirit of Jaspers' philosophy' (ibid., p. 391), and 'For Jaspers, Max Weber was like Socrates' (ibid., p. 369).

In discussing Merleau-Ponty's, but more particularly Schutz's, attitudes to Weber's work, the comparison with conceptual analytic attitudes must be kept in mind. There are three main areas of comparison. First, both phenomenologists and conceptual analysts assert that sociological knowledge is, or ought to be, one with the ordinary knowledge that each of us has of the social world and not distinct from it. They either criticise Weber for denying this, or compliment him for recognising it, but either way both schools assert the same kind of view. Second, and related to this, both accept Weber's concept of *Verstehen*, only in a modified form. The modification, for both schools, concerns the way that Weber appeared to write as if 'subjective meaning' was something which is somehow attached to, even glued on to, human actions. Their attempts to give a better understanding of the relationship of meaning to action than Weber gave, does not however lead the two schools in the same direction, as will be seen. And finally, both schools view Weber's concept of the 'causal adequacy' of sociological explanations, at the very least, with suspicion and, at the very most, with the unjustifiable hostility that can be seen in Winch's argument. In the analysis of the phenomenologists' discussions of Weber's work, these points of wider comparison with conceptual analysis must be borne in mind.

Winch and MacIntyre commented on Weber's methodological

concepts and his *Protestant Ethic* thesis respectively. There is a similar unwitting division of labour between the two main phenomenological commentators on Weber's work. Schutz was more concerned with Weber's methodology, while Merleau-Ponty was more concerned with his *Protestant Ethic* and with his philosophy of history in general. Schutz's work is by far the more detailed and consequential of the two phenomenological commentaries, but Merleau-Ponty's work is worth discussing briefly before we turn to Schutz.

Merleau-Ponty's main discussions of Weber are contained in two papers, one entitled 'Material for a theory of history', which was a résumé of his course of lectures at the College of France in 1953-4 (see Merleau-Ponty, 1968b) and the other entitled 'The crisis of the understanding' (see 1964a). His interest in Weber in the early 1950s coincided with his attempt to disentangle himself personally from Sartre and from responsibility for their journal *Les Temps Modernes*, and also to disentangle himself politically and theoretically from Marxism (see Rabil, 1967; Sartre, 1965c). His interest in Weber is therefore informed from a number of different sources in his own intellectual development. It is notable that any desire he may have had to clarify the nature of sociology was not one of these sources inspiring his interest in Weber. In fact, the papers he produced in this and in later periods specifically on the nature of sociology and the human sciences make no mention of Weber.

It was Weber the liberal politician and Weber the anti-dogmatic interpreter of Western civilisation who attracted Merleau-Ponty. The schizophrenic tension within the personality of one man of committed action and uncommitted thought was what attracted Merleau-Ponty about Weber. For Weber was not an exception, but rather was exceptionally frank about a tension which every intellectual must live with, not least French philosophers fresh from the anti-Nazi resistance movement.

In the *Phenomenology of Perception* Merleau-Ponty had taken on the empiricist-rationalist dichotomy in traditional philosophy. He had tried to show how each was an over-emphatic abstraction from what we know about the world and from the way we know what we know. The dichotomies can be reconciled, or alternatively bypassed and forced to relinquish their hold over our thought, if we only get back to perception, the perception of the embodied subject, living and acting in the world (see chapter 5 above).

A decade later Merleau-Ponty was still concerned with the dichotomies, contradictions, tensions and in general dialectical antinomies of philosophical thinking. Only now the emphasis was on the thought-action dichotomy, and the overcoming, or bypassing, of it was to be achieved by getting back to history. If perception was the ground and the arbiter of whatever validity might be contained in either empiricism or rationalism, so history was the ground and arbiter of the thought-action dichotomy.

On the one hand there is the historian who, we assume, detachedly and objectively reconstructs what happened in the past, while on the other hand there is the man of action who takes part in the goings-on of his present day, and so helps to 'make history'. One thinks about a given situation without committing himself to affecting that situation, while the other commits himself to affecting the situation without much thought about it, apart from calculations regarding the success or failure of his own practical project. The dichotomy it seems is absolute, and indeed one might be forgiven for believing that part of Weber's reputation rests on his clear recognition of it.

Weber wrote about history and he also helped to make it in his political roles in Wilhelmine and early post-war Germany (see Gerth and Mills, 1967; Bendix and Roth, 1971). The academic critic of ideology and the political ideologist were in tension within him. Merleau-Ponty's convoluted way with such dichotomies and tensions is to rename them dialectical reconciliations. And Weber, because he tacked (unhappily and 'heroically') back and forward between commitment and detachment, seems to become for Merleau-Ponty a dialectical reconciliation embodied. Merleau-Ponty exalts both the man and his work as examples of the dialectical unity of thought with action, of man with history, and of the historian with the historical actor.

Merleau-Ponty's biographer, A. Rabil, has pointed out that his critique of Marxism was couched in Weberian terms (Rabil, 1967, p. 150). The notion of a Marxist revolutionary, which Merleau-Ponty uses in his discussions of Trotsky and Lukacs, bears the imprint of Weber's notion of the charismatic leader who negates the present order. As opposed to that, Weber's account of the inevitable institutionalisation and bureaucratisation of social changes brought about through charismatic leadership is echoed in Merleau-Ponty's corresponding pessimism about the inevitable betrayal of revolutions and spontaneity in general, and about the Stalinist betrayal of the Russian Revolution in particular. Just as Merleau-Ponty came to believe that dogmatic allegiance to the French Communist Party was politically blind and therefore unacceptable, so he came also to believe that dogmatic allegiance to a Marxist perspective in the interpretation of history was intellectually blind and therefore unacceptable.

In the interpretation of history it was not that Marx was wrong but rather that the whole thing was more complicated than the Marxist schema would allow. The prime example of sensitivity to the complexities of history, in Merleau-Ponty's eyes, was Weber's

Protestant Ethic thesis. Weber's method in arguing this thesis, according to Merleau-Ponty, demonstrated both the reconciliation of thought-about-history with historical action, and the essential historian's art of balancing and relating without reducing in any way different types of historical phenomena.

Concerning the first of these two points, Merleau-Ponty wrote in his 'Material for a theory of history' essay that, while Weber distinguished absolutely between the historian's activity and the activity of the historically significant man, there was, none the less, a 'profound analogy'. Although Merleau-Ponty does not refer to Weber's use of the method of *Verstehen* in so many words, it is this that he is getting at. But it is a rather empathic version of *Verstehen*, which Merleau-Ponty was to qualify later, which he attributed to Weber. Thus the historian tries to understand the past by 'getting inside the skin', so to speak, of the actors who are involved in the relevant situations. He must think what they thought, feel what they felt, and reconstruct all of this for his readers. He must imaginatively enter into the historical situation, and thus historical understanding is 'an action in the imagination'. Historical understanding is not detached thought, but rather the reconstruction of action. On the other hand, the thought-action dichotomy is undermined, or overcome, or whatever, from the other direction also, according to Merleau-Ponty. That is, not only is thought (here specifically historical understanding) action-like, but equally action is thoughtful. Thus 'action is an anticipation of knowledge, we become historians of our own life' (1968b, p. 48) by thinking back and forward in time over what we have done and will do, by rehearsing and understanding the actions and thoughts of others in relation to us and so on.

In his later paper, 'The crisis of the understanding', Merleau-Ponty repeated this theme in his discussion of Weber. 'History is the same whether we contemplate it as a spectacle or assume it as a responsibility' (1964a, p. 195). But here he qualified the possible implications of this that history was therefore some kind of empathy with the 'great men' of the past by emphasising, in Weberian style, that understanding remains ideal-typical and has to reconstruct the objective context of any action as well as the subjective project of that action.

The second point that Merleau-Ponty wanted to stress about Weber's method, particularly in his *Protestant Ethic* thesis, was that it is a criterion of a good historian and of a good historical reconstruction that it both maintains the uniqueness and irreducibility of phenomena while at the same time showing how they were related and how they affected one another. Entwined with this aspect of method is the epistemological aspect that the historical phenomena and their relation-without-reduction to other historical phenomena are both objectively 'out there in the past' and also created and constructed by the historian in his account. So the historian must be sensitive on the one hand to the independence and interdependence of phenomena, and on the other to his own role in recreating and reconstructing them. On both counts Merleau-Ponty extols Weber's historical work.

On the epistemological point we have already discussed how Weber thought that criteria both of causal and meaning adequacy were relevant to historical and sociological accounts and explanations. Meaning adequacy referred to the rational comprehensibility of the phenomena as human actions and thoughts which had, and therefore which must be given by the historian, their meaning. Causal adequacy simply referred to the distinction which must be made between imaginative history in the sense of fictional history, and imaginative history in the sense of rational reconstructions of actual history. Ideal types may be abstractions from the world, and they may be overemphatic constructions of elements from the world, but the important point here is that they must be 'from the world' or relevant to it. The criterion of causal adeqaucy simply asserts this relevance of ideal typical constructions and reconstructions to actual and objective historical processes and phenomena. Merleau-Ponty appreciated Weber's para-Kantian intuition of the dichotomy between the categorising knowing subject and the pre-categorised, pre-known existent world. Thus the subject's (the historian's) knowledge must be both rationally structured (adequate on the level of meaning) and empirical or objective (adequate on the level of cause).

Besides Weber's sensitivity to this point there was also his sensitivity on the point of maintaining at once the independence and interdependence of historical phenomena in any historical account. Merleau-Ponty, in his later essay, believes that the best exemplification of this can be seen in Weber's treatment of *The Protestant Ethic and the Spirit of Capitalism.* Weber's originality lies in relating two distinct types of phenomena, or rather in revealing a relation which is very far from obvious or commonsensical. His originality also lies in the subtlety with which he traced the relationship. Having seen the interdependence of the two types of phenomena, the Protestant Ethic as exemplified in the maxim 'idleness is sinful', and the spirit of capitalism as exemplified in the maxim 'time is money', Weber could have overstated his case in two ways. Had he wished to reintegrate his discovery into the Marxist framework he could have postulated antecedent changes in the economic relations of late feudalism to account for the Reformation. On the other hand, had he wished to do so he could have embroidered his thesis with idealist and Hegelian concepts. Either overstatement could have been phrased in a dialectical perspective of thesis, antithesis and synthesis. But here the historian would have become intoxicated with the theoretical meaning structure which he was imposing on the phenomena. He would have lost sight of the uniqueness of the phenomena, their contingency and their existence independent both of one another and of the theoretical scheme.

Merleau-Ponty is thus attracted by Weber's balance between his account of the interdependence and the independence of the Protestant Ethic and the spirit of capitalism. Weber balances their contingency and their necessity in a way calculated to please the open-minded dialectician freed from the Hegelian or Marxist frameworks, but calculated to confuse less subtle analysts. The latter search, in Weber's thesis, for a firm commitment to the idealist or to the materialist side of the fence, and of course find neither. The dialectician searches for ambiguity, and worse, for inconsistency, and sometimes finds both in Weber's thesis.

Weber's great discovery was to show that the Protestant Ethic had an important role to play in the genesis of capitalism and thus in the creation of the rational nature of modern Western societies. But he never asserted that such an ethic was the only factor, or that its genesis in prior states of society and of beliefs could not be traced. Furthermore, in the concluding remarks to his thesis he accepts that whatever influence it might once have had, that influence has long since passed away. If the Protestant ethic helped to get capitalism rolling, it no longer helps to keep it so. The secular rationalisation that religion helped to create has consumed it and now perpetuates itself in other ways.

Thus, as Merleau-Ponty asserts, the relation between Protestant morality and capitalism is 'supple and reversible'; the effect has turned back upon its cause, transforming it (1964a, pp. 199 and 201). The course of history takes contingent turns this way and that, evading an overall theoretical net thrown to catch it. And yet we can understand its contingent turns, they are meaningful, and we can rationalise and rationally reconstruct them.

MacIntyre in his analysis of Weber's thesis tried to show that on the level of meaning the thesis was consonant with our everyday understanding of the relations between beliefs and actions. Merleau-Ponty similarly tried to emphasise the unity of the historian's reconstruction with the historian's and others' ordinary actions. MacIntyre reconstructed this consonance in terms of a practical syllogism; as we have seen, Merleau-Ponty simply asserts as a dialectical unity what he could also appreciate, in Weber's terms, to be a simple dichotomy between the observer and the actor, between detached observation and committed action.

But on the other hand, Merleau-Ponty had no qualms, as had MacIntyre, Winch, and as will be seen, Schutz, over the use of the term 'causality' in historical accounts. For Weber the connection between Protestant Ethic and the spirit of capitalism was both a contingent causal one, and a rational meaningful one. Merleau-Ponty saw in this the contradiction of contingency and necessity in human history and embraced the contradiction with dialectical fervour. MacIntyre too saw a contradiction here, and so provided a reinterpretation of what Weber must have, or 'could only have', meant by 'causal adequacy'. We must, however, reserve further comparative comment on Merleau-Ponty and MacIntyre until the areas of comparison between Schutz and Winch's analysis become clear regarding Weber's general methodological concepts. Therefore we turn next to Schutz.

The discussions of Winch, MacIntyre and Merleau-Ponty on Weber have either had to be excavated from more wide-ranging arguments, or from collections of relatively short papers. In the case of Schutz the situation is very different, there is almost too much material. In Schutz's postumous *Collected Papers* (1962-6, 3 vols) the implicit references to Weber's sociological concepts are as numerous and obvious as the explicit references. But, more important, Schutz's first and major work, *The Meaningful Construction of the Social World* (1932) (the adapted and translated title of which is *The Phenomenology of the Social World*, 1967) was devoted to an analysis and mild critique of Weber's work. We will limit our discussion mainly to this piece of Schutz's writings, as the later and shorter papers, in the main, tend to clarify, build upon, and elaborate rather than to change, its arguments.

In spite of the volume and depth of his analyses of Weber, Schutz, like Winch and unlike MacIntyre and Merleau-Ponty, sticks mainly to Weber's sociological concepts. He is not at all interested in discussing whether and to what extent Weber's concepts are exemplified in such socio-historical works as *The Protestant Ethic and the Spirit of Capitalism.* In fact, in *The Phenomenology of the Social World,* Schutz almost exclusively refers to Weber's methodological introduction to *The Theory of Social and Economic Organisation* (1957), the chapter called 'Basic sociological terms'.

Schutz's main terms of reference in his analysis of Weber were the philosophical arguments of Husserl, and to a lesser extent, Bergson, on the nature of man's consciousness. Husserl provided Schutz with the concept of the 'natural attitude', which we have already discussed in chapter 1, and with the concept of a phenomenological analysis of consciousness and meaning, which attempts to show how the intersubjective natural attitude arises in, and is partly constructed by, the subject. And both Bergson and Husserl provided Schutz with the concept of consciousness as an onrushing stream of experience, which man lives-through rather than knows-about, and which is tied to some concept of time.

These concepts Schutz analyses in a very careful and painstaking manner, expanding and exploiting them in his critique of Weber. But before we give a more detailed account of their exploitation and application it is relevant to summarise the overall direction Schutz's thesis takes and the stages it passes through. There are five main sections of which the first and the last are directly concerned with Weber's concepts, particularly, that of the meaningfulness of social action. Criticisms of the inadequacy of Weber's concept are couched in terms of the analysis given in the other three sections. These elaborate first, what meaning is all about and how it comes about in the subject's own experience, second, what understanding other people and their meanings is all about and third, how the world of others and social facts, in which the subject lives, is structured.

Schutz's thesis is a mixture of pure and existential phenomenology, in the sense of those terms we have outlined in chapter 1. In his analysis of the nature of meaning and of how it comes about in the subject's own experience, it may be said that he is nearer to a pure phenomenological method. He brackets away the taken-for-granted world of the subject, and tries to analyse what the meaning-endowing activity of consciousness amounts to, from this 'phenomenologically reduced' standpoint. But even here Schutz is not concerned with the meaning-endowing activities of a transcendental Pure Ego. Rather, he is concerned with the meaning-endowing activities of the mundane organic/social self-entity. His phenomenological reduction does not bring Schutz to the transcendental level, but rather to some very primitive level of the ordinary man's experience (here, like Heidegger, he uses Husserl's analysis of internal time consciousness (1964b)). This primitive level is that of the stream of undifferentiated experience in which and through which the ordinary man lives and acts. It is the level or stratum (Schutz has a liking for archeological and geological metaphors when describing consciousness) of pre-reflective experience.

The similarity here with Merleau-Ponty's imperative to philosophy to return to perception, that is to pre-reflective and pre-scientific experience, is considerable. And the similarity increases when Schutz's accounts of the understanding of other people, and of the social world in general, are considered. For while we may not have here a precise forerunner of Merleau-Ponty's 'embodied social subject', we certainly do have a descriptive and analytical account of the mundane social subject. And just as analysis of perception is, for Merleau-Ponty, analysis of the world-as-perceived, similarly for Schutz analysis of subjective social knowledge is an analysis of the social world-as-known. For both phenomenologists the reference of philosophical analysis to the subject involves necessarily a descriptive and analytical recapture and reconstruction of the objective world, the objective correlate of subjectivity.

If we thus see Schutz as nearer the existentialist end of the phenomenological spectrum this is not intended to be a crude categorisation which ignores Schutz's reductive/reconstructionist method, or which ignores his search for the eidetic/essential structures of consciousness. Quite the reverse, as we noted with Merleau-Ponty, the existential phenomenologist does not eschew the search for, and assertions of, essences, but merely locates such essences in the structures of existence, in the structures of knowledge with which the mundane subject relates to the mundane world. Unlike the pure phenomenologist who locates essences in the transcendental realm, the existential turn in phenomenology means that essences must be discovered and located within, or at least in relation to, the natural attitude. In a nutshell the existential turn in phenomenology has meant that now it explicitly deals with man, instead of with the pure phenomenological angelic presumption.

The experience of time—the fleeting present, the past one recognises as such, and the future one envisages—is introduced by Schutz at every stage of his analysis of consciousness, from the solitary self to the social self. At the solitary self level, the level of the undifferentiated lived-through stream of experience, time comes in as an essential feature of one's meaning-endowing activity. The thesis is that the stream of lived-through experience is, strictly speaking, meaningless. Men bring meaning into the world when they think about what they have done, differentiate it, categorise it and make sense of it (see also Husserl, 1964b). Of course one can think about what one 'is doing' also, but one only grasps that reflectively in the instant after 'it is done'. The subject cannot grasp and make sense of the fleeting present he is immersed in. The repercussions that this thesis has for our knowledge of others, according to Schutz, are important, and we must look at them in more detail. But first, some equally important additions and qualifications to the meaning-endowing thesis must be made.

Even if meaning is established by acts of attention which the subject pays to his stream of lived-through experience, Schutz does not want to leave us with the impression that meaning is blind. Meaning-endowment would be blind if the past, defined by the fleeting present, were its only area of application. The impression would be that man can know what he has done, can snatch at an understanding of what he is doing, and fails totally even to orient himself towards what he will do. The picture of meaning-endowment would then be comparable to the illuminating activity of a spotlight facing backwards and mounted on a car moving forwards. That Schutz suggests this metaphor himself is an indication of the inadequacies of the resources of metaphor in this area rather than an indictment of the thesis. The road behind the car would be illuminated while we must presume that the road in front of it would remain in darkness. We may well conclude that therefore the car would not get anywhere very fast, if it got anywhere at all.

The Husserl-Schutz thesis of meaning-endowment by attentional modification would be in sad straits if this were its metaphorical conclusion. For it would mean that the question implied earlier (about whether, on this theory, one can know what one is doing), had not received a satisfactorily answer. If 'knowing what one is doing' means being appraised of what one is up to while one is up to it, then this is not consonant with the idea that one can only know, in the sense of 'make meaningful', what one is doing fractionally after one has done it.

Thus an equal half of the thesis must be that meaning is brought into the world by the subject paying attention to the future in some sense, as well as to the past. But meaning-endowment is reflective and therefore oriented to past and passing experiences. Therefore future-orientation by the subject is recognised, by Schutz, as becoming meaningful due to the reflective acts of attention that the subject pays to it. Plans for the future, projects which the subject wants to realise, are all future-oriented but at the same time they are all past and passing experiences lit upon with an act of attention directed from the fleeting present. To revert to the metaphor of the spotlight on the car once more, it is not quite the case that another spotlight has been acquired which faces forward in the direction that the car is going. Rather the situation is this. The backward-facing spotlight illuminates the receding road, but part of the road is composed in a way different from the rest. Let us use the picture of an irregular crystaline structure; it could then be conceived how the receding road could in part act like a mirror for the spotlight, and reflect its light back past it and beyond it, to illuminate the road in front of the car also. This is just about conceivable, but, like all over-stretched metaphors it totters on the brink of humorous nonsense. Once again this should be held to indict the resources of the metaphor, and not the resources of Schutz's thesis.

So meaning as a subjective endowment has two forms at least. On the one hand it is simply making sense of one's passing and past experiences by lighting upon them, distinguishing them, attending to them and categorising them as discrete individuals within some ordering scheme. And on the other hand, in a more complex mode, it is an attending to past and passing experiences, which are future-oriented and which are attended to as projects and plans for the subject's future.

It is this latter more complex mode of meaning-endowment which is most relevant to the discussion of the nature of meaningful action, and thus Schutz devotes considerable effort to its analysis. It is, in fact one of the major foci of his critique of Weber. Weber, Schutz asserts at many points throughout his thesis, gives a completely inadequate account of the nature of meaningful action (1967, pp. 3-4, 15, 38, 40, 63-6, 215, etc.). In the opening paragraph of his 'Basic sociological terms' chapter, Weber defined meaningful action as follows: 'We shall speak of "action" in so far as the acting individual attaches a subjective meaning to his behaviour' (1968, vol. 1, p. 3-4), and left it at that. Schutz thinks that virtually all of the terms of the definition should have been clarified, and in particular regards the term 'attach' as a gross and misleading metaphor. But most of all Weber's crime was in leaving things at that, when all the spadework remained to be done in the analysis of the meaning-endowing activity of consciousness and in the analysis of the manifold ways the actor and observer conceive of, and relate to, the action. It may be recalled that it was precisely at this issue of the inadequacy of Weber's treatment of the meaning of actions that Winch directed his critique. When we come to compare Schutz's and Winch's accounts, however, it will be seen, if it is not already clear, that this putative similarity did not issue from a similar line of argument.

Meaning, for Schutz is neither an attachment, or appendage of an action, and nor is it an undifferentiated process. 'Attachment' suggests contingent association, and Schutz believed that nothing would be further from the truth than such an interpretation of the relationship between the meaning-endowing subject and his action. And similarly subjective meaning-endowal is far from simple and undifferentiated. Quite the reverse, Schutz presents a fairly complex analysis of the different ways an action can be meaningful for the subject. One of the main differentiations he makes once again utilises the dimension of time, and of the subject's temporal standpoint from which he reflects upon, grasps and generates the significance and meaning of his actions. There are at least the temporal standpoints, before and after. These make a great difference to the 'subjective meaning' which Weber blithely glues on to his concept of rational action.

Before and during an action the subject must at least be conscious of the action as a whole, as already over-and-done-with, that is in the future-perfect tense of 'I will have done *X*'. He may also be conscious of the stages and sub-actions he has to go through in order to achieve the total action. He may be conscious of choices and alternatives of means in the process of executing some of the stages of a total action which he had not thought of to begin with. The total plan may be with him all of the time, or he may forget it, and merely recall it from time to time and so on.

Similarly, after the total project has been completed, there are at least the judgements 'success' or 'failure' to be passed on it, or a judgement graded between these two poles. There are the unintended and unforeseen consequences of the action to be noted and judged. And on a more abstract level what can best be called the memory of the act, the subject's description of it when it has been completed may well be very different from his description of it before and during its completion in the following sense. As was pointed out, before and during the action the subject's experience must be differentiated into numerous sub-plots, stages to be gone through and alternatives to be considered, relative to the overall conception he has of the finished project. But when the action has been completed the subject's remembering of the action is more synthetic and continuous, stages disappear, and the completed action seems to unfold necessarily out of the past. The sense of contingency, the discontinuities, the possibility of failure and so on, which were experienced before and during, now, after let us say a successful completion of an action, are lost and changed, according to Schutz's analysis (1967, pp. 64-5).

Thus there are at least temporally different standpoints from which the action has different meanings for the subject, a point that Weber did not take into consideration. There is also the difference between the observer's and the actor's conception of the meaningfulness of an action to be taken account of. And while this was something that Weber presented an analysis of, needless to say Schutz considers it to be inadequate, and presents a far more detailed and painstaking analysis. But before this methodological topic concerning the possibility of and nature of the sociological observer's knowledge is delved into, the seed-bed from which such knowledge arises, and to which it is intrinsically related, according to Schutz, requires some statement. From his nearest approximation to pure phenomenology, that is from his *non*-transcendental phenomenological reduction to, and analysis of, the *non*-transcendental mundane ego, Schutz turns away completely from Husserl's path (ibid., p. 77). In expanding his account of the socially situated self, Schutz preoccupies himself with the descriptive analysis of the natural attitude, or *Lebenswelt*, something which the pure phenomenologist would hardly bother himself with at all. To the latter the natural attitude is something to be reduced or thought-away to facilitate the analysis of consciousness in the transcendental mode; Schutz is interested, on the other hand, precisely in the mundane and this-wordly mode of consciousness, and thus makes the natural attitude his thematic object, instead of attempting to think it away.

The two topics then that Schutz turns to are first the subject's knowledge of other people, that is the basic possibility of intersubjective knowledge and second, the dimensions, levels and structures of this social knowledge.

Schutz's account of the subject's knowledge of other selves, which he calls the 'Thesis of the Alter Ego', is both original and controversial, (ibid., ch. 3; 1962, pp. 172-5). It relies on the intrusion of the temporal dimension into consciousness which Schutz first presented in his analysis of the meaning-endowing activities of the solitary self. Meaning depends on reflection, and reflection can only grasp elements of the stream of experience as they are just past and passing, never as they really are, now, in the fleeting present.

However, while the subject cannot grasp his own present flow of experience, Schutz argues that another self *can* catch the subject's present flow of experience. Similarly, the subject can catch the other self's present flow of experience. There is no sense to be given to the notion of solipsism in the natural attitude. Others are there, and they are structures like myself, first physically, second as regards social role and social definition, and finally as regards their conscious experience. There is, in fact, no doubt about this; I communicate with them, and they with me, and we live in time together. As Schutz is fond of putting it, we 'grow old together', Ego and Alter, I and Thou, we pass a common time together in our interaction, we both age in it.

In Bergson's terms there is a simultaneity between my stream of consciousness, my lived experience, and yours. I experience your spontaneous experience directly as you talk, for instance, but you can only recapture your own spontaneity after it has flowed away, in a self-conscious reflective turn. Any my own awareness of my expressions and performances are similarly indirect relative to your knowledge of them. This is not to say necessarily that I know you, or even understand your expressions, better than you do. There is still a necessary inferential and interpretive effort involved in my direct knowledge of your present, and I can interpret and infer wrongly. In a conversation I may be using a concept to mean one thing and you may be using it to mean something else; our presumptions are not congruent and we become aware that each of us is being wrong about the other. But then, more often than not we *can* use a concept in the same way, our assumptions are congruent and we do understand one another. Indeed, it is a commonplace for one partner in a discussion to understand the other's use of a concept well enough to be able to point out to the other that his (the other's) use of the concept has undergone a change in the course of the discussion. And the other may not have been as aware of the drift of his own expressions and usage as was his partner. The observing partner would have been, in this case, more 'on top of', more synchronised with, the drift of the other's meanings, and with the flow of the other's stream of experience, than was the other himself.

It is not the place here to attempt a detailed review and critique of Schutz's analysis of the thesis of the Alter Ego, tortuous and guarded as it is. It is enough to have established that, as a description of the structure of intersubjective knowledge, his account of it has a certain plausibility. Schutz uses this account as a take-off point for the core of his thesis, which is a descriptive analysis of the dimensions and structures of the social world. In the natural attitude the consciousness of Everyman operates at the very least on the thesis of the Alter Ego, according to Schutz, that is on the principle that there are other men, and that everyman is like every other and like myself. Given this secure social ontology, are there within it any major differences in the modes of being that other men have for the subject? Are there different dimensions of Others for the subject, and does he know of them in different ways? These are the kinds of questions to which Schutz now addresses himself. His answers have methodological consequences for sociology, and for Weber's concept of an interpretative sociology in particular.

Just as Schutz introduced his analysis of the meaning-endowing activity of the solitary mundane consciousness through a critique of Weber's concept of meaning-attachment, so similarly he introduces his analysis of the structures of social knowledge through a critique of Weber. Schutz lights upon Weber's definition of social relationship, and shows that it confuses and conflates at the least the participants' understanding of the relationship with the interpretation that the sociological observer may make of it (1967, p. 152). And further, Weber's concept of social action in general does not distinguish clearly enough between subjective attitudes that are merely oriented towards the other, and subjective attitudes of wanting to affect the other's behaviour. When I speak to another, I want at the very least to get him to understand what I am talking about; I want to affect his behaviour and his understanding. However, when I listen to somebody speaking to me I am merely heeding what he is saying, and am merely oriented towards him. Furthermore, Weber never really understood how his definitions of social action and social relationship were rooted in the presumption that all of social knowledge is of a face-to-face and direct kind. It is on this issue that Schutz bases his descriptive analysis of the dimensions of the mundane subject's social knowledge.

He wants to show that there are levels of direct and indirect social knowledge. And from this he is able to provide a more consistent account of the differences, pointed to above in Weber's concept of social relationships, between direct participant knowledge and indirect sociological knowledge. He is able to integrate sociological knowledge with the mundane social actor's knowledge without committing such knowledge to being simply a re-run of face-to-face interactions. That is, he is able to integrate sociological knowledge with the ordinary man's knowledge because this latter knowledge has at least two dimensions, direct and indirect. And sociological integration with indirect social knowledge carries with it no necessary integration with direct social knowledge. Before we raise some questions as to the validity of this rather artificial boundary-drawing in relation to sociological knowledge, we must first see in a little more detail what these boundaries contain and what they exclude.

Schutz asserts that men's ordinary common-sense social knowledge, their natural attitude, contains three dimensions of social objects and other selves (ibid., ch. 4). The dimensions are distinguished by time and by social proximity, relative to any given subject. The subject is aware that men have lived before him who are now dead, that men live in the world with him now, and that men will live in the world after he is dead. The subject thus recognises his predecessors, his contemporaries and his successors, respectively. These are distinctions according to subjectively relative time. The main distinction according to subjectively relative social proximity is one we have already mentioned, and it operates within the realm of the subject's contemporaries. Basically it is the distinction that there are people living now who I know, and people who I do not know; there are those who I interact with often and who I know very well, and there are those who I never interact with at all and am never likely to. These latter are a dimension which Schutz would call the subject's true contemporaries, they just happen to occupy the same historical period as the subject without coming into contact with him, and without direct knowledge between the subject and this dimension of his social world ever arising. The other dimension, that of face-to-face interaction and direct knowledge of others, occurs with what Schutz calls the subject's 'consociates' or 'associates'. We have intimate 'We-relationships' with our consociates, while we have anonymous 'They-relationships' with our contemporaries.

How does the subject view these different dimensions and the men they contain? At the risk of over-simplifying Schutz's account we may say that the problems addressed by this question revolve around the concept of freedom. Schutz conceives of freedom in the romantic sense of unbridled spontaneity, and of man's ability to be unpredictable in the eyes of his fellow men. Thus the world of our predecessors is seen by us as unfree, all of its possibilities have been used up, all of the options taken, all of the choices made. The past is what it is, it cannot now be any different, it is a closed book. In contrast to this, the world of our successors is totally free and totally unpredictable; every possibility, every choice and option is there to be taken, it is an open book.

The world of our contemporaries, for Schutz, is more like the world of our predecessors, while the world of our consociates is more like the world of our successors. We experience our consociates as free and unpredictable, while we experience our contemporaries as unfree and predictable. Freedom is related to the possibility of prediction, and that is related to the adequacy of one's conceptual scheme in terms of which the prediction can be made. The conceptual schemes, and in particular the ideal types, which we attempt to apply to the actions of our consociates, are always destined to remain inadequate, according to Schutz. It is like trying to catch the free flow of a stream with a fishing net. With our contemporaries, however, the case is very different. The subject knows too much to conceptualise about his consociates, but he knows so little about his contemporaries that it is easy to structure that knowledge, particularly into stereotypes and other anonymous and minimally informed ideal-types.

Our knowledge, or mine at least, of what royalty, millionaires, Chinese peasants, Russian soldiers or whatever are like is very stereotyped. We have fairly clear expectations of how persons who fill such roles ought to act. In the small amount of time that the average person may have to observe such people, if indeed he ever bothers to, they appear much as he expects. They appear in fact like puppets on the strings of his expectations. More socially important forms of such anonymous ideal-typing of one's contemporaries might be seen in the spheres of social class stereotyping, and black-white racial stereotyping. The actions of our consociates, by contrast is what Schutz calls 'type-transcendent'.

Ideal-types are deterministic schemes which present actions as typical, that is to say, as predictable. In so far as they have an application to reality, then the implication is that there are objectively real things and aspects of things which have some of the determined and predictable features of the ideal-type. Thus it may be that ideal-types reify social reality, or it may be that they reveal and reflect the already reified nature of social activity. Either way, Schutz associates freedom with spontaneous type-transcendence, and unfreedom with type-conformity and, further links the scientific perspective on human action with the latter (ibid., pp. 219-20). (The scientific perspective in question here, of course, is that of Weber's interpretative sociology, not that of the natural sciences.) The scientific perspective on human action is integrated with unfree type-conformity, while any perspective that attempts to understand human action in terms of free type-transcendence is debarred, by Schutz, from the sphere of scientific sociology.

Before going into more detail about Schutz's application of his analysis of the dimensions of ordinary social knowledge to the methodological problems of Weber's interpretative sociology, some problems may be raised. Briefly, far from the dichotomy between contemporaries and consociates being a dichotomy between unfree conceptualisable and predictable action on the one hand, and free unconceptualisable and unpredictable action on the other, the reverse could be true. My anonymous and impersonal stereotype of a pop-star or a millionaire includes the feature that they live in a dimension of possible courses of action that is not open to the ordinary person, solely by virtue of their great wealth. Equally, the face-to-face interaction that a man has with his wife, or his best friends, more often than not generates a very rigid rather than a too flexible stereotype. Intimacy does not always correlate highly with spontaneous idiosyncracy. Quite the reverse; the most intimate relationships can be the most predictable for both partners and, further, they are probably so intimate because they are so predictable. Thus the millionaire's courses of actions may appear to me to be virtually inconceivable, while, on the contrary, my close friend's actions may appear to me to be easily conceivable and highly predictable. Thus, on Schutz's own definition of freedom, the millionaire must appear, to me, to be more free than my close friend, and yet this is the opposite of what Schutz would want to assert.

Similarly it is not self-evident that we conceive of the past as closed, unfree and predicted (as opposed to predictable), and that we contrast this with the future which we conceive of as open, free and unpredictable. Once again, quite the reverse may be true. It is possible to see the past as a realm of freedom, to see that choices between real alternatives were actually made, that what a person said he was going to do he actually went ahead and did, etc. It is also possible to see the future as a realm of determinism, as a realm where certain processes which are now developing will continue to grow and to preoccupy man's actions in dealing with them. At the present time it is possible to say that future generations will be tied to solving the population and pollution problems on this planet, and that there is a calculable possibility that the present or future generations may annihilate the future in an atomic war. That is, certain eventualities are predictable or have a certain degree of probability. Also, in a more abstract sense, it is possible to argue that men necessarily act on the assumption that the future is closed and predictable in so far as they act upon plans, intentions and predictions, at all.

We need not elaborate on these objections to Schutz's analysis to see that one of the main problems lies in his equation of free action with unpredictable action. Of course, it could not in any case be acceptable that free action could be equated with behaviour that the actor himself could not predict, and presumably Schutz never would have intended his analysis to be understood in this light. But then some relevant equation of freedom with predictability must be admitted, even if only on the actor's part. But how different from this actor's awareness is the observer's awareness that a certain entity in the field of his social perception is a free actor, and that this entity is freely acting? What if the subject informs the observer about what he intends to do, and thus in doing so makes more or less conditional predictions about his own (the actor's) immediate future? How could the predictability of, let us say, the sequences of movements involved in the course of the act, and possibly its consequences also, from the observer's point of view, detract from the observer's knowledge that this was a free act freely done? Must action transcend the observer's concepts and stereotypes in order to be called 'free'? Is Schutz right to implicitly equate freedom with anarchic spontaneity? For the moment it is less important to have in mind a clear answer to these questions than it is to be aware that they can be asked.

Social scientific knowledge can be understood, according to Schutz, in terms of the analysis of the dimensions of social knowledge he has provided. Thus 'social science is through and through an explicit knowledge of either mere contemporaries or predecessors; it nowhere refers back to the face-to-face experience' (ibid., p. 223). Thus sociological knowledge is integrated with, and in most respects the same as, ordinary social knowledge. But of course what he calls 'meaning-context' is very different in each case.

The context of our ordinary knowledge of contemporaries, the criteria in terms of which we build it up and so on, relate to our practical involvement in social life. The sociologist's 'meaning-context', on the other hand, is that of a deliberate neutralisation of such involvement, the adoption of a detached scientific standpoint, the commitment to critical observation of the world and critical reflection on theories and hypotheses and so on. Schutz's use of the term 'meaning-context' here is almost the equivalent of the concept of a game (or a 'form of life?'). Thus the game of everyday living is a different game from that of science, having a different point to it and different ways of proceeding. And though the social scientist's knowledge is ideal-typical in more or less the same way as is the ordinary person's (regarding his contemporaries) yet the context of it is very different.

In the everyday world one's knowledge of contemporaries is affected by, and can possibly transmute into, the direct knowledge of face-to-face interaction. Thus any given actor's ideal-typical knowledge is constantly being changed, becoming more informed and flexible here, while becoming less informed and more rigidly stereotypical there, in the flux of the face-to-face interaction of everyday life. In the scientific world, on the other hand, any given ideal typical knowledge only undergoes changes and modifications, according to Schutz, relative to other systems of ideal-typical knowledge. Thus a system of ideal-types becomes more or less adequate, and more or less appropriate to a certain area of social reality, as more information, more theories and more ideal-types are discovered or are constructed.

Schutz calls the scientific game, an 'objective meaning-context'. Thus the basic methodological problem of Weber's interpretative sociology, according to Schutz, was how an 'objective meaning-context' of 'subjective meaning-context' could be possible (ibid., p. 241). As Weber's own analysis was unclear we have seen that Schutz based the possibility of a scientific understanding of subjective meanings on the actuality of our everyday ideal-typical knowledge of our contemporaries.

Schutz proposes that, like everyday knowledge, sociological ideal-type knowledge can take the forms of either 'personal-types' or 'course-of-action' types. It can concern itself with, among other things, both the immediate goal 'in-order-to' achieve which a type of action was undertaken, and the more profound motive 'because-of' which it was undertaken. And finally, to resort back to Weber's theme, instead of elaborating upon it, ideal-type knowledge must be adequate both on the levels of meaning and of causality. It will be recalled that it was the causal criterion of adequacy to which MacIntyre and Winch objected, and Schutz too registers some objections to it in the course of his discussion of Weber's concepts. But first, the other aspects of ideal-type knowledge mentioned above must be examined.

Our everyday knowledge of our contemporaries and social scientific knowledge of social actions are both equally 'objective meaning-contexts' of subjective meanings. And this is the same, according to Schutz, as saying that they are both equally ideal-typical. Social science follows mundane knowledge then, in distinguishing two classes of ideal-type, one class which refers to types of persons and one class which contains types of courses-of-action, or action-patterns (like social rules, roles and games), (ibid., p. 187). The class of personal types is probably more important in life and in social science also. Schutz writes of them as 'puppets' (1964, p. 81), which in social science are carefully constructed, whereas in everyday life they are casually picked up one way or another. In the former case they can easily be changed and reconstructed, whereas in the latter less rational case of everyday life the process of changing ideal-types may also be less rational. The personal ideal-type, or puppet, is totally artificial, a total construct, a non-human robot of the sociologist's imagination.

Schutz conceives of personal ideal-types very much in terms of the occupation of social roles or functional positions in the institutional hierarchies and networks of society. Thus a personal ideal-type might be 'the typical postman' or 'the typical politician'. As such, Schutz proposes that they are derivative from action-pattern or course-of-action ideal-types which state the relevant features of the institutional context of any role (1967, p. 188). Whatever 'subjective' features may then be attributed to the role-player, such as the intention to regularly play this role, can be inferred from the more independent and objective features of the typified institutional context. This is how far Schutz has taken Weber's concept of *Verstehen* from any of the associations with emotion, empathy or sympathy that it might have had in the work of Dilthey and others. The sociologist is not interested in metaphorically getting inside the skin of any given actor. If the term *Verstehen* should suggest that to any critic of interpretative sociology, then Schutz wants to remind them that one cannot 'get inside the skin' of a rationally constructed puppet, and neither would there be the slightest point in doing so.

We must leave aside the question of the wisdom and the worth of such a treatment of *Verstehen*, to consider further points of Schutz's analysis of 'subjective meaning-contexts'. He distinguishes between 'because-of' and 'in-order-to' motives or subjective meaning-contexts. This distinction is introduced after a consideration of the ambiguities in Weber's conception of motive (ibid., p. 87). Weber is held to have conflated the *orientation* of actions to further events with the *relation* of actions to past lived experiences. Weber is held to have failed to make clear the difference between explaining an action in terms of what the action was designed 'in-order-to' achieve (i.e. the conscious intention), and explaining it in terms of the actor's past experience, 'because-of' which the action is being performed (i.e. possibly habitual, conditioned or 'latently unconscious' factors).

Involved in this distinction in types of motive, then, are dimensions of time and dimensions of freedom. We can give an example of the former as follows. A churchgoer might be asked why he kneels and prays in church. He might reply 'in order to get to Heaven', this is his conscious intention and it is future-oriented. But an alternative explanation of his action might refer to his childhood socialisation into a religious community, a sequence of events in his past experience to which his action is related and 'because-of' which it occurs. There is a future-past time distinction between in-order-to and because-of motives respectively.

The freedom dimension enters in when we take into account the actor's awareness of the 'because' motive we attribute to him. We must have evidence, as in the example above, that the actor at some time or another experienced in his socialisation what we assert that he is acting 'because-of'. But is it necessary that he remember, or be aware of, these sources of motivation when he acts? Schutz is not clear on this. He is not even clear that the actor must in principle be able to have such recall of his own past experiences. Schutz's presumption, at the very least, is that the 'because' motive is more profound and deeply hidden than the 'in-order-to' motive, implying that it is more effective, and even mechanically effective. The 'in-order-to' motive is more shallow, vividly present in the actor's awareness, and Schutz leaves us with the Freudian suspicion that it may even be more of a hindrance than a help in understanding any given course of action. He also hints at, but does not make explicit, the possibility that the demonstration of effective because-motives lends credence to a deterministic view of man, while the demonstration that man lives in and through his often actualised projects lends itself to an overall 'free will' view of man (1962, p. 172; 1970, pp. 45-52).

Thus the sorts of motives or subjective meaning-contexts which the social scientist may decide to attribute to his constructed personal ideal-type may be either typical goal or future oriented in-order-to motives or they may be typical past oriented because-of motives.

Having seen how Schutz's analysis of ideal-types has proceeded in part through a critique of Weber's ambiguities, we may now turn to Schutz's judgements on Weber's criteria of meaningful and causal adequacy in ideal-typical sociological explanation. We have discussed Schutz's analysis of meaning and of meaningful ideal-typical explanation at some length already, so we may just record here that Schutz's whole thesis is virtually an attempt to save Weberian interpretative sociology from its own ambiguities and obscurities, and that it is important to stress the word 'save'. Schutz is very far from presenting a destructive critique.

As regards the criterion of causal adequacy, Schutz concludes this is 'only a special case of meaning adequacy' (1967, p. 234). That is, he interprets it in the sense in which we have already analysed it, as ensuring the empirical reference and empirical relevance of the ideal-type *Verstehen* approach in sociology. He does not interpret it as implying the importation of any inductivist method of discovery, any empiricist exaltation of contingent association, or any materialistic determinism. Causal adequacy simply means 'relevant to reality'. Thus Schutz argues that it means that in a type construct of ordinary means-ends rational action, the means that the sociologist ascribes to the type must be, 'in the light of our past experience', appropriate to the goal. Similarly, he argues that an ideal type construct is causally adequate 'when it turns out to predict what actually happens, in accord with all the rules of frequency'. But Schutz then immediately withdraws this over-emphatic interpretation of causal adequacy in terms of predictive accuracy on the basis of statistical probabilities, as follows: 'But this does not mean that what it predicts must always happen.' Thus he feels that it is better to interpret it more generally as 'the consistency of the type construct of a human action with the total context of our past experience'. Whatever Weber meant by causal adequacy Schutz does not think that he was talking about 'causal necessity in the strict sense', and thus was not committing himself to any kind of deterministic view. Rather, he was talking about 'the so-called "causality of freedom", which pertains to the ends-means relation'. Schutz felt generally that 'there are weighty objections against the use of the word "causal" in sociological discourse' (ibid., pp. 231-3), a point on which he bears a comparison with Winch and MacIntyre.

In conclusion we note Schutz's opinion (1970, p. 49) that 'With respect to human action, in short, any statement of causal relevancy can be easily translated into terms of motivational relevance, and the adherent systems of interpretational relevance'. Bearing this in mind we may now turn to an overall review of the discussions of Weber that have been analysed in this chapter.

Conclusion

In this chapter discussions of Weber's sociology by two conceptual analytic philosophers, Winch and MacIntyre, have been juxtaposed with discussions by two phenomenological philosophers, Merleau-Ponty and Schutz. We have already traced the common humanistic form and content of critiques of the reductionist features of psychology by other philosophers of these schools. In this chapter we have been looking in the same way for areas of similarity between the discussions of the two schools. However, since the topic here was sociological rather than psychological then the two schools could be expected to be less critical. The reason for this is that sociological explanation is committed in divers implicit and explicit ways to humanistic modes of explanation rather than to reductionist ones. One illustration of the consequently relatively harmonious relationship between humanistic philosophy and sociology was given in our discussion of phenomenological psychiatry and the sociology of deviance. And Weber's sociology is another, historically and theoretically more significant, illustration of this harmony.

This is not of course to say that the discussions of Weber by the two humanistic schools of philosophy have not been critical; quite the reverse. But the criticism has been constructive and fraternal compared with the destructive and dismissive criticism by these schools of the reductionist features of psychology.

The feature of Weber's sociology of which Winch, MacIntyre and

Schutz were most critical was that of the criterion of causal adequacy. Some of this criticism was generated simply by the ambiguous nature of Weber's original argument, and so had the function of presenting an interpretation, and hopefully a clarification, of that argument. This would be the case with much of Schutz's discussion of this topic. However, some of the criticism was undoubtedly inspired by a certain sensitivity, even squeamishness, over the very concept of causality having anything to do with the understanding of human action.

All three commentators shared, to a greater or lesser extent, in this sensitivity. Winch appeared to go to the furthest lengths in denying the usefulness and even the very possibility of causal concepts by a critique of inductive, empirical and observational knowledge in sociology. Schutz's comments were more balanced and attempted to elucidate and to reinterpret Weber's criterion in terms of a wider elucidation and reinterpretation of Weber's whole set of sociological concepts. Winch exorcised any concept of causality because of the opposition between such a concept and the concept of understanding meanings. Causality on the Humean model is meaningless, contingent association. Thus Winch exorcised it from sociological relevance through a curious argument which conflated philosophy and sociology, and which presented the resultant mutation with an armchair and a blindfold to help it understand the world. Schutz, on the other hand, did not exorcise causal adequacy but rather integrated it with the meaning adequacy as a sub-species of the latter. MacIntyre like Winch and unlike Schutz, analysed causal adequacy as the importation of a criterion of meaningless contingent association, specifically with reference to Weber's *Protestant Ethic* thesis. But equally, like Schutz and unlike Winch, he did try to present some account of what Weber 'must have', or 'ought to have', meant, by causal adequacy. In MacIntyre's case this meant giving some account of the status and relevance of statistical information to sociology. We have mentioned once or twice already, and it might be mentioned here once more, that MacIntyre has since changed his attitude to causality in the explanation of human action. He would not now have to try hard to find a place for it in sociology, and would possibly allow the sociologist even to refer to the beast by name. And finally, Merleau-Ponty, far from criticising any possible inconsistency in Weber's concepts between the criterion of meaning adequacy and the criterion of causal adequacy, with characteristic dialectical enthusiasm, embraced the contradiction.

But this general antipathy to the concept of causality in Weber's sociological concepts and his historical writings, by these philosophical commentators, is more than balanced by their sympathy with his concept of *Verstehen* and of an interpretative sociology.

Indeed, it is *because* they sympathise with his concept of meaningfully adequate sociological explanation that they are suspicious of the possible inconsistency, or dilution, of this with causal criteria.

However, sympathy with Weber's project does not mean an acceptance of it as it stands. Thus Winch on the one hand and Schutz on the other tried to present an interpretation of what Weber meant, or rather what he should have meant, by *Verstehen* and by the understanding of meaning. Therefore both Winch and Schutz turn the spotlight of their attention on the inadequacies of Weber's concept of meaningful action, and of how meaning is somehow 'attached' to action by the subject. Similarly, both Winch and Schutz argue first that Weber should have presented a far more informed and detailed analysis of ordinary meanings, and of ordinary meaningful action. And secondly, they both argue that sociological knowledge and understanding of human action is basically no different from the everyday understanding that any actor has of any other actor and of the actions that are going on around him. That is that sociological knowledge is in some sense 'one with' ordinary everyday understanding of meanings and knowledge of the social world.

But there the explicit similarity between Schutz and Winch ends. Their analyses of what ordinary meanings are all about, and of what meaningful action is all about, take paths that appear to be very different. One is Husserl's path and the other is Wittgenstein's; one locates the analysis of meaning in the analysis of the subject's attention to his own stream of consciousness, and the other locates the analysis of meaning in the analysis of language games, ordinary linguistic and conceptual schemes, intersubjective communication games and so on. But Schutz does not remain long at the analysis of the subjective stream of consciousness, and devotes more attention to the subject's intersubjective knowledge, his knowledge of and communication with others, the dimensions and structures of his social experience and so on. Thus it is not impossible to link the sort of analysis that conceptual analysts in general might make. One interesting and important point of comparison, for instance, would then be between, on the one hand, Schutz's concept of personal types and its relation with action-pattern types, and on the other, the conceptual analytic concept of the rule-governed actor and its relation with language-games and forms of life.

But leaving conceptual analysts in general, and dealing with Winch in particular, the potential similarities dissolve. It is hard to see how his conception of sociology as an unsystematic and lackadaisical type of philosophical analysis compares with Schutz's conception of sociology as a systematic construction of ideal-types. It is true that they both wish to integrate sociological knowledge with everyday knowledge, but in very different ways and with different ends.

Schutz proposes the rather artificial thesis that sociological knowledge must be modelled solely on our anonymous and impersonal knowledge of our contemporaries. It must eschew face-to-face personal knowledge. Winch implies that sociological knowledge ought just to sink back into the kind of informed actor's social awareness from which it arose. And this would be a melange of personal and impersonal knowledge, social rules and games of universal application and those of small-scale and specific application to small intimate groups of actors. Schutz's guarded modelling of sociological knowledge with one's ideal-typical knowledge of one's contemporaries would be a systematic, reflective, changeable and criticisable pursuit specialised in by sociologists. It may be over-emphatic, but there is nevertheless some truth in the assertion that Winch's integration of sociological knowledge with ordinary everyday knowledge is designed to reduce the aspirations of sociologists to the unsystematic and unreflective attitudes of the ordinary man. It is designed to abolish sociology as any kind of systematic and specialised pursuit. As a final word it might be noted that Winch's rather nihilistic conclusions are not the only conclusions that the conceptual analytic school could have come to regarding sociology.

9 Conclusion: Humanistic philosophy and sociology

A considerable amount of philosophical, psychological and sociological ground has been covered so far in the demonstration of similarities between conceptual analysis and phenomenology. In this concluding chapter the more general points in this demonstration will be summed up, and their implications for the identity and practice of sociology, for its theory and research, will be indicated.

Thus there are three sections to the chapter. The first summarises the foregoing arguments of the thesis and indicates other writers and commentators who have held a similar or tangential picture of the comparability of conceptual analysis. The second examines the common humanistic presuppositions of the two schools in terms of the concepts 'experiential empiricism' and 'personalistic ontology'. These concepts help to clarify the sorts of theories of philosophical method, of knowledge and of being that the two schools rely upon, whether explicitly or implicitly. And finally, in the third section we will be interested in pointing out the ways in which the identity, theories and, to some extent, the methods of sociology can be seen to be humanistic and consonant with the presuppositions of humanistic philosophy. Naturally, this section can only present a sketch of an analysis of sociology, a more comprehensive analysis being outside of our terms of reference. In it, however, we have attempted to select the most humanistic of recent developments in sociological research. Here, as in chapter 7, the point has been to provide a concrete sociological ground and focus for our philosophical arguments which might otherwise be thought to be incurably abstract and inapplicable in practice.

Phenomenology and conceptual analysis

The last decade has seen a considerable growth in commentaries on phenomenology and conceptual analysis and comparisons between them. Some of the conclusions reached have been at odds with, or irrelevant to, our conclusions. But it is worth while just to indicate in passing some of the more interesting discussions (see Bibliography).

As superficial as his discussion is, Colin Wilson was one of the first English writers to have devoted much attention to a comparison between the two schools (C. Wilson, 1965), and his *Introduction to the New Existentialism* (1966) remains virtually the only attempt to synthesise various aspects of the two schools into a new philosophical approach. Ayer's and Taylor's discussions, although shorter, are less superficial and of more academic interest; and the discussions between the schools recorded in Mays and Brown (1972) represents a substantial first step in philosophical dialogue.

Both Bochenski (1965) and Kohl (1965) have discussed the two schools at some length in their reviews of modern philosophy. Tillman (1966, 1967) has devoted two papers to comparisons. And recently S. Rosen (1970) has produced a long comparative study which, however, comes to some arguable conclusions about the common nihilism of the two schools. Philosophers who have made more than passing comments about the comparability of the two schools include Murdoch (1970), van Peursen (1966), Radnitzky (1968), Mohanty (1964) and Cerf (1966). From within conceptual analytic philosophy itself, awareness of phenomenology, mostly critical, has come from Hamlyn, Hampshire, Austin, Ryle and others (see chapter 2).

On more specific points of comparison, Bochenski (1965) for instance, has noted the comparison between two precursors of the two schools, Moore and Brentano respectively. Indeed, Moore (1965, Introduction) was explicit about the similarity of his intuitionist theory of moral knowledge with that of Brentano. Austin's intriguing use of the term 'linguistic phenomenology' to characterise his philosophical approach produced general discussions by Furberg (1963) and Cerf (1966) on Austin as a phenomenologist. It also inspired Spiegelberg's (1967) comparison of Austin with the phenomenologist, Pfander.

Wittgenstein has been discussed in comparison with Heidegger by Horgby (1959), Weil (1960) and at some length by Erickson (1970). Comparisons between Wittgenstein and Husserl have been more forthcoming, including papers by van Peursen (1959-60), Munson (1959), Ricoeur (1967b), Spiegelberg (1968). On this, and in general, see Specht's excellent analysis of Wittgenstein's late philosophy. Murdoch (1953) noted a comparison between Ryle's and Sartre's treatment of emotions, as did Dilman (1963-4). Ryle himself, early in his career had been a keen student of Husserlian phenomenology (see Ryle, 1970). He became disillusioned, particularly with Heidegger's philosophical developments, and produced a critical review of *Being and Time* in 1929. There followed two critical discussions of phenomenology in 1932 and 1946. And finally, he contrasted rather than compared his *Concept of Mind* with phenomenology, and would only allow his approach to be called phenomenological as a trivial gesture to humour those who felt the need to rename things in such a 'misleading' way. One such would presumably have been Ayer who in his 1959 paper had argued that the *Concept of Mind* was precisely a phenomenological work.

But none of these discussions follow the same route we have followed, and before we turn to a discussion of sociology we must recap on that route.

The differences between phenomenology and conceptual analysis are vivid and obvious, as they have remained in mutual isolation historically, geographically and linguistically. The former has been mainly a Franco-German preserve, while the latter has been mainly an Anglo-American one. The former originated in the late nineteenth and early twentieth century, while the latter originated in the 1930s and most conspicuously in the post-1945 British philosophy.

Until recently there had been remarkably little translation of phenomenological work into English, and it is a fair presumption that there was just as little translation of conceptual analytic work into French and German (discounting Wittgenstein's work which was and has been simultaneously published in German and English). The feeling has arisen that this mutual isolation should be overcome, as the two schools of philosophy could have much of value to say to each other. And in a sense this book is in part a response to and a manifestation of this feeling. Philosophy cannot afford to be an insular activity, inward-looking and unaware of the seas of society, of science and of argument in which it must in any case flourish. Ultimate thought cannot be insular thought.

Thankfully, the situation from the point of view of the English-speaking reader has now greatly improved. Most of Husserl's major works have now been translated, or are in the process of being translated. Virtually all of Heidegger's and Merleau-Ponty's work has now been translated, and the same goes for Aron Gurwitch's and Schutz's work. The most important work of Sartre which is still untranslated is his *Critique of Dialectical Reason* (1960, vol. 1) but there are a number of synposes of his arguments in this book available (see Laing and Cooper, 1964), and the introduction to it has been translated (Sartre, 1963b).

Apart from this linguistic gulf between the schools, which is at least bridgeable through translations, there remains a stylistic gulf which it could be said is virtually unbridgeable. To greatly oversimplify the picture, conceptual analysis affects a trivialising attitude to what have always been considered to be philosophical and metaphysical problems. It aspires to a commonsensical dissolution of such problems through detailed description and analysis of ordinary language. Phenomenology, on the other hand, affects pious solemnity and great awe in the face of metaphysical problems. There could hardly be more of a contrast than between a philosophy which coats everything with triviality and which deals with everything trivially, and one which coats everything with profundity and deals with everything profoundly. The conceptual analyst seems to locate sense in commonsense and nonsense in metaphysics, while the phenomenologist could conceivably be said to locate sense in metaphysics and nonsense in common sense (pure phenomenology, that is; this would not apply to the existential version, even if it could be said to apply to the pure version).

At the very least this characterisation of the contrast between the two schools eradicates the variety and richness of individual perspectives within each school. Thus Strawson and Hampshire could not be accused of conspicuous triviality, or of fear of generalising about metaphysical problems. Neither could Schutz and Merleau-Ponty be accused of under-rating the importance of analysing everyday beliefs and actions, since it is precisely the 'natural attitude' and the existence of the subject in his world which are the respective foci of their philosophical efforts.

Thus differences between the two schools may well be superficial features, and are certainly capable of being overstated so as to present a very misleading contrast.

Even more moderately stated, is the stylistic difference a significant one? Does it imply that the exponents of the two schools go about their philosophising in very different ways, and with very different underlying presumptions? The argument of this thesis has been that it does not. Rather, it has been argued that both schools use a similar method of descriptive analysis which deals with the facts of ordinary social experience, particularly with facts concerning the experience of social interaction and the experience of action. We can call this approach 'experiential empiricism', as it is an empirical, i.e. descriptive and factual, account of experience. The unadorned term 'empiricism' would not do at all, because, if the two schools have one clear area of similarity, then it lies in their critical attitudes to sensationalistic empiricism and the various philosophical positions associated with this position.

The other major class of presuppositions common to both schools constitutes what may be called either an 'anthropomorphic or personalistic ontology'. This ontology is most in evidence where the schools deal with human action. But since most of their respective doctrines refer, in one way and another, to the realm of human action, this ontology is a pervasive feature. This is not of course to say that it is an explicit feature. It is certainly an explicit feature of much phenomenological writing, but the same could not be said for most conceptual analysis. Most writers of this school tend to be evasive about the most innocuous of generalities, let alone metaphysical and ontological ones. But once again the writings of Strawson and Hampshire are notable exceptions to this rule. But explicit or implicit, we have tried to identify elements of a personalistic ontology, elements of a certain taken-for-granted theory of being, in the writings of Wittgenstein and Ryle, besides those of Strawson and Hampshire. The same kind of ontology, at times vividly explicit, but at other times not at all clearly expressed and rather taken for granted, was also traced in the writings of the phenomenologists Husserl, Sartre, Merleau-Ponty, Heidegger and Schutz.

None of the common moral associations, uses and implications of the term 'humanistic' have any necessary relevance to the way we have used the term in this book. Humanistic philosophy describes and analyses man's experience and thus proceeds on the basis of experiential empiricism and a personalistic ontology respectively.

In Part 1 we indicated the importance of such presuppositions in general in the broad themes of most of the major philosophers in each school. In Part 2 we could see these presuppositions more distinctly in the concern of the two schools for a correct account of human action.

The account in Part 1 stressed the controversial nature of both the explicit doctrines and the implicit presuppositions of the two humanistic schools, which were highlighted by a contrast with logical empiricism. This latter school of philosophy, and the long tradition with which it is associated, proceed explicitly on the basis of a sensationalistic empiricism, and implicitly, it was argued, on the basis of a materialistic ontology. Both of these features were held to be at odds with the underlying features of the two humanistic schools.

The discussion in Part 2 focused this contrast on the field of human action, and on the disciplines of psychology, psychiatry and sociology, which offer explanations in this field. The contrast was then between the affinities of these disciplines with humanistic philosophy on the one hand, and their affinities with logical empiricism on the other. To be more precise, it was argued that logical empiricism proposed a certain conception of what the explanation of human action is and ought to be all about. Using the term 'social science' in its widest sense to include psychology and psychiatry as well as sociology, this logical empiricist conception was called the 'reductionist' idea of a social science. It was argued that physiologically interpreted psychology, and psychologistically interpreted sociology, conformed more or less to such an idea. On the other hand, humanistic principles of explanation and comprehension of action emphasised the need to conceive of action as purposive, conscious and social.

It was argued that behaviourist psychology, to a lesser extent Gestalt psychology, and also to a lesser extent Freudian psychology, more or less conformed to, or aspired to conform, to the reductionist idea. On the other hand, it was argued that post-Freudian humanistic psychiatry and sociology conformed more to humanistic principles of explanation. (This argument still has to be developed further with regard to sociology.)

In broad terms, then, we have been concerned in this book much more with the knowledge of sociology, than with any kind of sociology of knowledge. We have been trying to characterise both sociology as a humanistic discipline and two schools of philosophy as humanistic schools, in order better to understand the kind of useful give and take which could go on between them. This is one reason why, apart from the extra analytical work involved, we have hardly pursued the sociology of knowledge route at all. Had the historical and social context of the recent development of humanistic philosophy been methodically outlined, then the life of the philosophy would have been frozen. The sociologist's interest in its theoretical and methodological implications for his theory and practice would have been overbalanced by his interest in its antecedents, its causes and its context.

To greatly oversimplify the issue, it could be said that philosophy is interested in analysing the nature of (sociological) knowledge; whereas sociology is interested in the causes of (philosophical) knowledge. Thus, while the two enterprises are interlocked, it could be argued that philosophy takes the claims to knowledge that it analyses at face value. The questions it poses about these claims are 'internal' ones concerning their coherence, consistency and implications. 'What kind of claim is being made?', 'How are the concepts being used?', 'Are there any illogical deductions?', 'Are relevant implications being ignored?' and so on.

'External' questions concerning the physical, psychological or sociological nature of the claimant are usually excluded from philosophic interest as a form of debunking or *ad hominem* argument. But it is precisely this 'external' aspect, the socio-historical situation of the claimant and his claim, which interests the sociology of knowledge. Questions of truth and consistency, and of whether theological, religious or scientific claims are 'objective', or 'correspond' to reality, are 'suspended' in precisely a phenomenological fashion by the sociology of knowledge.

Such questions no longer matter; the claim directs the sociologist's attention not to its referent, but to the social conditions and organisation of its production as a claim.

Traditionally this direction of attention has produced a causal and deterministic account by sociologists of the claim to knowledge which, if only implicitly, 'debunks' and 'refutes' the claim. In this way the political philosophy of Locke, for instance, could be held to be an ideological reflex stimulated by the rise of the eighteenth-century English bourgeoisie. Such an analysis easily transfers from a sociological to an explicitly polemical context, and Locke's analysis may thus stand 'refuted'.

But, as Sartre put it 'Valéry is a petit bourgeois intellectual, no doubt about it. But not every petit bourgeois intellectual is Valéry' (ibid., p. 56). The sociology of knowledge cannot with any integrity opt for some kind of reflex structural or economic determinism. Its project cannot be simplification in the interests of theory, but rather the grasping of the complex mediations between the piece of literature or the claim to knowledge and its socio-historical situation and context. Neo-Marxism, particularly in the work of Sartre and Goldmann, has attempted to come to terms with the epistemological and methodological difficulties of understanding, as opposed to explaining, knowledge-claims sociologically. They adopt a 'dialectical' approach, which relates the social bit to the social whole in continuous progressive and regressive movements in their accounts.

Reservations about the precisely methodic nature of this 'method' have prohibited me from employing it in this work. On the other hand, its anti-deterministic, anti-debunking features I wholly sympathise with. And my own effort here has been precisely to try to preserve the interest and relevance of humanistic philosophy for sociology. That job could not have been done by adopting a sociology of knowledge approach which, instead of merely explaining the philosophy, actually explained it away. Hence, I have stayed with more or less 'internalist' philosophical explication and criticism in my account.

The relevance of experiential empiricism and of personalistic ontological axioms for sociology, then, will be discussed in the third section. But first the term 'personalistic ontology' must be clarified, along with humanistic presuppositions in general.

Humanistic presuppositions

The humanistic presuppositions of conceptual analysis and phenomenology at which we have directed attention throughout this book can be gathered together as constituting a 'personalistic ontology' and an 'experiential empiricism'. Our discussion of these presuppositions will mainly concern itself with the former class, as it can be argued that the latter class is inextricably bound up with, and even a derivative of, the former. This general point can be developed as follows.

Let us first distinguish between presuppositions that are methodological or procedural, those that are epistemological and those that are ontological. Methodology refers to how knowledge ought to be acquired and built up in a specific field. Epistemology refers to how knowledge is actually acquired and built up in general. Ontology refers to the nature of what is known, that is, to the nature of that to which reality and existence is ascribed.

The presuppositions of humanistic philosophy which can be gathered together as constituting an 'experiential empiricism' are mainly methodological or procedural, but some also are epistemological. Thus most are presumptions about the correct way that the particular discipline of philosophy (together with psychology and/or sociology, in some accounts) ought to proceed in its analysis and description of its chosen subject matter. Also some presuppositions concern the general nature of how man knows what he claims to know, of how he knows the world, and are thus epistemological.

The most important procedural presuppositions are that it is right to describe accurately, and if needs be minutely, the meanings that men use and that they see in the world, and facts about action and interaction. The most important epistemological presupposition is the negative one that however men acquire and build up knowledge in general they do *not* do it in the way that the sensationalistic theorists tell us. The more positive theory of knowledge that the two humanistic philosophies have is essentially tied to their conception of what a human being is, and of the kind of context it develops and acts within. Similarly it is true to say that the sensationalistic theory of knowledge is also tied essentially to some more ontological theory of what kind of an entity it is that happens to acquire knowledge in the specified way. The theory of knowledge and the theory of being, epistemology and ontology, are inseparably, linked. If there is an over-emphasis on ontology in this book it is to balance the traditional post-Cartesian philosophic over-emphasis on epistemology. And it is to counter the traditional misconception that problems concerning how one knows what one does can be discussed in isolation from problems concerning what it is that does the knowing and also what it is that is known.

Thus 'experiential empiricist' presuppositions are inextricably bound up with 'personalistic ontological' presuppositions, in the structure of humanistic philosophy, in so far as it is oriented to giving an account of thought and action in the lived-world. But what sense could be given to the argument that the former can be, or rather have been, derived from the latter? In what sense are the latter more primary or more fundamental? Only in the sense that the presupposition underlying my knowledge is that I exist and *can* know X, and only in the sense that the presupposition underlying my awareness that, You too know X is that You exist and can know such things. But the primacy argument is not crucial. What is crucial is to recognise the importance of ontology to epistemology. We can then be in a position to accept, and to understand in a better light than much modern philosophy gives us, the reciprocal importance of epistemology for ontology.

So we must now present a fuller analysis of the personalistic ontological presuppositions which underly humanistic philosophy. And this will be done in general terms, as in the identification of elements of a model or ideal-type, to which we will not wish to pin any particular conceptual analyst or phenomenologist. This degree of abstraction is necessary also if we are to explore the relevance of humanistic philosophy and humanistic presuppositions for sociology.

The personalistic ontology which underlies humanistic philosophy presupposes that there exist such entities as persons and that such entities have the attributes of being (a) embodied, (b) temporal, (c) intentional and (d) social. Little need be said about embodiment and temporality. While we may find, later, some use for the concept of a disembodied pseudo-person, it is not controversial to assume that indication of a specific type of organism is necessarily associated with the correct use of the term person. And embodiment imposes temporality, in the minimal sense of a birth-death cycle, upon any basic idea of what a person is. It is an entity that lives in time and must die, and which knows this. Merleau-Ponty and Schutz, as has been seen, analyse the experiential aspects of embodiment and temporality respectively, thereby explicitly basing their work on these presuppositions. No conceptual analyst does so with anything approaching this explicitness, but then these presumptions are innocuous and non-controversial. They could be said to underly non-humanistic materialistic accounts of the nature of man, and deterministic accounts of the correct method of understanding his behaviour, just as well as they could be said to underly humanistic accounts. By contrast, the attributes of sociality and intentionality are by no means philosophically non-controversial and require much more clarification. My general argument has been that *the social and intentional attributes of persons which humanist philosophy presupposes are very much those of everyday common sense*. I have tried to show the profound commonsensicality of humanist philosophies of common sense, showing them as members of a modern Western community of rationality and theorising, through the of reconstructing their ‘implicit’ and ‘explicit’ commitments. method

Humanistic philosophies' personalism is reflexive upon that of everyday commonsense; while the latter is often the former's topic, it is more deeply and generally its resource. Thus persons can be held to be social entities in as much as they have a consciousness of themselves as selves, existing in the midst of, and relating to, and communicating with, other selves. The sociality of persons is their tendency to believe that there are other persons in the world besides themselves. This sociality, this consciousness of being one self among many, arises socially, through the person growing from infancy under the influence of other selves. Not only is sociality developed socially, it is also manifested socially. That is, it is manifested in the person's social actions and interactions involving others, and in the person's linguistic and para-linguistic communications with them.

Persons are held to be intentional entities in as much as they can always think what they want, they can always think about what they want to do, and sometimes they actually do what they want to do. In this formulation intentionality involves the concepts of thought and action. And to attribute intentionality to an entity means attributing thought and action to it. The most important interpretation of intentionality for much humanistic philosophy has been that relating to action. Thus a person is an entity which can formulate plans, projects and purposes concerning the future and which can act to implement them. This is not in any way to avoid the intentionality of thought (as action can only ever be more or less thoughtful, while thought itself is a form of activity); it is merely to lay an emphasis.

Just as it is conceptually difficult to comprehend action and thought as anything but inextricably fused, so it is equally difficult to maintain any important analytic distinction between the intentional and the social attributes of persons. Sociality and intentionality are bound up together in humanistic presumptions about the nature of persons. And one of the most important ways of understanding how they are bound up together is through the concept of skill (or Techné).

A skill-employing entity necessarily must be social, and equally it necessarily must be intentional also. The major class of skills we may think of are linguistic skills—Logos, Dialectic, the abilities and competences involved in speaking a language. Such skills are socially learnt and socially manifested by persons. A skill is something which is possessed and performed by others before any given person comes to learn it. The person learns it from others, and the person exercises the skill in interaction with others. The person learns rules of correct and incorrect procedure which apply to all prospective users of the skill. In the case of language these rules structure a use-context which includes a performer and an audience, a speaker and a listener. The person who possesses linguistic abilities and who uses them, conforms in divers gross and subtle ways to specially given rules of communication (rules need not dictate and specify what conforms to them, they may merely govern). Furthermore the person orients to achieving such manifold conformity, and perhaps more important, to demonstrating and showing such orientation and achievement to others in his talk and action. He necessarily orients himself to another person whom he believes to be really there and to be the same kind of entity as hiself. Part of what is necessarily involved in the attribution of skills to a person is the presumption of the social nature of the person-entity and of its context, (of man and the Polis).

Intentionality is also necessarily involved in the attribution of skills to the person. A skill is an ability to do something, to achieve something by proceeding in a certain sort of manner. A person uses these words in this order and with this emphasis in order to communicate what he intends to communicate. The exercise of a skill always has a point or a purpose. There can be no sense given to the notion of a pointless or purposeless exercise of skills. Skills exist and are possessed in order to manifest purposes and intentions, and to promote the achievement of goals and ends. The only occasions on which purposes seem to be cut adrift from skilful performance are those when we say that for the person to have performed in a certain way was 'unnecessary', 'redundant flamboyance', 'merely showing off', etc. Thus the skilful performance would be called 'pointless' even though it demonstrably had a point, which was that of confirming for the performer himself, or demonstrating to an audience, the performer's competence in the particular skill.

We may conceive of skills as means which logically and conventionally imply certain ends or goals. Thus the skill of playing a musical instrument may be said to be a means implying the end of producing music. Similarly, the skill of playing chess is a means implying the end of beating somebody at chess. Thus skills as means imply goal-oriented or intentional actions. The possibility of 'pointless' skilful performance mentioned earlier would then be the possibility of the actors occasionally treating the skill not as a means but as an end in itself, and they may do this for a number of social, aesthetic or personal reasons. A man may speak, not to communicate anything, but 'just to hear the sound of his own voice', a chess player may play not caring whether he wins or loses, just because he likes to participate in the ebb and flow of a chess game and so on. The exercise of a skill, then, is never non-intentional, and most often the intention with which a skill is performed is that to which it is logically and conventionally related, that to which it could be said to be a means.

The sociality and the intentionality of persons is thus fused in the concept of the person as a user of skills and of the person as a skilful performer. Skills are social acquisitions, exercised in respect of social rules and of other people, and they necessarily imply intention and purpose on the part of the user.

It is worth mentioning at this point that the humanistic presupposition that persons are intentional entities, which is philosophically controversial at the very least in its implications for the understanding of personal action, is not bound up with any presupposition about the intuited or introspective nature of person's self-knowledge. We have said that sociality and intentionality are attributes of persons which persons themselves are more or less conscious of, and which they can be conscious of. Thus, regarding their sociality, persons are prone to believe that they are one among many persons and, regarding intentionality, persons are prone to believe that they can intend to do something and then do it.

Sociality and intentionality are not only fused in the concept of a person as a skill-user, they are also fused in the concept of a person's self-knowledge. The view that self-knowledge is something private, inaccessible and incommunicable to others, something which is intuited, introspected or somehow the object of some 'inner sense', is *not* a necessary part of the humanistic position. Thus the objections which philosophers have raised, particularly to the interpretation of persons as intentional entities, apply to those arguments which base this interpretation on, or ally it to, incommunicable 'inner feelings' and so on. They do not apply to the humanistic presuppositions we have been discussing.

It is true that each person does know himself in a direct way which is inaccessible to others. We happen to be organically different and we happen to have discrete cortico-nervous systems. We do not happen to be capable of switching ourselves into some physical system linking all of us, whereby I can feel precisely what you can feel and vice versa. But then self-knowledge is not based on the mere primitive fact of organic individuality and of inter-organic inaccessibility. What self-knowledge *is* so based is minimal and incapable of conceptualisation and it is probably not correct to call such suspicions and confused feelings 'self-knowledge' in any full sense of that term. 'Inner twinges', incapable of conceptualisation and communication, are not the basis of a person's self-knowledge as far as the humanist is concerned.

On the other hand, personal identity and self-knowledge can be founded upon the person's consciousness-of what has happened to him in the past, of why he did certain things and did not do others, of what he intends to do in the future, of how his own judgements of the worth and importance of features of the world differ from or are similar to those of other people and so on. All of these things the person can conceptualise, and is capable of giving some account of linguistically. In fact, the humanist presupposition is that the great bulk of what a person knows about himself is in principle communicable to others. Whether or not it is in fact communicated is another matter, about which we say things like 'I know him like the back of my hand', or 'I've worked with him for all of these years, and I still don't *really* know him'. The general presumption of interpersonal or intersubjective accessibility is not the same as a guarantee of specific interpersonal access.

The attribute of intentionality is thus not associated with any thesis concerning the incommunicability and privacy of the subject's access to his own mind and motives. Quite the reverse, it is associated with a thesis concerning the communicability and accessability of the subject's mind and motives to those he interacts with. Intentionality is thus not to be associated with any incommunicable sense of agency which may be asserted to be a feature of each individual. Rather, it is associated with the fact that the actor and others can describe his intentions. Indeed, persons, particularly sociological persons, formulate motives and intentions precisely as observers' descriptions of courses of actions and not as individual agents' possessions (see chapter 2 above and Blum and McHugh, 1971). And, unlike the privacy of access thesis, the thesis of intersubjective access has no solipsistic implications. The attribute of intentionality is entwined with the non-solipsistic attribute of sociality in the concept of the person as a skill-user. Thus intentionality is associated with the thesis that a person's intentions consciously conform with, or break with, procedures, rules and roles which he believes can and do apply to others besides himself, and it is associated with the thesis that a person's intentions consciously conform with or break with expectations and pictures which he believes others have of how he and people like him, or people 'in his position' ought to act.

One of the main features of the humanistic presupposition that persons are intentional entities, to which some philosophers and psychologists have objected, is the implication that persons are the 'final cause' of their own action. The objection is that this is a teleological presupposition, and that a causal or lawful explanation of behaviour must ultimately go beyond this, to locate the determinants of behaviour in intra-organic micro-structures. We have already discussed this position at some length when analysing behaviourist and Gestalt psychology. This position is partly justified in the eyes of its proponents, by the consideration that it is scientific, rational and empirical to investigate and to look for the causes of action. While on the other hand, it is anti-scientific, irrational and non-empirical to simply assert that something is a final cause, an uncaused cause, and thus to 'explain' by fiat, as it were.

The humanistic counter to this must be along the lines that, while the actor's conscious intention *is* an ultimate beyond and behind which it is wrong to go, still there remains the need to investigate the intention itself. And far from this being a short and simple task, this can in fact be a long and complex task. When the humanist presupposes that the person is an intentional actor he is presupposing that action is thoughtful, that action is a function of thinking, and thus that action is a function of mind, (of Reason, Theoria).

Earlier we analysed the humanistic position that intentionality was not founded upon an individual's incommunicable feelings of individuality or of agency. Rather it was related to a different interpretation of self-identity, one which was more social and accessible. In analysing their broader position that intentionality is founded on and related to 'mind', similarly it will be seen that mind is interpreted in terms of linguistically accessible conceptualisation, and not in terms of incommunicable privacy. Furthermore, to repeat a point that has been made on a number of different occasions already in the course of this thesis, mind is not visualised as being 'in' a person in any sense. Thus no sense can be given to private introspective fishing for thoughts in some subjective container. On this, both the conceptual analysts and the phenomenologists are explicit.

Rather mind has to be understood as a field of meanings within which the person is situated. Mind has to be understood as the person's beliefs and knowledge. The person believes-that *A,B... Y,Z;* the person claims to know-that *a,b...y,z. A,B... Y,Z* are objects of belief, they are believed-in realities, which the subject experiences as external and objective. Similarly *a,b...y,z*, are known-about realities, which the subject experiences as external and objective. To talk about a person's mind is thus to talk about the meaningful objectivities which he believes and knows to be about him. It is to talk about the world of his experience, his experienced world.

An investigation and analysis of the main features of the experienced world of modern man, a descriptive phenomenology of his *Lebenswelt*, would be in itself a considerable task, and one which cannot be embarked upon here. However, the sorts of directions that such a study could involve can be briefly stated here. Experienced realities could be classified in terms of two highly general types, physical and social. The relationship of the experiencing agency to his experienced world could be approached through an analysis of the actor's projects and actions. Thus the experienced world could be understood, at least these preliminary investigations, in terms of its practical significance for, and relevance to, actor's practical projects. It could be analysed according to whether it was positively, negatively or neutrally project-relevant, that is respectively according to whether it helped, hindered or was 'just there' for the actor.

Some general points about experienced physical reality for the typical modern actor would then relate to its instrumentality, and its non-religious nature. It could be argued that one kind of teleology and purpose, God's, has been abolished and no longer haunts the physical goings-on we experience. Modern man now experiences a physical world which has been socially constructed to serve a *diversity* of *human* purposes, and not a world which has been constructed to serve *one* divine purpose. This analysis of the humanisation of the physical world should not be taken to conflict with the argument that our socially constructed environment is also experienced as 'de-humanised'. (Indeed, the latter argument is only possible because of the former, but limits of space and relevance preclude the development and clarification of this point here.)

The general points which would need to be made about experienced social as compared with physical reality would relate to the clearly purposive and possibly coercive nature of the former as against the latter. The actor uses physical realities as instruments for his projects, as means for his ends. This instrumental mode of experience is not the dominant one in relation to social realities. These realities fall into two general types, persons and pseudo-personal social organisations. They can be experienced by the actor as coercive, that is as using the actor as a means and as an instrument in the achievement of personal or organisational purposes. Of course, actors *can* put persons and organisations to work as means and instruments also. But in modern society, where there is this continual interaction, in the relation between the typical actor and the typical social realities that he experiences, between 'using' and 'being used', it is arguable that the latter is more dominant than the former.

It can be noted in passing that it is here that a Marxist analysis of alienation and exploitation of the worker in capitalist society becomes relevant. So too does the Weberian analysis of the progressive rationalisation and bureaucratisation of capitalist society. But the existence of these theories, and the existence of the structures and processes they claim to isolate, must be humanistically and phenomenologically *grounded*. That is, first, how is Marxist and Weberian theory produced, so to speak, by and from the everyday world of social actors? (1) How and why did Marx and Weber themselves generate their theories? (2) How and why can Marxist and Weberian analyses get re-generated by successive, intellectual groups up to the present day? and (3) In what sense can the theories be said to be actually generated and potentially generatable in and from the ordinary everyday experience of any man?

Second, how are the structures and processes described, talked-about, lived, endured, experienced, suffered, used, misused, negotiated and changed from day to day by actors in everyday life? Humanistic and phenomenological grounding of theory thus requires reflexivity on the part of the theorist, a self-conscious attention to the lived grounds of his own intellectual productions. And it requires phenomenological description of everyday life in order to read whether or not the theory is exemplified there, and further whether it is exemplifi*able* by ordinary actors.

These then are some directions that could be taken in any description and analysis of the experienced world, or the *Lebenswelt*. Earlier we closely associated the concept of the experienced world with the concept of mind, in the way that Merleau-Ponty has associated the concept of the perceived world with the concept of perception, and what we have tried to indicate here is how the humanistic manoeuvre, in the understanding of action, of asserting the actor's mind as some kind of final cause, is not an irrational attempt to forestall further inquiry and investigation. On the contrary, it calls precisely for inquiry and investigation in the field of the actor's mind, i.e. the field of the realities that the actor believes, thinks, wants to, hates to, doubts, etc., that he lives among. That is it calls for inquiry into his world, and to his constitution of his world, both concretely and analytically.

So far we have attempted to identify the humanistic presuppositions which could be said to underlie both phenomenology and conceptual analysis. These presuppositions are concerned with philosophic method, with how knowledge is acquired, and with what kinds of things that both know (i.e. persons) and are known about. The methodological and epistemological presuppositions have been discussed as forms of 'experiental empiricism', while the ontological ones have been discussed in terms of a 'personalistic ontology'. That this kind of humanism underlies, not just the two schools of philosophy under consideration, but also sociology is an argument we may now take up.

Sociology and humanism

Sociology and psychology

A major theme in this book has been the development of a critical perspective on psychology. The purpose of such a perspective is that through it we can come to an understanding of the nature of sociology. No worthwhile analysis of the nature of sociology can afford to ignore the challenge that is presented by the existence of psychology. We aim to do no more in this conclusion than present merely a brief sketch of sociology and a few indications of the ways in which it is a humanistic discipline. But even this limited task requires a critical comparison between psychology and sociology.

Why is the very existence of psychology something of a standing challenge to sociology? The answer to this is that the two disciplines have traditionally held competing claims, and dynastic ambitions, over the explanation of identical and similar ranges of phenomena. This competition has usually been quite conscious and explicit. Psychologists have often portrayed sociological explanations and social phenomena as reducible to psychological explanations and phenomena respectively. On the other hand, sociology (*most* of the brands that is) has equally often asserted its autonomy from psychology. Indeed in recent years it has successfully challenged the validity of psychological explanations in many fields.

The fields of mental illness which we discussed in chapter 7 is only the most striking. Other examples of the superiority of sociological over psychological explanations would not be hard to find in the fields of crime, industry and education. In the latter field, for instance, psychology endorsed the measuring of ability by I.Q. tests, and the consequent segregation of children into streams, classes and schools, allegedly catering for children of allegedly different intelligence and potential. This application of a characteristic piece of psychological pseudo-science is now giving way, in the British educational system, at least to a more sociologically informed practice.

Classes and ethnic groups provide different social environments and different types of socialisation for their young. The educational institutions themselves are social environments which socialise children in many more and subtle ways than merely those relating to academic performance. This involves recognition of the social nature of the self, of its development through social interaction, and of academic performance as *consequence*, and not by any means the only or most important consequence, of its developments. These more sociologically informed perspectives have been manifested most clearly in the 'comprehensive' schools movement in Britain. But they are also manifested in the pre-school play-group movement, in the 'learning through play' movement in British primary schools, in the attempt to involve parents in their child's education, and to involve schools in the social problems of their local communities.

There are, admittedly, shades of grey between the black and white of sociology and psychology. Perhaps the 'discipline' of social psychology is the most important of these intermediary areas, but even this is often merely an undigested mixture of sociological and psychological perspectives without much demonstration of their compatibility. Where it is not a mixture, then it is micro-sociology, dealing with such things as socialisation processes, the social development of the self, of its linguistic abilities, moral convictions, stereotypical perceptions, organisation of attitudes, interaction in small-group situations and so on. But given that there are shades of grey in some sense or the other, the contrast between sociology and psychology can usefully be highlighted, and even exaggerated, as a black-white contrast.

This contrast runs deep into the very presuppositions beneath the two disciplines, and into the aspirations that lie unquestioned behind their ongoing activities. Psychology's aspiration is to become a natural science, or failing that, at least to look like one. Thus much psychology at least takes on the apparel of rigorous quantitative and mathematical techniques in pursuit of reductive integration with physiological and ultimately physical science. It is true that the construction of mathematical models and also statistical analysis have found a place in modern sociology. But even where there is this desire to be hard-headed, positivistic and all of the rest, sociologists, whether from principle or expediency, hardly ever bring themselves to associate this desire with the further one of reductive integration with natural science.

Scientistic rigour in psychology has required an abandonment and scrupulous avoidance of the explanatory significance of the concepts of mind and purpose. But these concepts and their explanatory significance have an unshakable place in sociology, just as much in the work of some of the 'founding fathers', like Weber, Durkheim, Mead, and arguably Marx, as in the more recent work of Schutz, Parsons, Berger and others. Thus whatever concept of science sociologists may aspire to, it is not the reductionist idea we have outlined above in chapter 3, and to which it is possible to say that psychology aspires.

The analysis we have provided, in chapters 4, 5 and 6, of behaviourist, Gestalt and Freudian psychology respectively, is a little uncharitable in this respect. It attempts to tar them all with the same brush of materialism and determinism. But being uncharitable is not the same as being unfair, and this kind of characterisation of some of the major forms of psychology is very far from an artificial construction of a straw man. Rather the features of psychology against which the humanistic philosophies objected were features asserted by the psychological practitioners themselves and not imposed on them totally from without.

The behaviourists explicitly hold a picture of man, and of the type of explanation relevant to human action, which abolishes the concepts of mind and purpose. On their own account man is little more than a reflexive organism. The Gestalt account of man is more sophisticated in that it analyses perceptual consciousness and considers the distinctive importance of the human brain. But ultimately the only coherent interpretation of the principle of 'psychophysical isomorphism' is some kind of neurological determinism. The Freudian account is even less internally coherent than the Gestalt account, and thus the decision to portray it as a materialist and determinist one is even more uncharitable and difficult, but it is hard to see what else to do with it. On the one hand, its materialism is an explicit and ponderous assertion of the importance for human behaviour of sexual physiology but, on the other hand, there are symbols and meanings, mind, society and culture, present in the Freudian account of thought and action.

Freudian psychology in particular, but also Gestalt psychology to some extent, could be said to *rely* on an ambivalence between a humanistic and a reductionist account. So the characterisation of them both as reductionist may not capture this ambivalence, but it is not on that account invalid. In the case of behaviourism there is no such ambivalence to capture, and the characterisation fits well.

Reductionism in psychology means that no absolutely irreducible levels of analysis are established beyond which it would be wrong and inappropriate to take explanation. There may be pragmatic divisions of labour, stipulations and restrictions of subject matter and so on. But it is always accepted that the integration of explanations relating to different areas and levels of behavioural phenomena—with one another and with physiological and other types of explanation—is possible and desirable in principle. Quite the reverse is true in sociology. Indeed, the great contrast between sociology and psychology can be seen highlighted in this difference over whether phenomena and explanations are reducible or not.

The irreducibility of levels in sociological theory

Most surveys of sociological theory claim to reveal a dichotomy between those theories which emphasise social action and those which emphasise social structure (see for instance Cohen, 1968, chs 3 and 4). In the eyes of action theorists, structure theorists present men's actions as mere epiphenomena of structures of norms and values, and thus social structures are given the appearance of Hobbesian Leviathans. On the other hand, in the eyes of structure theorists, action theorists present an individualistic account of society which might even be a thinly disguised psychologistic account. If this interpretation of action theory were right, it would, of course, undermine the autonomy of sociology and allow the reduction of its explanations and subject matter to those of psychology.

Structure theorists might well accept the characterisation of themselves as conceiving of society as Leviathan-like. Indeed they state the central problem that they see confronting sociology precisely in Hobbes' terms as the 'problem of order' (see Parsons, 1937, p. 89; Cohen, 1968a, p. 18). That is, sociology's central problem is held to be how to account for the fact that social life is *not* the individualistic nightmare of a war of all against all. Hobbes invented the extra-societal Leviathan to account for order; structure theorists seem to imply that we do not need to go outside of society to account for order; rather we live in a Leviathan-like structure of norms and values, with which each new member of the society is socialised to conform.

On the other hand, action theorists would not accept the characterisation of themselves as atomistic or psychologistic reductionists. They would assert that, no less than structure theorists, they too have a commitment to irreducibility. While structure theorists assert that social structure is an emergent or irreducible phenomen similarly action theorists assert that social actions are emergent or irreducible phenomena. According to whatever theory you choose in sociology, either social action or social structure is held to be irreducible to the parts which go to make it up. Thus structure is irreducible to individual actions and actions are irreducible to physiological processes.

We will argue in the next section that, phenomenologically, structure and action theories are less competitive than has normally been thought. But on the brief analysis we have given so far it is clear that they have irreducibility and non-psychologism in common at the very least. This means that, from the logical point of view, explanations at the action level and those at the structure level have a distinctly similar form. They are both types of teleological explanation (see in particular Taylor, 1967; Wright, 1971).

Teleological explanation posits some end or purpose of a phenomenon as the 'final cause' of that phenomenon's behaviour. This contrasts with a truly causal explanation. Here the decision to trace the efficacy of causal linkages 'only so far and no further' (or to explain macro-behaviour in terms of macro-behavioural laws rather than micro-structural ones (see chapter 3)) is a purely pragmatic one. In principle, every cause is itself caused, and the linkages can be traced back in time *ad infinitum*. Truly causal explanation accepts this, if only in principle; teleological explanation denies this both in principle and in practice by positing 'final causes' and 'uncaused causes'.

There are two variations of teleological model which have been used as analogies in sociological theory. One is that of Free Will, and the other is that of the Organism. When the philosopher asserts that an action is done through Free Will, he is attributing a kind of causal significance to some kind of mental act, which itself cannot have been caused or it would not have been free. Similarly, the biologist can explain the behaviour of some part of an organism in terms of the need of the total organism for its part to function in specific ways in order to maintain the life of the whole. Thus he is attributing to the total organism a kind of causal significance in relation to the part, while positing the total organism itself as some kind of uncaused cause, or final cause.

Social action teleology is not merely modelled on but to some extent based upon Free Will teleology. And social structure teleology has been to a considerable extent modelled on Organism teleology. The point about making these forms of teleological explanation explicit here, is in order to understand what sociological theory is up to and to say 'so be it'. Too often, particularly from logical empiricist philosophy of science, such a demonstration is preparatory to giving advice to sociology on how to make its explanations conform to 'more scientific' causal and lawful forms (see Hempel, 1969; Rudner, 1966; see also chapter 2 below). Such advice, generally speaking, attempts to reorient sociology away from its involvement with teleological forms of explanation, and to enforce the barren 'waiting for Newton' posture on sociology. Sociologists do not need to believe that their teleological theories are very clear, or valid, or even that they are as much as they could aspire to, in order to reject the natural scientific aspiration proferred by logical empiricism.

The teleology involved in explanations at the social action level is that of attributing goal-orientation and purposiveness to actors. This necessarily invokes some concept of mind (that is unless recourse is made to the Freudian mumbo-jumbo about an unconscious mind and purposes which the actor does not know that he has). This is explicit, as we have seen, in Weber's account of the social action approach (chapter 8). On the other hand, the teleology involved in explanations at the social structure level involves attributing goals and 'preferred states' to the structure. And it might be argued that this does not involve any human concept of purpose, nor any concept of mind. Merton has contributed to this kind of argument in his distinction between the 'manifest' and 'latent' functions of social phenomena (1957). This distinction is basically that between the seen and unseen aspects of social phenomena respectively, or more specifically, between foreseen and unforeseen aspects. Thus, on this latter interpretation, Merton's endorsement of the study of latent functions for sociology is equivalent to Popper's definition of sociology as the study of the unintended consequences of intentional action (1961, p. 158). Popper's presumption is that most of the important things that go on in society are unintended. And Merton's presumption, we must assume, is that there exists alongside of the manifest purposes and structures of a society, a latent unseen and unforeseen structure produced by the former.

Latent functions presuppose latent structural requirements and, ultimately, a latent social structure. But this extrapolation of Merton's argument goes much further than he himself would have wanted to go. Indeed, he presents no clear analysis of the way in which the social context of a latently functional item is latently structured. Thus the question regarding any item pronounced 'latently functional' by Merton is 'functional for what?'. He cannot resort to characterising the item's social context as organisations and structures of manifest purposes and interests and he cannot say that *that* is what the item is functional for. This would simply be self-contradictory. And yet many of the social phenomena he attempts to grasp with the concept of latency lead him precisely towards this kind of contradiction. Merton wants, for instance, to characterise criminal organisations and political rackets as 'latently functional' items in American social structure, when all he really can indicate is that they are 'unofficial' items. They may be the unintended and unforeseen consequences of omissions and failings in the official political structure, but they are surely the intended and foreseen consequences of the action of the political bosses and their organisations. It may be that crime and racketeering *ought* not to be seen and to be in some sense recognised. and perhaps it is in this way latent for *some* members of the society. But the fact is that it *is* seen and recognised by many members of society, including those running it, those affected by it and those fighting it. It is thus a demonstrably manifest feature of the society, and not a latent one; it serves manifest and not latent functions.

Merton's manifest-latent distinction, where it slips loosely like this into legitimate-illegitimate, above-ground/underground distinctions, cannot be used to prop up the abolition of mind and purpose from the sociologist's conception of social structure. This is all the more so because Merton's latent functions do not, although logically they should, imply a latent social structure. Merton was in fact involved in covertly redefining the concept of 'function' to liberate it from the concept of structural determinism, which at least is clear, whether right or wrong. Merton's revision, embodied in his motto 'structure affects function and function affects structure (1957, p. 82) is not particularly clear and might even be vacuous.

The whole concept of a totally 'latent' social structure has always been too difficult to sustain consistently in sociology. Even the concept of economic structure and its contradictions in Marx's analysis (the true form of which is held to be often obscured by ideology, false consciousness and alienation, not only from the proletariat but also from the bourgeoisie) is wheeled out of the shadows of the theorist's knowledge and into the light of everyman's everyday knowledge in the revolutionary period. Durkheim's conception of normative structure even more clearly locates society-as-church in the minds of participants. Even in closed tribal societies part of the structural iceberg had to be manifest in the minds of actors. In modern society-as-bureaucracies it is defensible to locate the bulk of the social structural iceberg in men's minds, as manifest and not latent. If society determines the individual actor by appearing to him, as Durkheim argued (1965, ch. 1), as external and coercive, then clearly society determines precisely by being manifest as coercive, and not by being latent, unknown and unrecognised by the actor.

Social structures, then, are not 'realities' and 'objective' because social theorists say they are: rather, they are 'real' and 'objective' in so far as ordinary social actors say they are. The sociologists reifications are a reflection of the reification experienced and attributed by ordinary actors in everyday life, but they are refracted through the sophistications of his academic community's modes of living, speaking and thinking. These issues, the ordinary actor's everyday knowledge of society as a form of practical sociology on the one hand, and the professional sociologist's knowledge of society as a form of common-sense on the other, present sociologists with topics to study and methodological problems to worry about. In so far as sociologists have explicitly addressed these topics and problems they are involved in humanistic thinking in a way that psychology never has been. But even where these topics and problems remained explicit or obscured as they do in classical and conventional sociology of the kind sketched in this section, sociology remains fundamentally humanistic and distinct from psychology's reductionism. Thus, sociology holds either structure or action to be irreducible, and its explanations have either a holistic or a personalistic/mentalistic teleological form respectively. Psychology, by contrast is reductionist and thus, anti-teleological in its explanatory form; at least, it hopes and says that it is, although it is arguable that in practice it fails to be. Sociology, whether structural-functionalist, Marxist or 'actionist' ('phenomenological' is a more informative name for this latter approach), preaches teleology in one form or another and succeeds in practising it.

The 'action-structure' dichotomy in sociological theory

(a) *Dichotomies abound in sociological theory.* The flogging of such horses, dying and dead, as conflict-consensus, holism-individualism, objectivism-subjectivism and so on, has become the substance as well as the ritualised form of university courses in the 'subject'. There are a number of reconciling and/or dissolving manoeuvres available in relation to these dichotomies. One which is not too well explored on conventional courses is the Marxist dialectical option. Another unexplored option is the humanistic or phenomenological one. The similarities between these two options, particularly in their focus on the role of action and consciousness cannot be gone into here. Let us look briefly instead at what sense can be made of the action-structure dichotomy as a dichotomy in 'theory', from the humanistic or phenomenological point of view.

(b) *That this is supposed to be a dichotomy between theories is interesting.* At the back of it is the scientistic idea that scientific knowledge is a theoretical contruct, and that sociological knowledge is or can be similarly scientific. The fact that further at the back of this lies the reductionist idea of science, to which teleology and mentalism are anathema, has never generated the sense of dissonance and paradox that it ought to have done among social theorists.

(c) *We can distinguish between two types of theory, first-order, which takes features of the world as its objects, and second-order, which takes theories of the world as its objects.* Both types of theorising can be divided into what can be called 'substantive' and 'methodological' varieties. The former is descriptive and explanatory, the latter is advisory and procedural, producing imperatives concerning how best to proceed. First-order theory is substantive in so far as it provides a description of a structure, process or phenomenon, and offers explanations of it. It is methodological in so far as it advises the investigator how to proceed. Second-order theory is substantive in so far as it provides a model or framework which integrates the main features of lower-level and first-order laws and theories. It is methodological in so far as it advises the theorist how best to construct and integrate theories.

(d) *This analysis might well be illuminating in relation to physics, which has generated first-and second-order theories of both varieties.* But it does not fit sociology too well which has generated many pseudo-scientific 'theories', taxonomies, schemes, languages and what not, but precious little else. In physics there are numerous corroborated first-order theories. There is thus much point to second-order formalisation and integration into wider theories and deductively unified schemes. There is also much point to methodological theorising and advising at both levels. The contrast with sociology is glaring; sociology has no rigorously corroborated and testable first-order theories; thus its sparse collection of empirical generalisations and correlations remain theoretically unintegrated, mute and meaningless. Sociology can therefore, have no second-order theorising in the sense in which physics can: there are no laws and low-level theories to formalise and integrate. We seem to be left with first-order methodology, advice on how best to study hypothesise and theorise about social reality, and also with the question 'what is social reality'? Sociologies, of whatever persuasion, operate implicitly or explicitly with some kind of answer to that question.

Thus in fact there are first-order 'substantive' as well as 'methodological' theories in sociology: these are untestable theories, or convictions, that social reality is of a certain kind and has certain features. One is that 'social reality is given in, and produced by, men's actions'. Another is that 'social reality has structured and holistic features which make it emergent and irreducible to men's actions'. We can call the first 'action theory' and the latter 'structure theory' for the moment. From the humanistic or phenomenological viewpoint these two are linked by a third, first-order, but none the less similarly abstract, theoretical conviction swimming in sociological circles; this is that 'society is all in the mind'.

(e) *Action theory and structure theory appear to be conflicting claims about social reality, one of which thus must be true and the other false.* Of course, nothing is so black and white in this world, so let us rather see how one could be said to be superior to the other and in what senses. Phenomenologically, action theory is superior to structure theory because of the following considerations. Take the third conviction mentioned above, 'society is all in the mind'. This seems to me to be incontestable; the only problem is, whose mind? It could be reformulated as 'society exists in so far as men know and believe that it does', and the problem would then be, which men? There are numerous candidates possible, but we need only consider two, the native and the anthropologist, or the ordinary man and the sociological observer. The conviction has been both denied and endorsed by both groups. But denial by the latter is most relevant here, particularly in terms of 'latent functions', 'unintended consequences' and 'false consciousness'. The denial thus takes the form 'social reality is not that known by ordinary actors, it is that known by sociological observers'. We need hardly point out that this demonstration of the falsity of 'society is all in the mind' is only possible given its truth and acceptance, i.e. that 'society is all in the (sociologist's) mind'.

(f) *The humanistic-phenomenological view, then, accepts the general truth of this conviction, and specifically asserts that 'society is all in the (ordinary actor's) mind.'* Further, it denies the arrogant élitist and scientistic assumption present in some sociology that social reality is accessible to *it* and to nobody else, that it is in it's mind, and in no one else's. Acceptance of this general conviction helps to mediate between the apparently conflicting claims of action and structure theories. It is fully consistent with action theory, (which holds that social reality equals men acting in terms of their purposes and experiences) to say that: (i) men experience structures and wholes; (ii) they act in terms of this and that therefore; (iii) social reality has important structured and emergent features. Action theory is not an atomism, nor is it a scientistic élitism. On the other hand, structure theory is very often in the position of saying that social reality is manifested in the unwitting behaviour of actors, of which only the sociologist knows the 'real truth'. Structuralism can be a scientistic élitism, which not only has no conception of social reality as historical, but also has no conception of it as human, that is as both continually re-made by and always re-makeable by social actors.

(g) *From this viewpoint the truth of structure theory depends on the prior truth of action theory.* That is, the existence of social structures depends on the existence of conscious actors capable of conceiving and perceiving structures and acting in terms of them. The existence of structural determination depends on, and is given in, actor's experiences of 'being ordered', 'forced', 'coerced' and so on. To repeat, action theory is not an atomism, it is social study from and in terms of the point of view of social actors. Descriptively this means that it necessarily continually encounters social structures. Class, nation, bureaucracy and so on *are* present, but in actors' experiences, formulated in their linguistic descriptions, their talk, as 'my class', 'their nation', 'bloody red-tape' and so on. Social structures are accessible for the sociologist through actors' experiences and talk. The sociologist has no other access to them; his armchair speculation cannot substitute for confrontation with actors, just as his theoretical constructions and conceptions of structure cannot substitute for actors' talk, for their linguistic construction and reconstruction of their experiences of structure.

(h) *This is not to say that the sociologist, having abandoned the reifications and objectivism of structuralist sociology, then accepts and endorses the reifications and objectivism of ordinary actors' accounts.* The sociologists' research has not ended when he has elicited and revealed actors' understandings and meanings. He has just begun; he must now find out how they 'do' their 'class-consciousness', their 'nation-consciousness' their 'red-tape consciousness' in everyday life. How do they enact it? What methods do they use? How do they give and receive information, and negotiate the interactions of their daily lives by using such 'structuralist' terms? The sociologist must study the methods actors employ of talking about, using and doing 'my class', 'their nation' and so on, which actors take for granted. The sociologist must study this 'taken-for-grantedness' of experienced structures; but he must not join the everyday actor in taking them for granted. He must strive to make commonsense understanding his explicit topic and not his unexplicated resource.

(i) *The action-structure theory dichotomy, then, from the humanistic phenomenological point of view, resolves itself in the process of doing sociological work and research.* The distinctiveness of structure theory can only be maintained by both a scientistic arrogance and an unwillingness to confront actors' theories, typifications and constructions in research. Apart from this, structure theory collapses into the implications of action theory, as we have argued.

History, as a discipline including social and economic history, has always been able, without undue strain, to describe and explain the realities of class, nation and international relations through a discussion of the realities of what men claimed to have done and why they claimed to have done so. It has required no heavy-handed structuralist alternative to a humanistically informed account. It has got by without the gross obliteration of freedom and meaning that structuralism has too often imposed on sociology.

Sociology, hopefully, is coming to learn what history has never forgotten, that not only does history make man, but man makes history in his thought and in his actions. Structure can be read in men's social life, whereas too often it has been impossible to read man's social life in sociological accounts of structure.

The phenomenological turn in sociology

(a) *Much of what we say here about research methods will by now be fairly clear.* The phenomenological turn in sociology, which has become increasingly influential in recent years, embodies features we have described in this book as humanistic, and which have been latent and repressed in sociology for a long time. The two ideological factors in sociology which generated this repression and which are now slowly losing their grip, are the positivist reductionist ideal which we have discussed at length, and the structuralist movement which we have discussed briefly in the preceding section. But both as 'abstracted empiricism' (now, 'scientifically' serving the agencies of government and big business) and as 'grand theory' (now with an alleged added ingredient-'application to the world') they are still firmly entrenched in the tribal beliefs and practices of the American sociological profession.

(b) *In spite of the growing political and methodological critiques of these beliefs and practices, their loss of power has not yet anywhere near matched their loss of authority.* However, their loss of authority means that both humanism and Marxism, long repressed, are now at least heard in sociology. I would include in the repressed humanism, Weber's concept of an interpretive sociology, Schutz's elaboration of this and his own contributions in more recent years, and symbolic interactionism and the whole influence of George Herbert Mead's thought. Stock is now being taken of these contributions as well of the newer developments in the work of Goffman and Garfinkel in particular. These newer developments have not only drawn on the humanistic sources ignored and repressed within sociology, they have also turned outside the conventional boundaries of sociology to phenomenological philosophy and to the conceptual analysis of ordinary language, the two schools of philosophy with which we have mainly been concerned. At the very least these schools have bequeathed to phenomenological sociology their ontological commitments and their descriptivist method, besides their anti-reductionism.

(c) *The phenomenological turn in sociology requires experiential-linguistic description, sociological reconstruction, and sociological reflexivity*. Put as briefly and as simply as possible, these points can be re-stated as four methodological imperatives for the sociologist.

The sociologist must: (1) describe the meanings, purposes and communications of men's interactions in great detail; (2) attempt to reveal and to understand what the actors take for granted in all of this; (3) attempt to be reflexive or self-conscious, accounting his own interpretations and procedures *as part of* the presentation of the research project; and (4) attempt to provide the script, plan, recipe or whatever, which would allow actors to reconstruct both the researched reality and his research presentation, if they followed it.

The humanistic approach in sociology, in so far as it calls for a theoretical structure, calls for a minimal one. On the other hand, it calls for maximum attention to and descriptions of, social phenomena *for their own sakes*, not for the sake of some abstract and general theoretical comprehension. In this sense it is more of an idiographic than a nomothetic approach. But it also calls for systematic analysis, in the provision of an account from which the sense of the reality could be reconstructed, and for typical accounts of typical realities. Furthermore it calls for theoretical awareness and explication of the sociologist's grounds and rules. And in this sense it is more nomothetic than idiographic. We must now fill out the four points mentioned above regarding these descriptive and reconstructionist implications.

The first imperative is for sociology to pay close descriptive attention, much after the fashion of anthropologists (particularly those in semantics and language studies), to social meanings and interactions. The bulk of interaction is linguistic communication between actors, for which field-notes, or much better, tape-recording, are essential tools. Much communication, however, can also be paralinguistic, in such things as facial movements, bodily posture, physical gesturing and so on. Video-tape seems to be the most promising research tool in spite of the problems of its obtrusiveness and its cost. Other methods, long frowned upon as 'uncontrolled', 'subjective', etc., such as participant observation, extended interviewing of participants and so on, are also available for descriptive phenomenological sociology. The sociological imagination has hopefully not been stuck in the mass-questionnaire groove for so long that it can learn nothing from anthropological, psychiatric and social psychological practices, let alone from the descriptive and investigatory practices of the ordinary social actor.

Similarly, it is to be hoped that sociology has not brainwashed itself of the importance of secondary accounts of actions, interactions and structures. In particular there are those provided in autobiographical, biographical, psychiatric, historical and journalistic writings (see Becker, 1970). Even literary fiction has a relevance here. On the one hand, stories, plots and plays invariably reflect and magnify some real aspect of the social situation in which they are produced, and on the other hand, they may construct imaginary and fantastic worlds of interaction, or extrapolate features of a given real social situation to produce a *1984* or a *Brave New World.* All literature and art, in the exploration of human possibilities, the invention of futures and pasts, persons, situations and societies, as well as in the innovation of new modes of communication and sociality are sociologically relevant. There is no better way to expose features and presuppositions of social situations (otherwise unremarked and not seen for what they are) than by getting a perspective either from a fictional construction, or from a cross-cultural comparison. There is a precedent for this in classical sociology, Weber's 'ideal-type' method was a construction of what he called 'utopias' with which to compare reality.

Thus the second imperative is for sociology to reveal what the grounds of members theorizing and practice, that is to formulate what the actors in any social situation take for granted in the generation and acting out of their plans, purposes and projects. If the first imperative could be said to advise sociology to record the messages that are communicated, that is to hear what members say, then the second imperative could be said to advise attention to that which provides for the sensible character of their speech. This would involve attention to the structures of men's language and their linguistic competences, the most basic presuppositions of men's experience and action in any social situation. But also the sociologist would have to attend to the various features of the experienced world that Schutz referred to as the 'stock of knowledge at hand', 'sediments of meaning' and the actor's 'structures of relevances'. Messages presuppose not only media, but also contexts. Thus the sociologist must formulate the describable experience that the actor has of what constitutes his relevant and significant context, an experience that the actor himself may rarely articulate, or be unable or unwilling to articulate coherently and in detail. Where collective interactions have a game-like character, then the sociologist must formulate the rules and criteria of right/wrong, good/bad and successful/unsuccessful moves which the actors are taking-for-granted. Where the actor claims 'truth' or 'objectivity' or talks of 'reality' the sociologist may describe this. He must not endorse or accept such judgements at face-value, but he must always record how they are enacted, how such terms are used, how the rules of use of the terms that the actor takes for granted are applied to and mapped on to situations considered 'the same' and 'different' by the actor. He must treat the actor's common-sense meanings (as much as he can, and as involved in them himself as he is) as an explicit topic and not as an unexplicated resource.

The third imperative is for sociology to be reflexive and self-conscious when engaged in its researches. Humanistic sociology must at least engage in an ongoing critique of positivist methods in sociology, both in general but more especially in their specific research applications. Here relevant questions concern how much existing quantitative and statistical data, and the practices, and beliefs which generated them, take for granted about the experiences and purposes of actors and types of actors they are related to. What do existing and ongoing sociological theories, hypotheses, classifications, generalisations, data and methods of data-collection presuppose about their own meaningfulness, viability and validity, and about actors' meanings, minds and purposes? Some presuppositions stand explicitly stated by the authors of theories and methods, but most (reminiscent of the extra-contractual social bases of contract to which Durkheim drew attention) are not. It may be useful in this respect to approach a single social phenomenon or process, using a variety of different tools and procedures, from participant observation to quantitative analysis. This would assist the sociologist in maintaining the necessary sensitivity to the implications and to the theoretical presuppositions of different research procedures. Research conducted under the humanistic rule of reflexivity must become an occasion for displaying the very possibility of research. That is it must become an occasion for disengaging from any naive grasp of a world of social facts (*pace* Durkheim), and for addressing different methods of constituting the social world as a researchable and factual world. Sociologists have ignored for too long the fact that the sociology of knowledge necessarily implies the possibility of a sociology of sociology. It is not too circular to be aware that sociological understanding of actions must also cover understanding the class of actions called 'sociological research techniques and methods' (see below, and Phillipson *et al.*, 1972).

The fourth imperative was for the sociologist to attempt to provide the script, plan or recipe which would allow actors to reconstruct the researched reality, and which would allow other sociologists to understand and conceivably reproduce the research project, in some sense. I am aware that this is the humanist's version of the positivist notion of the replicability of any study by any scientist in the democratic community of science. But the analogy with positivism is diminished if reconstruction and replicability are conceived of as occasions for interpretation, that is playfully and creatively. The sociologist must construct types of actors, of interaction sequences, and of operations of social organisations and structures. Society and social processes are thus seen as more or less distinct games or plays, and contexts of games and plays. And the sociologist, like the players and participants themselves, is continually involved in post-mortems on the games. How was the result achieved? How could it have been changed, avoided, enhanced? The sociological understanding aimed at by such questions is a family relative of the participant's questions such as 'where did we go wrong/right?' etc; it is a recognition of the historical 'it-could-have-gone-differently', and of the active 'we-could-have-done-it-differently'; it is a recognition of possibilities and potentialities in the players and in the game.

There could be said to be a division of labour within the humanities in the study of social games and plays. Thus the sociologist studies very common, highly repetitive and very general games. The historian tells the story and narrative of events and sequences that are never exactly repeated; the anthropologist studies exotic tribal games, highly repetitive in their own context, but disappearing under the impact of the modern world; and the psychiatrist studies highly repetitive, sometimes highly subtle, games, plots and plays between a small number of people who know one another intimately and often interact.

But then again, as against this division of labour, historians study many phenomena and processes that repeat themselves, like wars, the emergence of nations and empires and so on. Similarly, anthropologists, faced with a dwindling supply of the exotic, have turned their attentions to the mundane, that is to such things as kinship structure in modern urban communities. Also psychiatrists like to pronounce not only on the sanity and madness of individuals but also on the sanity and madness of societies and civilisations (see for example, Freud, 1930; Reich, 1940; Fromm, 1956; Laing, 1967). And finally, sociology, while it must study regularities and create ideal-types to capture typical processes, has an investment in the unique and particular, that is, an investment in history. Sociology is necessarily informed about society to a great extent through the study of history and, in any case, studies a unique social present that is forever becoming history.

Many of the plays and games that sociology studies have runs which stretch for centuries. Many are played on the most important social stages, but equally, many have only a few performances, and in the societal provinces at that. Some of the plays may be repeated only once or twice a century, like revolutions, international wars, international economic depressions, civil wars and so on. Similarly, the scale of the play is not necessarily a distinguishing feature of sociological interests. For instance, mental illness may or may not be wide-spread in a society, and in this sense may or may not be a large-scale social phenomena. In either eventuality, as we saw in chapter 7, the processes involved tend to be relatively small-scale, centring on intra-family, family-agencies, and intra-asylum interaction. But it is none the less available for sociological study for all that. Indeed, in so far as sociology requires some conception of the social self, as we have argued that it does, it necessarily has an interest in small-scale social interaction. So in general, the divisions of effort between the various disciplines of the humanities are pragmatic and changeable, unlike the division between the humanities as a whole and the natural sciences.

To see these methodological implications in action we might look very briefly at some recent sociology. This 'brief look' ignores the brilliant contribution of Erving Goffman at the descriptive phenomenological level, in his accounts of interaction. This is partly to keep the look brief. But also, Goffman does not exhibit as much concern with reflexivity as the others will be seen to do. He tends to trade on his own members knowledge, and his readers' presumed members knowledge of society. He rarely addresses this membership to provide in any way for the comprehensibility of his descriptions. It is rare that his implicit commonsense methods become his explicit topics.

In American sociology, in particular, the underlying influence of Mead has provided a basis for the recognition of the importance of Schutz's phenomenological approach to sociology, part of which was discussed above in chapter 8. Two of the most important and interesting areas of impact of Schutz's influence can be found in the writing of Cicourel and Garfinkel respectively.

Cicourel has provided, in his *Methods and Measurement in Sociology* (1964) a fundamental critique of sociological research methods. He has demonstrated that sociologists simply take for granted the 'reality' of the social realities they study and the 'appropriateness' of their ways for studying, describing and explaining them. They engage in no critique, or self-consciousness, of their own methods. In particular, questionnaire methods merely make a gesture at understanding the meanings of social actors (they do, after all, 'ask actors questions'). At the same time, they merely make a gesture towards scientific rigour (they do, after all, quantify and statistically collate what they purport to measure). Cicourel's critique implies that, as opposed to this gesturing, the sociologist must get down to a painstaking approach to social phenomena. In particular, he must have a detailed and sensitive approach to actors' meanings. And this same sensitivity must be extended to sociological research methods in any given area. It is not only the actor's presuppositions about meaning, but also the sociological researcher's which must be brought to light and made evident. Explication of the actor's game(s) must be entwined with explication of the sociologist's game.

Cicourel (1968) has tried to apply this phenomenologically inspired approach in a study of juvenile justice, where he proceeds through a critique of the application of traditional sociological research techniques in this field. He addresses macro or structural theories and micro theories, even of the apparently descriptively phenomenological 'labelling' and 'societal reaction' kind we discussed in chapter 7 above. These use both allegedly 'hard' statistical data on age, sex, ethnicity, income, class, type of offence, number of offences and so on, and more impressionistic observations of oral character, good and bad family backgrounds, good and bad attitudes to authority on the part of the deliquent, and so on. The different kinds of traditional theories, typically use these divers kinds of material to produce objective or verified accounts of the 'underlying' patterns and processes explaining crime and deviance. Cicourel, however, shows how this invokes researchers' ideals which preclude seeing how it is that members, including the sociologist, do deciding, describing, judging, and all of the other practices that produce the very social organisation that the sociological researcher is supposed to be attending to. Bureaucratically produced statistical 'data' on crime, for instance, cannot possibly show its day to day negotiated character. Rather, sociologists need to orient themselves to a theory of social organisation which would generate or provide for both the statistical materials and the activities that such materials truncate and transform. Thus Cicourel orients to the problem of theorising members' interpretive procedures, in his account, and provides detailed conversational material of police-delinquent interactions for his reader's inspection and reference.

Garfinkel's work has developed under the stimulus of his association with Cicourel (and vice versa) and his acknowledgement of the importance of Schutz's phenomenological approach. Garfinkel's contribution in what he calls 'ethnomethodology' is certainly that of a new word, probably that of a new concept and programme, and possibly that of a new substantive discipline within the humanities (see Garfinkel, 1967; Garfinkel and Sacks, 1970; Douglas, 1971). 'Ethnomethodology' as a concept has a meaning which the occasionally dense and ponderous style of Garfinkel's prose obscures, and it is open to changes of emphasis in his and his associates work. His most well-known, original position holds ethnomethodology to be the study of the taken-for-granted levels and meanings of ordinary everyday actions and interactions. It studies 'the routine grounds of everyday activities', and 'common-sense knowledge'. The study is relatively descriptive and founded upon the actors' or natives' terms and concepts rather than on externally imposed sociological ones. The similarity of this to certain aspects of social anthropology and ethnography accounts for the 'ethno-' part of Garfinkel's concept. Apart from this, the similarity of such a study to the sociological implications of Winchean and Wittgensteinian conceptual analysis has been noted by both Cicourel (1964, pp. 184, 225, etc.) and more distantly by Garfinkel himself (1967, p. 70; see also bibliography for works by Blum and McHugh).

But 'ethnomethodology' refers to, and offers, an area of study rather than a method of study. That is, the '-methodology' part of the concept must not be misconstrued as offering a methodology. The whole concept indicates the study of a substantive area much as the concept 'sociology' refers to the study *of* society, or 'phenomenology' refers to the study *of* experienced phenomena, or 'biology' refers to the study *of* animate matter. Of course the '-logy' part of all of these concepts leads us to expect some kind of a rational and systematic account, and in that sense a scientific account. But phenomenology, sociology and biology are different enough for us to appreciate that no one method of study is being implied in this expectation. Ethnomethodology, then, is a rational study of ethnic methods, or of the ordinary man's methodologies, projects, plans and intentions in social action and interaction.

Such work can be somewhat similar to a psychiatric case-study of, let us say, the interactive organisation of sexual identity (see Garfinkel, 1967, ch. 5), or it can concern itself with more conventional bureaucratic organisational methods; that is, with the ways that members of organisations make what they do rationally accountable to outsiders and, indeed, to any observer (ibid., chs 4,

6, and 7). This would be a study of the ways that actors create meanings for their own and outsiders' consumption, and this would also be a study of what actors rely upon and take for granted, apart from official and manifest rules and injunctions governing what they do and how they do it. Cicourel refers to these unspecified competences (which enable members to appear as applying rules to specific changing situations which are not and cannot be detailed by the rule itself, no matter how qualified by 'if... then...' conditions it is) as 'interpretive procedures'. And he generalises the argument to consider the interpretive procedures members use in mapping 'norms' and 'roles' on to specific changing social circumstances (1970) (see also Cicourel and Zimmerman in Douglas, 1971).

Garfinkel has recently used the terms 'indexicality' and 'reflexivity' to characterise ethnomethodology's interests (see Garfinkel and Sacks, 1970). Just as Wittgenstein thought that all 'meaning is in use', so Garfinkel thinks that language is an inherently situated and context-bound phenomenon. All language and meaning depends on conversational context and on interpretive work speakers and hearers do in conversing. Context dependence, or 'indexicality', is most clearly seen in pronominal devices like 'he', 'they', 'there' and so on, the meaning of which depends on the hearer 'knowing' or interpreting who 'he' refers to, or where 'there' is. 'Indexicality' signifies speakers taking things for granted. 'Reflexivity', in the rather concrete sense in which Garfinkel uses it, signifies the work men do to make sure that what is being taken for granted 'actually is' being taken for granted. That is, it is the ongoing attempt in conversational contexts to specify the meaning of those contexts, to formulate what the conversation is about and what it is for. Without going into this subject further, it can be seen that 'indexicality' and 'reflexivity' are intimately related, and speak to the dialectical relationship between man and language, between consciousness-purposiveness and its linguistic form and content.

In the light of these wide-ranging concepts, research implications for the sociologist are the necessity for him to study everyday conversational interaction. He must relinquish the point of view of the ordinary member concerning the existential reality of a bureaucratic organisation, for instance. He must instead study how members talk about and 'do' bureaucracy, in this way revealing *the way in which* the bureaucracy is real—as opposed to taking that reality for granted and instead studying 'its' (presumed) relationships with other such 'structural elements'. Not that these relationships are not also available in their conversational display for the sociologist (in principle if not in practice). In modern bureaucratic, legalistic and contractual society official and manifest rules of procedure are virtually the *sine qua non* of the very 'official' existence of social organisations. But a 'work to rule' in a firm virtually amounts to a strike against the firm's activities. Most social organisations in general are 'sustained' in mystifying ways, and to always historically problematic degrees, by a host of informal 'rule-breaking' everyday actions. And while the organisation may be itself sustained in this way, its official purposes may not be; the organisation can both wittingly and unwittingly be doing very different things that it thinks it ought to be doing (for an overview of sociological work on bureaucracy, see Mouzelis, 1967; Silverman, 1970).

Thus Garfinkel is interested in social phenomena which have an explicit charter, a defined programme and aim, and he devotes particular attention to the various social organisations of inquiry, selection, decision-making and so on. These have explicit rules of procedure, that is methodologies, for investigating the world. Thus Garfinkel states that he is interested in all kinds of methodologies, 'from divination to theoretical physics', and he is interested in them *as* 'socially organized artful practices' (1967, p. 32). All stations from sorcery to science naturally takes in sociological methods on the way. So, together with his accounts of decision-making on juries, of record-keeping in clinics, of patient-selection practices in psychiatric clinics and so on, Garfinkel also gives accounts of presuppositions involved in similar investigatory, classifying and decision-making activity in sociology and sociological research (1967, chs 1 and 3; see also Cicourel, 1968; Scott, 1968).

In all of this Garfinkel is interested in what we have mentioned above as the 'interpretive procedures' (Cicourel) or the 'reflexive' methods for remedying the inherent 'indexicality' of meanings. 'Officially' defined methods of investigating, or whatever, provide a wonderful stamping ground for this interest. How do bureaucrats (or any class of members) actually go about applying the rules they are supposed to be following and, further, providing for the reading of what they do by others as 'demonstrably rule-following'. For these methods constitute the everyday existential reality of bureaucracy, or of any other social phenomenon. It is this topic that ethnomethodology is raising for sociological consideration.

Matza's work resonates to a limited extent the descriptive orientation to meanings, and the reconstructionist accounting of member's methods and recipes sounded in ethnomethodology. The idea of reconstruction, is exemplified in Matza's account of 'becoming deviant'. It could be said that it is basically the idea of a sociology modelled on the principles of a cookery book. Thus the operative principle is to provide an account of the constitution of a phenomenon, be it a cake or a social interaction process, which would enable someone to reconstitute the phenomenon. From this kind of knowledge of the constitution of a cake a cook could advise us 'how to bake a cake'. Similarly, from a knowledge of the social interactions involved in the process of generating a deviant career a sociologist could advise us on 'how to become deviant'. He could advise us on the kind of social situation to get ourselves in, the appropriate self-conception to have, and the most appropriate modes of interacting with people (see chapter 7 and Matza, 1969, p. 110).

Thus Matza would hold that the sociologist only understands the social phenomena of a deviant and his career when he could advise a person and other relevant actors how to co-operate in helping the person become deviant. The sociological understanding is valid when it can reconstruct the script of a typical deviance-achievement play, appropriately assigning responsibilities and important parts to a cast of players. This reconstructionist aspect of sociological humanism is closely allied with its descriptive aspect. In their different ways this is so in Matza's as in Cicourel's and Garfinkel's cases.

Matza's general perspective is what he calls 'naturalism' (ibid., ch. 1). That is, the sociologist must study man and society as they naturally occur. He must not impose perspectives and concepts prematurely on the natural phenomena. Now this naturalism is a very different creature from that which is normally denoted by this word. For the more usual denotation of naturalism refers to the position which we have called 'reductionism'. That is, it usually refers to an attempt to understand the humanities in terms of the natural sciences, as proto-natural sciences. But Matza's use of the term is exactly the opposite and more in line with what we have discussed here as the humanistic perspective.

Thus, according to Matza, man is *naturally* a choosing subject (ibid., pp. 108-17) and society is *naturally* meaningful. Thus a reductionist idea of man and of social science is profoundly *un*natural. The two uses of the term 'naturalism' can equally well be expressed in terms of the Cartesian dualism of mind and matter, using the term 'realism'. Thus for reductionists man as matter is real (i.e. sensorily given, objective, etc.), whereas man as mind is an unreal abstraction. For humanists, on the other hand, man as matter is an unreal abstraction, whereas man as mind (albeit embodied, active, expressive and so on) is real (i.e. sensorily and in other ways given objective, etc.). In fact, Matza's position is basically no more and no less than that of existential phenomenology. Just as phenomenology has as its basic imperative 'study of the phenomenon', 'being true to the things themselves' and 'getting back to the things themselves as we know them', so the basic commitment of Matza's naturalism is 'fidelity to the phenomenon under consideration'. For him this means that 'Naturalism in the study of man is a disciplined and rigorous humanism' (ibid., p. 8; see also pp. 93, 131, etc. where Matza acknowledges Sartre's influence).

The reorientation of sociological theory and method which we have been discussing, then, is self-consciously humanistic in the senses outlined in this book. Further, indications of this reorientation can be found within social psychiatry. The British school of Laing, Esterson, Cooper, Phillipson, Lee and others has adopted a very sensitive descriptive approach to interactions and communications involving actors labelled as schizophrenic with other actors who are labelling them. It makes extensive use of tape-recordings in patient-doctor and more particularly, doctor-patient-patient's family interviews. It has also tried to represent and reconstruct, both in ordinary language and neutral symbol schemes, the complexities of interaction and communication between twos, threes and groups of actors (see Laing, Phillipson and Lee, 1966).

A more conventionally sociological study consonant with this humanistic turn in psychiatry and the sociology of deviance, has been Douglas's critique (1970) of Durkheim's classic study of suicide (1951). Douglas criticises Durkheim's too easy reliance on official suicide statistics, this being but one aspect of a general lack of sensitivity to the moral and social meanings of suicide. For all his statistics Durkheim observed too little, and imposed and pre-supposed too much. He observed too little of the differences between communities concerning the meanings attached to the suicide act and its context by the suicidal actor himself and relevant others. He presupposed an invariant meaning for suicide, and imposed upon his 'material' his theory of anomie and of the normative nature of social life. Douglas thus advocates, in this particular case, what Cicourel argued in general, that before any dubious methods are used to collect dubious statistical material for generating or testing a theory, the sociologist must be 'really empirical', in the sense of 'experiental empiricism' which we have discussed above, and he must be prepared to face the reflexity of his empirical practice as a commonsense practice. He must be phenomenological, or ethno-methodological in Garfinkel's terminology He must at least get down to describing and reconstructing what social phenomena, in this case the act of suicide, mean to different actors in different social contexts of rules and of other actors, and how 'suicide' is talked about and socially managed. And he must address the sense of these descriptive and reconstructive practices.

The humanistic turn in modern philosophy, which has been the main subject of this book has its counterpart in the phenomenological turn in sociology briefly illustrated above. My aim has been both to show that sociology coexists with this humanistic philosophy in a common context, and to say something about the nature of this context.

Notes

1 Phenomenology

1 This is the most comprehensive analysis of the movement available at the present time. For other introductory works see Pivčevic (1970), Kockelmans (1967) and Farber (1966).

2 Not a lot of Brentano's work has been translated into English; most of what has can be found in the bibliography. See also Bergmann (1967b), Chisholm (1956; 1967a), Grossman (1960; 1969), Morrison (1970), Spiegelberg (1969, vol. 1, pp. 27-50), and Srzednicki (1965). Rancurello 1968 is the most useful modern commentary on Brentano's work.

3 A good deal of Husserl's work has been translated recently, see the bibliography. The best introductions to Husserl's work, besides those mentioned in note 1 above, are Ricoeur (1967a), Welch (1965) and Farber (1940; 1943).

4 Husserl's *Philosophy of Arithmetic* (1891) remains untranslated; on his clash with Frege over the correct analysis of the concept of number see Pivčevic (1970, ch. 2; see also 1969, p. 86).

5 See Husserl (1967, p. 30; 1969, pp. 232-44; 1960a, p. 89); see also Schutz (1962, pp. 165, 167 and 197; 1966, pp. 51-84).

6 On Husserl's later philosophy see Husserl (1960; 1965; 1970a); see also Gurwitsch (1966, ch. 18), Schutz (1966, pp. 15-50), Merleau-Ponty (1964b, pp. 159-81), and Kockelmans (1967, pp. 237-51).

7 Regarding Dilthey and Husserl, see Ricoeur (1967a, pp. 68-9), and Spiegelberg (1969, vol. I, pp. 122-4). Dilthey's early direct but not necessarily influential relationship with Husserl later became more indirect, but possibly more influential. Specifically, Dilthey influenced Heidegger (see Spiegelberg, 1969, vol. 1, p. 323 and 327; Heidegger, 1962, pp. 449-55, etc.). On Heidegger's influence on Husserl see Spiegelberg (1969, vol. 1, ch. 6, pp. 275-91). The anthropologist Lévy-Bruhl also influenced Husserl's later writings (see Merleau-Ponty, 1964a, p. 90).

2 Conceptual analysis

1 Mehta (1965) gives one view of the controversy following the publication of Gellner's attack. For other general accounts of conceptual analysis

see Mundle (1970), Cornforth (1965), Pole (1956), Russell (1953) and Waismann (1965).

2 See bibliography for Wittgenstein's main writings. See also Moore (1954-5), Waismann (1965), Gill, Copi and Beard in Fann (ed.) (1967a; 1967b), Morick (1967), Pitcher (1964; 1966) and (1966), Winch (1969), Fodor and Chihara (1967), Hartnack (1962), Hunnings (1968), Malcolm (1966), Pears (1966; 1969; 1971), van Peursen (1969), Pole (1958), Quinton (1970), Specht (1969), Winch (1968), von Wright (1969).

3 Gellner (1959, pp. 53-6) for instance. Austin denies this type of charge, see the section on him in this chapter. It is more strenuously denied by Warnock and Urmson in their discussions of Austin's philosophy (see Fann, 1969).

4 Wittgenstein (1963, pp. 102-3), by arguing in terms of grammar and linguistic behaviour, is not self-consciously trivialising philosophical problems. Quite the reverse. He sees himself as addressing profundity by taking this line. 'Grammar tells us what kind of an object anything is' (ibid., section 373, p. 116). 'Essence is expressed by grammar' (ibid., section 371, p. 116). 'Like everything metaphysical, the harmony between thought and reality is to be found in the grammar of the language' (1967, section 55, p. 12). On this see Specht (1969).

5 Below it will be seen that Ryle wants to interpret reasons and of consciousness, reductively, as types of dispositions. Wittgenstein, on the other hand, differentiated between dispositions and states of consciousness, see for instance (1967, p. 15; see also Geach, 1957).

6 For further critical comments on Ryle's *Concept of Mind* arguments see the Bibliography for Beloff (1962), Campbell (1953), Ewing (1952-3), Hanson (1952), Hicks (1961), J. Smart (1959), Mandelbaum (1958), Wisdom (1949-50), J. Wright (1959); see also the essays in Wood and Pitcher (1970).

7 Variations on position A can also be found in the following: Hart (1961), Hart and Honore (1959), Louch (1966), Malcolm (1964), Peters and Tajfel (1957) and Silber (1963-4). The philosophy of action has been the subject of much debate in and around positions A and B (see Adams (1966), Alston (1967), Bennett (1965), Brandt and Kim (1963), Brodbeck (1963), D. Brown (1968), R. Brown, (1965), Care and Landesman (1968), Danto (1965), Dodwell (1960), Forguson (1969), Gustafson (1967), King-Farlow and Hall (1965), Kolnai (1965-6), Levison and Thalberg (1969), McCracken (1952), Margolis (1964), Meiland (1963), Peters (1952), Potts (1965), Ritchie (1951-2), Schwayder (1965), Searle (1969), N. Smart (1964), Smythies (1965), Strawson (1968), Sutherland (1959), R. Taylor (1967), Vesey (1965; 1968), Warnock (1963), White (1968b) and Whiteley (1961; 1968)).

3 Logical empiricism and the reductionist idea of psycho-social science

1 Mach succeeding in intriguing Husserl (1970b, vol. I, p. 197) and dismaying Lenin (1964). We have already mentioned that Husserl had a certain regard for sensationalistic empiricists like Hume, Locke and Mach, as naive and proto-phenomenologists. Chapman and Cowley provide

modern phenomenological discussions of this school. Lenin's 'dialectical materialist' position saw either an impractical agnosticism *vis-à-vis* the objective world, or an ultimately theistic idealism lurking behind such empiricism. The idealism is certainly there, from Berkeley through Kant to Husserl, but together with an increasing detachment from empiricism. However, the anti-idealist existentialist critique of both idealism and empiricism seems to me to return to a dialectical unity of man and the world, or subject and object, through the practical activity of the body, which is comparable with the materialist epistemology and ontology of the young Marx (e.g. Merleau-Ponty, 1962; Sartre, 1963b).

2 See Kraft (1953), Ayer (1971; 1959a), Carnap (1937), Reichenbach (1938), Achinstein and Barker (1969), and Schilpp (1963). Relevant discussion of logical empiricism, mainly critical, from the point of view of a humanistic sociology are Apel (1967), and Schutz (1962, pp. 48-66).

3 Critiques of empiricism and logical positivism by conceptual analysts are numerous and trenchant, seee Austin's attack on Ayer (1971), Peters attack on Hobbes (1957; 1958), Winch's attack on Mill (1968), Wittgenstein's critique of his *Tractatus* views (1963), Hampshire (1959, ch. 1) and so on.

4 See bibliography for Neurath, Lundberg and Hummell and Opp. Furfey (1953, p. 40) states the sociological relevance of physicalism as follows: 'Physicalism demands that all sciences including the social sciences should speak a common language and that this common language should be the language of physics. Thus all science is, in a sense, reduced to physics.' But the 'language of physics' is a mythical and mystifying ideal. The actual languages of the various theoretical communities in physics require sociological and linguistic description, together with their methods of intertranslation and substitution, if only to provide the basis for an adequate philosophy of science: see Kuhn (1970a; but particularly 1970b, pp. 266-77). It need hardly be added that the present sociologically inadequate philosophy of science, 'verificationist' or 'falsificationist', cannot expect its model of physics to be taken seriously as normative for sociology.

5 See Lenin (1964) and Althusser (1969, ch. 6). For more humanistic interpretations see Schmidt (1962), Lukacs (1922), Sartre (1963b), Gramsci (1959), Meszaros (1970), Lefebvre (1966), and Goldmann (1964), besides Marx (1844; 1857). All Marxist and Leninist concepts are humanistic in that they address and call for action by men. Similarly they are all teleological in either the personalistic or holistic senses I have been using. But they are also 'dialetical'. The changing import of this term within Marxism, and its alleged superiority to both the positivism and the humanism I am discussing, would require much more detailed analysis than can possibly be given it here.

5 Gestalt psychology

1 See Koffka (1935, pp. 570-1, and also pp. 18-21) on the importance of what was ultimately Husserl's analysis of the ideality of meaning structures. Allport discusses Husserl and Kohler (1955, pp. 91-2 and

141-2). The phenomenological psychologist, Carl Stumpf, Husserl's colleague, was an important influence on Kohler, Koffka, Wertheimer, Lewin, and others, see Spiegelberg (1969), vol. I, p. 54. H. Rorschach, originator of the famous visual test method, was influenced by phenomenology, see Ellenberger (1970, p. 842). Tangential to Gestalt psychology, E. Strauss (1963) evinces Husserl's influence.

2 Wittgenstein (1963, p. 204); he warns against the description or reference to sensations or inner experience on many occasions in the *Philosophical Investigations*. See for instance, ibid., p. 71 (the 'experience' of deliberation); ibid., p. 87 (the 'experience' of acting according to a rule); ibid., pp. 102-3 (the 'inner mental process' of remembering); ibid., p. 161 (the 'experience' of doing); ibid., pp. 175-6, 181 and 217 (the 'experience' of meaning); and ibid., p. 231 (the 'experience' of remembering). This approach is none the less descriptive of facts which he would call conceptual and grammatical, and which we consider to be experiential and phenomenological. Regarding his descriptivism, see ibid., p. 31: 'don't think, but look!', and Wittgenstein (1967, p. 80).

3 Chomsky is very much in the *nature* ('innate structures of the mind') rather than the *nurture* (environmental stimuli) camp in relation to psychology. And this, together with his stress on the organisation and 'deep structure' of the language possessed and used by all humans, makes the affinities of his position with that of Gestalt psychology quite clear. His position is far closer to that of the Gestaltists than it is to either that of the phenomenologists or that of the conceptual analysts. However, it must be said that Chomsky himself has nowhere acknowledged such an affinity.

Bibliography

This bibliography contains works cited either in the text or in the notes. The works most frequently quoted are marked with an asterisk.

Abbreviations

A.P.Q. *American Philosophical Quarterly*
I.P.Q. *International Philosophical Quarterly*
P.A.S. *Proceedings of the Aristotelian Society*
P.P.R. *Philosophy and Phenomenological Research*
P.Q. *Philosophical Quarterly*

ABELSON, R. (1965), 'Because I want to', *Mind*, 74, 540-53.

ACHINSTEIN, P. and BARKER, S. F. (1969), *The Legacy of Logical Positivism: Studies in the Philosophy of Science* (Baltimore: Johns Hopkins).

ADAMS, E. M. (1966), 'Mental causality', *Mind*, 75, 552-63.

ADDIS, L. and LEWIS, D. (1965), *Moore and Ryle: Two Ontologists* (The Hague: Nijhoff).

ALEXANDER, P. (1955), 'Psychoanalysis and cure symposium with A. MacIntyre', *P.A.S.* Supplement, xxix, 25-42.

ALEXANDER, P. (1962), 'Rational behaviour and psychoanalytic explanation', *Mind*, 71, 326-41.

ALEXANDER, P. (1963), *Sensationalism and Scientific Explanation* (London: Routledge & Kegan Paul).

ALLERS, R. (1961), *Existentialism and Psychiatry* (Springfield, Ill.: C. C. Thomas).

ALSTON, W. (1967), 'Wants, actions and causal explanation', in CASTENADA, H. (ed.) (1967).

ALTHUSSER, L. (1969), *For Marx* (London: Allen Lane).

AMES, V. M. (1954-5), 'Mead and Husserl on self', *P.P.R.*, xiv, 320-31.

ANSCOMBE, G. E. M. (1968), 'Intentions', in WHITE, A. R. (ed.) (1968b).

APEL, K.-O. (1967), *Analytic Philosophy of Language and the Geisteswissenschaften* (Dordrecht: Reidel).

ARGYLE, M. (1957), *The Scientific Study of Social Behaviour* (London: Methuen).

ARMSTRONG, D. M. (1961), *Perception and the Physical World* (London: Routledge & Kegan Paul).

ARMSTRONG, D. M. (1967), *A Materialist Theory of the Mind* (London: Routledge & Kegan Paul).

ARTISS, K. L. (1962), *Milieu Therapy in Schizophrenia* (New York: Grune & Stratton).

ASCH, S. E. (1968), 'The doctrinal tyranny of associationism: or what is wrong with rote learning', in DIXON, J. R. and HORTON, D. L. (eds.) (1968).

AUSTIN, J. L. (1968), 'A plea for excuses', in WHITE, A. R. (ed.) (1968b); also in AUSTIN, J. L. (1970a).

AUSTIN, J. L. (1970a), *Philosophical Papers* (Oxford University Press).

AUSTIN, J. L. (1970b), *Sense and Sensibility* (Oxford University Press).

AUSTIN, J. L. (1971) *How to Do Things with Words* (1955 lectures) (Oxford University Press).

AYER, A. J. (1956), *The Problem of Knowledge* (Harmondsworth: Penguin).

AYER, A. J. (ed.) (1959a), *Logical Positivism* (New Jersey: Free Press).

AYER, A. J. (1959b), 'Phenomenology and linguistic analysis', *P.A.S.*, xxxiii, 111-24.

AYER, A. J. (1967), 'Man, as a subject for science', in LASLETT, P. and RUNCIMAN, W. G. (eds.) (1967).

AYER, A. J. (1971), *Language, Truth and Logic* (Harmondsworth: Penguin).

BARRAL, M. R. (1965), *Merleau-Ponty: The Role of the Body-subject in Interpersonal Relations* (Pittsburgh: Duquesne University Press).

BATESON, G., JACKSON, D., HALEY, J. and WEAKLAND, J. (1956), 'Toward a theory of schizophrenia', *Behavioural Science*, 1, 251.

BECK, L. W. (1966) 'Conscious and Unconscious Motives', *Mind*, 75, 155-79.

BECKER, E. (1962), *The Birth and Death of Meaning: A Perspective in Psychiatry and Anthropology* (New York: Free Press).

BECKER, E. (1964), *The Revolution in Psychiatry: The new Understanding of Man* (London: Collier-Macmillan).

BECKER, E. (1968), 'Socialisation, command of performance and mental illness', in SPITZER, S. P. and DENZIN, N. K. (eds.) (1968).

BECKER, H. S. (ed.) (1964), *The Other Side: Perspectives on Deviance* (New York: Free Press).

BECKER, H. S. (1966), *Outsiders* (London: Collier-Macmillan).

BECKER, H. S. (1970), 'The life history', in WORSELEY, P., *et al.* (eds.) (1970), *Modern Sociology: Introductory Readings* (Harmondsworth: Penguin).

BELOFF, J. (1962), *The Existence of Mind* (London: MacGibbon and Kee).

BENDIX, R. (1960), *Max Weber* (New York: Doubleday Anchor).

BENDIX, R. and ROTH, G. (1971), *Scholarship and Partisanship: Essays on Max Weber* (London: University of California Press).

BENNETT, D. (1965), 'Action, reason and purpose', *Journal of Philosophy*, 62, 85-96.

BERGER, P. (1967), *The Sacred Canopy: Elements of a Sociological Theory of Religion* (New York: Doubleday).

BERGER, P. and LUCKMANN, T. (1967), *The Social Construction of Reality* (London: Allen Lane).

BERGMANN, G. (1944-5), 'Brentano', *P.P.R.*, 5.

BERGMANN, G. (1967a), *The Metaphysics of Logical Positivism* (University of Wisconsin Press).

BERGMANN, G. (1967b), *Realism: A critique of Brentano and Meinong* (University of Wisconsin Press).

BERGMANN, G. and SPENCE, K. W. (1951), 'Operationism and theory construction', in MARX, M. H. (ed.) (1951).

BERNE, E. (1961), *Transactional Analysis in Psychotherapy—A Systematic Individual and Social Psychiatry* (New York: Grove Press).

BERNE, E. (1968), *Games People Play: The Psychology of Human Relationships* (Harmondsworth: Penguin).

BEVER, T. G., FODOR, J. A. and GARRETT, M. (1968), 'A formal limitation of associationism', in DIXON, T. R. and HORTON, D. L. (eds.) (1968).
BICKFORD, A. R. (1968), 'Is most mental illness an illusion?', *New Society*, 9 May.
BINSWANGER, L. (1945a), 'The case of Ellen West', in MAY, R., *et al.* (eds.) (1958).
BINSWANGER, L. (1945b), 'Insanity as a life-historical phenomenon, and as mental disease: the case of Ilse', in MAY, R., *et al.* (eds.) (1958).
BINSWANGER, L. (1946), 'The existential analysis school of thought' in MAY, R. *et al.* (eds.) (1958).
BINSWANGER, L. (1963), *Being-in-the-world* (New York: Basic Books).
BLACK, M. (1969), 'Austin on performatives', in FANN, K. T. (ed.) (1969).
BLUM, A. F. (1970), 'The sociology of mental illness', in DOUGLAS, J. (ed.) (1970).
BLUM, A. F. and MCHUGH, P. (1971), 'The social ascription of motives', *American Sociological Review*, 36, 98-109.
BOCHENSKI, I. M. (1964), *Contemporary European Philosophy* (Berkeley: University of California Press).
BOCHENSKI, I. M. (1965), *The Methods of Contemporary Thought* (Dordrecht: Reidel).
BORING, E. G. *et al.* (1945), Symposium on Operationism', *Psychological Review*, 52, 241-94.
BOSS, M. (1949), *The Meaning and Context of Sexual Perversions: an Existentialist Account* (New York: Grune & Stratton).
BOTTOMORE, T. B. and RUBEL, M. (eds.) (1962), *Karl Marx: Selected Writings in Sociology and Social Philosophy* (Harmondsworth: Penguin).
BRAITHWAITE, R. B. (1953), *Scientific Explanation* (London: Cambridge University Press).
BRANDT, R. and KIM, J. (1963), 'Wants as explanations of actions', *Journal of Philosophy*, 60, 425-35.
BRENTANO, F. (1924), *Psychologie vom empirischen Standpunkt;* published as *Psychology from an Empirical Standpoint* (London: Routledge & Kegan Paul, 1972).
BRENTANO, F. (1960a), 'The distinction between mental and physical phenomena', in CHISHOLM, R. M. (ed.) (1960).
BRENTANO, F. (1960b), 'Genuine and fictitious objects', in CHISHOLM, R. M. (ed.) (1960).
BRENTANO, F. (1960c), 'Presentation and judgement form two distinct fundamental classes', in CHISHOLM, R. M. (ed.) (1960).
BRENTANO, F. (1966), *The True and the Evident:* and *Letters to Husserl* English ed. by R. M. CHISHOLM (London: Routledge & Kegan Paul).
BRENTANO, F. (1969), *The Origin of our Knowledge of Right and Wrong* (English translation by R. M. CHISHOLM) (London: Routledge & Kegan Paul).
BRIDGMAN, P. W. (1927), *The Logic of Modern Physics* (New York: Macmillan).
BRODBECK, M. (1963), 'Meaning and action', *Philosophy of Science*, 30, 309-24.
BROWN, D. G. (1968), *Action* (London: Allen & Unwin).

BROWN, J. A. C. (1961), *Freud and the Post-Freudians* (Harmondsworth: Penguin).

BROWN, R. (1965), 'The explanation of behaviour, re. C. Taylor's book', *Philosophy*, 40, 344-8.

BROWN, R. and FRASER, R. (1963), 'The acquisition of syntax', in COFER, C. N. and MUSGRAVE, B. S. (1963).

BUCKLEY, W. (1967), *Sociology and Modern Systems Theory* (New Jersey: Prentice-Hall).

CAMERON, N. (1943), 'The paranoid pseudo-community', *American Journal of Sociology*, 46, 33-8.

CAMPBELL, C. A. (1953), 'Ryle on the intellect', *P.Q.*, iii, 115-38.

CARE, N. and LANDESMAN, C. (eds.) (1968), *Readings in the Theory of Action* (Bloomington: Indiana University Press).

CARNAP, R. (1937), *The Logical Syntax of Language* (London: Routledge & Kegan Paul).

CARNAP, R. (1951), 'Physicalism in psychology', in AYER, A. J. (ed.) (1951).

CARNAP, R. (1967), *The Logical Structure of the World* (London: Routledge & Kegan Paul).

CARNAP, R. (1963), 'Discussion of critics', in SCHILPP, P. (ed.) (1963).

CASTENADA, H. (ed.) (1967), *Intentionality, Minds and Perception* (Detroit: Wayne State University Press).

CATTELL, R. B. (1965), *The Scientific Analysis of Personality* (Harmondsworth: Penguin).

CERF, W. (1966), 'Critical review of *How to Do Things with Words*', in FANN, K. T. (ed.) (1969).

CHAPMAN, H. M. (1966), *Sensations and Phenomenology* (Bloomington: Indiana University Press).

CHISHOLM, R. M. (1955-6), 'Sentences about believing', *P.A.S.*, lvi, 125-48.

CHISHOLM, R. M. (1960), *Realism and the Background of Phenomenology* (London: Allen & Unwin).

CHISHOLM, R. M. (1967a), 'Brentano on descriptive psychology and the intentional', in LEE, E. N. and MANDELBAUM, M. (eds.) (1967).

CHISHOLM, R. M. (1967b), 'Intentionality', in EDWARDS, P. (ed.) (1967), *The Encyclopedia of Philosophy* (London: Collier-Macmillan).

CHISHOLM, R. M. (1969), 'Austin's philosophical papers', in FANN, K. T. (ed.) (1969).

CHOMSKY, C. (1970), *The Acquisition of Syntax in Children from* 5 *to* 10 (Cambridge, Mass: M.I.T. Press).

CHOMSKY, N. (1964), 'Review of B. F. Skinner's *Verbal Behaviour*', in FODOR, J. and KATZ, J. (eds.) (1964).

CHOMSKY, N. (1966), *Cartesian Linguistics: a Chapter in the History of Rationalist Thought* (New York: Harper & Row).

CHOMSKY, N. (1968), *Language and Mind* (New York: Harcourt, Brace & World).

CHOMSKY, N. (1971), 'Interpreting the world: the philosophy of Russell', *Cambridge Review*, 29 January.

CICOUREL, A. (1964), *Method and Measurement in Sociology* (New York: Free Press).

CICOUREL, A. (1968), *The Social Organisation of Juvenile Justice* (New York: Wiley).

CICOUREL, A. (1970), 'Basic and normative rules', in DREITZEL, H. P. (ed.) (1970).

CICOUREL, A. (1972), 'Ethnomethodology', in SEBEOK, T. *et al.* (eds.), *Current Trends in Linguistics*, vol. 12.

CLINARD, M. B. (1963), *Sociology of Deviant Behaviour* (revised edition) (New York: Holt, Rinehart & Winston).

COFER, C. N. and MUSGRAVE, B. S. (eds.) (1963), *Verbal Behaviour and Learning: Problems and Processes* (New York: McGraw-Hill).

COHEN, A. K. (1966), *Deviance and Control* (New Jersey: Prentice-Hall).

COHEN, P. (1968a), *Modern Social Theory* (London: Heinemann).

COHEN, P. (1968b), 'The very idea of a social science', in LAKATOS, I. and MUSGRAVE, A. (eds.) (1968).

COOLEY, C. H. (1922), *Human Nature and the Social Order* (revised edition) (New York: Scribner's).

COOPER, D. (1968), *Psychiatry and Anti-Psychiatry* (London: Tavistock).

COOPER, D. (1971), *The Death of the Family* (New York: Pantheon).

COPI, L. M. and BEARD, R. W. (1966), *Essays on Wittgenstein's Tractatus* (London: Routledge & Kegan Paul).

CORNFORTH, M. (1965), *Marxism and the Linguistic Philosophy* (London: Lawrence & Wishart).

COWLEY, F. (1968), *A Critique of British Empiricism* (London: Macmillan).

CROCKETT, R. and ST BLAIZE-MOLONY, R. (1964), 'Social ramifications of the therapeutic community approach in psychotherapy', *British Journal of Medical Psychology*, 37, 153.

CROWCROFT, A. (1967), *The Psychotic* (London: Pelican).

DAHRENDORF, R. (1968), *Essays in the Theory of Society* (London: Routledge & Kegan Paul).

DANTO, A. C. (1965), 'Basic actions: and theory of action', *A.P.Q.*, 2, 141-8.

DAVENEY, T. F. (1966-7), 'Intention and action', *Analysis*, 27, 23-8.

DAVENEY, T. F. (1967), 'Feelings, causes and Mr. Myers', *Mind*, 76, 592-4.

DAVIDSON, D. (1968), 'Actions, causes, reasons', in WHITE, A. R. (ed.) (1968b).

DESAN, W. (1966), *The Marxism of Jean-Paul Sartre* (New York: Anchor).

DEVEREAUX, G. (1939), A sociological theory of schizophrenia', *Psychoanalytic Review*, 26, 315-42.

DILMAN, I. (1959), 'The unconscious', *Mind*, 68, 446.

DILMAN, I. (1963-4), 'Examination of Sartre's theory of the emotions re. modern British philosophy', *Ratio*, 5, 190-212.

DINGLE, H. (1949), 'The logical status of psychoanalysis', *Analysis*, 9, 63-6.

DIXON, T. R. and HORTON, D. L. (eds.) (1968), *Verbal Behaviour and General Behaviour Theory* (New Jersey: Prentice-Hall).

DODWELL, A. (1960), 'Causes of behaviour and explanation in psychology', *Mind*, 69, 1-13.

DOUGLAS, J. D. (1967), 'The moral meanings of suicide', *New Society*, 13 July.

DOUGLAS, J. D. (1970a), *The Social Meanings of Suicide* (Princeton University Press).

DOUGLAS, J. D. (ed.) (1970b), *Deviance and Respectability: The Social*

Construction of Moral Meanings (New York: Basic Books).

DOUGLAS, J. D. (ed.) (1971), *Understanding Everyday Life* (London: Routledge & Kegan Paul).

DRAY, W. (1957), *Laws and Explanations in History* (New York: OUP).

DRAY, W. (1964), *Philosophy of History* (New Jersey: Prentice-Hall).

DREITZEL, H. P. (ed.) (1970), *Recent Sociology 2. Patterns of Communicative Behaviour* (New York: Macmillan).

DUNLAP, K. (1965), 'Psychoanalysis and the unconscious', in SARASON, I. G. (ed.) (1965).

DURKHEIM, E. (1951), *Suicide* (London: Routledge & Kegan Paul).

DURKHEIM, E. (1965), *The Rules of Sociological Method* (New York: Free Press).

EISENSTADT, S. N. (ed.) (1968), *The Protestant Ethic and Modernisation* (New York: Basic Books).

ELIOT, T. D. (1956), 'Interactions of psychiatric and social theory prior to 1940', in ROSE, A. (ed.) (1956).

ELLENBERGER, H. F. (1959), 'A clinical introduction to psychiatric phenomenology and existential analysis', in MAY, R., *et al.* (eds.) (1958).

ELLENBERGER, H. F. (1970), *The Discovery of the Unconscious: The History and Evolution of Dynamic Psychiatry* (London: Allen Lane).

ERICKSON, S. A. (1970), *Language and Being: An Analytic Phenomenology* (Yale University Press).

ESTERSON, A. (1970), *The Leaves of Spring: A Study in the Dialectics of Madness* (London: Tavistock).

EWING, A. C. (1952-3), 'Against Ryle's attack on dualism', *P.A.S.*, liii, 47-78.

EYSENCK, H. J. (1954), *The Psychology of Politics* (London: Routledge & Kegan Paul).

EYSENCK, H. J. (1965), *Fact and Fiction in Psychology* (Harmondsworth: Penguin).

EYSENCK, H. J. (1970), *Crime and Personality* (London: Paladin).

FANN, K. T. (1967a), 'A Wittgenstein bibliography', *I.P.Q.*, vii, 311-39.

FANN, K. T. (ed.) (1967b), *Wittgenstein, the Man and his Philosophy. An Anthology* (New York: Dell).

FANN, K. T. (ed.) (1969), *Symposium on J. L. Austin* (London: Routledge & Kegan Paul).

FARBER, L. H. (1966), *The Ways of the Will. Essays Towards a Psychology and Psychopathology of the Will* (London: Constable).

FARBER, M. (ed.) (1940), *Philosophical Essays in Memory of Edmund Husserl* (Connecticut: Greenwood Press).

FARBER, M. (1943), *The Foundation of Phenomenology: Edmund Husserl and the Quest for a Rigorous Science of Philosophy* (University of New York Press).

FARBER, M. (1966), *The Aims of Phenomenology: the Motives, Methods and Impact of Husserl's Thought* (New York: Harper & Row).

FEIGL, H. (1963), 'Physicalism, the unity of science and the foundation of psychology', in SCHILPP, P. (ed.) (1963).

FENICHEL, O. (1945), *The Psychoanalytic Theory of Neurosis* (New York: Morton).

FINN, D. R. (1967), 'Determinism and the explanation of behaviour' (unpublished Ph.D. thesis, University of London).

FLEW, A. (ed.) (1953), *Logic and Language*, 2nd Series (Oxford: Blackwell).

FLEW, A. (1960), 'Philosophy and psychopathology', in HOOK, S. (ed.) (1960).

FODOR, J. and CHIHARA, C. S. (1967), 'Operationalism and ordinary language—a critique of Wittgenstein', in PITCHER, G. (ed.) (1967).

FODOR, J. and KATZ, J. (eds.) (1964), *The Structure of Language: Essays in the Philosophy of Language* (New Jersey: Prentice-Hall).

FORGUSON, L. W. (1969) 'Austin's philosophy of action', in FANN, K. T. (ed.) (1969).

FOUCAULT, M. (1967), *Madness and Civilisation* (London: Tavistock).

FREEMAN, H. (1969), 'Community care', *New Society*, 10 April.

FREIDSON, E. (ed.) (1963), *The Hospital in Modern Society* (New York: Free Press).

FREUD, S. (1930), *Civilisation and its Discontents* (London: Hogarth Press and Institute of Psycho-analysis).

FREUD, S. (1938), *Basic Writings* (New York: The Modern Library).

FREUD, S. (1949), *Collected Papers*, vol. III (London: Hogarth Press).

FREUD, S. (1950), *Collected Papers*, vol. IV (London: Hogarth Press).

FREUD, S. (1953), *A General Selection from the Works of Sigmund Freud*, ed. by J. RICKMAN (London: Hogarth Press).

FREUD, S. (1962), *The Ego and the Id* (London: Hogarth Press).

FREUD, S. (1965), *The Psychopathology of Everyday Life*, translated by A. TYSON (New York: Norton).

FREUND, J. (1968), *The Sociology of Max Weber*, translated by M. ILFORD (London: Allen Lane).

FRIEDMAN, M. (ed.) (1964), *The Worlds of Existentialism* (New York: Random House).

FROMM, E. (1956), *The Sane Society* (London: Routledge & Kegan Paul).

FURBERG, M. (1963), *Locutionary and Illocutionary Acts* (Stockholm: Alquist & Wiksell).

FURFEY, P. H. (1953), *The Scope and Method of Sociology* (New York: Cooper Square).

GARDINER, P. (ed.) (1959), *Theories of History* (Chicago: Free Press).

GARFINKEL, H. (1956), 'Some sociological concepts and methods for psychiatrists', *Psychiatric Research Reports*, 6, 181-950.

GARFINKEL, H. (1967), *Studies in Ethnomethodology* (New Jersey: Prentice-Hall).

GARFINKEL, H. and SACKS, H. (1970), 'On the formal structures of practical actions', in MCKINNEY, J. and TIRYAKION, E. (eds.) (1970), *Theoretical Sociology* (New York: Appleton-Century-Crofts).

GEACH, P. T. (1957), *Mental Acts* (London: Routledge & Kegan Paul).

GELLNER, E. (1950-1), 'Analysis and ontology', in *P.Q.*, 1, 407-15.

GELLNER, E. (1959), *Words and Things* (London: Gollancz).

GELLNER, E. (1968), 'The new idealism—cause and meaning in the social sciences', in LAKATOS, I. and MUSGRAVE, A. (eds.) (1968).

GELLNER, E. (1970), 'Concepts and Society', in WILSON, B. (ed.) (1970).

GERTH, H. and MILLS, C. WRIGHT (1967), *From Max Weber: Essays in*

Sociology (London: Routledge & Kegan Paul).

GILL, J. H. (1967), 'The contents of Wittgenstein's *Philosophical Investigations*', *I.P.Q.*, vii, 305-10.

GILLIE, O. (1969), 'Freedom Hall', *New Society*, 27 March.

GLASER, B. G. and STRAUSS, A. L. (1967), *The Discovery of Grounded Theory: Strategies for Qualitative Research* (Chicago: Aldine).

GOFFMAN, E. (1961), *Encounters* (New York: Bobbs-Merrill).

GOFFMAN, E. (1968a), 'The moral career of the mental patient', in SPITZER, S.P. and DENZIN, W. K. (eds.) (1968).

GOFFMAN, E. (1968b), *Asylums* (Harmondsworth: Penguin).

GOLDMANN, L. (1964), *The Hidden God* (London: Routledge & Kegan Paul).

GOLDMANN, L. (1969), *The Human Sciences and Philosophy* (London: Cape).

GOUGH, H. G. (1968), 'A sociological theory of psychopathy', in SPITZER, S. P. and DENZIN, N. K. (eds.) (1968).

GRAMSCI, A. (1959), *Modern Prince and Other Writings* (New York: International Publishers).

GREEN, R. W. (ed.) (1959), *Protestantism and Capitalism* (New York: Heath).

GRODDECK, G. (1961), *The Book of the It* (London: Vision Press).

GROSSMAN, R. (1960), 'Acts and relations in Brentano', *Analysis*, 21, 1-5.

GROSSMAN, R. (1969), 'Non-existent objects: recent work on Brentano and Meinong', *A.P.Q.*, 6, 17-33.

GUNTRIP, H. (1968), *Schizoid Phenomena: Object Relations and the Self* (London: Hogarth Press and Institute of Psycho-analysis).

GURWITSCH, A. (1929), 'Phenomenology of thematics and of the pure ego: Studies of the relation between gestalt theory and phenomenology', in GURWITSCH, A. (1966).

GURWITSCH, A. (1964), *The Field of Consciousness* (Pittsburgh: Duquesne University).

GURWITSCH, A. (1966), *Studies in Phenomenology and Psychology*(Evanston: North Western University Press).

GUSTAFSON, D. F. (ed.) (1967), *Essays in Philosophical Psychology* (London: Macmillan).

HALEY, J. (1963), *Strategies of Psychotherapy* (New York: Grune & Stratton).

HAMLYN, D. W. (1951), 'Psychological explanation and the Gestalt hypothesis', *Mind*, lx, 506-20.

HAMLYN, D. W. (1961a), *The Psychology of Perception* (London: Routledge & Kegan Paul).

HAMLYN, D. W. (1961b), *Sensation and Perception: A History of the Philosophy of Perception* (London: Routledge & Kegan Paul).

HAMLYN, D. W. (1964), 'Causality and human behaviour', *P.A.S.*, Suplement, xxxviii, 125-42.

HAMLYN, D. W. (1970), 'Knowing people', *Birkbeck Philosophy Faculty Magazine*, Autumn, 3, 1-12.

*HAMPSHIRE, S. (1959), *Thought and Action* (London: Chatto & Windus).

HAMPSHIRE, S. (1965), *Freedom of Mind* (Lecture at Kansas University).

HANSON, N. R. (1952), 'Professor Ryle's "Mind"', *P.Q.*, 2, 246-8.

HART, H. L. A. (1961), *The Concept of Law* (Oxford University Press).

HART, H. L. A. and HONORE, A. M. (1959), *Causation in the Law* (Oxford: Clarendon Press).

HARTNACK, J. (1962), *Wittgenstein and Modern Philosophy*, translated by M. CRANSTON (London: Methuen).

HEIDEGGER, M. (1949), *Existence and Being* (Chicago: Henry Regnery).

HEIDEGGER, M. (1962), *Being and Time* (London: S.C.M.).

HEIDEGGER, M. (1970), *Hegel's Concept of Experience* (New York: Harper & Row).

HEMPEL, C. (1959), 'The function of general laws in history', in GARDINER, P. (ed.) (1959).

HEMPEL, C. (1965), *Aspects of Scientific Explanation and Other Essays in the Philosophy of Science* (New York: Free Press).

HEMPEL, C. (1966), *Philosophy of Natural Science* (New Jersey: Prentice-Hall).

HEMPEL, C. (1969), 'Logical positivism and the social sciences', in ACHINSTEIN, P. and BARKER, S. F. (eds.) (1969).

HEMS, J. M. (1968), 'Husserl and Wittgenstein', in *I.P.Q.*, viii, 547-77.

HICKS, J. R. (1961), 'Language games and inner experience' (unpublished Ph.D. thesis, University of London).

HILGARD, E. R. (1965), 'The scientific status of psychoanalysis', in SARASON, I. E. (ed.).

HODGES, H. A. (1969), *Wilhelm Dilthey: An Introduction* (London: Routledge & Kegan Paul).

HOLBOROW, L. C. (1967), 'Wittgenstein's kind of behaviourism' in *P.Q.*, 17, 345-57.

HOOK, S. (ed.) (1959), *Psychoanalysis, Scientific Method and Philosophy* (New York: Grove Press).

HORGBY, I. (1959), 'The double awareness in Heidegger and Wittgenstein', *Inquiry*, 2, 235-64.

HUGHES, H. S. (1959), *Consciousness and Society* (London: MacGibbon & Kee).

HULL, C. L. (1943), *Principles of Behaviour* (New York: Appleton-Century-Crofts).

HULL, C. L. (1951), 'The uniformity point of view', in MARX, M. H. (ed.) (1951).

HULL, C. L. (1952), *A Behaviour System* (Yale University Press).

HUME, D. (1735), *A Treatise on Human Nature*, 1969 edition ed. by E. L. MOSSNER (Harmondsworth: Penguin).

HUMMEL, H. S. and KARL-DIETER OPP (1968), 'Sociology without sociology: the reduction of sociology to psychology; a program, a test and the theoretical evidence', *Inquiry*, ii, 205-26.

HUNNINGS, G. (1968), 'Wittgenstein's theories of language' (unpublished Ph.D. thesis, University of London).

HUSSERL, E. (1931), *Ideas*, translated by E. GIBSON (London: Allen & Unwin); revised edition, 1962.

HUSSERL, E. (1960a), *Cartesian Meditations* (The Hague: Nijhoff).

HUSSERL, E. (1960b), 'Phenomenology', in CHISHOLM, R. M. (ed.) (1960).

HUSSERL, E. (1960c), 'Phenomenology and anthropology', in CHISHOLM, R. M. (ed.) (1960).

HUSSERL, E. (1964a), *The Idea of Phenomenology* (The Hague: Nijhoff).

HUSSERL, E. (1964b), *The Phenomenology of Internal Time-Consciousness* (The Hague: Nijhoff).

HUSSERL, E. (1965), *Phenomenology and the Crisis of Philosophy* (New York: Harper & Row).

HUSSERL, E. (1967), *Ideas: General Introduction to Pure Phenomenology* (London: Allen & Unwin).

HUSSERL, E. (1969), *Formal and Transcendental Logic* (The Hague: Nijhoff).

HUSSERL, E. (1970a), *The Crisis of European Sciences and Transcendental Phenomenology* (Evanston: North Western University Press).

HUSSERL, E. (1970b), *Logical Investigations*, vols 1 and 2 (London: Routledge & Kegan Paul).

ISAJIW, W. (1968), *Causation and Functionalism in Sociology* (London: Routledge & Kegan Paul).

JACKSON, D. D. (ed.) (1960), *The Etiology of Schizophrenia* (New York: Basic Books).

JACKSON, D. D. (1964), *Myths of Madness: New Facts for Old Fallacies* (New York: Macmillan).

JAMES, W. (1890), *Principles of Psychology*, 2 vols (New York: Dover Publications).

JANSEN, E. (1969), 'Therapeutic communities', *Sunday Times*, 23 March.

JASPERS, K. (1913), *General Psychopathology*, 1963 edition translated by J. HOENIGMAN and M. HAMILTON from 1942 revised edition (Manchester University Press).

JONES, E. (1964), *The Life and Work of Sigmund Freud*, ed. and abridged to one vol. by L. TRILLING and S. MARCUS (Harmondsworth: Penguin).

JONES, J. R. (1958-9), 'Two concepts of mental contexts', *P.A.S.*, lix, 105-24.

JONES, J. R. (1967), 'How do I know who I am?', *P.A.S.* Supplement, xli, 1-18.

KAAM, A. van (1969), *Existential Foundations of Psychology* (New York: Doubleday, Image Books).

KENNY, A. (1963), *Action, Emotion and Will* (London: Routledge & Kegan Paul).

KING-FARLOW, J. and HALL, E. (1965), 'Man, beast and philosophical psychology', *British Journal for Philosophical Science*, 16, 81-101.

KITSUSE, J. I. (1968), 'Societal reaction to deviant behaviour: problems of theory and method', in SPITZER, S. P. and DENZIN, N. K. (eds.) (1968).

KOCH, S. (1964), 'Psychology and emerging conceptions of knowledge as unitary', in WAHN, T. W. (ed.) (1964).

KOCKELMANS, J. (ed.) (1967), *Phenomenology: The Philosophy of Edmund Husserl* (New York: Doubleday Anchor).

KOESTLER, A. (1967), *The Ghost and the Machine* (London: Pan Books).

KOESTLER, A. and SMYTHIES, J. R. (1969), *Beyond Reductionism: The Alpbach Symposium* (London: Hutchinson).

KOFFKA, K. (1928), *Growth of the Mind* (revised edition) (New York: Harcourt, Brace & World).

KOFFKA, K. (1935), *Principles of Gestalt Psychology* (New York: Harcourt, Brace & World).

KOHL, H. (1965), *The Ages of Complexity* (New York: Mentor).

KOHLER, W. (1938), *The Place of Value in a World of Facts* (New York: Liveright).

KOHLER, W. (1940), *Dynamics in Psychology* (New York: Liveright).

*KOHLER, W. (1947), *Gestalt Psychology: An Introduction to New Concepts in Modern Psychology* (New York: Mentor).

KOLNAI, A. (1965-6), 'Games and aims', *P.A.S.*, lxvi, 103-28.

KÖRNER, S. (1966), *Experience and Theory* (London: Routledge & Kegan Paul).

KRAFT, V. (1953), *The Vienna Circle: The Origin of Neo-positivism: A Chapter in the history of recent philosophy* (New York: Philosophical Library).

KUHN, T. (1970a), *The Structure of Scientific Revolutions*, second edition (University of Chicago Press).

KUHN, T. (1970b), 'Reflections on my critics', LAKATOS, I. and MUSGRAVE, A. (eds.) (1970), *Criticism and the Growth of Knowledge* (Cambridge University Press).

KULLMAN, M. and TAYLOR, C. (1966), 'The pre-objective world', in NATANSON, M. (ed.) (1966).

KURTZ, R. M. (1969), 'A conceptual investigation of Witkin's notion of perceptual style', *Mind*, 78, 522-33.

LAING, R. D. (1961), *The Self and Others: Further Studies in Sanity and Madness* (London: Tavistock).

LAING, R. D. (1965a), *The Divided Self: An Existential Study in Sanity and Madness* (Harmondsworth: Penguin).

LAING, R. D. (1965b), 'Family and individual structure', in LOMAS, P. (1965), *Psychoanalytic Approaches to the Family* (London: Hogarth Press).

LAING, R. D. (1965c), 'Mystification, confusion and conflict', in BOSZORMENYI-NAGY, I. and FRAMO, J. L. (eds.) (1965), *Intensive Family Therapy: Theoretical and Practical Aspects* (New York: Hocker; Harper & Row).

LAING, R. D. (1967), *The Politics of Experience and the Bird of Paradise* (Harmondsworth: Penguin).

LAING, R. D. (1969a), *Intervention in Social Situations* (London: Association of Family Caseworkers).

LAING, R. D. (1969b), *Self and Others* (London: Tavistock).

LAING, R. D. (1970), *Knots* (London: Tavistock).

LAING, R. D. (1971), *The Politics of the Family* (London: Tavistock).

LAING, R. D. and COOPER, D. (1964), *Reason and Violence: A Decade of Sartre's Philosophy* 1950-1960 (London: Tavistock).

LAING, R. D. and ESTERSON, A. (1958), 'The collusive function of pairing in analytic groups', *British Journal of Medical Psychology*, 31, 117.

LAING, R. D. and ESTERSON, A. (1964), *Sanity, Madness and the Family* (London: Tavistock; New York: Basic Books).

LAING, R. D., PHILLIPSON, H. and LEE, A. R. (1966), *Interpersonal Perception: A Theory and a Method of Research* (London: Tavistock).

LAKATOS, I. and MUSGRAVE, A. (eds.) (1968), *Problems in the Philosophy of Science* (Amsterdam: North-Holland Publishing).

LAPLANCHE, J. and PONTALIS, B. (1968), 'Fantasy and the origins of sexuality', *International Journal of Psychoanalysis*, 49, 1-18.

LASLETT, P. and RUNCIMAN, W. G. (eds.) (1962), *Philosophy, Politics and Society: second series* (Oxford: Blackwell).

LEE, E. N. and MANDELBAUM, M. (eds.) (1967), *Phenomenology and Existentialism* (Baltimore: Johns Hopkins).

LEFEBVRE, H. (1966), *The Sociology of Marx*, English translation 1968 (London: Allen Lane).

LEMERT, E. M. (1951), *Social Pathology* (New York: McGraw-Hill).

*LEMERT, E. M. (1967), *Human Deviance, Social Problems and Social Control* (London: Prentice-Hall).

LENIN, V.I. (1964), *Materialism and Empirio-Criticism: Critical Comments on a Reactionary Philosophy* (Moscow: Progress Publishers).

LEVISON, A. B. (1966), 'Knowledge and society', *Inquiry*, 9-10, 132-46.

LEVISON, A. B. and THALBERG, I. (1969), 'Essential and causal explanations of action', *Mind*, lxxviii, 91-102.

LEWIN, K. (1942), 'Field theory and learning', *Forty-first Yearbook of the National Society for the Study of Education*, pp. 215-42.

LOCKE, J. (1690), *An Essay concerning Human Understanding*, 1964 edition abridged and ed. by A. D. WOOZLEY (London: Collins, Fontana).

LORENZ, K. (1966), *On Aggression*, translated by M. LATZKE, (London: Methuen).

LOUCH, A. R. (1966), *Explanation and Human Action* (Oxford: Blackwell).

LUIJPEN, W. A. (1963), *Existential Phenomenology* (Pittsburgh: Duquesne University Press).

LUKACS, G. (1922), *History and Class Consciousness: Studies in Marxist Dialectics*, English translation 1967 (London: Merlin).

LUNDBERG, G. (1939), *Foundations of Sociology* (New York: McKay).

MCCLELLAND, D. C. (1953), *The Achievement Motive* (New York: Appleton-Century-Crofts).

MCCRACKEN, D. J. (1952), 'Motives and causes', *P.A.S.* Supplement, xxvi, 163-78.

MACH, E. (1914), *The Analysis of Sensations* (London: Open Court).

MACHOTKA, O. (1964), *The Unconscious in Social Relations: an Analysis of Unconscious Processes in Personality, Society and Culture* (New York: Philosophical Library).

MCHUGH, P. (1968), *Defining the Situation* (New York: Bobbs-Merrill).

MCHUGH, P. (1970), 'A common-sense perception of deviance', in DREITZEL, H. P. (ed.) (1970).

MACINTYRE, A. (1955), 'Psychoanalysis and cure symposium with P. Alexander', *P.A.S.* Supplement, xxix, 43-58.

MACINTYRE, A. (1957), 'Determinism', *Mind*, lxvi, 28-41.

MACINTYRE, A. (1960), *The Unconscious—a Conceptual Analysis* (London: Routledge & Kegan Paul).

MACINTYRE, A. (1962), 'A mistake about causality in social science', in LASLETT, P. and RUNCIMAN, W. G. (eds.) (1962).

MACINTYRE, A. (1966), 'The antecedents of action', in MACINTYRE, A. (1971).

MACINTYRE, A. (1967), 'The idea of a social science', in MACINTYRE, A. (1971).

MACINTYRE, A. (1968), 'Materialism Revisited', *New Society*, 1 February (review of D. M. Armstrong, 1967).

MACINTYRE, A. (1971), *Against the Self-Images of the Age* (London: Duckworth).

MACINTYRE, A. and NOWELL-SMITH, P. H. (1960), 'Symposium: Purpose and intelligent action', *P.A.S.* Supplement, 34, 79-112.

MCKINNEY, J. C. (1970), 'Sociological theory and the process of typification', in MCKINNEY, J. C. and TIRYAKIAN, E. A. (eds.) (1970).

MCKINNEY, J. C. and TIRYAKIAN, E. A. (eds.) (1970), *Theoretical Sociology: Perspectives and Developments* (New York: Appleton-Century-Crofts).

MACNAB, F. A. (1965), *Estrangement and Relationship: Experience with Schizophrenics* (London: Tavistock).

MADELL, G. C. (1964), 'Causal explanation and human behaviour' (unpublished Ph.D. thesis, University of London).

MADELL, G. C. (1967), 'Action and causal explanation', *Mind*, 76, 34-48.

MALCOLM N. (1964), 'Behaviour as a philosophy of psychology', in WAHN, T. W. (ed.) (1964).

MALCOLM, N. (1966), *Ludwig Wittgenstein: A Memoir* (with bibliographical sketch by G. von WRIGHT (Oxford University Press).

MALCOLM, N. (1967), 'Explaining behaviour', *Philosophical Review*, 76, 97.

MANASSE, E. M. (1957), 'Jaspers' relation to Max Weber', in SCHILPP, P. (ed.) (1957).

MANDELBAUM, M. (1958), 'Professor Ryle and psychology', *Philosophical Review*, lxvii, 522-30.

MANDLER, C. and KESSEN, W. (1964), *The Language of Psychology* (New York: Wiley).

MARGOLIS, J. (1964), 'Motives, causes and action', *Methodos*, xvi, 83-9.

MARTIN, M. (1964), 'The explanatory value of the unconscious', *Philosophy of Science*, 31, 122-32.

MARX, K. (1844), *Economic and Philosophical Manuscripts*, English translation, 1970 (London: Lawrence & Wishart).

MARX, K. (1857), *Marx's Grundrisse*, English translation 1971, ed. by D. MACLELLAN (London: Macmillan).

MARX, M. H. (ed.) (1951), *Psychological Theory* (New York: Macmillan).

MATZA, D. (1969), *Becoming Deviant* (New York: Prentice-Hall).

MAY, R. (1967), *Psychology and the Human Dilemma* (New York: Van Nostrand).

MAY, R. (1970), *Love and Will* (New York: Souvenir Press).

*MAY, R., ANGELE, E. and ELLENBERGER, H. F. (eds.) (1958), *Existence: A New Dimension in Psychiatry and Psychology* (New York: Basic Books).

MAYS, W. and BROWN, S. C. (eds.) (1972), *Linguistic Analysis and Phenomenology* (London: Macmillan).

*MEAD, G. H. (1967), *Mind, Self and Society* (Chicago University Press).

MECHANIC, D. (1962), 'Some factors in identifying and defining mental illness', in SPITZER, S. P. and DENZIN, N. K. (eds.) (1968).

MEHTA, V. (1965), *The Fly and the Fly Bottle* (Harmondsworth: Penguin).

MEILAND, J. W. (1963), 'Motives and ends', *P.Q.* 13, 64-71.

MELDEN, A. I. (1967), *Free Action* (London: Routledge & Kegan Paul).

*MERLEAU-PONTY, M. (1962), *Phenomenology of Perception* (London: Routledge & Kegan Paul).

MERLEAU-PONTY, M. (1964a), *The Primacy of Perception: And Other Essays* (Evanston: North Western University Press).

*MERLEAU-PONTY, M. (1964b), *Signs*, translated by R. C. MCCLEARY (Evanston: North Western University Press).

MERLEAU-PONTY, M. (1964c), 'Phenomenology and the science of man', in MERLEAU-PONTY, M. (1964a).

MERLEAU-PONTY, M. (1964d), 'The child's relations with others', in MERLEAU-PONTY, M. (1964a).

*MERLEAU-PONTY, M. (1965), *The Structure of Behaviour* (London: Methuen).

*MERLEAU-PONTY, M. (1968a), *Resume de cours College de France* 1952-62 (Paris: Gallimard).

MERLEAU-PONTY, M. (1968b), 'Matériaux pour une théorie de l'histoire', in MERLEAU-PONTY, M. (1968a).

MERTON, R. K. (1936), 'The unanticipated consequences of purposive social action', *American Sociological Review*, 1, 894-904.

MERTON, R. K. (1957a), *Social Theory and Social Structure* (Chicago: Free Press).

MERTON, R. K. (1957b), 'Manifest and latent functions', in MERTON, R. K. (1957a).

MERTON, R. K. (1957c), 'Social structure and anomie', in MERTON, R. K. (1957a).

MESZAROS, I. (1970), *Marx's Theory of Alienation* (London: Merlin).

MILLS, C. WRIGHT (1959), *The Sociological Imagination* (OUP).

MINKOWSKI, E. (1933), *Le temps vecu* (Paris: Artrey).

MINKOWSKI, E. (1958), 'Findings in a case of schizophrenic depression', in MAY, R., *et al.* (eds.) (1958).

MISES, R. von (1968), *Positivism: A Study in Human Understanding* (New York: Dover).

MOHANTY, J. N. (1964), *Edmund Husserl's Theory of Meaning* (The Hague: Nijhoff).

MOORE, G. E. (1954-5), 'Wittgenstein's lectures 1930-33', *Mind*, 63, 1-15, 289-315; 64, 1-27.

MOORE, G. E. (1965), *Principia Ethica* (Cambridge University Press).

MORICK, H. (ed.) (1967), *Wittgenstein and the Problem of Other Minds* (New York: McGraw-Hill).

MORRIS, G. O. and WYNNE, L. C. (1965), 'Schizophrenic and parental styles of communication—a predictive study using excerpts of family therapy recordings', *Psychiatry*, 28, 19-44.

MORRISON, J. (1970), 'Husserl and Brentano on intentionality', *P.P.R.*, 31, 27-46.

MOUSTAKAS, C. (ed.) (1966), *Existential Child Therapy: The Child's Discovery of Himself* (New York: Basic Books).

MOUZELIS, N. (1967), *Organisation and Bureaucracy* (London: Routledge & Kegan Paul).

MUNDLE, C. W. K. (1966), 'Private language and Wittgenstein's kind of behaviourism', *P.Q.*, 16, 35-46.

MUNDLE, C. W. K. (1970), *A Critique of Linguistic Philosophy* (Oxford: Clarendon Press).

MUNSON, T. N. (1962), 'Wittgenstein's phenomenology,' *P.P.R.*, 23, 37-50.
MURDOCH, I. (1953), *Sartre: Romantic Rationalist* (Cambridge: Bowes).
MURDOCH, I. (1970), *The Sovereignty of Good* (London: Routledge & Kegan Paul).
NAGEL, E. (1959), 'Methodological issues in psychoanalytic theory', in HOOK, S. (ed.) (1959).
NAGEL, E. (1961), *The Structure of Science* (New York: Harcourt, Brace & World).
NATANSON, M. (ed.) (1966), *Essays in Phenomenology* (The Hague: Nijhoff).
NEURATH, O. (1959), 'Sociology and physicalism', in AYER, A. J. (ed.) (1959).
NISSEN, H. W. (1964), 'The nature of the drive as innate determinant of behavioural organisation', in TEEVAN, R. C. and BIRNEY, R. C. (eds.) (1964) *Theories of Motivation in Learning* (London: Van Nostrand).
ODAJNYK, W. (1965), *Marxism and Existentialism* (New York: Anchor).
PARSONS, T. (1937), *The Structure of Social Action* (Chicago: Free Press).
PARSONS, T. (1966), *Societies: Evolutionary and Comparative Perspectives* (New Jersey: Prentice-Hall).
PARSONS, T. (1970), *The Social System* (London: Routledge & Kegan Paul).
PASSMORE, J. (1957), *A Hundred Years of Philosophy*, 1966 edition (Harmondsworth: Penguin).
PAVLOV, I. (1927), *Conditioned Reflexes* (Oxford University Press).
PEARS, D. (ed.) (1963), *Freedom and the Will* (London: Macmillan).
PEARS, D. (1966), 'Austin and Wittgenstein', in WILLIAMS, B. and MONTEFIORE A. (eds.) (1966).
PEARS, D. (1968), 'Desires as causes of actions', in VESEY, G. N. (ed.) (1968).
PEARS, D. (1969), 'The development of Wittgenstein's philosophy', *New York Review* Special Supplement, 16 January.
PEARS, D. (1971), *Wittgenstein* (London: Fontana, Collins).
PEARS, D., THOMSON, J. F. and WARNOCK (1963) 'What is the Will?', in PEARS, D. (ed.) (1963).
PETERS, R. S. (1952), 'Motives and causes', *P.A.S.* Supplement.
PETERS, R. S. (1956-7), 'Freud's theory', *British Journal for Philosophy of Science*, vii, 4-13.
PETERS, R. S. (1958), *The Concept of Motivation* (London: Routledge & Kegan Paul).
PETERS, R. S. and TAJFEL, H. (1957), 'Hobbes and Hull: metaphysicians of behaviour', *British Journal for Philosophy of Science*, viii, 36-40.
PEURSEN, C. A. van (1959-60), 'Husserl Wittgenstein', *PPR*, 20, 181-95.
PEURSEN, C. A. van (1966), *Body, Soul and Spirit: a Survey of the Mind-Body Problem* (Oxford University Press).
PEURSEN, C. A. van (1969), *Ludwig Wittgenstein: an Introduction to his Philosophy*, English translation by R. AMBLER (London: Faber & Faber).
PFAENDER, A. (1967), *Phenomenology of Willing and Motivation*, translated by H. SPIEGELBERG (Evanston: North Western University Press).
PHILLIPSON, M. *et al.* (1972), *New Directions in Sociology* (London: Collier-Macmillan).
PIAGET, J. *et al.* (1960), *The Moral Judgement of the Child*, 3rd impression (London: Routledge & Kegan Paul).
PIAGET, J. and INHELDER, B. (1969), 'The gaps in empiricism', in KOESTLER,

A. and SMYTHIES, I. R. (eds.) (1969).

PITCHER, G. (1964), *The Philosophy of Wittgenstein* (New Jersey: Prentice-Hall).

PITCHER, G. (ed.) (1966), *Wittgenstein: The Philosophical Investigations* (Notre Dame, Indiana: Notre Dame University Press).

PIVCEVIC, E. (1970), *Husserl and Phenomenology* (London: Hutchinson).

PLACE, U. T. (1956), 'Is consciousness a brain process?', *British Journal of Psychology*, xlvii, 44-50.

POLE, D. (1956), 'The therapeutic method in philosophy as in Wisdom and Ryle', unpublished Ph.D. thesis, University of London.

POLE, D. (1958), *The Later Philosophy of Wittgenstein* (London: Athlone Press, University of London).

POPPER, K. (1959), *The Logic of Scientific Discovery* (London: Hutchinson).

POPPER, K. (1961), *The Poverty of Historicism* (London: Routledge & Kegan Paul).

POPPER, K. (1965), *Conjectures and Refutations: the Growth of Scientific Knowledge* (London: Routledge & Kegan Paul).

POPPER, K. (1966), *Clouds and Clocks—an Essay on the Freedom of Man* (St Louis University Press).

POTTS, T. (1965), 'States, activities and performances', *P.A.S.*, Supplementary, xxxix, 65-84.

PRATT, C. C. (1939), *The Logic of Modern Psychology* (New York: Macmillan).

QUINTON, A. (1970), 'In conversations with philosophers', *Listener*, 10 December.

*RABIL, A. (1967), *Merleau-Ponty: Existentialist of the Social World* (New York: Columbia University Press).

RADNITZKY, G. (1968), *Contemporary Schools of Meta-science*, vols 1 and 2 (Goeteborg: Akademifoerlaget).

*RANCURELLO, A. C. (1968), *A Study of Franz Brentano: His Psychological Standpoint and his Significance in the History of Psychology* (New York: Academic Press).

RAPOPORT, R. N. (1960), *Community as Doctor: New Perspectives on a Therapeutic Community* (London: Tavistock).

REICH, W. (1940), *The Mass Psychology of Fascism* (New York: Orgone Institute Press).

REICHENBACH, H. (1938), *Experience and Prediction: An Analysis of the Foundations and the Structure of Knowledge* (Chicago University Press).

RESCHER, N. (ed.) (1967), *Logic of Decision and Action* (University of Pittsburgh Press).

RICKERT, H. (1962), *Science and History: A Critique of Positivist Epistemology* (Princeton: Van Nostrand).

RICKMAN, H. P. (1961), *Meaning in History* (London: Allen & Unwin).

RICKMAN, H. P. (1967), *Understanding and the Human Studies* (London: Heinemann).

RICOUER, P. (1967a), *Husserl: An Analysis of his Phenomenology* (Evanston: North Western University Press).

RICOUER, P. (1967b), 'Husserl and Wittgenstein on language', in LEE, E. N. and MANDELBAUM, M. (eds.) (1967).

RICOUER, P. (1970), *Freud and Philosophy: An Essay in Interpretation*, translated by D. Savage (Yale University Press).

RIEFF, P. (1959), *Freud, The Mind of the Moralist* (New York: Viking).

RIESMAN, D. *et al.* (1950), *The Lonely Crowd: A Study of the Changing American Character* (Yale University Press); reprinted in 1967.

RITCHIE, A. M. (1951-2), 'Agent and act in the theory of Mind', *P.A.S.*, lii, 1-22.

ROCK, P. E. (1968), 'Observations on debt-collecting', *British Journal of Sociology*, xix, 176-91.

ROGERS, C. R. (1951), *Client-centred Therapy: Its Current Practice, Implications and Theory* (Boston: Houghton-Mifflin).

ROGERS, C. R. *et al.* (eds.) (1967), *The Therapeutic Relationship and its Impact: a Study of Psychotherapy with Schizophrenics* (University of Wisconsin Press).

ROSE, A. M. (ed.) (1956), *Mental Health and Mental Disorder: A Sociological Approach* (London: Routledge & Kegan Paul).

ROSE, A. M. (1959), 'A socio-psychological theory of neurosis', in SPITZER, S. P. and DENZIN, N. K. (eds.) (1968).

ROSE, A. M. (ed.) (1962), *Human Behaviour and Social Processes* (London: Routledge & Kegan Paul).

ROSEN, G. (1968), *Madness in Society* (London: Routledge & Kegan Paul).

ROSEN, S. (1970), *Nihilism: A Philosophical Essay* (Yale University Press).

RUBINGTON, E. and WEINBERG, M. S. (1968), *Deviance: The Interactionist Perspective: Text and Readings in the Sociology of Deviance* (New York: Macmillan).

RUDNER, R. S. (1966), *Philosophy of Social Science* (New Jersey: Prentice-Hall).

RUITENBEEK, H. M. (ed.) (1962), *Psychoanalysis and Existential Philosophy* (New York: Dutton).

RUNCIMAN, W. G. (1970), *Sociology in its Place, and Other Essays* (Cambridge University Press).

RUSSELL, B. (1921), *The Analysis of Mind* (London: Allen & Unwin).

RUSSELL, B. (1926), *Our Knowledge of the External World* (London: Allen & Unwin).

RUSSELL, B. (1940), *An Inquiry into Meaning and Truth* (New York: Morton; London: Allen & Unwin) (1969, Harmondsworth: Penguin).

RUSSELL, B. (1948), *Human Knowledge, Its Scope and Limitations* (New York: Simon and Schuster).

RUSSELL, B. (1953), 'The cult of ordinary usage', *British Journal for Philosophy of Science*, 3.

RUSSELL, B. (1956), *Logic and Knowledge* (London: Allen & Unwin).

RUSSELL, W. A. and STAATS, A. W. (1970), 'Purpose and the problem of associative selectivity in language learning', in COFER, C. N. and MUSGRAVE, B. S. (eds.) (1963).

RYAN, A. (1970), *The Philosophy of the Social Sciences* (London: Macmillan).

RYLE, G. (1929), 'Review of Heidegger's *Being and Time*', *Mind*, xxxviii, 355-70.

RYLE, G. (1932), 'Systematically misleading expressions', *P.A.S.*, xxxii, 139-70.

RYLE, G. (1946), 'On Farber's version of Husserl', *Philosophy*, xxi, 263-9.

RYLE, G. (ed.) (1956), *The Revolution in Philosophy* (London: Macmillan).

RYLE, G. (1962), 'La phenomenologie contre The Concept of Mind', in *La philosophie analytique* (4th Symposium at Royaumont) (Paris: Editions de Minuit).

*RYLE, G. (1963), *Concept of Mind* (Harmondsworth: Penguin).

RYLE, G. (1970), 'Autobiographical', in WOOD, O. P. and PITCHER, E. (eds.) (1970).

RYLE, G., HODGES, H. and ACTON, H. B. (1932), 'Phenomenology', *P.A.S.* Supplement, xi, 68-83.

SAMPSON, H., MESSINGER, S. L. and TOWNE, R. D. (1968), 'Family processes and becoming a mental patient' in SPITZEL, S. P. and DENZIN, N. K. (eds.) (1968).

SARASON, I. G. (ed.) (1965), *Science and Theory in Psychoanalysis: An Enduring Problem in Psychology* (Princeton, New Jersey: Van Nostrand).

SARTRE, JEAN-PAUL (1947), *No Exit* (New York: Knopf).

SARTRE, JEAN-PAUL (1948a), *Anti-semite and Jew* (New York: Shoeken).

SARTRE, JEAN-PAUL (1948b), *Psychology of the Imagination* (New York: Philosophical Library).

SARTRE, JEAN-PAUL (1960), *Critique de la Raison Dialectique* (Paris: Gallimard).

*SARTRE, JEAN-PAUL (1962a), *Imagination—a Psychological Critique* (Ann Arbor: University of Michigan Press).

*SARTRE, JEAN-PAUL (1962b), *A Sketch for a Theory of the Emotions* (London: Methuen).

SARTRE, JEAN-PAUL (1962c), *The Transcendence of the Ego: an Existentialist Theory of Consciousness* (New York: Noonday Press).

SARTRE, JEAN-PAUL (1963a), *Baudelaire* (Paris: Gallimard).

SARTRE, JEAN-PAUL (1963b), *The Problem of Method* (London: Methuen).

SARTRE, JEAN-PAUL (1964a), *Words* (Harmondsworth: Penguin).

SARTRE, JEAN-PAUL (1964b), *Saint Genet: Actor and Martyr* (London: W. H. Allen).

SARTRE, JEAN-PAUL (1965a), *Existentialism and Humanism* (London: Methuen).

SARTRE, JEAN-PAUL (1965b), *Nausea* (Harmondsworth: Penguin).

SARTRE, JEAN-PAUL (1965c), *Situations* (London: Hamish Hamilton).

*SARTRE, JEAN-PAUL (1966), *Being and Nothingness: An Essay in Phenomenological Ontology* (New York: Washington Square Press).

SARTRE, JEAN-PAUL (1971), *L'Idiot de la Famille, Gustave Flaubert 1821-1857* (Paris: Gallimard).

SAUNDERS, J. T. and HENZE, D. F. (1967), *The Private Language Problem: A Philosophical Dialogue* (New York: Random House).

*SCHEFF, T. J. (1966), *Being Mentally Ill: A Sociological Theory* (London: Weidenfeld & Nicolson).

SCHEFF, T. J. (ed.) (1967a), *Mental Illness and Social Process* (New York: Harper & Row).

SCHEFF, T. J. (1967b), 'A theory of social coordination applicable to mixed-motive games', *Sociometry*, 30, 215-34.

SCHILPP, P (ed.) (1957), *The Philosophy of Karl Jaspers* (La Salle, Ill: Open Court).

SCHILPP, P. (ed.) (1963), *The Philosophy of Rudolf Carnap* (La Salle, Ill: Open Court).

SCHLICK, M. (1962), *Problems of Ethics* (New York: Dover).

SCHMIDT, A. (1962), *The Concept of Nature in Marx*, English translation 1971 (London: New Left Books).

*SCHUTZ, A. (1962), *Collected Papers, vol. I. The Problems of Social Reality* (The Hague: Nijhoff).

SCHUTZ, A. (1964), *Collected Papers, vol. II Studies in Social Theory* (The Hague: Nijhoff).

SCHUTZ, A. (1966), *Collected Papers, vol. III Studies in Phenomenological Philosophy* (The Hague: Nijhoff).

*SCHUTZ, A. (1967), *The Phenomenology of the Social World* (Evanston, Ill: North Western University Press).

SCHUTZ, A. (1970), *Reflections on the Problem of Relevance* (Yale U.P.).

SCOTT, M. B. (1968), *The Racing Game* (Chicago: Aldine).

SEARLE, J. (1969), *Speech Acts: An Essay in the Philosophy of Language* (Cambridge University Press).

SEARLES, H. F. (1959), 'The effort to drive the other person crazy—an element in the etiology and psychotherapy of schizophrenia', *British Journal of Medical Psychology*, 32, 1.

SHERIF, M. and SHERIF, C. W. (1956), *An Outline of Social Psychology* (New York: Harper & Row).

SHWAYDER, D. S. (1965), *The Stratification of Behaviour: A System of Definitions Propounded and Defended* (London: Routledge & Kegan Paul).

SIEGLER, F. A. (1967), 'Unconscious intentions', *Inquiry*, 10, 251-67.

SILBER, J. R. (1963-4), 'Human action and the language of volitions', *P.A.S.*, lxiv, 199-220.

SILVERMAN, D. (1970), *The Theory of Organisations* (London: Heinemann).

SKINNER, B. F. (1957), *Verbal Behaviour* (New York: Appleton-Century-Crofts).

SKINNER, B. F. (1964), 'Behaviourism at fifty', in WANN, T. W. (ed.) (1964).

SKINNER, B. F. (1965), 'Critique of psychoanalytic concepts and theories', in SARASON, I. G. (ed.) (1965).

SMART, J. J. C. (1959), 'Ryle on mechanism and psychology', *P.Q.*, 9, 349-56.

SMART, N. (1964), 'Causality and human behaviour', *P.A.S.* Supplement xxxviii, 143-8.

SMYTHIES, J. R. (ed.) (1965), *Brain and Mind* (London: Routledge & Kegan Paul).

SNYGG, D. and COMBS, A. W. (1959), *Individual Behavior: A Perceptual Approach to Behavior* (New York: Harper & Row.)

SONNEMAN, U. (1954), *Existence and Therapy—An Introduction to Phenomenological Psychology and Existential Analysis* (New York: Grune & Stratton).

SOROKIN, P. (1956), *Fads and Foibles in Modern Sociology* (Chicago: Henry Regnery).

SPECHT, E. K. (1969), *The Foundations of Wittgenstein's Later Philosophy* (translated by D. WALFORD) (Manchester University Press).

SPIEGEL, J. P. and BELL, N. W. (1959), 'The family of the psychiatric patient', in ARIETI, S. (ed.) (1959) *American Handbook of Psychiatry* (New York: Basic Books).

SPIEGELBERG, H. (1967), 'Linguistic phenomenology: John L. Austin and Alexander Pfaender', in Appendix to PFAENDER, A. (1967).

SPIEGELBERG, H. (1968), 'The puzzle of Wittgenstein's phaenomenologie', *A.P.Q.*, October, 5, 244-57.

*SPIEGELBERG, H. (1969), *The Phenomenological Movement*, 2 vols 2nd ed. (The Hague: Nijhoff).

SPITZER, S. P. and DENZIN, N. K. (eds.) (1968), *The Mental Patient: Studies in the Sociology of Deviance* (London: McGraw-Hill).

SRZEDNICKI, J. (1965), *Franz Brentano's Analysis of Truth* (The Hague: Nijhoff).

STAATS, A. W. (1968), *Learning Language and Cognition* (New York: Holt, Rinehart & Winston).

STAMMER, O. (ed.) (1971), *Max Weber and Sociology Today* (Blackwell: Oxford).

STEKEL, W. (1937), *La Femme frigide* (Paris: Gallimard).

STEVENS, S. S. (1951), *Psychology and the Science of Science*, in MARX, M. H. (ed.) (1951).

STORCH, A. (1924), *The Primitive and Archaic Forms of Inner Thought in Schizophrenia* (New York: Nervous and Mental Disorders Publishing).

STRASSER, S. (1963), *Phenomenology and the Human Sciences: A Contribution to a New Scientific Ideal* (Pittsburgh: Duquesne University Press).

STRAUS, E. (1963), *The Primary World of the Senses: A Vindication of Sensory Experience* (New York: Free Press).

STRAUSS, A. *et al.* (1963), 'The hospital and its negotiated order', in FREIDSON, E. (ed.) (1963).

*STRAWSON, P. F. (1959), *Individuals* (London: Methuen).

STRAWSON, P. F. (1968), *Studies in the Philosophy of Thought and Action* (Oxford University Press).

SUGARMAN, B. (1968), 'The Phoenix unit: alliance against illness', *New Society*, 6 June.

SULLIVAN, H. S. (1947), *Conceptions of Modern Psychiatry* (London: Tavistock).

SULLIVAN, H. S. (1955), *The Interpersonal Theory of Psychiatry* (London: Tavistock).

SULLIVAN, H. S. (1962), *Schizophrenia as a Human Process* (New York: Morton).

SUTHERLAND, M. S. (1959), 'Motives as explanations', *Mind*, 68, 145-59.

SZASZ, T. S. (1962), *The Myth of Mental Illness: Foundations of a Theory of Personal Conduct* (London: Secker & Warburg).

SZASZ, T. S. (1971), *The Manufacture of Madness* (London: Routledge & Kegan Paul).

TAYLOR, C. (1967), *The Explanation of Behaviour* (London: Routledge & Kegan Paul).

TAYLOR, C. and AYER, A. J. (1959), 'Phenomenology and linguistic analysis', *P.A.S.* Supplement, xxxiii, 93-100.

TAYLOR, D. M. (1970), *Explanation and Meaning* (Cambridge University Press).

TAYLOR, R. (1966), *Action and Purpose* (New Jersey: Prentice-Hall).

THOMAS, W. I. (1928), *The Child in America* (New York: Knopf).

TILLIETTE, X. (1970), *Merleau-Ponty: ou la mesure de l'homme* (Paris: Editions Seghers).

TILLMAN, F. (1966), 'Phenomenology and philosophical analysis', *I.P.Q.*, September, 6, 465-82.

TILLMAN, F. (1967), 'Transcendental phenomenology and analytical philosophy', *I.P.Q.* March, 7, 31-40.

TOULMIN, S. (1949), 'The logical status of psychoanalysis', *Analysis*, 9, 23-9.

TOULMIN, S. (1962), *The Philosophy of Science: An Introduction* (London: Grey Arrow).

URMSON, J. O. (1968), 'Motives and causes', in WHITE, A. R. (ed.) (1968a).

URMSON, J. O. (1969), 'Austin's philosophy', in FANN, K. T. (1969.)

van den BERG, J. H. (1955), *The Phenomenological Approach to Psychiatry* (Oxford: Blackwell).

VESEY, G. N. (1965), *The Embodied Mind* (London: Allen & Unwin).

VESEY, G. N. (ed.) (1968), *The Human Agent* (London: Macmillan).

VICO, G. (1944), *The Autobiography*, translated from the Italian by M. H. FISH and T. G. BERGIN) (New York: Cornell University Press).

WAHN, T. W. (ed.) (1964) *Behaviourism and Phenomenology: Contrasting Bases for Modern Psychology* (Chicago University Press).

WAISMANN, F. (1955), 'Language-strata', in FLEW, A. (ed.) (1953).

WAISMANN, F. (1965a), 'Notes on talks with Wittgenstein', *Philosophical Review*, 74, 12-16.

WAISMANN, F. (1965b), *The Principles of Linguistic Philosophy* (London: Macmillan).

WARNOCK, G. J. (1963), 'Actions and events', in PEARS, D. F. (ed.) (1963).

WATSON, J. B. (1928), *The Ways of Behaviourism* (New York: Morton).

WEAKLAND, J. H. (1960), '"The double-bind" hypothesis in schizophrenia and three-party interaction', in JACKSON, D. D. (ed.) (1960).

WEBER, M. (1930), *The Protestant Ethic and the Spirit of Capitalism* (New York: Scribner's).

WEBER, M. (1949), *The Methodology of the Social Sciences* (Chicago: The Free Press).

WEBER, M. (1957), *The Theory of Social and Economic Organisation* (London: Collier-Macmillan).

WEBER, M. (1968), *Economy and Society*, 3 vols, ROTH, G. and WITTICH, C. (eds.) (New York: Bedminster Press).

WEIL, G. M. (1960), 'Esotericism and the double awareness: reply to Horgby on Wittgenstein and Heidegger', *Inquiry*, 3-4, 61-72.

WEINBERG, S. K. (1967) *The, Sociology of Mental Disorders: Analyses and Readings in Psychiatric Sociology* (London: Staples Press).

WELCH, E. P. (1965), *The Philosophy of Edmund Husserl* (New York: Columbia University Press).

WERTHEIMER, M. (1912), 'Experimentalle Studien ueber das Sehen von Bewegung', *Zeitschrift für Psychologie*, 61, 161-265.

WHALLON, R. (1964-5), 'Unconscious mental events', *P.P.R.*, 25, 400-3.

WHITE, A. R. (1958), 'Language of motives', *Mind*, 67, 258-63.
WHITE, A. R. (1968a), 'On being obliged to act', in VESEY, G. N. (ed.) (1968).
WHITE, A. R. (ed.) (1968b), *The Philosophy of Action* (Oxford University Press).
WHITELEY, C. H. (1961), 'Behaviourism', *Mind*, 70, 164-740.
WHITELEY, C. H. (1968), 'Mental causes', in VESEY, G. N. (ed.) (1968).
WHORF, B. L. (1956), *Language Thought and Reality: Selected Writings of Benjamin Lee Whorf* (New York: Wiley).
WILD, J. (1969), *The Radical Empiricism of William James* (New York: Doubleday).
WILKINS, L. T. (1965), *Social Deviance* (New Jersey: Prentice-Hall).
WILLIAMS, B. and MONTEFIORE, A. (eds.) (1966), *British Analytical Philosophy* (London: Routledge & Kegan Paul).
WILSHIRE, B. (1968), *William James and Phenomenology: a study of 'The Principles of Psychology'* (Bloomington: University of Indiana Press).
WILSON, B. (ed.) (1970), *Rationality* (Oxford: Blackwell).
WILSON, C. (1965), *Beyond the Outsider* (London: Pan Books).
WILSON, C. (1966), *Introduction to the 'New Existentialism'* (London: Hutchinson).
WINCH, P. (1958), *The Idea of a Social science: And Its Relation to Philosophy* (London: Routledge & Kegan Paul).
WINCH, P. (1964), 'Understanding a primitive society', in WILSON, B. (ed.) (1970).
WINCH, P. (1968), 'Wittgenstein's treatment of the will', *Ratio*, June, x, 38-53.
WINCH, P. (ed.) (1969), *Essays on Wittgenstein's Later Philosophy* (London: Routledge & Kegan Paul).
WINTER, G. (1966), *Elements of a Social Ethic* (New York: Macmillan).
WISDOM, J. (1949-50), 'Review and criticism of *Concept of Mind*', *P.A.S.*, l, 189-204.
WISDOM, J. (1957), *Philosophy and Psychoanalysis* (Oxford: Blackwell).
*WITTGENSTEIN, L. (1933), 'Letter to the editor', *Mind*, xlii, 415.
WITTGENSTEIN, L. (1956), *Remarks on the Foundations of Mathematics* (Oxford: Blackwell).
*WITTGENSTEIN, L. (1961), *Tractatus Logico-Philosophicus* (London: Routledge & Kegan Paul).
*WITTGENSTEIN, L. (1963), *Philosophical Investigations* (Oxford: Blackwell).
WITTGENSTEIN, L. (1964), *The Blue and Brown Books: Preliminary Studies for 'The Philosophical Investigations'* (Oxford: Blackwell).
WITTGENSTEIN, L. (1965), 'Lecture on ethics', *Philosophical Review*, 74, 3-12.
*WITTGENSTEIN, L. (1966), *Lectures and Conversations: on Aesthetics, Psychology and Religious Belief* (Oxford: Blackwell).
*WITTGENSTEIN, L. (1967), *Zettel* (Oxford: Blackwell).
WITTGENSTEIN, L. (1969), *Notebooks* 1914-16 (Oxford: Blackwell).
WOOD, O. P. and PITCHER, G. (eds.) (1970), *Ryle: A Collection of Critical Essays* (London: Macmillan).
WRIGHT, G. von (1969), 'Survey of Wittgenstein's papers', *Philosophical Review*, October, lxxviii, 483-503.

WRIGHT, G. von (1971), *Explanations and Understanding* (London: Routledge & Kegan Paul).

WRIGHT, J. N. (1959), 'Against Ryle's *Concept of Mind*', *P.A.S.* Supplement, xxxiii, 1-22.

WRONG, D. (1966), 'The oversocialised conception of man', in INKELES, A. (ed.) (1966), *Readings on Modern Sociology* (New Jersey: Prentice-Hall).

WYNNE, L. C., RYCKOFF, I. M., DAY, J. and HIRSCH, S. (1958), 'Pseudo-mutuality in the family relations of schizophrenics', *Psychiatry*, 21, 205.

YOUNG, M. F. D. (1971), *Knowledge and Control* (London: Collier-Macmillan).

Index

International Library of Sociology

Edited by
John Rex
University of Warwick

Founded by
Karl Mannheim

as The International Library of Sociology
and Social Reconstruction

This Catalogue also contains other Social Science series published by Routledge

Routledge & Kegan Paul London and Boston

68-74 Carter Lane London EC4V 5EL
9 Park Street Boston Mass 02108

Contents

● *Books so marked are available in paperback*

All books are in Metric Demy 8vo format (216 × 138mm approx.)

GENERAL SOCIOLOGY

Belshaw, Cyril. The Conditions of Social Performance. *An Exploratory Theory. 144 pp.*

Brown, Robert. Explanation in Social Science. *208 pp.*

● Rules and Laws in Sociology.

Cain, Maureen E. Society and the Policeman's Role. *About 300 pp.*

Gibson, Quentin. The Logic of Social Enquiry. *240 pp.*

Gurvitch, Georges. Sociology of Law. *Preface by Roscoe Pound. 264 pp.*

Homans, George C. Sentiments and Activities: *Essays in Social Science. 336 pp.*

Johnson, Harry M. Sociology: *a Systematic Introduction. Foreword by Robert K. Merton. 710 pp.*

Mannheim, Karl. Essays on Sociology and Social Psychology. *Edited by Paul Keckskemeti. With Editorial Note by Adolph Lowe. 344 pp.*

Systematic Sociology: *An Introduction to the Study of Society. Edited by J. S. Erös and Professor W. A. C. Stewart. 220 pp.*

Martindale, Don. The Nature and Types of Sociological Theory. *292 pp.*

● **Maus, Heinz.** A Short History of Sociology. *234 pp.*

Mey, Harald. Field-Theory. *A Study of its Application in the Social Sciences. 352 pp.*

Myrdal, Gunnar. Value in Social Theory: *A Collection of Essays on Methodology. Edited by Paul Streeten. 332 pp.*

Ogburn, William F., and **Nimkoff, Meyer F.** A Handbook of Sociology. *Preface by Karl Mannheim. 656 pp. 46 figures. 35 tables.*

Parsons, Talcott, and **Smelser, Neil J.** Economy and Society: *A Study in the Integration of Economic and Social Theory. 362 pp.*

● **Rex, John.** Key Problems of Sociological Theory. *220 pp.*

Urry, John. Reference Groups and the Theory of Revolution.

FOREIGN CLASSICS OF SOCIOLOGY

● **Durkheim, Emile.** Suicide. *A Study in Sociology. Edited and with an Introduction by George Simpson. 404 pp.*

Professional Ethics and Civic Morals. *Translated by Cornelia Brookfield. 288 pp.*

● **Gerth, H. H.,** and **Mills, C. Wright.** From Max Weber: *Essays in Sociology. 502 pp.*

Tönnies, Ferdinand. Community and Association. *(Gemeinschaft und Gesellschaft.) Translated and Supplemented by Charles P. Loomis. Foreword by Pitirim A. Sorokin. 334 pp.*

SOCIAL STRUCTURE

Andreski, Stanislav. Military Organization and Society. *Foreword by Professor A. R. Radcliffe-Brown. 226 pp. 1 folder.*

Coontz, Sydney H. Population Theories and the Economic Interpretation. *202 pp.*

Coser, Lewis. The Functions of Social Conflict. *204 pp.*

Dickie-Clark, H. F. Marginal Situation: *A Sociological Study of a Coloured Group. 240 pp. 11 tables.*

Glass, D. V. (Ed.). Social Mobility in Britain. *Contributions by J. Berent, T. Bottomore, R. C. Chambers, J. Floud, D. V. Glass, J. R. Hall, H. T. Himmelweit, R. K. Kelsall, F. M. Martin, C. A. Moser, R. Mukherjee, and W. Ziegel. 420 pp.*

Glaser, Barney, and **Strauss, Anselm L.** Status Passage. *A Formal Theory. 208 pp.*

Jones, Garth N. Planned Organizational Change: *An Exploratory Study Using an Empirical Approach. 268 pp.*

Kelsall, R. K. Higher Civil Servants in Britain: *From 1870 to the Present Day. 268 pp. 31 tables.*

König, René. The Community. *232 pp. Illustrated.*

● **Lawton, Denis.** Social Class, Language and Education. *192 pp.*

McLeish, John. The Theory of Social Change: *Four Views Considered. 128 pp.*

Marsh, David C. The Changing Social Structure of England and Wales, 1871-1961. *288 pp.*

Mouzelis, Nicos. Organization and Bureaucracy. *An Analysis of Modern Theories. 240 pp.*

Mulkay, M. J. Functionalism, Exchange and Theoretical Strategy. *272 pp.*

Ossowski, Stanislaw. Class Structure in the Social Consciousness. *210 pp.*

SOCIOLOGY AND POLITICS

Hertz, Frederick. Nationality in History and Politics: *A Psychology and Sociology of National Sentiment and Nationalism. 432 pp.*

Kornhauser, William. The Politics of Mass Society. *272 pp. 20 tables.*

Laidler, Harry W. History of Socialism. *Social-Economic Movements: An Historical and Comparative Survey of Socialism, Communism, Co-operation, Utopianism; and other Systems of Reform and Reconstruction. 992 pp.*

Mannheim, Karl. Freedom, Power and Democratic Planning. *Edited by Hans Gerth and Ernest K. Bramstedt. 424 pp.*

Mansur, Fatma. Process of Independence. *Foreword by A. H. Hanson. 208 pp.*

Martin, David A. Pacificism: *an Historical and Sociological Study. 262 pp.*

Myrdal, Gunnar. The Political Element in the Development of Economic Theory. *Translated from the German by Paul Streeten. 282 pp.*

Wootton, Graham. Workers, Unions and the State. *188 pp.*

FOREIGN AFFAIRS: THEIR SOCIAL, POLITICAL AND ECONOMIC FOUNDATIONS

Mayer, J. P. Political Thought in France from the Revolution to the Fifth Republic. *164 pp.*

CRIMINOLOGY

Ancel, Marc. Social Defence: *A Modern Approach to Criminal Problems. Foreword by Leon Radzinowicz. 240 pp.*

Cloward, Richard A., and **Ohlin, Lloyd E.** Delinquency and Opportunity: *A Theory of Delinquent Gangs. 248 pp.*

Downes, David M. The Delinquent Solution. *A Study in Subcultural Theory. 296 pp.*

Dunlop, A. B., and **McCabe, S.** Young Men in Detention Centres. *192 pp.*

Friedlander, Kate. The Psycho-Analytical Approach to Juvenile Delinquency: *Theory, Case Studies, Treatment. 320 pp.*

Glueck, Sheldon, and **Eleanor.** Family Environment and Delinquency. *With the statistical assistance of Rose W. Kneznek. 340 pp.*

Lopez-Rey, Manuel. Crime. *An Analytical Appraisal. 288 pp.*

Mannheim, Hermann. Comparative Criminology: *a Text Book. Two volumes. 442 pp. and 380 pp.*

Morris, Terence. The Criminal Area: *A Study in Social Ecology. Foreword by Hermann Mannheim. 232 pp. 25 tables. 4 maps.*

● **Taylor, Ian, Walton, Paul,** and **Young, Jock.** The New Criminology. *For a Social Theory of Deviance.*

SOCIAL PSYCHOLOGY

Bagley, Christopher. The Social Psychology of the Epileptic Child. *320 pp.*

Barbu, Zevedei. Problems of Historical Psychology. *248 pp.*

Blackburn, Julian. Psychology and the Social Pattern. *184 pp.*

● **Brittan, Arthur.** Meanings and Situations. *224 pp.*

● **Fleming, C. M.** Adolescence: Its Social Psychology. *With an Introduction to recent findings from the fields of Anthropology, Physiology, Medicine, Psychometrics and Sociometry. 288 pp.*

● The Social Psychology of Education: *An Introduction and Guide to Its Study. 136 pp.*

Homans, George C. The Human Group. *Foreword by Bernard DeVoto. Introduction by Robert K. Merton. 526 pp.*

Social Behaviour: *its Elementary Forms. 416 pp.*

Klein, Josephine. The Study of Groups. *226 pp. 31 figures. 5 tables.*

Linton, Ralph. The Cultural Background of Personality. *132 pp.*

Mayo, Elton. The Social Problems of an Industrial Civilization. *With an appendix on the Political Problem. 180 pp.*

Ottaway, A. K. C. Learning Through Group Experience. *176 pp.*

Ridder, J. C. de. The Personality of the Urban African in South Africa. *A Thematic Apperception Test Study. 196 pp. 12 plates.*

● **Rose, Arnold M.** (Ed.). Human Behaviour and Social Processes: *an Interactionist Approach. Contributions by Arnold M. Rose, Ralph H. Turner, Anselm Strauss, Everett C. Hughes, E. Franklin Frazier, Howard S. Becker, et al. 696 pp.*

Smelser, Neil J. Theory of Collective Behaviour. *448 pp.*
Stephenson, Geoffrey M. The Development of Conscience. *128 pp.*
Young, Kimball. Handbook of Social Psychology. *658 pp. 16 figures. 10 tables.*

SOCIOLOGY OF THE FAMILY

Banks, J. A. Prosperity and Parenthood: *A Study of Family Planning among The Victorian Middle Classes. 262 pp.*
Bell, Colin R. Middle Class Families: *Social and Geographical Mobility. 224 pp.*
Burton, Lindy. Vulnerable Children. *272 pp.*
Gavron, Hannah. The Captive Wife: *Conflicts of Household Mothers. 190 pp.*
George, Victor, and **Wilding, Paul.** Motherless Families. *220 pp.*
Klein, Josephine. Samples from English Cultures.
1. Three Preliminary Studies and Aspects of Adult Life in England. *447 pp.*
2. Child-Rearing Practices and Index. *247 pp.*

Klein, Viola. Britain's Married Women Workers. *180 pp.*
The Feminine Character. *History of an Ideology. 244 pp.*
McWhinnie, Alexina M. Adopted Children. *How They Grow Up. 304 pp.*
Myrdal, Alva, and **Klein, Viola.** Women's Two Roles: *Home and Work. 238 pp. 27 tables.*
Parsons, Talcott, and **Bales, Robert F.** Family: Socialization and Interaction Process. *In collaboration with James Olds, Morris Zelditch and Philip E. Slater. 456 pp. 50 figures and tables.*

SOCIAL SERVICES

Bastide, Roger. The Sociology of Mental Disorder. *Translated from the French by Jean McNeil. 260 pp.*
Carlebach, Julius. Caring For Children in Trouble. *266 pp.*
Forder, R. A. (Ed.). Penelope Hall's Social Services of England and Wales. *352 pp.*
George, Victor. Foster Care. *Theory and Practice. 234 pp.*
Social Security: *Beveridge and After. 258 pp.*
● **Goetschius, George W.** Working with Community Groups. *256 pp.*
Goetschius, George W., and **Tash, Joan.** Working with Unattached Youth. *416 pp.*
Hall, M. P., and **Howes, I. V.** The Church in Social Work. *A Study of Moral Welfare Work undertaken by the Church of England. 320 pp.*
Heywood, Jean S. Children in Care: *the Development of the Service for the Deprived Child. 264 pp.*
Hoenig, J., and **Hamilton, Marian W.** The De-Segration of the Mentally Ill. *284 pp.*
Jones, Kathleen. Mental Health and Social Policy, 1845-1959. *264 pp.*

King, Roy D., Raynes, Norma V., and **Tizard, Jack.** Patterns of Residential Care. *356 pp.*

Leigh, John. Young People and Leisure. *256 pp.*

Morris, Mary. Voluntary Work and the Welfare State. *300 pp.*

Morris, Pauline. Put Away: *A Sociological Study of Institutions for the Mentally Retarded. 364 pp.*

Nokes, P. L. The Professional Task in Welfare Practice. *152 pp.*

Timms, Noel. Psychiatric Social Work in Great Britain (1939-1962). *280 pp.*

● Social Casework: *Principles and Practice. 256 pp.*

Young, A. F., and **Ashton, E. T.** British Social Work in the Nineteenth Century. *288 pp.*

Young, A. F. Social Services in British Industry. *272 pp.*

SOCIOLOGY OF EDUCATION

Banks, Olive. Parity and Prestige in English Secondary Education: a Study in Educational Sociology. *272 pp.*

Bentwich, Joseph. Education in Israel. *224 pp. 8 pp. plates.*

● **Blyth, W. A. L.** English Primary Education. *A Sociological Description.*

1. Schools. *232 pp.*
2. Background. *168 pp.*

Collier, K. G. The Social Purposes of Education: *Personal and Social Values in Education. 268 pp.*

Dale, R. R., and **Griffith, S.** Down Stream: *Failure in the Grammar School. 108 pp.*

Dore, R. P. Education in Tokugawa Japan. *356 pp. 9 pp. plates*

Evans, K. M. Sociometry and Education. *158 pp.*

Foster, P. J. Education and Social Change in Ghana. *336 pp. 3 maps.*

Fraser, W. R. Education and Society in Modern France. *150 pp.*

Grace, Gerald R. Role Conflict and the Teacher. *About 200 pp.*

Hans, Nicholas. New Trends in Education in the Eighteenth Century. *278 pp. 19 tables.*

● Comparative Education: *A Study of Educational Factors and Traditions. 360 pp.*

Hargreaves, David. Interpersonal Relations and Education. *432 pp.*

● Social Relations in a Secondary School. *240 pp.*

Holmes, Brian. Problems in Education. *A Comparative Approach. 336 pp.*

King, Ronald. Values and Involvement in a Grammar School. *164 pp.*

School Organization and Pupil Involvement. *A Study of Secondary Schools.*

● **Mannheim, Karl,** and **Stewart, W. A. C.** An Introduction to the Sociology of Education. *206 pp.*

Morris, Raymond N. The Sixth Form and College Entrance. *231 pp.*

● **Musgrove, F.** Youth and the Social Order. *176 pp.*

● **Ottaway, A. K. C.** Education and Society: An Introduction to the Sociology of Education. *With an Introduction by W. O. Lester Smith. 212 pp.*

Peers, Robert. Adult Education: *A Comparative Study. 398 pp.*

Pritchard, D. G. Education and the Handicapped: *1760 to 1960. 258 pp.*
Richardson, Helen. Adolescent Girls in Approved Schools. *308 pp.*
Stratta, Erica. The Education of Borstal Boys. *A Study of their Educational Experiences prior to, and during Borstal Training. 256 pp.*

SOCIOLOGY OF CULTURE

Eppel, E. M., and **M.** Adolescents and Morality: *A Study of some Moral Values and Dilemmas of Working Adolescents in the Context of a changing Climate of Opinion. Foreword by W. J. H. Sprott. 268 pp. 39 tables.*
● **Fromm, Erich.** The Fear of Freedom. *286 pp.*
The Sane Society. *400 pp.*
Mannheim, Karl. Essays on the Sociology of Culture. *Edited by Ernst Mannheim in co-operation with Paul Kecskemeti. Editorial Note by Adolph Lowe. 280 pp.*
Weber, Alfred. Farewell to European History: *or The Conquest of Nihilism Translated from the German by R. F. C. Hull. 224 pp.*

SOCIOLOGY OF RELIGION

Argyle, Michael. Religious Behaviour. *224 pp. 8 figures. 41 tables.*
Nelson, G. K. Spiritualism and Society. *313 pp.*
Stark, Werner. The Sociology of Religion. *A Study of Christendom.*
Volume I. *Established Religion. 248 pp.*
Volume II. *Sectarian Religion. 368 pp.*
Volume III. *The Universal Church. 464 pp.*
Volume IV. *Types of Religious Man. 352 pp.*
Volume V. *Types of Religious Culture. 464 pp.*
Watt, W. Montgomery. Islam and the Integration of Society. *320 pp.*

SOCIOLOGY OF ART AND LITERATURE

Jarvie, Ian C. Towards a Sociology of the Cinema. *A Comparative Essay on the Structure and Functioning of a Major Entertainment Industry. 405 pp.*
Rust, Frances S. Dance in Society. *An Analysis of the Relationships between the Social Dance and Society in England from the Middle Ages to the Present Day. 256 pp. 8 pp. of plates.*
Schücking, L. L. The Sociology of Literary Taste. *112 pp.*

SOCIOLOGY OF KNOWLEDGE

Mannheim, Karl. Essays on the Sociology of Knowledge. *Edited by Paul Kecskemeti. Editorial Note by Adolph Lowe. 353 pp.*

Remmling, Gunter W. (Ed.). Towards the Sociology of Knowledge. *Origins and Development of a Sociological Thought Style.*

Stark, Werner. The Sociology of Knowledge: *An Essay in Aid of a Deeper Understanding of the History of Ideas. 384 pp.*

URBAN SOCIOLOGY

Ashworth, William. The Genesis of Modern British Town Planning: *A Study in Economic and Social History of the Nineteenth and Twentieth Centuries. 288 pp.*

Cullingworth, J. B. Housing Needs and Planning Policy: *A Restatement of the Problems of Housing Need and 'Overspill' in England and Wales. 232 pp. 44 tables. 8 maps.*

Dickinson, Robert E. City and Region: *A Geographical Interpretation. 608 pp. 125 figures.*

The West European City: *A Geographical Interpretation. 600 pp. 129 maps. 29 plates.*

● The City Region in Western Europe. *320 pp. Maps.*

Humphreys, Alexander J. New Dubliners: *Urbanization and the Irish Family. Foreword by George C. Homans. 304 pp.*

Jackson, Brian. Working Class Community: *Some General Notions raised by a Series of Studies in Northern England. 192 pp.*

Jennings, Hilda. Societies in the Making: *a Study of Development and Redevelopment within a County Borough. Foreword by D. A. Clark. 286 pp.*

● **Mann, P. H.** An Approach to Urban Sociology. *240 pp.*

Morris, R. N., and **Mogey, J.** The Sociology of Housing. *Studies at Berinsfield. 232 pp. 4 pp. plates.*

Rosser, C., and **Harris, C.** The Family and Social Change. *A Study of Family and Kinship in a South Wales Town. 352 pp. 8 maps.*

RURAL SOCIOLOGY

Chambers, R. J. H. Settlement Schemes in Tropical Africa: *A Selective Study. 268 pp.*

Haswell, M. R. The Economics of Development in Village India. *120 pp.*

Littlejohn, James. Westrigg: *the Sociology of a Cheviot Parish. 172 pp. 5 figures.*

Mayer, Adrian C. Peasants in the Pacific. *A Study of Fiji Indian Rural Society. 248 pp. 20 plates.*

Williams, W. M. The Sociology of an English Village: *Gosforth. 272 pp. 12 figures. 13 tables.*

SOCIOLOGY OF INDUSTRY AND DISTRIBUTION

Anderson, Nels. Work and Leisure. *280 pp.*

● **Blau, Peter M.,** and **Scott, W. Richard.** Formal Organizations: *a Comparative approach. Introduction and Additional Bibliography by J. H. Smith. 326 pp.*

Eldridge, J. E. T. Industrial Disputes. *Essays in the Sociology of Industrial Relations. 288 pp.*

Hetzler, Stanley. Applied Measures for Promoting Technological Growth. *352 pp.*

Technological Growth and Social Change. *Achieving Modernization. 269 pp.*

Hollowell, Peter G. The Lorry Driver. *272 pp.*

Jefferys, Margot, *with the assistance of Winifred Moss.* Mobility in the Labour Market: *Employment Changes in Battersea and Dagenham. Preface by Barbara Wootton. 186 pp. 51 tables.*

Millerson, Geoffrey. The Qualifying Associations: *a Study in Professionalization. 320 pp.*

Smelser, Neil J. Social Change in the Industrial Revolution: *An Application of Theory to the Lancashire Cotton Industry, 1770-1840. 468 pp. 12 figures. 14 tables.*

Williams, Gertrude. Recruitment to Skilled Trades. *240 pp.*

Young, A. F. Industrial Injuries Insurance: *an Examination of British Policy. 192 pp.*

DOCUMENTARY

Schlesinger, Rudolf (Ed.). Changing Attitudes in Soviet Russia.

2. The Nationalities Problem and Soviet Administration. *Selected Readings on the Development of Soviet Nationalities Policies. Introduced by the editor. Translated by W. W. Gottlieb. 324 pp.*

ANTHROPOLOGY

Ammar, Hamed. Growing up in an Egyptian Village: *Silwa, Province of Aswan. 336 pp.*

Brandel-Syrier, Mia. Reeftown Elite. *A Study of Social Mobility in a Modern African Community on the Reef. 376 pp.*

Crook, David, and **Isabel.** Revolution in a Chinese Village: *Ten Mile Inn. 230 pp. 8 plates. 1 map.*

Dickie-Clark, H. F. The Marginal Situation. *A Sociological Study of a Coloured Group. 236 pp.*

Dube, S. C. Indian Village. *Foreword by Morris Edward Opler. 276 pp. 4 plates.*

India's Changing Villages: *Human Factors in Community Development. 260 pp. 8 plates. 1 map.*

Firth, Raymond. Malay Fishermen. *Their Peasant Economy. 420 pp. 17 pp. plates.*

Gulliver, P. H. Social Control in an African Society: a Study of the Arusha, Agricultural Masai of Northern Tanganyika. *320 pp. 8 plates. 10 figures.*

Ishwaran, K. Shivapur. *A South Indian Village. 216 pp.*

Tradition and Economy in Village India: *An Interactionist Approach. Foreword by Conrad Arensburg. 176 pp.*

Jarvie, Ian C. The Revolution in Anthropology. *268 pp.*

Jarvie, Ian C., and **Agassi, Joseph.** Hong Kong. *A Society in Transition. 396 pp. Illustrated with plates and maps.*

Little, Kenneth L. Mende of Sierra Leone. *308 pp. and folder.*

Negroes in Britain. *With a New Introduction and Contemporary Study by Leonard Bloom. 320 pp.*

Lowie, Robert H. Social Organization. *494 pp.*

Mayer, Adrian C. Caste and Kinship in Central India: *A Village and its Region. 328 pp. 16 plates. 15 figures. 16 tables.*

Smith, Raymond T. The Negro Family in British Guiana: *Family Structure and Social Status in the Villages. With a Foreword by Meyer Fortes. 314 pp. 8 plates. 1 figure. 4 maps.*

SOCIOLOGY AND PHILOSOPHY

Barnsley, John H. The Social Reality of Ethics. *A Comparative Analysis of Moral Codes. 448 pp.*

Diesing, Paul. Patterns of Discovery in the Social Sciences. *362 pp.*

Douglas, Jack D. (Ed.). Understanding Everyday Life. *Toward the Reconstruction of Sociological Knowledge. Contributions by Alan F. Blum. Aaron W. Cicourel, Norman K. Denzin, Jack D. Douglas, John Heeren, Peter McHugh, Peter K. Manning, Melvin Power, Matthew Speier, Roy Turner, D. Lawrence Wieder, Thomas P. Wilson and Don H. Zimmerman. 370 pp.*

Jarvie, Ian C. Concepts and Society. *216 pp.*

Roche, Maurice. Phenomenology, Language and the Social Sciences. *About 400 pp.*

Sahay, Arun. Sociological Analysis.

Sklair, Leslie. The Sociology of Progress. *320 pp.*

International Library of Anthropology

General Editor Adam Kuper

Brown, Raula. The Chimbu. *A Study of Change in the New Guinea Highlands.*

Van Den Berghe, Pierre L. Power and Privilege at an African University.

International Library of Social Policy

General Editor Kathleen Jones

Holman, Robert. Trading in Children. *A Study of Private Fostering.*
Jones, Kathleen. History of the Mental Health Services. *428 pp.*
Thomas, J. E. The English Prison Officer since 1850: *A Study in Conflict. 258 pp.*

Primary Socialization, Language and Education

General Editor Basil Bernstein

Bernstein, Basil. Class, Codes and Control. *2 volumes.*
1. *Theoretical Studies Towards a Sociology of Language. 254 pp.*
2. *Applied Studies Towards a Sociology of Language. About 400 pp.*

Brandis, Walter, and **Henderson, Dorothy.** Social Class, Language and Communication. *288 pp.*
Cook-Gumperz, Jenny. Social Control and Socialization. *A Study of Class Differences in the Language of Maternal Control.*
Gahagan, D. M., and **G. A.** Talk Reform. *Exploration in Language for Infant School Children. 160 pp.*
Robinson, W. P., and **Rackstraw, Susan, D. A.** A Question of Answers. *2 volumes. 192 pp. and 180 pp.*
Turner, Geoffrey, J., and **Mohan, Bernard, A.** A Linguistic Description and Computer Programme for Children's Speech. *208 pp.*

Reports of the Institute of Community Studies

Cartwright, Ann. Human Relations and Hospital Care. *272 pp.*
Parents and Family Planning Services. *306 pp.*
Patients and their Doctors. *A Study of General Practice. 304 pp.*
● **Jackson, Brian.** Streaming: *an Education System in Miniature. 168 pp.*
Jackson, Brian, and **Marsden, Dennis.** Education and the Working Class: *Some General Themes raised by a Study of 88 Working-class Children in a Northern Industrial City. 268 pp. 2 folders.*
Marris, Peter. The Experience of Higher Education. *232 pp. 27 tables.*
Marris, Peter, and **Rein, Martin.** Dilemmas of Social Reform. *Poverty and Community Action in the United States. 256 pp.*
Marris, Peter, and **Somerset, Anthony.** African Businessmen. *A Study of Entrepreneurship and Development in Kenya. 256 pp.*
Mills, Richard. Young Outsiders: *a Study in Alternative Communities.*

Runciman, W. G. Relative Deprivation and Social Justice. *A Study of Attitudes to Social Inequality in Twentieth Century England. 352 pp.*

Townsend, Peter. The Family Life of Old People: *An Inquiry in East London. Foreword by J. H. Sheldon. 300 pp. 3 figures. 63 tables.*

Willmott, Peter. Adolescent Boys in East London. *230 pp.*

The Evolution of a Community: *a study of Dagenham after forty years. 168 pp. 2 maps.*

Willmott, Peter, and **Young, Michael.** Family and Class in a London Suburb. *202 pp. 47 tables.*

Young, Michael. Innovation and Research in Education. *192 pp.*

● **Young, Michael,** and **McGeeney, Patrick.** Learning Begins at Home. *A Study of a Junior School and its Parents. 128 pp.*

Young, Michael, and **Willmott, Peter.** Family and Kinship in East London. *Foreword by Richard M. Titmuss. 252 pp. 39 tables.*

The Symmetrical Family.

Reports of the Institute for Social Studies in Medical Care

Cartwright, Ann, Hockey, Lisbeth, and **Anderson, John L.** Life Before Death.

Dunnell, Karen, and **Cartwright, Ann.** Medicine Takers, Prescribers and Hoarders. *190 pp.*

Medicine, Illness and Society

General Editor W. M. Williams

Robinson, David. The Process of Becoming Ill.

Stacey, Margaret. *et al.* Hospitals, Children and Their Families. *The Report of a Pilot Study. 202 pp.*

Monographs in Social Theory

General Editor Arthur Brittan

Bauman, Zygmunt. Culture as Praxis.

Dixon, Keith. Sociological Theory. *Pretence and Possibility.*

Smith, Anthony D. The Concept of Social Change. *A Critique of the Functionalist Theory of Social Change.*

Routledge Social Science Journals

The British Journal of Sociology. *Edited by Terence P. Morris. Vol. 1, No. 1, March 1950 and Quarterly. Roy. 8vo. Back numbers available. An international journal with articles on all aspects of sociology.*

Economy and Society. *Vol. 1, No. 1. February 1972 and Quarterly. Metric Roy. 8vo. A journal for all social scientists covering sociology, philosophy, anthropology, economics and history. Back numbers available.*

Year Book of Social Policy in Britain, The. *Edited by Kathleen Jones. 1971. Published Annually.*

Printed in Great Britain by Lewis Reprints Limited
Brown Knight & Truscott Group, London and Tonbridge

1373